MW00789056

HOLMES AND FRANKFURTER

HOLMES

AND

FRANKFURTER

Their Correspondence, 1912–1934

Edited by

Robert M. Mennel and Christine L. Compston

UNIVERSITY OF NEW HAMPSHIRE

PUBLISHED BY UNIVERSITY PRESS OF NEW ENGLAND

HANOVER AND LONDON

University of New Hampshire
Published by University Press of New England, Hanover, NH 03755
© 1996 by the Trustees of the University of New Hampshire
All rights reserved
Printed in the United States of America
5 4 3 2 1
CIP data appear at the end of the book

Excerpts found in the Harvard Law Library's collections titled the Oliver Wendell Holmes, Jr., Papers, the Grant Gilmore Papers, the Mark DeWolfe Howe Papers, and the Correspondence of Rosika Schimmer are published herein by the kind permission of the Harvard Law School Library.

In memory of Paul A. Freund

CONTENTS

ACKNOWLEDGMENTS ix

INTRODUCTION xi

THE CORRESPONDENCE 3

FREQUENTLY CITED WORKS 281

SUBJECT INDEX 283

INDEX TO COURT CASES 299

ACKNOWLEDGMENTS

"You've made me pretty shy about expressing my indebtedness to you," wrote Felix Frankfurter in an early letter to Justice Oliver Wendell Holmes. Of course, it wasn't so. Frankfurter was anything but restrained in his praise and Holmes often responded in kind. Their correspondence, rich in so many ways, was above all characterized by a warm admiration that extended to their many other friendships. In this spirit, it is a pleasure to acknowledge the institutions and individuals who made our work possible.

This volume is dedicated to the memory of Professor Paul A. Freund of Harvard Law School. In the earliest and most difficult stage of editing and annotation, he encouraged us with careful reading and commentary that reflected both his unsurpassed knowledge of American constitutional law and his sensitive recollections of Frankfurter and Harvard. We remember with fondness his legendary knack of plucking just the right source from the mountains of articles surrounding his desk in Langdell Hall. If this work furthers understanding about Holmes and Frankfurter and the role of law in American life, we hope that it will also recall Paul Freund's contribution to the ongoing search for justice infused with mercy.

We are deeply grateful to a dedicated group of librarians and archivists whose patience and helpfulness enriched our study. David de Lorenzo, Curator of Manuscripts and Archives at Harvard Law School, gave permission to publish the Holmes-Frankfurter correspondence, which is located in the Oliver Wendell Holmes, Jr. Papers, and to publish other excerpts from the Holmes Papers, the Felix Frankfurter Papers, the Grant Gilmore Papers, the Mark DeWolfe Howe Papers, and the Correspondence of Rosika Schwimmer. Erika S. Chadbourn, Curator Emerita at Harvard Law School, and Judith W. Mellins of the Special Collections Department were both knowledgeable and forbearing in answering our numerous inquiries; their generous assistance made research a pleasure. The staffs of the Boston Public Library, Harvard Law School Library, and the Dimond Library at University of New Hampshire were also unfailingly helpful. At UNH, Reference Librarian Deborah E. Watson provided invaluable assistance, and computer specialist Terri S. Winters unerringly guided our text through several waves of technological change.

The support of fellow historians and scholars has been crucial to our work. Research grants from the University of New Hampshire Graduate School assisted our initial verification of the letters. Harvard Law School's award of a Liberal Arts Fellowship to Christine Compston greatly facilitated completion of the research. Stuart Palmer, Dean of the College of Liberal Arts at the University of New Hampshire, aided our work at all stages. Gerald Gunther and Nadine Strossen read the entire manuscript and gave us the benefit of their incisive commentary. Robert H. Bremner, Susan Mennel, and Lucy Salyer read the introduction and raised important questions which we hope have been addressed. David Andrew, Robert N. Hudspeth, J. Willard Hurst, Sheldon M. Novick, John Rouman, and Jack Yeager gave us the benefit of their knowledge on particular subjects.

We wish to offer special thanks to those who have assisted our research and helped us to complete the task of organizing the manuscript. We acknowledge with appreciation Barbara Eggers, Petra A. Harris, and Carrie L. Leighton, who provided research support with intelligence and care. We are also grateful for the calm and effective assistance of Lee A. Calderone, Virginia M. Fish, Jane Fogarty, and Jeanne A. Mitchell.

The staff of the University Press of New England has encouraged us at every turn, though all errors of fact and of judgment are, of course, the responsibility of the editors.

Prefaces often conclude with thanks to long-suffering spouses—a description that we hope does not apply to Susan Mennel and Stephen Senge. This formal acknowledgment of their support also seems inadequate, because love and devotion cannot be measured.

Durham, New Hampshire R.M.M.
Bellingham, Washington C.L.C.
December 1995

INTRODUCTION

To all appearances, the friendship between Justice Oliver Wendell Holmes (1841–1935) and Felix Frankfurter (1881–1965) was an unlikely one. The elderly jurist, a hero of the Civil War, with his dignified manner and distinguished New England lineage, was strikingly different from the excitable, youthful Jewish lawyer. Liva Baker, biographer of both, pictures them tramping the streets of pre-World War I Washington, "a tall man with a thatch of snowy hair, matching mustaches, and a long stride, accompanied by a short man half running to keep up and breathlessly talking."[1] Their very dissimilarities, however, helped to kindle a relationship that grew closer as the years passed.

The Holmes-Frankfurter correspondence, which began in 1912 and ended in late 1934 shortly before Holmes died, displays the vitality of their friendship and also offers insights into the practice of Constitutional law and the character of intellectual life in early twentieth-century America. The views they exchanged on the meaning of law in general and American law in particular found expression in their work, which influenced legal and political change in their own lifetimes and in ours as well. The letters written by Holmes are especially distinguished by his reflections on the role of the judge as philosopher and his effort to convey these thoughts to Frankfurter.

Holmes, who was seventy-one at the time the two men met, had completed his first decade on the Supreme Court. He was the author of several liberal opinions, particularly two dissents, in *Lochner v. New York* and *Adair v. U.S.*, and a unanimous decision, *Noble State Bank v. Haskell.*[2] These

1. Liva Baker, *Felix Frankfurter: A Biography* (New York: Coward-McCann, 1969), 36; *The Justice from Beacon Hill: The Life and Times of Oliver Wendell Holmes* (New York: Harper, 1991), 454–55.

2. *Lochner v. New York*, 198 U.S. 45 (1905); *Adair v. U.S.*, 208 U.S. 161 (1908); *Noble State Bank v. Haskell*, 219 U.S. 104 (1911). Holmes had also issued a famous dissent in *Northern Securities Co. v. U.S.*, 193 U.S. 197, 400 (1904), in which he declined to find a railroad holding company, owned by J. P. Morgan, acting to restrain interstate commerce. For contrasting views on this case, see Sheldon M. Novick, *Honorable Justice: The Life of Oliver Wendell Holmes* (Boston: Little, Brown, 1989), 268–72, 461n, and G. Edward White, *Justice Oliver Wendell Holmes: Law and the Inner Self* (New York: Oxford, 1992), 330–32, 557n.

articulated a philosophy of judicial restraint by taking a tolerant view of legislative efforts to regulate the economy. Conservatives were enraged, but reformers such as young Felix Frankfurter lionized the Justice's writings and crusty New England personality. Nonetheless, Holmes had not yet achieved the public recognition that accorded with his own sense of his accomplishments as a judge and legal scholar—the editor of the twelfth edition of Chancellor James Kent's *Commentaries on American Law* (1873) and the author of *The Common Law* (1881) and several other important essays on the meaning of the law.[3] Furthermore, he had begun to brood upon the passage of time as many of his friends passed away. In the process, his gloomy Malthusian philosophy of life, which placed little faith in the laws that his decisions sought to uphold, deepened into dogma.

Felix Frankfurter's effervescent personality helped to slow the development of Holmes's pessimism. Frankfurter had come to Washington in 1911 as Law Officer, Bureau of Insular Affairs, U.S. Department of War. Just thirty years old, he had already gained considerable recognition for his achievements. Born in Vienna, he immigrated to New York City with his parents in 1894. He learned English by reading newspapers in the New York Public Library and in Public School 25 from the stern Miss Hogan, "a redoubtable Irish lady who not only believed in corporal punishment for intellectual indolence but threatened the other students with uppercuts when they conversed with Felix in German." He had established a brilliant academic record at College of the City of New York (A.B., 1902) and Harvard Law School (LL.B., 1906). At Harvard, he was particularly influenced by the work of James B. Thayer and the teaching of Holmes's old friend John Chipman Gray. Thayer argued for strict limits on judicial authority in the area of social policy, in effect strengthening legislative efforts to regulate the economy. Gray, like Holmes, held that legal rules were more likely to be the product of shifting social forces than of judicial logic as orthodox legal thinking prescribed.[4]

Following graduation, Frankfurter joined the prestigious Wall Street firm of Hornblower, Byrne, Miller and Potter. Private practice, however, was pervaded by anti-Semitism and, in addition, curtailed his time for reform activity. Thus, he eagerly accepted an offer from the patrician statesman Henry L. Stimson to join the U.S. Attorney's Office, Southern Dis-

3. The most significant articles were: "Privilege, Malice and Intent" (1894); "The Path of the Law" (1897); "Law in Science and Science in Law" (1899); and "The Theory of Legal Interpretation" (1899). These and other scholarly writings were brought together in *Collected Legal Papers* (New York: Harcourt, Brace and Howe, 1920).

4. Michael E. Parrish, *Felix Frankfurter and His Times: The Reform Years* (New York: Free Press, 1982), 12, 20–21.

trict of New York. When in 1911 Stimson was named Secretary of War by President Taft, Frankfurter followed him to Washington, carrying to Holmes a letter of introduction from John Chipman Gray.

Justice and Mrs. Holmes invited Frankfurter to call. Fanny Holmes presided on Monday afternoons at the I Street home just west of Lafayette Square. Frankfurter soon became a regular visitor, sitting by the fire and listening to Holmes's "wonderful stream" of ideas.[5] The Holmeses also visited Frankfurter and his lively friends, who included the brilliant journalist Walter Lippmann, at their bachelor quarters, which they called "The House of Truth." The home was owned by U.S. Commissioner of Indian Affairs Robert G. Valentine, and the young men who lived there enjoyed entertaining and talking politics.[6] Holmes found them enchanting. In an early letter to Frankfurter, he wrote, "It will be many years before you have the occasion to know the happiness and encouragement that comes to an old man from the sympathy of the young."[7]

Scholars have found a variety of motivating factors shaping the development of the relationship between Holmes and the young reformers. G. Edward White has stressed Holmes's desire for recognition growing out of public indifference to his scholarship—"the fruits of his earlier ambition." Liva Baker portrays Holmes, sadly watching his old friends pass away, seeking a sense of security from a new generation "unlikely to desert him by dying." This view of Holmes savors the contrast between the active reformism of the young men and his own more scholarly and isolated life in the 1870s. David Hollinger has written that the ties binding Holmes to Frankfurter and his friends were forged partly by their admiration of his judicial philosophy, but more importantly, by the need of both parties to separate themselves from parochial cultures—for Holmes, Brahmin Boston with its anti-Semitism and, for the young men, the orthodox Jewry of their parents.[8] All scholars agree, however, that as the web of relationships de-

5. *Felix Frankfurter Reminisces*, as recorded by Dr. Harlan B. Phillips (New York: Reynal, 1960), 58.

6. Jeffrey O'Connell and Nancy Dart, "The House of Truth: Home of the Young Frankfurter and Lippmann," *Catholic University Law Review* 35 (1985): 79.

7. Holmes to Frankfurter, March 8, 1912. Several years later, Holmes wrote to John Chipman Gray: "I am all alone except for some of the young fellows, especially Frankfurter who you introduced to me." Holmes to Gray, May 10, 1914, Box 33, folder 25, Oliver Wendell Holmes, Jr., Papers, Harvard Law School Library. Hereinafter Holmes Papers.

8. White, *Justice Oliver Wendell Holmes*, 354–77; Baker, *Justice from Beacon Hill*, 454–55; David A. Hollinger, "The 'Tough-Minded' Justice Holmes, Jewish Intellectuals, and the Making of an American Icon," in Robert W. Gordon, ed., *The Legacy of Oliver Wendell Holmes, Jr.* (Stanford: Stanford University Press, 1992), 216–28. The culture of nineteenth-century Boston was shaped in good part by the genteel poetry and essays of Holmes's father, Oliver

veloped, Frankfurter was at the center. In an essay written many years later, Matthew Josephson caught the warmth, energy, and excitement that Frankfurter imparted to the social circles that formed around him: "Wherever Frankfurter is, there is no boredom. As soon as he bounces in—he never walks, he bounces—the talk and the laughter begin, and they never let up. He brings with him the sweep of national affairs and the human interest of personal gossip."[9]

The correspondence began in 1912, in the context of social calls, and continued until the end of 1932 when Holmes was no longer able to write. Several letters from Frankfurter, then a professor at Harvard Law School and leading New Dealer, exist for the period 1933–34. A total of 373 letters, 243 from Holmes to Frankfurter and 130 from Frankfurter to Holmes, have been preserved, and nearly all are included in this volume. In both quantity and quality, Holmes's contribution is superior. The numerical imbalance may be explained by the fact that many Frankfurter letters were either destroyed or removed, perhaps by Holmes but possibly by Frankfurter himself. This latter possibility is based in part upon our study of the pattern of letters remaining, which we discuss below, but also upon the evidence uncovered by Melvin Urofsky and David Levy that Frankfurter may have destroyed nearly all of his letters to Louis D. Brandeis.[10] In any case, although some remarkable individual letters from Frankfurter to Holmes remain, Paul Freund's comment, in correspondence with one of the editors, is apt: "In number and significance the letters are of course strongly weighted on Holmes's side, a bias that is actually fortunate, in view of Frankfurter's constant deference to his idol."[11]

The collection may be conveniently divided into three parts, the first running through World War I and its immediate aftermath, the second covering the 1920s, and a final section marked by Holmes's decline following the death of Mrs. Holmes on April 30, 1929. Each period is shaped by unique concerns that can be clarified by editorial comment.

In 1931, Holmes chose Frankfurter, in an equivocal way, to write his bi-

---

Wendell Holmes, who lived until 1894 when Holmes was fifty-three. Many scholars have commented on the psychological tension and intellectual rivalry that characterized relations between the two men.

9. Wallace Mendelson, ed., *Felix Frankfurter: A Tribute* (New York: Reynal, 1964); *The New Yorker* 16 (November 30, 1940): 25.

10. See below, xix; Melvin I. Urofsky and David W. Levy, eds., *"Half Brother, Half Son": The Letters of Louis D. Brandeis to Felix Frankfurter* (Norman: University of Oklahoma Press, 1991), 10, 13: "It is our suspicion that Frankfurter destroyed a majority of his letters to Brandeis in the early 1940s."

11. Paul Freund to Robert M. Mennel, February 23, 1984.

ography, a development that has further complicated the task of editing. Frankfurter never wrote the "authorized" work, but he outlived Holmes by thirty years, during which time he campaigned relentlessly to enhance Holmes's reputation as well as his own. As part of that effort, Frankfurter passed on to Mark Howe the task of writing Holmes's biography. Frankfurter closely supervised Howe while simultaneously promoting other biographical projects on Louis D. Brandeis and himself. In this somewhat tense atmosphere, Howe deferred publication of the Holmes-Frankfurter correspondence. This decision, while understandable, had further ramifications since Howe died in 1967, only two years after Frankfurter had passed away. In the aftermath, Paul Freund, Holmes's literary executor, continued the "authorized" biographer format until 1982. This story too deserves to be told.

The letters during the initial period, from 1912 until after World War I, are intermittent because Frankfurter spent much of his time in Washington, thus allowing for face-to-face visits. He supported Theodore Roosevelt in the 1912 Bull Moose campaign but remained in the War Department following Stimson's departure in the aftermath of Woodrow Wilson's victory. In 1914, Frankfurter joined the Harvard Law faculty, but returned to wartime Washington in 1917 to serve the Wilson administration as Chairman of the War Labor Policies Board. He advocated strong federal controls over labor-management relations and sought, with little success, to establish the eight-hour day in basic industries. In 1919, Frankfurter returned to Harvard, where he continued to build a legendary career as a teacher and advocate of liberal causes.

The correspondence between Holmes and Frankfurter soon reflected a deepening and reciprocal affection—from Frankfurter's side, an exuberant, filial devotion approaching deification. "My Justice! March 8 is one of my votive days, and a very happy one" began a birthday greeting. "Noblest of Friends" opened another letter. Holmes's tone was in general more formal—"Dear Frankfurter"—but on occasion he too showed deep emotion: "Felicissime! Or, oh my most particular Felix (Felix=special)" ran one salutation.[12]

Several events help to explain the deepening friendship. In 1916 Frankfurter introduced Holmes to the British polymath, Harold Laski.[13] The ensuing Holmes-Laski correspondence, which constitutes one of the great

12. Frankfurter to Holmes, undated, Box 30, folder 1, Holmes Papers; Frankfurter to Holmes, December 23, 1917; Holmes to Frankfurter, March 27, 1917.

13. Mark DeWolfe Howe, ed., *Holmes-Laski Letters: The Correspondence of Mr. Justice Holmes and Harold J. Laski, 1916–1935* (Cambridge: Harvard University Press, 1953).

collections in western letters, further strengthened the connection between Holmes and an entire generation of young political thinkers. An equally important tie between Holmes and Frankfurter was formed by Frankfurter's marriage to Marion Denman in 1919. The daughter of a Congregationalist minister and a graduate of Smith College, Marion Frankfurter balanced her husband's ebullience with a cool intelligence and refined nature. Her sensitivity resulted periodically in mental anguish requiring professional care, but the marriage remained a devoted one.[14] Holmes named her "Luina" after a portrait by the Renaissance artist Bernardino Luini. Her beauty, wit, and charm also impressed Mrs. Holmes and created a bond between the couples.

At first, the subjects of the letters ran more to personal, social, and philosophical topics than to discussion of legal questions. Holmes dispensed familiar opinions; for example: "The American public seems to believe that the Sherman Act and smashing great fortunes are roads to an ideal—which seems to me open to debate." Frankfurter praised Holmes's ideas, offered suggestions for leisure reading and, somewhat disingenuously, sought career advice. "And now I want the help of your reaction," he wrote regarding Harvard's offer of a professorship. Although Holmes was invigorated by the praise and intellectual breadth of his new friend, he was not shy about offering wry rejoinders. His lengthy response to Frankfurter's request for advice concluded "with an impression superadded that you have already made up your mind." G. Edward White aptly observes the reciprocal nature of the exchange: "Holmes is flattered in being consulted by a far younger man, and Frankfurter is flattered in being permitted to consult Holmes about his future."[15]

The beginning of Frankfurter's career at Harvard Law School provided a new basis for the relationship and developed patterns and themes that would come to characterize the correspondence in the 1920s. Starting in the spring of 1915, Frankfurter annually selected Holmes's secretary from the Law School's graduating class. Holmes routinely warned that the man—and all of the secretaries were men—must serve, "subject to my right to die or resign." He much preferred bachelors to married men: "I want a free man, and one who may be a contribution to society."[16] Over the years,

14. Baker, *Frankfurter*, 49–50, 75–76, 89–90; Parrish, *Frankfurter and His Times*, 76–78, 123–24, 176–77. See also, H. N. Hirsch, *The Enigma of Felix Frankfurter* (New York: Basic Books, 1981), 37, 49–51, 81–85, 208. Hirsch portrays an unhappy marriage, the principal cause of which was Frankfurter's "dominant, aggressive personality."

15. Holmes to Frankfurter, April 8, 1913; Frankfurter to Holmes, July 4, 1913; Holmes to Frankfurter, July 15, 1913; G. Edward White, "Holmes as Correspondent," *Vanderbilt Law Review* 43 (1990): 1707, 1725.

16. Holmes to Frankfurter, February 11, 1920, and January 6, 1925.

a number of the clerks—the eminent New Dealers Thomas G. Corcoran and James Henry Rowe, Jr., Holmes's future biographer Mark DeWolfe Howe, and the alleged communist spy Alger Hiss—went on to achieve fame of their own.

Frankfurter initiated another ongoing practice by promoting Holmes's influence through commemorative publications, the first being the April 1916 issue of the *Harvard Law Review*, which celebrated Holmes's seventy-fifth birthday. Frankfurter's own contribution, "The Constitutional Opinions of Justice Holmes," relied heavily on the Justice's own words, but the publication was itself significant for several reasons. First, it demonstrated what G. Edward White has termed "the ubiquity of Frankfurter's presence" in Holmes scholarship. Here began a relentless campaign to lionize Holmes in various publications, articles, books, and the new liberal journal *The New Republic*. Second, the Holmes portrayed in these forums was the leader of a revolution in constitutional law whose rulings widened the regulatory power of the Commerce Clause and restricted the use of the Fourteenth Amendment's Due Process Clause to frustrate legislative reform. That Holmes's actual decisions were inconsistent on these issues did not disturb Frankfurter in the least.[17]

Beginning in 1914, Holmes and Frankfurter corresponded more frequently about Court cases and the decision-making process. Writing to Holmes about his dissent in a labor case, Frankfurter exclaimed, "I *am* stirred up about the decision as a student of Constitutional law and how she is made." In addition to praising Holmes, Frankfurter encouraged him to gossip about his fellow Justices. Responding to Frankfurter's query about a decision by the idiosyncratic Joseph P. McKenna, Holmes remembered in another McKenna decision "a distinct sentence that is delightfully distorted by taking it alone—'It is misleading to say that men and women have rights.' I told him that I should make it the text of a destructive sociological discourse."[18] In the next decade, this confiding tone would become more prominent.

The letters during the 1920s are shaped by American reaction to the shattering impact of World War I and its aftermath. The triumph of Bolshevism in Russia, and the collapse of Woodrow Wilson's Peace Plan combined with nativist American fear of immigration to set off a wave of antilabor and antiradical activity throughout the United States. Attorney General

17. White, *Justice Oliver Wendell Holmes*, 361–65. Frankfurter did not comment upon most Holmes decisions with which he disagreed, making the rare moment of documented discord between the two all the more revealing. See below, xxiii–xxv.

18. Frankfurter to Holmes, January 27, 1915; Holmes to Frankfurter, December 19, 1915.

A. Mitchell Palmer's Red Raids in January 1920 served as a model for local and state campaigns against dissidents. In the face of these crusades, Frankfurter helped to found the American Civil Liberties Union and staunchly defended the right of free speech and the right of workers to organize. These activities provoked the wrath of the Boston Brahmins dominating Harvard's Board of Overseers, who pressured President A. Lawrence Lowell to fire him.

Holmes also supported civil liberties. Indeed, with Justice Louis D. Brandeis, he provided the benchmark for the expanded, modern meaning of the subject in his famous *Abrams* dissent where his phrase—"we should be eternally vigilant against attempts to check the expression of opinions that we loathe"—tacitly suggested a "preferred" place for the Bill of Rights in Constitutional law.[19] By the mid-twentieth century, expansive interpretations of individual rights would be joined to a permissive attitude toward economic legislation to form the two legs of modern judicial liberalism. Frankfurter's own jurisprudence remained based upon judicial restraint toward laws regulating the economy and to legislative efforts curtailing civil liberties.[20]

In 1920, however, judicial liberalism was an unarticulated, minority view. In fact, Holmes's civil liberties record was decidedly mixed—belated, inconsistent, and, like his philosophy of judicial restraint, tinged with cynicism.[21] He pragmatically urged Frankfurter to pursue a cautious course so as not to endanger his position at Harvard: "Of course, I believe in academic freedom but, on the other hand, it is to be remembered that a professor's conduct may affect the good will of the institution to which he belongs."[22] Frankfurter repeatedly sought to assure Holmes that his defense of free speech did not encompass support for communism and, despite several confrontations with the Overseers, he was not fired.[23] Frankfurter's

19. *Abrams v. U.S.*, 250 U.S. 616, 630 (1919). See Richard Polenberg, *Fighting Faiths: The Abrams Case, the Supreme Court, and Free Speech* (New York: Viking, 1987), 224–27.

20. On the evolution of Frankfurter's thought on judicial review of economic and civil liberties legislation, see Hirsch, *Enigma*, 127–76, and Melvin I. Urofsky, *Felix Frankfurter: Judicial Restraint and Individual Liberties* (Boston: Twayne, 1991), 58–59, 102.

21. White, *Justice Oliver Wendell Holmes*, 348–53, 438–50. Of a later case, *Gitlow v. New York*, 268 U.S. 652 (1925), Holmes wrote, "I gave an expiring kick on the last day (Brandeis was with me) in favor of the right to drool on the part of believers in the proletarian dictatorship." Holmes to Frankfurter, June 14, 1925.

22. Holmes to Frankfurter, December 4, 1919.

23. Holmes's concern about Frankfurter's susceptibility to radical causes did not end with this incident. In 1921, responding to Holmes's query, Frankfurter vehemently denied that he was involved in the series of events that permitted Leon Trotsky to leave the United States and return, via Canada, to Russia in 1917. See Holmes to Frankfurter, November 26, 1921,

friend Harold Laski was not so lucky, losing his Harvard instructorship after a series of episodes tinged with anti-Semitism.[24]

The correspondence during the 1920s forms the core of the collection, in both length and thematic substance. The extant letters comprise nearly two-thirds of the whole, an indication of the enormous size the collection would have achieved had all of Frankfurter's letters been included. The exchanges for 1921, the most complete of the decade, are the exception that proves the point. There are eighteen letters from Holmes in that year and fourteen from Frankfurter; even here, at least three Frankfurter letters are missing. In the following two years there are only five letters from Frankfurter and thirty-three from Holmes, an imbalance in the record that did not change for the remainder of the decade.

In reflecting upon the subjects of the missing Frankfurter letters as well as the character of the extant letters, we must consider the possibility that Frankfurter winnowed his part of the correspondence, perhaps shortly after Holmes died. The Holmes letters themselves indicate that the missing Frankfurter letters contained remarks on important events—the Presidential election of 1916, the Sacco-Vanzetti case, and key Court decisions such as *Gilbert v. Minnesota* (1920) and, as discussed below, *Pennsylvania Coal Co. v. Mahon* (1922). On political matters especially, Frankfurter's reformism was often at odds with Holmes's staunch Republicanism. Thus, Frankfurter may have removed some of his own letters in order to deflect attention from their differences. Also, the surviving Frankfurter letters generally endorse opinions of Holmes with which Frankfurter agreed, or respond to Holmes's praise of his scholarly work. Several Frankfurter letters probably also owe their preservation to his ongoing effort to establish his judicial lineage from Holmes. In these, Frankfurter lauds the legal opinions, literary essays, and personal qualities of Judge Benjamin N. Cardozo, who sat on the New York Court of Appeals. Cardozo took Holmes's seat in 1932; when Cardozo died in 1938 Frankfurter replaced him.[25]

The volume of letters in this period may also be explained by the phys-

---

and Frankfurter to Holmes, December 1, 1921. It is worthwhile noting that the Frankfurter letters preserved in this collection often display terse, even unsympathetic opinions about labor issues.

24. Holmes to Frankfurter, February 11 and 17, 1920; Frankfurter to Holmes, April 19, 1920.

25. See Holmes to Frankfurter, November 5, 1916 (election of 1916), March 18 and September 9, 1927 (Sacco-Vanzetti), December 22, 1920, and February 14, 1923, and below, xxiii–xxv (*Gilbert* and *Pennsylvania Coal* cases). On Cardozo, see Holmes to Frankfurter, April 29, 1916, January 22, 1925. July 12, 1930, and Frankfurter to Holmes, April 18 and 25, 1921, May 2, 1921, June 30, 1925, and June 13, 1928.

ical distance separating the correspondents for most of each year. Frankfurter saw Holmes when he came to Washington on business, as when he argued the important Washington, D.C., minimum wage case before the Supreme Court.[26] He occasionally visited the Justice at his Beverly Farms summer home north of Boston. Holmes hated the telephone, so, for most of the year, letters were the only way to maintain the personal bond that had grown strong in the wartime years.

The necessity of relying upon letters encouraged a deeper, more nuanced relationship—allowing for discussion of legal philosophy and permitting both Holmes and Frankfurter to omit discussion of sensitive matters. Holmes, for example, ignored a caustic comment about his close friend, the British scholar James Bryce, of whose two-volume *Modern Democracies* (1921) Frankfurter wrote: "They are not as dull as he is."[27] Likewise, when Holmes wrote inviting endorsement of a heterodox opinion or attitude, Frankfurter either remained silent or praised other opinions. Such was his response to Holmes's defense of his notorious *Buck v. Bell* decision: "I think my cases this term have been of rather a high average of interest e.g., the Virginia Sterilizing Act."[28]

Holmes's letters, bearing nearly the entire narrative burden for the decade, are distinguished by acute observations about cases before the Court and by his ruminations on the meaning of the judicial role. Prodded by Frankfurter, he also commented regularly on an extraordinary range of literary and artistic topics, sharing memories both recent and long past.

26. *Adkins v. Children's Hospital*, 261 U.S. 525 (1922).

27. Frankfurter to Holmes, May 2, 1921. Frankfurter's criticism mirrored Laski's more severe evaluation, which Holmes tepidly endorsed. Bryce was, however, one of Holmes's oldest friends. He had introduced Holmes to British society and corresponded with him on the challenges of legal scholarship. Of a forthcoming visit to the United States, Bryce wrote: "It is delightful, dear old friends, to think of seeing you so soon." Howe, ed., *Holmes-Laski Letters*, 325, 327, 329; Novick, 142–46, 151, 155–56, 196–97.; White, *Justice Oliver Wendell Holmes*, 130–31, 198, 205, 226; Bryce to Holmes, August 4, 1921, Box 38, folder 13, Holmes Papers.

28. Holmes to Frankfurter, May 14, 1927; Frankfurter to Holmes, June 5, 1927; *Buck v. Bell*, 274 U.S. 200, 207 (1926). Holmes's majority opinion, upholding the law with the rationalization, "Three generations of imbeciles are enough," may have caused Frankfurter discomfort, but it exemplified the philosophy of judicial restraint. However, Brandeis and Frankfurter apparently did not discuss the case either, perhaps because Brandeis had supported Holmes. Also, Brandeis and Frankfurter were then fully occupied with efforts to appeal the murder conviction of the Massachusetts anarchists Nicola Sacco and Bartolomeo Vanzetti. The appeal proved unsuccessful and the two men were executed on August 27, 1927. Holmes complimented Frankfurter's criticisms of the Massachusetts justice system, but remained unsympathetic to the cause that, he believed, exemplified "the undue prominence given to red opinions which interest more than black skins." Holmes to Frankfurter, September 9, 1927; Parrish, *Frankfurter and His Times*, 176–96.

How astonishing to read the musings of a man who, as a boy, remembered Herman Melville "dimly as a neighbor of ours at Pittsfield," who knew both the painter William Morris Hunt and the philosopher William James as "Bill," who could read Homer, "*not* in a translation," and who could respond to a Frankfurter reading tip: "Think not, my son, to introduce me to Marcel Proust. I read *Du Cote de Chez Swann* soon after it came out and another of the series."[29]

The capaciousness of Holmes's mind and the acuity of his observations make these letters a delight to read. They are particularly fascinating because they show Holmes trying, with little success, to communicate to Frankfurter his conception of what it meant to be a judge. White argues that Holmes "was much more interested in receiving flattery that confirmed his continued importance to a younger generation of lawyers than he was in actually having any impact on Frankfurter's career."[30] Holmes certainly enjoyed the attention, but several of his 1920s letters to Frankfurter are characterized by a serious tone that merits further consideration. In commenting upon cases before the Court but also in more philosophical remarks, Holmes sought to teach Frankfurter the central importance of a judge striking a careful balance on the question of the independence of the judiciary. Holmes had addressed this issue decades earlier in the well-known opening lines of *The Common Law*: "The life of the law has not been logic; it has been experience. The felt necessities of the time, the prevalent moral and political theories, institutions of public policy, avowed or unconscious, *even the prejudices which judges share with their fellow men*, have had more to do than the syllogism in determining the rules by which men should be governed"[31] (italics added). This passage, because it joined "institutions of public policy" with "felt necessities," has often been cited as endorsing judicial restraint toward legislative regulation of the economy. It rejects the syllogistic reasoning of conservatives who believed that judges were oracular guardians of property or "natural" rights specifically protected by the Constitution's Due Process Amendments.

The emphasized clause, however, also supports a modified definition of the oracular role. By characterizing judges as both human and fallible, Holmes deflated conservative intimations of judicial autonomy while continuing to insist that judges do respond to "the felt necessities of the time." He would later define this obligation as an essential part of the duties of the

29. Holmes to Frankfurter, April 16, 1921; September 3, 1921; July 8, 1923; August 9, 1921; July 12, 1923.

30. White, "Holmes as Correspondent," 1722.

31. Holmes, *The Common Law*, 1. For a thorough analysis of *The Common Law*, see White, *Justice Oliver Wendell Holmes*, 148–95.

"jobbist." Edmund Wilson's description links Holmes's conception of the role with the tradition of New England Calvinism: "The jobbist is one who works at his role without trying to improve the world or make a public impression. He tries to accomplish this professional job as well as it can be accomplished, to give it everything of which he is capable. The jobbist is alone with his job and with the ideal of touching the superlative—which in his grandfather Abiel Holmes's time would have been called being chosen for salvation."[32]

Utilizing the idea of jobbism, Holmes fashioned a place for judicial review even as his definition of "prevalent moral and political theories" changed. Morton Horwitz has shown that by the late 1890s Holmes abandoned his faith in society as an organic whole governed largely by custom and came to accept the new industrial order where property was increasingly defined as a construct of state policy and hence subject to legislative regulation.[33] This intellectual shift reflected Holmes's increasing skepticism regarding change, but did not signify his abdication of the judicial role to the legislative or executive branches of the state.[34] The "prejudices" that he shared with his fellow man diminished but did not negate the authority of judicial review. As Wilson notes, the "jobbist," disliking the laws that society made him enforce, "would . . . sometimes seize upon the benefit of a doubt to declare himself in the opposite sense."[35] In other words, Holmes could question both syllogistic conservatism when it ignored the historical dimension of the law and liberal reformism when it placed undue faith in legislation.

Exchanges between the two men regarding two cases illustrate Holmes's effort to explain his judicial philosophy and Frankfurter's relentlessly political focus. In one, *Duplex Co. v. Deering* (1921), Holmes supported the position of restraint, in the other, *Pennsylvania Coal Co. v. Mahon* (1922), he did not. In *Duplex*, a ruling on the Clayton Antitrust Act (1914), the majority opinion of Justice Mahlon Pitney found that the Act's prohibition against labor injunctions did not protect unions engaged in a secondary boycott from damage suits. Holmes joined Brandeis's dissent, which held that the conflict was "not for judges to determine."[36]

32. Edmund Wilson, *Patriotic Gore: Studies in the Literature of the Civil War* (New York: Oxford, 1962), 789–90.

33. Morton J. Horwitz, "The Place of Justice Holmes in American Judicial Thought," in Gordon, ed., *The Legacy of Oliver Wendell Holmes, Jr.*, 31–71.

34. Several scholars, especially Yosal Rogat, "The Judge as Spectator," *University of Chicago Law Review* 31 (1964): 213, noting Holmes's fatalism and sense of cosmic loneliness, have questioned his reputation as a defender of civil liberties.

35. Wilson, *Patriotic Gore*, 794.

36. *Duplex v. Deering*, 254 U.S. 443, 479 (1921).

Frankfurter bemoaned Pitney's decision by praising a famous Holmes essay urging latitude for legislative action: "I have been curious to try to pierce below the surface of Pitney's opinion in the Clayton Act case. Why did he decide as he decided, why does he live in a world into which, apparently, your 'Privilege, Malice and Intent,' with all its implications has never intruded[?]" Holmes answered by noting his distaste for the Clayton Act—"a piece of legislative humbug." Agreeing with Brandeis that the conflict should have been initially litigated in state rather than federal courts, he had little sympathy with the sociological tone of the dissent. "I think it pretty doubtful that the Court of Appeals would hold this [the boycott] O.K.," he remarked pointedly to Frankfurter. Holmes concluded, "I went the whole hog with Brandeis but I am not inclined to be severe on the opposite view, even while I think it a public misfortune." Frankfurter responded to this and another decision weakening the Clayton Act by praising the dissenters and excoriating the "appalling result," adding that the labor movement's real need was "expert assistance." Caught up in his advocation of labor's political goals, Frankfurter failed to grasp Holmes's implicit suggestion that judges should take a long view of the issues and not tie themselves to the immediate interests of one party or the other.[37]

Holmes's majority opinion in *Pennsylvania Coal* further demonstrated the differing philosophies of the two men. This case ruled unconstitutional a 1921 Pennsylvania law that prohibited mining beneath improved lands as a violation of the Contracts and Due Process Clauses, which, Holmes held, protected subsurface rights that the company had obtained at an earlier time. Conceding that the police power could qualify the property protections of the Fifth and Fourteenth Amendments, Holmes concluded: "The natural tendency of human nature is to extend the qualification more and more until at last private property disappears. But that cannot be accomplished in this way under the Constitution of the United States." Brandeis's dissent supported the law as a public safety measure and therefore an integral contribution to "living and doing business in a civilized community."[38]

37. Frankfurter to Holmes, January 26, 1921; Holmes to Frankfurter, January 30, 1921. Frankfurter's views on this and other subjects often appeared as unsigned editorials in *The New Republic*. See Parrish, *Frankfurter and His Times*, 164, 301. A similar exchange followed *Nickel v. Cole*, 256 U.S. 222 (1921), where Holmes wrote the majority opinion favoring restraint. Frankfurter to Holmes, April 18, 1921; Holmes to Frankfurter, April 20, 1921.

38. *Pennsylvania Coal Company v. Mahon*, 260 U.S. 393, 415, 422 (1922). White, *Justice Oliver Wendell Holmes*, 401–403; Levy and Urofsky, eds., *Half Brother, Half Son*, 127–28, 130–31. Commenting on this case, Paul Freund wrote, "For me, the main interest in the letters for that year [1922] is the cleavage between Holmes and Brandeis on the extent of protection to property rights. It is interesting that when these occasional cleavages occurred, Frankfurter refrained from his usual exuberant resonance." Paul Freund to Robert M. Mennel, June 20, 1985. A recent study, Mary Ann Glendon, *A Nation Under Lawyers* (New York:

Frankfurter did not mention the case when he next wrote to Holmes, but an article in *The New Republic*, written by Brandeis's former secretary Dean Acheson, termed the dissent "the superior statesmanship."[39] Brandeis suspected the conservative influence of Holmes's current secretary, Robert M. Benjamin. He and others even speculated that the decision was a result of the Justice's recent illness.[40] Aware that he had displeased his liberal friends, Holmes was unrepentant. Statesmanship, he grumbled to Laski, is "an effective word but needs caution using it."[41]

Frankfurter's letters for this period are almost entirely missing, but he must have mentioned the subject for Holmes to have made the following remark:

> Let me timidly suggest caution in the use of the word statesmanship with regard to judges. Of course, it is true that considerations of the same class come before their minds that have to be or ought to be the motives of legislators, but the word suggests a more political way of thinking than is desirable and also has become slightly *banal*. . . . A statesman would consider whether it was wise to bring to the mind of Congress what it might do in this or that direction—but it seems to me wrong to modify or delay a decision upon such grounds. When economic views affect judicial action I should prefer to give such action a different name from that which I should apply to the course of Wilson or Lodge.[42]

Here and elsewhere, Holmes tried to show that judicial "statesmanship" meant something more than agreeing with the laws that reformers convinced legislatures to pass. Excessive Court interventions against economic regulation could weaken the legislative branch, he conceded, but the "fundamental responsibilities" of the Supreme Court remained. He added

---

Farrar, Straus and Giroux, 1994), 44–45, has suggested that Holmes may have been favorably disposed to the company because he admired the skill of its counsel, John W. Davis.

39. White, *Justice Oliver Wendell Holmes*, 403. When Brandeis joined the Court in 1916, Frankfurter began to supply his secretaries who included Acheson, James M. Landis, Paul Freund, Henry J. Friendly, Henry M. Hart, Louis L. Jaffee, David Riesman, and Willard H. Hurst.

40. Urofsky and Levy, eds., *Half Brother, Half Son*, 130–33. Paul Freund remembered: "In discussing the *Coal* case in his classes, Professor [Thomas Reed] Powell ascribed what he regarded as Holmes' aberration to the effects of his recent operation." Freund to Mennel, June 20, 1985.

41. Howe, ed., *Holmes-Laski Letters*, 473–74.

42. Holmes to Frankfurter, September 9, 1923. Holmes may have been responding to Frankfurter's "Twenty Years of Mr. Justice Holmes' Constitutional Opinions," *Harvard Law Review* 36 (June 1923): 909, 919, which described Holmes's work as "in the school of statesmanship. He is philosopher become king." Frankfurter dissembled, however, since he pointedly restricted analysis to cases "actually decided" before December 8, 1922. *Pennsylvania Coal* was announced on December 11.

a wry note of attribution: "The best defence [of due process] I ever heard came from Brandeis many years ago—that constitutional restrictions enable a man to sleep at night and know that he won't be robbed before morning—which, in days of legislative activity and general scheming, otherwise he scarcely would feel sure about."[43]

Judges, in other words, had no choice. Unlike politicians, who can defer or refuse to take action, judges must rule on the cases that come before them and their decisions will likely offend one of the parties. For Holmes, this duty was tempered by another "fundamental fact": "that . . . all questions are ultimately questions of degree"—a view that conservatives such as Justice McKenna, he thought, failed to recognize.[44] But it was just right for a judge who saw himself upholding the concept of judicial review—performing the role of oracle in a world of fragmentation and disbelief. As he wrote to Frankfurter at the end of the decade: "I see no reason for expecting to touch bottom. I accept my limitations and bow my head."[45]

Holmes expressed these opinions numerous times in letters and published writings, but Frankfurter constructed another Holmes whose decisions invariably supported Frankfurter's reformist predilections. During the 1920s and indeed throughout their relationship, Frankfurter simply ignored those of Holmes's decisions with which he disagreed while enthusiastically citing those that supported his views. Although he claimed to disdain the label of "onward and upwarder," Frankfurter remained in essence the progressive, "interested in having some pet ideas accepted by the courts," hoping to encourage "organized effort towards more life" and "disinterested expert guidance."[46] Joseph Lash's comparison of the two men remains persuasive:

> If any Justice served him as a model, Holmes did, and yet Frankfurter's espousal of Holmes's Olympian philosophy seems a little forced. Holmes was a genuine Olympian. He never read newspapers; Frankfurter devoured them. . . . Holmes really was above politics. Frankfurter was deeply involved. . . . For Holmes, law served as a jumping-off place for larger cosmic speculations; for Frankfurter, philosophy was of interest only if it helped to solve legal issues. Holmes never crusaded. . . . Frankfurter was always promoting many causes. Holmes was an ironist, Frankfurter an enthusiast.[47]

43. Holmes to Frankfurter, April 20, 1921.

44. *Id.*

45. Holmes to Frankfurter, February 21, 1929.

46. Frankfurter to Holmes, January 27, 1915; April 19, 1920; March 28, 1914; November 11, 1915. For a contrary view of Frankfurter, see Glendon, *A Nation Under Lawyers*, 128–29.

47. Joseph P. Lash, *From the Diaries of Felix Frankfurter* (New York: Norton, 1975), 77. Hirsch, *Enigma of Frankfurter*, 128–32, has suggested that Brandeis rather than Holmes ful-

This comparison explains Frankfurter's success as a New Deal reformer as well as his subsequent frustrations as a Supreme Court Justice. Not long after his appointment in 1939, he began to lecture his colleagues, particularly Hugo Black and William O. Douglas, on the significance of Holmes's ideas. His interpretation soon came to include a strained reading of Holmes's record in civil liberties cases where he took his cue from a 1923 dissent, *Bartels v. Iowa*, in which Holmes argued that statutes forbidding children from speaking languages other than English in the public schools did not deny their liberty under the Fourteenth Amendment.[48] Justices Hugo Black and William O. Douglas refused to support this kind of judicial restraint and, ignoring Frankfurter, went on to develop the doctrine of preference for individual rights that defined the Supreme Court in the mid-twentieth century. Whether or not Frankfurter's career on the Court is ultimately considered a "failure," his contemporaries saw his accomplishments as falling well short of the attainments of his idols, Holmes and Brandeis.[49]

Holmes may have detected the difficulties to come. At the conclusion of the debate on statesmanship and in the course of expressing regret at a missed opportunity to visit with Frankfurter, he remarked with more wistfulness than conviction: "No matter—you and I are philosophers and to a certain extent can transcend time and space."[50] The correspondence of the 1920s shows, on the contrary, two archetypes of the American mind,

---

filled the definition of Frankfurter's "statesman" in that he, like Frankfurter, believed that the judiciary could encourage intelligent social policy by allowing legislation to stand. Although close to both men, Frankfurter worshipped Holmes, who represented the establishment whose approval he so desperately sought. Thus, in Hirsch's view, he conflated the two men's judicial philosophies, distorting Holmes in the process.

48. *Bartels v. Iowa*, 262 U.S. 404 (1923); Holmes to Frankfurter, June 6, 1923; Richard M. Abrams, "The Reputation of Felix Frankfurter," *American Bar Foundation Research Journal* (1985): 647. Lash, *Diaries of Frankfurter*, 68–72, and others have suggested that Frankfurter's conservatism in civil liberties cases—arguing, for example, that school children could be required to salute the flag, overriding the tenets of their religious faith—came from his intense patriotism as a naturalized citizen.

49. Urofsky, *Frankfurter: Judicial Restraint and Individual Liberties*; Melvin I. Urofsky, "The Failure of Felix Frankfurter," *University of Richmond Law Review* 26 (1991): 175. On reconsidering the significance of Frankfurter's ideas, see Michael J. Klarman's review of Urofsky's biography, *Law and History Review* 12 (1994): 407: "From the perspective of the 1990s, when judicial activism is as likely to mean judicial invalidation of affirmative action . . . as it is to mean invalidation of abortion restrictions or school prayer, one wonders if the time has not arrived to begin contemplating a revisionist rehabilitation of Frankfurter."

50. Holmes to Frankfurter, September 20, 1923.

one magisterial and the other politically engaged, deeply enjoying their personal bond but passing each other intellectually like shadows in the twilight.

The last phase of the relationship may be dated from the death of Mrs. Holmes in April of 1929. Holmes's ability to meet the demands of work was already declining and slipped further by the early 1930s. He talked increasingly of retirement. "I feel as if my first bell had rung," he wrote to Frankfurter shortly after Mrs. Holmes's passing. He revived in early 1930 when he was called upon to act briefly as Chief Justice after William Howard Taft fell mortally ill. His letters remained perceptive. The philosopher George Santayana was "good sauce to have on hand, but not a food." Jerome Frank and the Yale Legal Realists were confused about "the emotional reaction of judges—as if it were all to be set against the rules. . . . Frank's prejudice against the rules seems to forget how great a body of conduct is determined by them and how many cases they keep out of Court." Holmes no longer read Virgil by himself but listened to his secretary read a translation as he followed along in the Latin.[51]

The Justice's physical and emotional decline accelerated as the 1930–31 Term approached. "I feel as if it were time for me to die," he wrote to Laski.[52] G. Edward White has pointed out that this "method of warding off a fear by stating it openly" mingled with Holmes's increasing guilt about meeting the demands of work to form what became the standard lament of his last years.[53] "My uneasiness increases and the fear that I am not pulling my weight," he wrote Frankfurter in early 1931. After suffering what was probably a mild stroke in August, he struggled to write opinions and dozed on the Bench. At the end of the year, he was "thinking more than ever that I am finished."[54] His colleagues agreed and, following a visit on January 12, 1932, from Chief Justice Charles Evans Hughes, Holmes resigned. In retirement, he described himself as "a blank paper . . . an empty bottle." In his last letter to Frankfurter he remarked, "I have dropped into the final obscurity."[55]

Throughout these years, the younger man remained the jolly, newsy

51. Holmes to Frankfurter, May 31, 1929, October 17, 1930; Howe, ed., *Holmes-Laski Letters*, 1375.

52. Howe, ed., *Holmes-Laski Letters*, 1278.

53. White, *Justice Oliver Wendell Holmes*, 474.

54. Holmes to Frankfurter, January 27, 1931, and December 7, 1931. On Holmes's stroke or "cave in," see White, *Justice Oliver Wendell Holmes*, 458–59.

55. Holmes to Frankfurter, November 12, 1932, and November 26, 1932.

companion. "Frankfurter brings fire and invites to new adventures," said Holmes.[56] Frankfurter's ebullience was no doubt fueled by his renewed friendship with "Frank" Roosevelt, who had been elected Governor of New York in 1928. As an adviser to FDR in New York and during the New Deal, the now middle-aged reformer at last achieved influence as one of the principal architects of the welfare state.[57]

For this period, Frankfurter left a larger number of his letters to Holmes—eight in 1930 alone—in the collection. These equal, perhaps even surpass, the adulatory tone of his early correspondence. Frankfurter aimed primarily to sustain Holmes's self-confidence. The Justice's opinions were "like sparkling wine in a dry age . . . pungent and definitive . . . brave truth and luminous insight . . . A 1 ." Near career's end, Frankfurter found "the power and fire of old wholly unimpaired." Your leavetaking, he assured Holmes on the day of his resignation, was "in the grand manner."[58]

In the early 1930s, Frankfurter's political activity increased and his fame spread. In 1932 he declined a nomination to the Massachusetts Supreme Judicial Court—"a mistake" according to Holmes.[59] After Roosevelt's election, he was offered the U.S. Solicitor Generalship, which he also turned down. During the academic year 1933–34, he was George Eastman Visiting Professor at Balliol College, Oxford, where he wrote several chatty letters from "the very Hall that Wolsey built." The year concluded with a trip to Palestine, "a most inspiring and glorious adventure."[60]

The Frankfurters returned to Cambridge in the autumn of 1934, and Felix resumed his shuttling between the Law School and Washington, visiting Holmes when he came. When Holmes contracted pneumonia in late February 1935, Frankfurter left immediately for his bedside. On March 2, Holmes smiled and thumbed his nose when Frankfurter told a joke. He repeated the gesture three days later when oxygen tanks were brought in and his secretary, James Rowe, saluted him for the last time: "Every soldier to his tent, Captain Holmes." He died early in the morning of March 6, two days before his ninety-fourth birthday.[61]

In a memorandum written in the summer of 1932, Felix Frankfurter noted Holmes's increasing remoteness—his profound skepticism that he

56. Howe, ed., *Holmes-Laski Letters*, 1102.

57. See Max Freedman, *Roosevelt and Frankfurter, Their Correspondence, 1928–1945* (Boston: Little, Brown, 1967).

58. Frankfurter to Holmes, May 22, 1928, September 9, 1928, May 28, 1930, May 6, 1931, February 6, 1931, and January 12, 1932.

59. Howe, ed., *Holmes-Laski Letters*, 1406.

60. Frankfurter to Holmes, October 30, 1933, and May 7, 1934.

61. White, *Justice Oliver Wendell Holmes*, 471; Baker, *Justice from Beacon Hill*, 642.

had made any difference at all. In an addendum, Marion Frankfurter concluded that "his isolation now could only be mitigated by children to play about him."[62] Holmes told his secretary for that year: "What I want is that my days should pass as a rock in a bed of a river, with the water flowing over it."[63] But in fact Holmes wanted to spend his days in the company of loved ones, foremost of whom were Felix and Marion Frankfurter. On one of their later visits, Marion recalled Holmes reading a favorite Civil War poem: "He was terribly moved by it, and before the end the tears were streaming down his face and his voice broke and trembled. I couldn't control myself either, and at the end he turned to me and I to him, just openly crying."[64] The grace note, also from Marion Frankfurter, was supplied at the bier: "Looking at him had the strange effect of healing my grief. I saw not the ruins of Holmes' glory but the figure of death—it conveyed the impenetrability, the mystery and majesty of death itself. His absence was accidental—what I ever had of him was in me."[65]

The history of the Holmes-Frankfurter correspondence is as long and complex as the relationship itself. In 1931, Holmes informed his lawyer and executor, John Gorham Palfrey, that Felix Frankfurter would be his biographer. Holmes's decision evoked a typical, effusive response from Frankfurter: "I'm bowed with zest and humility." Holmes, also characteristically, reflected gloomily on the wisdom of his own decision, writing to Laski: "While Felix seems to me the man for the law part I can't help thinking that there well might be another part dealing with the old Yankee that could perhaps better be managed by some other Yankee. . . . I blush to assume so much interest in me—nor do I expect it."[66]

The task was additionally complicated by Holmes's wish that correspondents either destroy his letters or refrain from quoting from them for

62. White, *Justice Oliver Wendell Holmes*, 473–74. Holmes, who pretended to endorse infant damnation whenever visitors brought their children, might have agreed with Marion Frankfurter. In correspondence with the pacifist Rosika Schwimmer, whose petition for naturalization he and Brandeis had supported in a minority opinion, *United States v. Schwimmer*, 279 U. S. 644, 653–54 (1929), Holmes thanked her for sending him a copy of her sister's book, *Great Musicians as Children* (1929): "I say charming and I mean charming. I became a child again on reading them and sentimental tears drop from my eyes as I follow the boy chasing the rainbow or the youth of the other boys who followed the rainbow music. The law also is a rainbow, but you have made me forget it. I am truly obliged to you both." Holmes to Schwimmer, February 5, 1930, file 274, Small Manuscript Collection, Harvard Law School Library.

63. Baker, *Justice from Beacon Hill*, 639.

64. Memorandum, August 10, 1932, Box 54, folder 5, Holmes Papers.

65. Marion Frankfurter memorandum, March 8, 1935, Box 54, folder 5, Holmes Papers.

66. Frankfurter to Holmes, August 4, 1931; Howe, ed., *Holmes-Laski Letters*, 1320–21.

publication. In 1921, he had noted to Frankfurter: "I forget what I have written to you about my letters, but if you have not burned them, I should feel easier if you would assure me that none of them should be published after my death." Frankfurter agreed—"any wish of yours is sacred to me"—but added: "I do hope you will let me talk to you about your general attitude towards your correspondence when next we meet."[67] Some accommodation appears to have been reached, as Holmes did not pursue the issue, perhaps because he was later assured by Frankfurter and others that the biographical undertaking would be entrusted to an "authorized" scholar. The "authorized biography" approach to legal scholarship, critically termed "constitutional theosophy" by Clyde Spillenger, has of course not been able to stifle the appearance of unflattering portraits of major Supreme Court figures, particularly of Frankfurter.[68]

Holmes underestimated interest in his own life and career, but his doubts about Frankfurter's suitability as a biographer were not without foundation. Throughout the 1930s, Frankfurter was preoccupied with shaping the New Deal program; he placed many Harvard Law graduates in the new alphabet agencies and two of his "boys," Thomas G. Corcoran and Benjamin V. Cohen, crafted key pieces of federal regulatory legislation.[69] Frankfurter's scholarship continued to be respectable, but not extensive. He jointly authored several important works with younger colleagues, but his own writings on Holmes—principally, *Mr. Justice Holmes and the Supreme Court*

67. Holmes to Frankfurter, November 26, 1921, and Frankfurter to Holmes, December 1, 1921. "Perhaps when I die my executor (John Palfrey and/or Felix Frankfurter) may do something, with more materials, but I have done my best to destroy illuminating documents," Holmes wrote to the American diplomat and scholar Lewis Einstein. See, James Bishop Peabody, ed., *The Holmes-Einstein Letters: Correspondence of Mr. Justice Holmes and Lewis Einstein, 1903–1935* (New York: St. Martin's Press, 1964), 349. Also, Mark Howe omitted several *Holmes-Laski* letters in which the Justice requested that his letters be destroyed. See Isaac Kramnick and Barry Sheerman, *Harold Laski: A Life on the Left* (New York: Penguin, 1993), 585–86.

68. Clyde Spillenger, "Lifting the Veil: The Judicial Biographies of Alpheus T. Mason," *Reviews in American History* 21 (1993): 733. See Hirsch, *Enigma of Frankfurter*, and Bruce Allen Murphy, *The Brandeis/Frankfurter Connection: The Secret Political Activities of Two Supreme Court Justices* (New York: Oxford, 1982).

69. Frankfurter's influence has extended to the present time. A partial list of his law clerks from 1939 to 1962 includes Joseph L. Rauh, Jr., Philip L. Graham, Philip B. Kurland, Elliot L. Richardson, William L. Coleman, Albert M. Sacks, Abram L. Chayes, Alexander M. Bickel, James Vorenberg, John H. Mansfield, Richard N. Goodwin, David P. Currie, and Peter Edelman. For a recent analysis, see G. Edward White, "Felix Frankfurter, the Old Boy Network, and the New Deal: The Placement of Elite Lawyers in Public Service in the 1930s," in White, ed., *Intervention and Detachment: Essays in Legal History and Jurisprudence* (New York: Oxford, 1994), 149–74.

(1938)—were essentially glosses that relied heavily on the Justice's own words.[70] Prospects for Frankfurter assuming the biographical task dimmed further when Franklin Roosevelt appointed him to the Supreme Court in January 1939.

Throughout the late 1930s, scholarly work on Holmes remained difficult because the material was scattered and unorganized. In 1936, John Palfrey retrieved some letters inserted in books in the Holmes library that had been sent to the Library of Congress, which was the residual legatee in Holmes's will.[71] He stored these and other papers in his Boston law office where they were partially catalogued. Frankfurter was evidently concerned about the haphazard nature of the organizational effort as well as his own ability to do the job, for as early as 1937 he began to look for assistance. At that time, he literally ordered Mark DeWolfe Howe, who was Holmes's secretary in 1933–34, to leave private practice and go to the University of Buffalo, which, at Frankfurter's urging, had just established a law school. Frankfurter and Palfrey together assigned Howe a scholarly task—editing the correspondence between Holmes and the British legal scholar Sir Frederick Pollock.[72] Howe's wife, Mary Manning Howe, recalling the forceful impact of Frankfurter's personality, observed: "He loved his proteges, but he also owned them. It was very bad for Mark."[73]

Howe nonetheless rose to the challenge and soon completed the two-volume *Holmes-Pollock Letters*, which opened the initial era of Holmes scholarship.[74] Howe did not recognize Frankfurter in the preface, but he did acknowledge the assistance of John Palfrey, who also wrote the introduction. Palfrey was losing patience with Frankfurter, writing Howe, "Neither Laski nor Felix have yet sent in their letters, although they are doubtless avail-

70. Parrish, *Frankfurter and His Times*, 159–60, 168–75. *Mr. Justice Holmes*, reprinted in 1961 by Harvard University Press, has had little impact on scholarship. White's bibliographical essay in *Justice Oliver Wendell Holmes*, 591–609, does not mention it.

71. [Undated] Memorandum, *Material Relating to Holmes in Possession of Mark Howe at Time of His Death*, Box 1, folder 3, Grant Gilmore Papers, Harvard Law School Library. Hereinafter Gilmore Papers.

72. [Undated] Memorandum, Box 1, folder 3, Gilmore Papers; Mark DeWolfe Howe, ed., *Holmes-Pollock Letters: The Correspondence of Mr. Justice Holmes and Sir Frederick Pollock, 1874–1932* (Cambridge: Harvard University Press, 1941).

73. Lash, *From the Diaries of Felix Frankfurter*, 54–55.

74. On Holmes bibliography see White, *Justice Oliver Wendell Holmes*, 591–609, and James A. Thomson, "Playing with a Mirage: Oliver Wendell Holmes, Jr. and American Law," *Rutgers Law Journal* 22 (1990): 123. Holmes was controversial in death as in life. His letters to Pollock were attacked by Catholic scholars, who saw in his ethical relativism encouragement for the totalitarianism threatening the world in 1941. See Edward A. Purcell, Jr., *The Crisis of Democratic Theory: Scientific Naturalism and the Problem of Value* (Lexington: University Press of Kentucky, 1973), 167–68.

able."[75] Dumas Malone, editor of Harvard University Press, was also anxious to build upon the publicity of *Holmes-Pollock* by publishing more from the Holmes collection. He urged Howe to edit Holmes's letters to Nina Gray, wife of John Chipman Gray, but Howe demurred, indicating willingness to undertake the project only if he were given responsibility for publishing all of the major correspondences in the collection.[76] Writing directly to Frankfurter, Howe said that "if there is still a real chance that you will do what the Justice hoped you might . . . others should stand aside."[77] At the same time, several commercial publishers were attempting to induce Howe to write Holmes's biography, and Catherine Drinker Bowen was seeking permission to use the letters for what would become *Yankee from Olympus*, her well-known fictionalized account of Holmes's life.[78]

As a result of these exigencies, Dumas Malone and Howe's father, New England writer Mark Antony DeWolfe Howe, joined with Palfrey to induce Frankfurter to relinquish formal control of the letters to young Howe. By October 1941 an agreement had been reached wherein Howe would be responsible for writing a multivolume biography and also editing significant collections of letters as he went along. Frankfurter retained the right to contribute a "later" volume of the biography. After the arrangement was formalized in February 1942, Howe wrote to Frankfurter, "Your abdication came to me as an enormous disappointment," adding that, "If our partnership cannot be overt it may still, I hope, be an actuality—at least to the extent of giving me a feeling that I can turn to you for aid." A memorandum tracing the history of the Holmes papers states, "in the course of time Frankfurter withdrew from the project, perhaps reluctantly." In any case, Palfrey sent Howe the Holmes collection, which included "Letters to

75. Palfrey to Howe, February 17, 1941, Box 62, folder 12, Holmes Papers.

76. Howe to Malone, April 18, 1941, Box 62, folder 12, Holmes Papers.

77. Howe to Frankfurter, July 30, 1941, Box 2, folder 7, Mark DeWolfe Howe Papers, Harvard Law School Library. Hereinafter Howe Papers.

78. Howe to W. W. Norton, April 19, 1940, Box 61, folder 13, and Roger Scaife of Little, Brown to Howe, June 12, 1941, Box 62, folder 12, Holmes Papers. Bowen's request was granted but with several restrictions including no access to personal correspondence without the explicit approval of the person writing to Holmes. Frankfurter called Bowen "a writer of perception and delicacy of feeling" but added, "One can give her encouragement without giving her confidential materials." Palfrey, with Howe's agreement, required her to submit her manuscript "for comment and criticism without prejudice and without sponsorship." See Frankfurter to Palfrey, February 1, 1941, and February 17, 1941, Box 62, folder 12, Holmes Papers. *Yankee from Olympus: Justice Holmes and His Family* (Boston: Little, Brown, 1944) served as a source for Emmet Lavery's popular Broadway play, "The Magnificent Yankee" (1946), and the 1951 movie of the same title.

OWH from" many individuals including Felix Frankfurter. Howe then began to describe himself as the "official" biographer of Justice Holmes.[79]

By this time, of course, World War II had intervened. "It would . . . seem safe to predict," Howe wrote to Frankfurter, "that my first duty will not be to my task as biographer."[80] Heavily burdened by administrative duties at Buffalo, he wanted to join the Army. He did so in late 1942 and, at that time, he returned the Holmes collection to Palfrey.[81] From 1943 to 1945 Howe served first in North Africa, Sicily, and Southern France and then in Washington on the War Department General Staff. He was awarded the Legion of Merit and the Distinguished Service Medal.

In 1945, Howe resumed custody of the Holmes papers and joined the faculty of the Harvard Law School. He soon published an edited volume: *Touched with Fire: Civil War Letters and Diary of Oliver Wendell Holmes, Jr., 1861–1864* (1946). Also in 1945, John Palfrey died. Frankfurter replaced him as executor of the estate and named Harvard Law Professor Paul A. Freund, a former Brandeis law clerk and Assistant Solicitor General, as Holmes's literary executor. In 1948, Methyl Palfrey, wife of John Palfrey, on the suggestion of Mark Howe, deeded the Holmes collection to Harvard. Frankfurter and Freund controlled access to the papers but in effect delegated this authority to Mark Howe, in whose office the collection resided.[82]

Howe's position remained delicate. He had been allowed to return from

79. Malone to Howe, May 20, 1941, and October 27, 1941, Box 62, folder 12, Holmes Papers; Howe to Frankfurter, February 25, 1942, Box 2, folder 7, Howe Papers; *Material Relating to Holmes*, Box 1, folder 3, Gilmore Papers; Howe to Palfrey, August 14, 1942, Box 61, folder 12, Holmes Papers; Howe to Harry C. Shriver, May 16, 1942, Box 61, folder 14, Holmes Papers.

80. Howe to Frankfurter, December 17, 1941, Box 2, folder 7, Howe Papers. During the war, Holmes scholarship was advanced by Frankfurter's essay on Holmes in the *Dictionary of American Biography*, vol. 11 (supp. 1), 417, and by the publication of *The Mind and Faith of Justice Holmes: His Speeches, Essays, Letters and Judicial Opinions* (Boston: Little, Brown, 1943), which was edited, with introduction, commentary, and a "Note on the Holmes Literature" by the journalist Max Lerner, a friend of Frankfurter who later taught at Brandeis. Attorney General Francis Biddle, a former Holmes clerk, also published a biography, *Mr. Justice Holmes* (New York: Scribner, 1942), which was based in good part upon interviews and personal recollections. Howe disliked the aggressive research methods of Biddle and Catherine Drinker Bowen: "At the moment, I feel so uncharitable toward Philadelphians that I had better hold my tongue." Howe to Palfrey, June 8, 1942, Box 61, folder 12, Holmes Papers.

81. Howe to Palfrey, January 18, 1943, Box 61, folder 12, Holmes Papers.

82. Charles Stetson to Howe, January 21, 1946, and Howe to William J. Speers, April 13, 1946, Box 61, folder 12, Holmes Papers; *Material Relating to Holmes*, Box 1, folder 3, Gilmore Papers.

"exile" in Buffalo—the term is Mary Howe's.[83] But in addition to his writing and teaching responsibilities, he faced the major task of gathering and organizing letters and other materials from the many people with whom Holmes had corresponded. He also had to find a way to keep Justice Frankfurter at arm's length. Howe's strategy emerged in the research plan that he proposed to the President and Fellows of Harvard College:

> It has . . . become increasingly clear to me that I shall not be able to discharge my responsibility to scholarship if I permit this collection of materials to secure no higher degree of organization than is essential to my short-term obligations as biographer. The collection of materials in Harvard's possession is of extraordinary importance to all persons concerned with the intellectual history of the United States from 1860 to 1935. . . . It has, furthermore, become increasingly evident to me that many of these materials are deserving of early publication, not as part of the biography, but as self-sufficient and self-contained units.[84]

By giving priority to the publication of edited correspondence, Howe could write the biography in a methodical, chronological fashion, thereby conveniently deflecting Frankfurter's criticism of his work pace and also deferring discussion of the "later" volume that Frankfurter had promised to write. This of course was easier said than done, as Frankfurter did not hesitate to offer advice, including criticism of Howe's first draft on Holmes's early years.[85]

Howe nonetheless continued to follow his strategy by editing the massive Holmes-Laski correspondence, which came together in 1949 when Harold Laski's donation added Holmes's letters to him to the Laski letters in the collection. Frankfurter enthusiastically supported the Holmes-Laski project and wrote a spirited foreword to the two-volume work, which was completed in 1953. He continued, however, to complicate Howe's life, badgering him about the biography while at the same time urging him to publish an edition of Holmes's *Occasional Speeches*. Six months after the publication of the *Holmes-Laski Letters*, Frankfurter wrote to Howe: "Will you be able to do much on Holmes until you get your sabbatical?"[86]

83. Lash, *From the Diaries of Felix Frankfurter*, 55.

84. Howe to The President and Fellows of Harvard College, March 30, 1948, Box 12, folder 15, Howe Papers.

85. Frankfurter to Howe, May 11, 1949, Box 2, folder 8, Howe Papers. Somewhat later, a cheery letter from "Kitty" Bowen increased Howe's anxiety: "I look forward to your Holmes biography and Young Feller, there comes a time when a book must be WRITTEN." Catherine Drinker Bowen to Howe, February 28, 1951, and Howe to Bowen, March 8, 1951, Box 61, folder 9, Holmes Papers.

86. Frankfurter to Howe, October 1, 1953, Box 2, folder 11, Howe Papers. On *Occasion-*

Any scholarly criticism of Holmes was an occasion for Frankfurter to complain. He was particularly irritated by the "obtuse and unimaginative distortions" of Harvard Law Professor Lon L. Fuller, who believed, contrary to the purportedly amoral Holmes, that the law did have moral content.[87] Irving Bernstein's mildly critical essay, stressing Holmes's social conservatism and based to a considerable extent on the *Pollock* letters, caused Frankfurter to explode: "I have had to struggle with myself not to write either to Sam Morison or Perry Miller to ask why they should have printed that piece and, indeed, have given it pride of place."[88] While Howe agreed with Frankfurter's criticisms, his replies to Fuller and others were dictated not only by his convictions but also by his need to keep Frankfurter happy.[89]

---

al Speeches, see Frankfurter to Howe, December 21, 1951, March 25, 1957, and January 2, 1958; Howe to Frankfurter, June 2, 1958, December 12, 1959, and January 12, 1960, Box 185, folders 18–19, Felix Frankfurter Papers, Harvard Law School Library. Hereinafter Frankfurter Papers. *Occasional Speeches* was published originally by Little, Brown in 1891; it went through five editions, the last in 1913. Mark Howe's preface to the 1962 edition, published by Harvard, does not mention Frankfurter.

87. Frankfurter to Howe, June 16, 1950. Howe answered Fuller in a slashing essay, "The Positivism of Mr. Justice Holmes," *Harvard Law Review* 64 (1951): 529, that likened Fuller and Catholic critics of Holmes to the red-baiting columnist Westbrook Pegler. Frankfurter approved: "I thought that you dealt with the Jesuits just as you should have dealt with them—with a single keen and conclusive blow." Frankfurter to Howe, February 22, 1952, Box 185, folder 18, Frankfurter Papers. Frankfurter and Fuller had been allies in labor reform in the early 1930s. See Morton J. Horwitz, *The Transformation of American Law, 1870–1960: The Crisis of Legal Orthodoxy* (New York: Oxford, 1992), 183–84. On Fuller, see *The Law in Quest of Itself* (Chicago: Foundation Press, 1940), 63: "For him [Holmes] the notion that the law is something severable from one's notions of what it ought to be seems to have had a real and inhibitive meaning. One may admire his fidelity to a faith. But was it for the ultimate good of our law? I think there is reason to doubt it."

88. Irving Bernstein, "The Conservative Mr. Justice Holmes," *New England Quarterly* 27 (1950): 435, 452; Frankfurter to Howe, January 23, 1951, Box 185, folder 18, Frankfurter Papers. Bernstein concluded that liberals would continue to admire Holmes because he was "more liberal than reactionary colleagues," but then added a note that must have annoyed Frankfurter: "Finally, there was in Holmes an elusive, sometimes an impish quality that confounds any group that seeks to claim him entirely. He was, at bottom, himself." Samuel Eliot Morison and Perry Miller, leading lights of the Harvard history department, were members of the editorial board of *New England Quarterly*.

89. Frankfurter to Howe, June 16, 1950, Box 2, folder 9, Howe Papers. Howe too was sensitive to criticism. Rebecca West's brilliant review of the *Holmes-Laski Letters*, *Harvard Law Review* 67 (1953): 361, did not criticize Howe's editing but emphasized Laski's "rough housing of reality." Howe's irritation with "Becky Sharp," as he called her, stemmed in good part from the failure of his own plan to plant a favorable review: "More than a year ago I arranged to get galley proof to Max Lerner, so that he might complete a notice for the *HLR* as soon as possible after publication. He apparently got delayed, as one does, and had not sent in the review

After publication of the *Holmes-Laski Letters*, Howe devoted his energies to the biography. Volume I was published in 1957 and Volume II in 1963, but these carried the story only to 1882 when Holmes was appointed to the Supreme Judicial Court of Massachusetts.[90] During the 1950s, Frankfurter helped to support Howe's research program, which included reduced teaching responsibilities, by securing generous donations from two philanthropies, both controlled by Arthur W. A. Cowan, a wealthy Philadelphia lawyer. In addition to helping Howe, Cowan's donations were intended "to make possible an authoritative work on the judicial life of Mr. Justice Brandeis," whose "working papers" Frankfurter controlled.[91] In keeping with the "authorized" biographer tradition, Frankfurter designated his former clerk Alexander Bickel and Paul Freund as joint biographers of Brandeis. He also envisioned Bickel as his own biographer and soon expanded the Cowan grants to support a broadened research enterprise called the Holmes-Brandeis-Frankfurter project. Commenting on the future disposition of his papers to Bickel, whose appointment as a Research Associate at Harvard Law he had secured, Frankfurter wrote: "In view of the fact that the three of us, Holmes, Brandeis and I, were nurtured in the same tradition and that I was intimate with them and, through them, with the work of the Court for more than twenty-five years before I became one of its members, it seems desirable that my correspondence with Holmes and Brandeis, as well as my files pertaining to the Supreme Court and Federal Judiciary before I came on the Court, be included in the [Holmes] Papers."[92] In effect, the Holmes-Brandeis-Frankfurter project further isolated Frankfurter's correspondence with Holmes from prospective research-

by the time the old Board went out." The new editor "rudely pushed Max aside." Also, Howe's preface had pointed out Laski's tendency toward "exaggeration, distortion, and falsehood." See Howe to Frankfurter, January 6, 1954, Box 185, folder 18, Frankfurter Papers, and Howe, ed., *Holmes-Laski Letters*, vi.

90. Mark DeWolfe Howe, *Justice Oliver Wendell Holmes: The Shaping Years, 1841–1870* (Cambridge: Harvard University Press, 1957) and *Justice Oliver Wendell Holmes: The Proving Years, 1870–1882* (Cambridge: Harvard University Press, 1963). Volume I, vii, includes a tribute to Frankfurter; Volume II makes no mention of him. In 1955, Howe estimated that the first volume would take the story to 1883. See Howe to Frankfurter, April 20, 1955, Box 2, folder 11, Howe Papers.

91. Frankfurter to Cowan, March 20, 1954; Cowan to Frankfurter, April 28, 1954, Box 184, folder 11, Frankfurter Papers; Erwin N. Griswold to Cowan, October 11 and November 3, 1954, Box 61, folder 7, Holmes Papers; Box 1, folder 40, and Box 2, folder 11, Howe Papers. The philanthropies were the Jacob Brenner Foundation and the Philadelphia Community Foundation.

92. Frankfurter to Bickel, September 1, 1954, Case File, Holmes Papers; Financial Report, Holmes-Brandeis-Frankfurter project (1956/57), Box 63, folder 14, Holmes Papers.

ers by making it the domain of two "authorized" biographers, Howe and Bickel.

Frankfurter's control of Brandeis materials was also restrictive. He had written on Brandeis and, as with Holmes, regarded himself as the custodian of the Justice's reputation.[93] He was sharply critical of Alpheus T. Mason, the first biographer of Brandeis, and prevented him from consulting relevant judicial papers.[94] Yet, Frankfurter's protectiveness regarding the memoranda, notes, and letters relating to cases heard by himself, Holmes, and Brandeis must be set against his openness toward making available to the public his own personal papers, which are located in the Library of Congress. These include his long and intimate correspondence with Marion Frankfurter.

In the later years of his life, Frankfurter's involvement with the Holmes and Brandeis biographies became even more frenetic. He lobbied Harvard Law School Dean Erwin Griswold to retain Alexander Bickel while bombarding Mark Howe with memories of Holmes and queries about the biography.[95] Even after suffering a major stroke on April 5, 1962, Frankfurter continued to send memos, struggling to answer his critics and to pass along memories of Holmes and Brandeis.[96] Additional miscellany continued to arrive until Frankfurter's death, February 22, 1965.[97] His affection for

93. Felix Frankfurter, "Mr. Justice Brandeis and the Constitution," *Harvard Law Review* 45 (1931): 33; Felix Frankfurter, *Mr. Justice Brandeis* (New Haven: Yale University Press, 1932).

94. Spillenger, "Lifting the Veil," 725–27; Hirsch, *Enigma of Frankfurter*, 198. During the later 1950s, Mark Howe, too, discouraged other projects, turning down Holmes's old friend Lewis Einstein, who had asked Howe to edit his correspondence with Holmes, and then delaying the efforts of James B. Peabody to complete this work. See Howe to Einstein, March 4, 1960, Box 64, folder 8, Holmes Papers; Howe to Frankfurter, June 22, 1962, Box 185, folder 20, Frankfurter Papers; Peabody, ed., *The Holmes-Einstein Letters*.

95. Frankfurter to Griswold, April 10, 1956; Griswold to Frankfurter, April 11, 1956; Frankfurter to Griswold, April 13, 1956; Frankfurter to Howe, November 12, 1956, December 28, 1956, January 6, 1960, Box 2, folders 12, 14, Howe Papers. Frankfurter's efforts did not succeed; Bickel went to Yale Law School in the fall of 1956.

96. Box 2, folder 15, Howe Papers, is filled with these letters, written between April and October, 1963. See also, Frankfurter to Freund, March 12, 1963, November 5, 1963, and June 3, 1964, Box 184, folder 19, Frankfurter Papers.

97. Howe received Frankfurter material "at some time or times," noting shipments in 1947, 1949, 1950, 1954, 1957, and 1961. The Holmes-Frankfurter correspondence was assembled earlier, probably in 1946 and 1947, when Frankfurter sent his letters from Holmes to Howe, who joined them to the Frankfurter letters in the Holmes collection and made a rough typescript of the entire correspondence. A note in the Holmes to Frankfurter typescript file, dated 3/21/47 and initialed "ema," states: "Final copies of these letters have been made and are filed chronologically in the folder marked." See also, Howe to Francis X. Dwyer, November 19, 1945, and July 2, 1946; Dwyer to Howe, November 11, 1945, Box 64, Holmes Papers; Frankfurter to Howe, May 3, 1961, Box 2, folder 14, Howe Papers; *Material Relating to*

Howe remained strong through it all. "You are a grand lad, Mark," he wrote when he was nearly eighty, "you really are."[98]

Howe did not live much longer, passing away from cancer on February 28, 1967. It is difficult not to conclude that he had been emancipated by Frankfurter's illness. He did not, for example, inform Frankfurter of the leisurely pace of the Holmes biography until June 1962, several months after the stroke.[99] His work on Holmes slowed as he devoted increasing time to church/state issues and the Civil Rights movement.[100] He participated in the 1963 Civil Rights March on Washington and in 1966 spent the summer in Mississippi representing civil rights workers, who remembered him as the "little lawyer" who "spoke so beautiful about our constitutional rights."[101] He may never have been more himself than when he served in the cause of civil rights.

After Mark Howe's death, Mary Manning Howe returned all of his research material on Holmes, including the Holmes-Frankfurter letters, to Paul Freund, the literary executor of the estate. Freund, with Mary Howe's approval, decided to organize the collection and to make a final effort to secure a scholar to complete Holmes's "authorized" biography.[102] Freund selected Grant Gilmore, then at University of Chicago Law School. The logic of this choice lay in Gilmore's expertise in commercial law—a major focus of Holmes's career on the Massachusetts Bench that was to have been Mark

---

Holmes, Box 1, folder 3, and Erika S. Chadbourn to Gilmore, June 2, 1972, Box 1, folder 5, Gilmore Papers.

98. Frankfurter to Howe, August 30, 1961, Box 2, folder 14, Howe Papers.

99. Howe to Frankfurter, June 22, 1962, Box 185, folder 20, Frankfurter Papers. In the same letter, Howe informed Frankfurter that he would no longer object to James Peabody's effort to find a publisher for the Holmes-Einstein correspondence.

100. Howe also edited and wrote a new introduction to Holmes's *The Common Law* (Cambridge: Harvard University Press, 1963). He continued to complain about scholars whom he regarded as unfriendly to Holmes, adding to his list Yosal Rogat, who had criticized Holmes's uneven civil rights record. See Howe to Frankfurter, April 27, 1963, Box 185, folder 20, Frankfurter Papers.

101. "Mark DeWolfe Howe," Memorial Minute Adopted by the Faculty of Arts and Science, Harvard University, February 13, 1968. Howe's colleagues remembered his efforts as a reformer as much as his accomplishments as a scholar: "The best of the New England Tradition expressed itself in Mark Howe when he bore witness in the struggle for freedom of the mind and equality before the law."

102. The considerable archival task was accomplished by Erika S. Chadbourn, who became the head of special collections for the Law School Library. Mary Howe, who later became Mrs. Faneuil Adams, retained control over Mark Howe's correspondence relating to the biography. See Chadbourn to Frederic R. Kellogg, May 5, 1981, Box 1, folder 4, Gilmore Papers. Shortly before his death, Mark Howe described the state of the collection as "not systematically organized." Howe to Fred D. Ragan, November 11, 1966, Box 61, folder 1, Holmes Papers.

Howe's next topic. Gilmore was a curious choice since he did not appear to be interested in Holmes as a person. He generally ignored the rich correspondences, which remained at Harvard, and appears to have formed a negative opinion of his subject by studying the eight bound volumes of Holmes's Massachusetts opinions.[103] In a well-known passage, sounding not unlike the Catholic critics of the 1940s, Gilmore wrote:

> Holmes is a strange, enigmatic figure. Put out of your mind the picture of the tolerant aristocrat, the great liberal, the eloquent defender of our liberties, the Yankee from Olympus. All that was a myth concocted principally by Harold Laski and Felix Frankfurter about the time of World War I. The real Holmes was savage, harsh and cruel, a bitter, life-long pessimist who saw in the courts of human life nothing but a continuous struggle in which the rich and powerful impose their will on the poor and weak.[104]

The Jesuits had seen a philosophy based upon "struggle" or the chaos of the universe as a danger to be contested by a nation committed to religious values. Gilmore viewed the same ideas as indicative of the punitive quality of nineteenth-century private law that, he thought, Holmes fought to uphold.[105]

In the end, Gilmore's effort to continue Mark Howe's work came to nothing. He moved to Yale Law School in 1973, retired in 1978, and died in 1982 without publishing the next volume of the biography. Gilmore's papers contain a partial manuscript that begins as a critique of Holmes's jurisprudence but wanders into philosophical debates with his own contemporaries, Ronald Dworkin and Henry Hart.[106] He responded helpfully to some scholars seeking access to the Holmes papers, but he denied it to Liva Baker, who had already completed a biography of Frankfurter, judging her unqualified as a professional scholar because she was not a member of a university faculty.[107]

103. Chadbourn to Gilmore, October 16, 1968, Box 1, folder 4, Gilmore Papers.

104. Grant Gilmore, *The Ages of American Law* (New Haven: Yale University Press, 1977), 48–49. In *The Death of Contract* (Columbus: Ohio State University Press, 1974), 56, Gilmore also praised the work of Lon Fuller as an expert on contract.

105. G. Edward White, "Looking at Holmes in the Mirror," in White, ed., *Intervention and Detachment*, 106–31. White credits Gilmore with beginning the rediscovery of the history of private law.

106. Box 1, folder 7, Gilmore Papers.

107. Gilmore to Baker, January 30, 1968, Box 1, folder 4, Gilmore Papers. See Baker, *Felix Frankfurter*. In writing her Holmes biography, *The Justice from Beacon Hill* (1991), Baker acknowledges Erika Chadbourn and Judith Mellins of the Harvard Law School Library, "who made research a pleasure," and Mark Howe, whose scholarship "has helped all of us penetrate the impenetrable" (xiii).

Brandeis and Frankfurter scholarship proceeded more expeditiously. Alexander Bickel published several books, one on *The Unpublished Opinions of Mr. Justice Brandeis* (1957), but died in 1974 without making further progress on the biography.[108] Brandeis's private judicial papers were made "generally available" to scholars in 1976.[109] By this time, Melvin I. Urofsky and David W. Levy had begun to publish *The Letters of Louis D. Brandeis*, Urofsky had published a biography of Brandeis, and several other biographies were in progress.[110]

Frankfurter too received critical attention. Michael Parrish, who had studied under John M. Blum and Bickel at Yale, undertook a two-volume biography, publishing Volume I on the pre-Court years in 1982. H. N. Hirsch's critical psycho-biography of Frankfurter, published the same year, acknowledges Parrish, who had relinquished exclusive use of the Frankfurter Papers held by Harvard.[111] Leonard Baker's dual biography of Brandeis and Frankfurter was published a few years later to be followed by Urofsky's concise biography of Frankfurter and the Urofsky-Levy edition of Brandeis's letters to Frankfurter.[112]

After Gilmore's death, his wife, Helen Richter Gilmore, returned the Holmes papers to Harvard where, in accordance with the earlier agreement between Freund and Mary Howe, who was now Mrs. Faneuil Adams, they were deposited in the Law School archives and, in 1985, opened for scholarly research. The influence of Mary Howe Adams on this train of events was fitting, since the "authorized" biography approach particularly hin-

108. For the Holmes-Brandeis-Frankfurter project, Bickel described a book analyzing Brandeis and "the inner workings of the court," which was also never written. Memorandum, May 5, 1955, Box 63, folder 14, Holmes Papers.

109. Clyde Spillenger, "Reading the Judicial Canon: Alexander Bickel and the Book of Brandeis," *Journal of American History* 72 (1992): 132n14. Spillenger partially attributes the policy of restriction to Paul Freund, but the main incident, the denial of access to Alpheus T. Mason, was clearly Frankfurter's responsibility. Later biographers of Brandeis all cite Freund's willingness to help them in their research.

110. Melvin I. Urofsky and David W. Levy, eds., *Letters of Louis D. Brandeis*, 5 vols. (Albany: State University of New York Press, 1971–78); Louis J. Paper, *Brandeis* (Englewood Cliffs: Prentice-Hall, 1980); Melvin I. Urofsky, *A Mind of One Piece: Brandeis and American Reform* (New York: Scribner, 1971) and *Louis D. Brandeis and the Progressive Tradition* (Boston: Little, Brown, 1981); Phillipa Strum, *Louis D. Brandeis: Justice for the People* (Cambridge: Harvard University Press, 1983).

111. Parrish, *Frankfurter and His Times*; Hirsch, *Enigma of Frankfurter*. Grant Gilmore allowed Hirsch to use the Holmes papers and endorsed his work. See Gilmore to Hirsch, December 3, 1979, Box 1, folder 4, Gilmore Papers.

112. Leonard Baker, *Brandeis and Frankfurter: A Dual Biography* (New York: Harper & Row), 1984; Urofsky, *Felix Frankfurter: Judicial Restraint and Individual Liberties*; Urofsky and Levy, eds., *Half Brother, Half Son*.

dered Catherine Drinker Bowen and Liva Baker although it did not lessen the quality of their work. In the past decade, the outpouring of Holmes scholarship has increased exponentially. Three major biographies have been published along with numerous articles, a new volume of selections of Holmes's writing, and a collection of critical reassessments of Holmes "as an intellectual, a legal theorist, and an iconic public figure and culture hero."[113]

The volume of recent publishing activity suggests that Holmes has attained a transcendent place in American letters. As with Washington, Jefferson, Lincoln, the Roosevelts, and the Kennedys, his life and work continue to attract readers and writers of all persuasions, suggesting that the interpretive task will never be done. Among other signs of Holmes's enduring stature is the recent appearance of a new edition of his *Public Writings*, edited by Sheldon Novick.[114]

Our faith in continued interest in both Holmes and Frankfurter has animated this work. At the same time, we have tried to be responsive to both contemporary historiography and editorial tradition. Particularly, we have sought to uphold the method and philosophy of Mark Howe's editorial scholarship. To assist readers, we have provided minimal annotation to the text. In general, footnotes identify various personalities and writings and provide brief explanations of legal cases. Regarding methodology, we have been fortunate to have Howe's direct assistance. His rough typescript of the correspondence aided us immeasurably in verifying the original letters, which were sometimes nearly illegible. As to alterations, we have held to the standard Howe articulated in the preface to *Holmes-Laski*:

> In translating the informality of the handwritten originals to the formalities of the printed page . . . I have taken liberties which the purist may condemn. Paragraphing and punctuation have been added when they seemed manifestly called for; abbreviations have, for the most part, been eliminated. In all other respects the transcription is as accurate as my industry could make it, though I am sure that there are errors which other readers will discover.[115]

Adhering to Mark Howe's editorial philosophy has proven more challenging, given the subsequent swirl of historiography that has enveloped

113. Baker, *Justice from Beacon Hill*; Novick, *Honorable Justice*; White, *Justice Oliver Wendell Holmes*; Richard A. Posner, ed., *The Essential Holmes: Selections from the Letters, Speeches, Judicial Opinions and Other Writings of Oliver Wendell Holmes, Jr.* (Chicago: University of Chicago Press, 1992); Gordon, ed., *The Legacy of Oliver Wendell Holmes, Jr.*

114. *The Collected Works of Justice Holmes: Volumes 1–3: The Complete Public Writings of Oliver Wendell Holmes* (Chicago: University of Chicago Press, 1994). For a list of all published correspondences with Holmes, see Thomson, "Playing with a Mirage," 168–71.

115. Howe, ed., *Holmes-Laski Letters*, vii.

Holmes as well as Frankfurter. In editing the *Holmes-Laski Letters*, Howe eschewed the "hopeless task" of interpretation "in the light of my conviction that the two men are larger than their failings and that the record of their lives and thought is a record of their times which should speak for itself in its entirety."[116] In contrast, we have noted some controversies of scholarship and also have offered our own interpretation of the Holmes-Frankfurter relationship. The letters, we believe, soften White's rather bleak assessment that "Holmes's correspondence ultimately reveals his profound self-absorption and comparably profound detachment from the very humans with whom he was reaching out to communicate."[117] Yet they also support the observation of White and Hollinger that the two became close through their common desire to reject parochial cultures and their mutual need for admiration. Above all, we see Holmes vainly striving to convey cherished ideas to a younger man through whom he hoped to be known to subsequent generations. His disappointment, however, did not lessen the ties of love that bound them, friend to friend, subject to biographer. Such bonds reveal especially the emotional complexity of Holmes, self-described as "an empty bottle" but also, as Marion Frankfurter saw him, weeping over a Civil War poem.

The Holmes-Frankfurter letters, so long enchained by the friendships of the principals and between the biographers, are now available to all. Readers will form their own views of the Holmes-Frankfurter relationship. Yet the correspondence, filled as it is with observations on all facets of intellectual and cultural life, offers pleasure beyond the pursuit of interpretation. To be in the company of one of America's great minds and his close friend is a satisfaction in itself—an opportunity to indulge in what Thorstein Veblen called idle curiosity—that fanciful, inventive activity of the mind through which life takes on "dramatic character" and becomes worth living.[118]

116. *Id.*, vi.

117. White, "Holmes as Correspondent," 1761.

118. Thorstein Veblen, "The Place of Science in Modern Civilization," in Perry Miller, ed., *American Thought: Civil War to World War I* (New York: Holt, Rinehart and Winston, 1962), 310–13.

HOLMES AND FRANKFURTER

THE CORRESPONDENCE

Washington, D.C.
February 7, 1912

My dear Frankfurter,

Your friend's "stabs at truth" strike me as good.[1] The second is not much perhaps (the sturdier of our hypotheses), "sturdier" referring either to some unknown criterion or to the fact of our acceptance. The first, ability to fuse etc., touches the point that makes me say the system etc. The fourth and last—answer to desire for unity—is empirically good for you and me, though the question rises why should our desire be a criterion. Bill James preferred a pluralistic universe. I stick to mine as pointing to the arbitrary yet inevitable basis—our can't helps. The process of reasoning is good for me because I can't help yielding to it "so reason rooted in unreason stood," if I may parody Tennyson.[2] As we find that our neighbors' can't helps more or less coincide with ours, we can talk with them but only to a limited extent, as Newman pointed out in his *Grammar of Assent*.[3] Objective truth is a pure ideal that if everyone was as clever and educated as you they would agree with you and then the universe would be conquered. But even if we all agreed in everything, I don't see the guaranty that this universe would agree with us. We simply shouldn't think of the questions and be happy instead of unhappy dogmatists. The excellence of an ideal generally depends on its being unrealizable.

I am venturing to send you herewith my little book of speeches, which Biddle assures me you won't object to receiving.[4]

Sincerely yours,
O. W. Holmes

1. Frankfurter's friend was the poet and writer Gertrude King (1881–1923), who, with her husband, Stanley King (1883–1951), were frequent visitors at the House of Truth, the popular bachelor quarters shared by Frankfurter and a constantly changing cast of young lawyers, journalists, and government employees. Stanley King later served as President of Amherst College. Holmes sent this letter to Frankfurter, who was acting as an intermediary between Mrs. King and Holmes for an exchange on the nature of truth. Frankfurter enclosed a note to Mrs. King: "After you have formulated your own definition of truth, you may look inside and see the Justice's." Mrs. King responded: "1) The test of truth is its ability to fuse with former

experience. 2) Truth is that point of view from which man can make his most harmonious adjustment to reality. 3) Truth is the sturdier of our hypotheses. 4) Truth is the least incomplete answer to one's desire for unity." On the back, Frankfurter noted, "Holmes says that inasmuch as what he thinks, he is largely coerced into thinking by the nature of his being, etc. etc. etc., truth is 'the system of his limitations.'" Mrs. King rejoined, "I was honest and wrote mine first. Isn't this corking! Some of mine fit in with it rather interestingly." Subsequently, Mrs. King added a fifth definition: "Truth is the realization of the manageableness of facts." See Box 29, folder 2, Holmes Papers.

2. His honor rooted in dishonor stood,
And faith unfaithful kept falsely true.
Lancelot and Elaine, 871:72
Idylls of the King (1859)

3. In *An Essay in Aid of a Grammar of Assent* (London: Burns, Oates, 1870), John Henry, Cardinal Newman (1801–90) argued that individual belief could acquire a more dynamic character from social exchange but that perfect agreement was not a likely or even desirable outcome since belief was often not based upon empirical demonstration.

4. Oliver Wendell Holmes, *Speeches* (Boston: Little, Brown, 1900). Francis B. Biddle (1886–1968), Holmes's secretary (law clerk in contemporary usage), 1911–12, served as Attorney General of the United States, 1941–45, and was a member of the (Nuremberg) International Military Tribunal, 1945–46.

Washington, D.C.
February 10, 1912

My dear Justice Holmes,

Your suggestion that I may not be "unwilling" to receive your utterances of faith and doubt serves only to shrivel the expression of my gratitude, and makes me all the more dependent on expressive inarticulateness to convey what I feel.

It is, I think, a wise habit of our Puritanism to withhold appreciation from the living, for thus only the most purified sincerity will break through the dam of reticence. And so I do not even apologize for saying that from the time I first came in contact with you, as a freshman in the Law School, through your *Common Law*, you had for me the only sure canon of truth— "the gift of imparting ferment." That this bounty should be enriched by the passion and persuasiveness of the living fire is a good fortune that makes my indebtedness everlastingly alive.

Gratefully yours,
Felix Frankfurter

Washington, D.C.
February 16, 1912

My dear Frankfurter,

What quarrel is there between your correspondent and me beyond one as to the felicity of a phrase?[1] We both agree that for the moment the truth of a proposition rests on the immediate inability to dissent, in the long run it has to fit in more or less to our general system or it gets rejected. Perhaps, if, as I gather, she like me is a bettabilitarian (one who thinks you may bet more or less on the universe), she bets a little more cosmic importance on man's thought than I do—though in common with the dust we have all the importance there is, that of being part of it. I find that the weather has a good deal of effect on that as on other more articulate views. I gather that probably she agrees with my other formula that the great act of faith is when we decide that we are not God . . . we never can prove that our universe easily follows. And I for one believe in the *ding an sich*, (with modern improvements and electric darkness).[2] Hence I easily avoid pessimism without becoming an optimist. If I am in the universe, not it in me, I am in something that contains intellect, significance, ideals. True, I surmise, I bet, that these are all expressions of the finite, and that they are as unlikely to be cosmic categories as they are to apply to a prince with a genealogy of 1000 years. He doesn't live by his wits—He simply is—But I do not thereupon like the French sceptics put my hand into my bosom and rise in majestic superiority amid the ruins. I simply conclude that I am not big enough to think about it. The little god doesn't remain when the big one goes. I bow my head in the dust—I am content to live in my ultimates without requiring of the universe that it should be able to transcend them and I can find very good reasons for doing my best without being convinced that I am in on the ground floor with God.

Sincerely yours,
O. W. Holmes

1. Mrs. King continued her dialog with Holmes in a letter to Frankfurter (February 14, 1912). The letter read in part:

"In defense of 'the sturdier of our hypotheses,' sturdier refers both to the passion of acceptance and to the trial by fire of workability. So far as I know, we have only two tests (neither of which are absolute or capable of severe and accurate standardizing) for our 'can't helps' and these, both consciously and naively applied, constantly batter our limitations into some sort of system. One of these is—how does the new idea fuse with my previous mass, and the other is—how does it stand up under the pressure of further experience. Consequently, any new idea that applies for membership in the august company (generally a very close corporation) of our prejudices has to be judged by the old members as being in their class and he also must prove his sturdiness against the battering ram of experience. 'Sturdier,' then, comes down to the test of survival." See Box 27, folder 1, Holmes Papers.

2. Holmes defined *ding an sich* as a belief "somewhat independent" of consciousness, a phenomenon without phenomenal antecedents. See Howe, ed., *Holmes-Pollock Letters*, 1:122.

March 7, 1912[1]
Washington, D.C.

My dear Justice Holmes,

Even in these iconoclast days so venerable an institution as the calendar should be respected. And while you have made it difficult for me to think of you in terms of insignificant temporal measurements—so far as the dynamic realities of life are concerned—I'm glad that the occasion at least sanctions those expressions of warm wishes which a grateful heart so deeply feels. Your pipe *has* reached deep and permanently into the hearts of ever increasing passers in the crowd. May its tone find added joy in the ceaseless effort of it all that our own striving has a richer meaning and a deeper significance from your *being*. And may I add to this a fulsome measure of joys without effort, all the homely pleasures that add zest and give stimulating comfort.

A long-continued youth to you!

Gratefully yours,
Felix Frankfurter

1. Frankfurter wrote Holmes regularly around March 8, Holmes's birthday, and on December 8, the anniversary of his appointment to the Supreme Court in 1902. Most of these letters have been omitted because of their routine and sycophantic character.

Washington, D.C.
March 8, 1912

Dear Mr. Frankfurter,

It will be many years before you have occasion to know the happiness and encouragement that comes to an old man from the sympathy of the young. That, perhaps more than anything else, makes one feel as if one had not lived in vain, and counteracts the eternal gravitation toward melancholy and doubt. I am quite sincere in saying that you have done a great deal for me in that way and I send you my gratitude and thanks.

Sincerely yours,
O. W. Holmes

Washington, D.C.
May 24, 1912

My dear Mrs. Holmes,

My fondness for the Colonel may be only the undisciplined exuberance of youth.[1] At its best it is a stirring enthusiasm for the aspirations of the man rather than the man himself. But even at its worst, it only covers part of my yearnings and my relation to things, and helps me to cling all the more to the deep significance that the Justice means to me and the vital things that he has for me. I shall hold on to him—now beyond even *his* recall—long after the turmoil and noise of present-day politics will be even less than a memory. Your kindness will forgive this expression of faith.

Sincerely yours,
Felix Frankfurter

1. Frankfurter enthusiastically supported Theodore Roosevelt in the Presidential election of 1912. See Parrish, *Frankfurter and His Times*, 54–58.

Washington, D.C.
October 12, 1912

Dear Frankfurter,

The flag's come back to Knossus[1]—and I have a new Secretary—Stanley Clarke who seems a nice chap and I want to introduce him to you and Christie—not to ask you to do things but to give him a start as he knows no one.[2] If you chaps like him you probably will pass him around. . . . Our servants are not here but we still can talk.

Yours sincerely,
O. W. Holmes

1. Knossus or Gnossus was the ancient capital of Crete, home of Minos, a mythical king and lawgiver, the son of Zeus.

2. Stanley Clarke (1884–1955) later practiced law in New York City. Loring Christie (1885–1941), Harvard Law School graduate and Canadian diplomat, was a resident of the House of Truth. He was Minister to the U.S., 1939–41.

Washington, D.C.
April 8, 1913

Private

Dear Frankfurter,

What with a cold and many things to do, I don't think that I can attempt to contribute to the prospective seance.[1] I expressed my scepticism in a notice of Holdsworth's *English Law* in 25 *Law Quarterly Review* at p. 414.[2] Philosophers are apt to try to retain the dogmatic supremacy formerly accorded to theologians by assuming a mystic infinite value for morality as *point d'appui*.[3] But if one looks at ethics as a system of popular generalizations of the conditions of social welfare expressed in terms of emotion, one is led to ask for statistics that so far as I know are wanting. It may be true, as Pound says, that there has been a change of emphasis (such changes always are taking place and have led me to say that everything is dead after 25 years) and that we now articulately recognize that social welfare is the basis of individual rights—a principle always acted on whether recognized or not—e.g., eminent domain and conscription.[4] But if the emphasis has changed the question what social welfare is, and if we have agreed on that, which we haven't, which means tend to accomplish it seems to me very much in the air. The American public seems to believe that the Sherman Act and smashing great fortunes are roads to an ideal—which seems to me open to debate—so you see that if I do attempt to contribute I should not do much good. I will ask you to say that my occupation prevents my attempting to take part in the of course most interesting conference.

Ever yours,
O. W. Holmes

1. Morris Raphael Cohen (1880–1947), philosopher and teacher at City College of New York, had asked Frankfurter to invite Holmes to participate in a conference on the theme "The Nature of Law in Relation to Social Ends." See Cohen to Frankfurter, April 3, 1913, Box 27, folder 2, Holmes Papers.

2. In his review of W. S. Holdsworth, *A History of English Law*, vols. 2 and 3 (London: Methuen, 1909), Holmes commented: "No doubt the history of law encourages scepticism when one sees how a rule or doctrine has grown up, or when one notices the naivete with which social prejudices are taken for eternal principles. But it also leads to an unconvinced conservatism. For it points out that almost the only thing that can be assumed as certainly to be wished is that men should know the rules by which the game will be played."

3. Assumed starting point or place of leverage. Holmes also wrote the phrase in Greek.

4. Roscoe Pound (1870–1964), then Story Professor of Law at Harvard, was a founder of sociological jurisprudence. He was Dean of the Law School from 1916 to 1936.

Washington, D.C.
June 9, 1913

Dear Justice Holmes,

As I see your life-betting countenance, it tugs me hard to utter gratitude ever to mark the point.

So—a "whacking" trip to you![1]

Faithfully yours,
Felix Frankfurter

1. Holmes was about to embark upon his last trip to England.

On board the Cunard
"Mauretania"
June 15, 1913

Dear Frankfurter,

Your book was not handed to me until I had begun another, which accordingly I finished first like a good boy. Now I have just come to the end of Mary Antin's *Promised Land*.[1] It has stirred my vitals. But if everyone had her capacity for wonder and feeling things as they happen, life would be easy and all would succeed. It is a good thing, too, to be allowed to see another race from the inside and to learn to admire. You are a dear lad to have thought of me. Denison also sent me a telegram.[2] Please give my love to him—you chaps think you get something from me but I get quite as much from you and I am grateful.

The first 48 hours on this voyage I felt like a fog rather than a man but I have gradually recoagulated and have ascended like the race through victuals, drinks, standing about till I was tired and resting till I was bored, to your book and the potentiality of human converse. If you know or knew anything about the author in her external aspect, that is, her present fate and circumstances, I should like to hear it. I hope you will have a pleasant summer and that we shall meet again in the autumn. The dear Christie called on us in N.Y. and Olds enabled my wife to see me aboard in his company.[3] My bankers are Morgan, Grenfell and Co. London.

Sincerely and gratefully yours,
O. W. Holmes

It seems as if the gift of passionate enthusiasm were racial. It is a great one.

1. Mary Antin (1881–1949) was born in the Russian Pale. She migrated to America in 1894, settling in the Boston area. Her inspirational and popular autobiography, *The Promised*

Land (New York: Houghton, Mifflin, 1912), portrayed America as a land of freedom, hope, and opportunity.

2. Winfred T. Denison (1873–1919), one of Frankfurter's housemates, was Assistant Attorney General of the United States, 1910–1914, and a specialist in customs fraud prosecution.

3. Irving S. Olds (1887–1963), Holmes's secretary, 1910–11, became a leading New York attorney and philanthropist. He was Chairman of the Board of U.S. Steel, 1940–52.

Washington, D.C.
July 4, 1913

My dear Justice,

Today the Eagle screams—it's the fourth of July, but the deeper note of silence sounds from the Gettysburg field!

I don't know Mary Antin except through those who do. She is a passionate young person, of plain outwardness, according to ordinary canons of aesthetics, with an ego that sets her plainness a-fire and burns up aesthetic canons. (Some of the scribes have labelled her a "little egoist"—as well blame her for having a sense of her personality.) She has a pretty strong sense of making manifest the "soul of her race"—all the more so, I imagine, because she married a Gentile.[1] You know how deeply rooted the feeling against intermarriage is in us Jews.[2] She has felt herself isolated from some of her old associations, the old traditions grip her with a new tenacity and there is, I suspect, an unconscious sense of atonement in the endeavor to use her gifts for her People. She is particularly successful in her short stories—they have a first-handedness, a poignant actuality almost startling in its intimacy. Withal, she is a great artist. I think you may like them and I will get some of them to you in the Autumn. She has the freshness of a child towards expressions of appreciation for her book, so I hope you'll forgive me for having sent two or three of your sentences to Ellery Sedgwick of the *Atlantic* who "discovered" her.[3] (Really Israel Zangwill did—almost fifteen years ago).[4]

And now I want the help of your reaction! I have been asked by the Law School whether I would accept a professorship in criminology and other courses largely to be determined by Pound—should the necessary endowment for a new chair be secured, to be effective the academic year 1914–15. Of course, I'm not a scholar *qua* scholar but this thing doesn't hit me merely as a tempting bait for an academic career. The job to be done, as I think it, is to evolve this "sociological jurisprudence" that Pound has been talking about. I don't know whether I have the equipment for it but they seem to think so and perhaps I ought to give myself a try-out to see how much I *have* got. If I have enough to meet the potentialities of the work, my unscholarliness may be a help to save me and the students from Langdellian sterilization (I *do* appreciate his work as a pedagogic innovator but it strikes me the school has to do a bigger job than high technique.[5] I'm afraid if the Harvard nabobs heard this, I wouldn't long be confronted with the question of accepting or not). At all events, I wonder whether it isn't worthwhile as, say, a five years try—with the advantage of having done some systematic thinking and the opportunity of then deciding, at 35, whether that's my job. I'm looking at it either as end or preparation, leaving it to experience to decide. The alternatives are: 1) to stay here—I'm beginning to feel the point of saturation is fast being reached under this administration. My new chief is man-size but he hasn't the depth to utilize me to my full scope and Wilson doesn't seem to be alert in drawing on others.[6] Besides, the atmosphere is a good deal partisanly Democratic—they need the jobs (I'm glad, in a way, that the South is again drawn in the harness of national administration) or, 2) to enter private practice in New York. Well, I could get fun out of that, but to make the necessary livelihood out of it would absorb my vital powers most in lines not dominantly attractive to me.

I think I can fairly face my creator and say that, now at least, I have no concreter ambition than the realization of certain ideas—however vague—and the sharpening, enlargement of those ideas. I do, however, want to get some sustaining fun in the process of putting my personality to use without denying myself the joy of risks by demanding that my choice of conflicting doubts be safely underwritten. You once agreed that a young fellow should not bother about the advice of a man above thirty five. I respect that rule in asking you for *your* views! I shall be grateful for them with just a twinge of conscience to have broken in on your loaf.

Denison and I are happy tho' hot. I'm beginning to think Hell isn't all invention. Which reminds me to hope you will have an opportunity to convey the grateful pleasure of an unknown to Father Sheehan.[7]

We are looking forward to next autumn—even more than you might suspect. Our gratitude wings you wishes of joy.

Happily—one of your boys!
Felix Frankfurter

1. In 1901 Mary Antin married Amadeus William Grabau (1870–1946), a geologist at M.I.T. and Columbia. They had two children and then separated in 1919. Grabau lived the rest of his life in China.

2. Frankfurter penned in the phrase "in us Jews."

3. Ellery Sedgwick (1872–1960), editor of the *Atlantic Monthly*, 1908–38, had published one of Mary Antin's short stories in 1911 and serialized *The Promised Land*.

4. Israel Zangwill (1864–1926), playwright and novelist of ghetto life, had written a preface to Mary Antin's letters to her uncle in Russia: *From Plotzk to Boston* (Boston: W. B. Clarke, 1899).

5. Frankfurter recognized the value of the case study method of legal education as it had been developed by Christopher Columbus Langdell (1826–1906), Dean of Harvard Law School, 1870–95. However, he did not share Langdell's animating faith that the law could be scientifically purified by tracing precedents. Frankfurter and Pound wanted to humanize the law by incorporating economics, geography, government, history, psychology, and sociology into legal education. This approach so excited Frankfurter that his lectures often omitted discussion of cases altogether. See Baker, *Frankfurter*, 46–47; Parrish, *Frankfurter and His Times*, 64–66.

6. Woodrow Wilson's Secretary of War, 1913–16, was Lindley M. Garrison (1864–1932), a New Jersey lawyer and judge.

7. Canon Patrick Augustus Sheehan (1852–1913) of Doneraile (County Cork), poet and author, was an old friend whom Holmes visited shortly before his death. Holmes also assisted his biographer, Herman Joseph Heuser, *Canon Sheehan of Doneraile* (New York: Longmans, Green, 1917).

London, England
July 15, 1913

Dear Frankfurter,

It is delightful to hear from you and I begin by sending you and Denison my love. As to your question, I should answer with something of the reserve one would bring to a question of marriage, with an impression superadded that you already have made up your mind. I agree that you don't want to stay too long in a place that hardly offers a career for life. Much as I should miss you if you left, I should send you off if it were left to me. As to the place, the objection that occurs to me is that academic life is but half life—it is a withdrawal from the fight in order to utter smart things that cost you nothing except the thinking them from a cloister. My wife thinks I unconsciously began to grow sober with an inarticulate sense of limitation in the few months of my stay at Cambridge.[1] Academics hardly are a further preparation for active life and you would not be as fit for the fight at 35 after being a professor, as now—at least that would be my guess. Business in the world is unhappy, often seems mean, and always challenges your power to idealize the brute fact but it hardens the fiber and I think is likely to make more of a man of one who turns it to success.

On the other side, there is the question of your opportunities to break in—as to which I know nothing—of your health, which I sometimes have feared that you strained, but which very likely may have the wear-resisting quality—of your own judgment as to your native aptitudes—and of your desires—always assuming that the latter are not led by a feeling that a professorship is the line of least resistance. A man once wrote to me with some truth that the line of *most* resistance is the one to choose. The theme proposed is interesting and would open vistas to a mind like yours. Yet the criminal law, however improved, is rather an old gun and one can't help feeling that there is more of the future in the great economic organs forming outside the state—on which my friend Franklin Ford of New York likes to dwell and as to which, I gather from a book just sent to me, the French are quite alert.[2] The book is *Les Transformations du Droit Public* by Leon Duguit—one of many books by him and others that think something peculiar has happened.[3] I would not have you yield to the intellectual fashions of the moment—especially of France where fashion is so potent and changes so fast—but I think the suggestion worth considering. I should think you could get more nourishment from economics than from criminal law. But all these doubts are merely thinking aloud. I would not decide this question for you if I could and I might repeat to you what Brandeis said to me years ago—whichever you choose I think you will come out all right always provided you don't tax your health. I wish I could say better things, but I am too far out of it to be much good with all my solicitude for your welfare. I have been spending my time dining and lunching out with no improvement to my soul that I know of. The lawyers and judges, when I happen to meet them, treat me handsomely but I am primarily for agreeable women and run for luck on the men.

Your affectionate friend,
O. W. Holmes

1. Holmes was appointed Professor of Law at Harvard Law School in January 1882. He taught there from September to December 1882 when he was appointed Associate Justice, Supreme Judicial Court of Massachusetts.

2. Franklin Ford (1848–1918), publicist and director of the "General News Office," relentlessly promoted the idea that banks and news gathering organizations should be the main elements of political and economic authority. See Howe, ed., *Holmes-Laski Letters*, 118–25.

3. Leon Duguit (1859–1928) was a French legal philosopher.

Camp Burnt Rock Adirondacks
Blue Mountain Lake, New York
September 6, 1913

Dear Justice Holmes,

My articulation comes in inverse ratio to the momentum of the feelings behind the words. So often the very desire to convey dams my utterance. That's a goodly part of the wherefore back of my non-acknowledgment of your greedily welcome letter. You are very good to write to me as you do. My gratitude springs not from any concrete help in solving the question I put to you. The privilege that is mine is the temper of mind with which you help me to approach any answer and the sturdiness of deciding with an intensity as comprehensive as I am capable of, and a seasoned sense of perspective that decides all such questions with a view of the fullest exercise of one's personality, with a reverent sense of one's ignorance as to the wherefore of it all, yet a passionate desire to make life a vital thing and—not talk much about it.

Partly, I have wanted to be able to write you with definiteness as to my plans, Your solicitude for my welfare is at once comfort and spur. Well, things are yet *in nubibus*.[1] I have decided to go to Cambridge if they want me and now they are trying to raise an endowment to have me. I would not go up there for a conventional professorship. Academics are neither my aptitude nor the line of my choice so far as one chooses. This thing is rather different and what challenges me is to bring public life, the elements of reality, in touch with the university, and conversely, to help harness the law school to the needs of the fight outside. You know better than the rest of us how empirical, how inadequate the foundation of our legislative output, how unthoughtout much of social reform legislation is, how meager the data on which it is based. Practically no organized thought is available in this country as to the scope of legislative law; except, as Pound points out, the common lawyer's implicit distrust of legislation, law students leave the law schools ignorant and indifferent to legislation. Well, a big fact of the trend of things is statute-made law and it's up to the Law Schools to deal with the theories of legislation (I know it's a tough job) and in turn help shape the course. It sounds ambitious, but something I'm sure can be done to mediate between economist and social reformer in their demands for legislation but with little knowledge, either into the scope of legislative reforms inherent in the enforceability of laws or, illumined by the experience of history if proper study of cause and consequence can be made. At all events, the School feels the need of attempting something like that. They feel I can do the work with Pound and my own desire is very strong to try it on. My years in the Government have taught me the utter inability of thoroughgoing thinking while in office and I feel the need of correlating this kind of analysis and research with the living economic and social facts of the day. I can see only very few years ahead—for five years ahead. I hope to escape the softness of academic ease partly because I'm now conscious of its dangers, partly—with due regard to my heart and you more than anyone else have taught me sense about that—I hope to be active in some affairs outside the school to be effective within and, most hopeful of all, because by temperament I'm not a cloistered scholar and not even Cambridge, I think, can spoil my zest of life and my need of steering my boat through the currents of its rigorous realities. The economic clashes of the day are rich nourishment for me and it's with them that I want to deal but, with more scientific geometry, in a more tolerant temper and, a deeper sense of limitations though no less of the passion that is faith which animates the social reformer of the day. But enough of me except the thanks that are irrepressible as the nearest symbol of what is felt.

Christie and I went to Montreal. I can't say that the Bar Association proceedings fired us. Oh, if there were only a tax on words! Two talks *did* stand out—the Lord Chancellor spoke in an attractively impressive way though with some unnecessary verbiage and the central theme had more of an air than the reality of novelty.[2] Still, it's something to be remembered. Maitre Labori made me feel the crudities and emptiness of so much of our speaking—he spoke with the pace and flavor and felicity of France itself speaking.[3] The C.J. looked like a dominating Cardinal in his flaming red LL.D. robe, at McGill.[4] His response to the conferring of the degree was very happy. I think he made a massive impression on Canadians. His introduction of the Lord Chancellor was characteristically syllogistic. It was a complete demonstration of the proposition that he was assigned an impossible task in introducing the Lord Chancellor because he needed no introduction. Q.E.D. (You'll forgive my irreverence).

But I report with more eagerness another summer experience. Two of your children met—Mrs. Elizabeth Ellis and I had a rollicking time at Newport.[5] She is a most warm-hearted and generous-minded woman. I don't think we showed your non-teachings in our frolics.

I'm looking forward to the reconvening of court. My warmest to Mrs. Holmes.

Gratefully,
Felix Frankfurter

Dear Justice Holmes,

I can't resist the temptation of adding a line of heartiest greetings to you and Mrs. Holmes. Felix missed one address, Ezra Thayer's—a masterpiece of extemporaneous English that would have delighted you as it would have gratified his father.[6] But I doubt our wisdom in not following your example—of preferring a longer vacation in these woods, to a gathering of our professional brethren.

Faithfully yours,
Julian Mack[7]

1. Obscure or under clouds.

2. Lord Chancellor Richard Burdon, Viscount Haldane (1856–1928) of Great Britain, addressed the 36th annual meeting of the American Bar Association on "Higher Nationality: A Study in Law and Politics," emphasizing the need of Canada, England, and the United States to develop mutual interests on the basis of their common heritage. See *Proceedings* of the American Bar Association (1913): 393–417.

3. Fernand Labori (1860–1917), eloquent French lawyer who founded *La Gazette du Palais* and defended Dreyfus and Zola.

4. Edward D. White (1845–1921), Chief Justice of the U.S. Supreme Court, 1910–21.

5. Elizabeth Ellis (1875–1952), wife of socialite yachtsman Ralph Ellis (1852–1930), became a life-long friend of Felix and Marion Denman Frankfurter (1890–1975).

6. Ezra R. Thayer (1866–1915), Dane Professor and Dean of Harvard Law School, 1910–15, addressed the convention on "Law Schools and Bar Examinations." He challenged examiners to understand the "broad point of view" within legal education as a valuable antidote to the specialism that necessarily characterized practice. See *Proceedings*, 938–50. Thayer's father was James Bradley Thayer (1831–1909), expert on U.S. Constitutional law and a dominant figure at Harvard Law School from 1874 until his death.

7. Julian Mack (1866–1943), judge and early advocate of the juvenile court system, aided Frankfurter and Louis D. Brandeis in the moderate wing of the Zionist movement.

Beverly Farms, Massachusetts
September 19, 1913

Dear Frankfurter,

Your letter went to my heart though I have been slow in acknowledging it, not knowing where to direct. I assume that this will reach you in time. Your views as to your future and your intent give me a thrill. My uncertainty as to hitting you prevents my discoursing until we meet, but I feel very great sympathy for all that you say and long to talk to you. I have longed often—feeling that there were many observations, to wit, one or two, on life that I wished to pour forth to you. We will have a jaw before very long. Love to Denison and kindest regards to Judge Mack.

Yours ever,
O. W. Holmes

Can you recite on *Jean Christophe*?[1] If not, learn to. One of my remarks, suggested by him and that young man's poetry that you or Denison sent me last winter with its thought-transcending music or passion ("Damn Reason let's have our whack")[2] is that it calls up my often-quoted Hegel: False infinite of youth, potentially everything because actually nothing. We become persons by the increase of negations—of finite characteristics—but there is a cat walking over this as I write and I must stop for it gives me no chance.

1. Romain Rolland, *Jean Christophe*, 4 vols. (Paris: Ollendorff, 1904–12), a fictionalized biography of Beethoven that sought to reconcile French and German mentalities.

2. Possibly, Edward J. M. D. Plunkett (1878–1957), Baron of Dunsany, *Book of Wonder* (Boston: J. W. Luce, 1913). Plunkett's verse and plays, fantasies based upon his hunting and war experiences in Africa, were popular among Anglophiles and American college students.

Washington, D.C.
October 2, 1913

Dear Justice Holmes,

I'm here again and likely to be here for the coming official year.[1] Even if the Harvard thing goes through, it's not to commence until the academic year (I find myself sensitive to that word "academic") of 1914–15. So whatever be designed by Circumstances or Infinite Possibilities or God, or however we may label the Enthronement of our undefinable vision I feel eagerly sure of being here with you for these coming months.

I cursed my folly in not telling you I'm coming back, which deprived me of your goodness in writing me more; but found more than reward in the talk you beckon. Do pour forth—never was human bucket more eager and more grateful for the privilege. "Bucket" does scant justice to me (and one may, in this ameliorating age, be fair even to one's self) for it's a much more creative receptivity, I hope, that awaits you. The old Greek said glibly, "Know thyself"—it's a tough job for it partly involves a good deal of insight into a few other things. As perhaps no other influence, I feel you have what[?] is to give me to meet life (and give to it) with all the sanity and adventure and intensity that my irreducible limitations permit of.

Thank you, *ab viso pectore*.[2] My best to Mrs. Holmes.

Faithfully yours,
Felix Frankfurter

I'm now *in* Jean Christophe. This memo of Pound as to the Harvard work you may want to read at leisure.[3]

1. Frankfurter continued to work for the War Department until September 1914. See Parrish, *Frankfurter and His Times*, 57–61.

2. From the bottom of my heart.

3. Memo is missing.

Washington, D.C
December 22, 1913

Dear Frankfurter,

You make me happier by your letters as you always do whenever we encounter.[1] I don't fear that you will let yourself get soft, but I thought a word was permissible as I know how it is myself. I have thought of a last touch in this opinion that I showed you—a suggestion that the "*donatores*"—grantors—of Glanville led to the special forces given to *dedi* by Coke. The Statute de Bigamis, while attributing a warranty to *dedi et concessi*, says that the feoffor is held *ratione doni proprii* by force of his having made the grant not, it would seem, by force of the special word.[2] I have had a letter from Innes from which he has left out the first page probably by mistake.[3] So I don't know his address. If you do, please send it to me.

Yours ever,
O. W. Holmes

1. The letter referred to is missing.

2. In *Trimble v. City of Seattle*, 231 U.S. 683, 690 (1914), Holmes, writing for the unanimous Court, upheld a decision of the Washington State Supreme Court that denied the efforts of plaintiff to shift municipal taxation for improvements on leased property back to the lessor, which was the state. Holmes's opinion drew upon the first "Institute" of English jurist Sir Edward Coke (1552–1634), which held that a state's warranty against taxation did not have to be expressly stated: "When an interest in land, whether freehold or for years is severed from the public domain and put into private hands, the natural implication is that it goes there with the ordinary incidents of private property and therefore is subject to being taxed."

3. Alfred Mitchell-Innes (1864–1950), British diplomat and frequenter of the House of Truth, had been appointed Minister to Uruguay, where he served until his retirement in 1919.

Washington, D.C.
[March ?], 1914

Dear Justice Holmes,

It's high time to turn in, but I reward myself with a bit of late reading, having done two deeds today that make for happiness: paid some bills and listened to delightful music (thanks to the versatility and one's ability of life which rigid philosophers seek constantly to contract, the music that delighted me would bore another). And so I find myself reading your opinion in the *LeRoy Fibre Co.* case.[1] It's the dead of night—that corkscrew of truth even in a House of Truth—and you won't mind my saying that it's a gem—one of those pithy illuminations which give relation and harmony and human scope to apparently disconnected items of the law. And the method of your approval puts such an effective guide into one's possession as to other branches of the law. Thank you for it and good night.

Faithfully yours,
Felix Frankfurter

And I'm so grateful for your brevity. In the course of my employ, I had to read opinions today of fifty odd pages.

> " 'E liked it all
> Except when awful long."

1. *LeRoy Fibre Co. v. Chicago, Minneapolis and St. Paul Railway Co.*, 232 U.S. 340, 354 (1914). Plaintiff's straw, stored on company property but near the railroad, was burnt by a passing engine. The majority opinion, written by Joseph J. McKenna (1843–1926), held that plaintiff's storage practices could not be submitted to the jury as evidence of neglect. Holmes's concurring opinion, with which Chief Justice White agreed, concluded that distance was a plausible concern for the jury: "Negligence is all degree—that of the defendant here of the nicest sort; and between the variations according to distance that I suppose to exist and the simple universality of the rules in the Twelve Tables or the *Leges Barbarorum*, there lies the culture of two thousand years."

Washington, D.C.
March 24, 1914

Dear Frankfurter,

Your speech is stimulating and fine—and if, as I take it, it indicates the direction of your activities in the approaching future, I am very glad.[1] You know that I am rather sceptical, and still, as when I was editor of the *American Law Review*, regard most statutes that are called good as simply shifting the place where the strain or rub comes.[2] They are especially praised when the bill to be paid in detrimental reactions is concealed by the fact that the reactions are interstitial and hard to be detected. I quite agree that a law should be called good if it reflects the will of the dominant forces of the community even if it will take us to hell. But if one sees that result clearly, one may suspect that the community would change its will if it had the same wisdom. That is why I wish that the public thought in terms of the stream of products instead of ownership, rent, interest, money, taxes, etc. If all the world saw that a tax, however levied, ultimately means a diversion of part of that stream to government employees with so much less for those outside, they would see that in each case it was a question of the relative value of the government return, as a social investment, and that nothing was proved by showing that the tax began by socking it to the rich man e.g., inheritance tax, or income tax. They would see that extravagant returns from oil or railroads, if not going back to the employees in that industry, went to some other because the capitalist prophet saw, or thought he did, that greater returns were to be expected from that other, in other words, was doing what he could to hit the true equilibrium of social desires. They perhaps then would doubt whether a commission was as likely as self interest to be true prophet of the future. But this is not the fashion of the day. I am not sure that you even share my views. At all events, the first thing is to recognize the inevitable and to try to put what rationality one can into the semirational prejudices that govern the world. In that effort, I expect you to take a noble part.

Ever sincerely yours,
O. W. Holmes

I have done nothing in this note but repeat my old saws but repetition hardly is a match for oblivion.

1. Probably, "The Zeitgeist and the Judiciary," *Survey* 29 (1912–13): 542. Reprinted in Archibald MacLeish and E. F. Prichard, Jr., eds., *Law and Politics: Occasional Papers of Felix Frankfurter, 1913–1938* (New York: Harcourt, Brace, 1939), 3–9. Frankfurter urged the judiciary to respect legislative efforts to deal with social and economic problems in order to avoid further stimulating the movement for popular recall of judicial decisions, most forcefully advocated by Theodore Roosevelt in the Bull Moose campaign of 1912.

2. From 1870 to 1873, Holmes edited the *American Law Review* with Arthur G. Sedgwick (1844–1915), who later wrote for the *Nation* and the *New York Evening Post.*

Washington, D.C.
March 28, 1914

Dear Justice Holmes,

I should like to be able to tell you how much your letter about that speech goes to my heart and reinforces the fibre of effort. Whatever the reason, very very few people have ever helped to give me direction, to stimulate purpose. And since early Law School days, you are one of those I'm so deeply indebted to and contact with you here will be the most precious thing I shall carry from Washington. Therefore, it is that I rejoice in your hopes as to the line of my activities for the next few years at any rate. You cannot express your point of view too often for me. It always comes with insights and stirs my own thinking into fresher activity. The truth is, I don't know enough as yet to know how far I *do* agree with you. I know I do in a good deal of your scepticism—I prefer to think it as critical undeluding regard for the facts and forces of society deeper than party platform or temporary shibboleths. As so I *am* pretty wary of how little, after all, legislation can go beneath the surface of things. Perhaps tho', I *am* more hopeful tho' of the area of conscious readjustments. So much of legislation does not at all deal with economic changes, does not involve redistributions. I do think a lot of our life is muddled, there is large room for inventiveness and legislation should be an instrument of imagination. I try not to think of these aims in ethical terms. It isn't a question of better or onward and I certainly do not believe in any determinable standard of "progress." I do think, I do hope that life can be a finer, in the sense of a richer, more teeming sort of spectacle, not only on a more extensive basis, but in its intricate and intensive manifestation. In other words, an organized effort towards more life.

At all events this persisting phenomena of legislation, as you so encouragingly agree, should be studied much in the spirit that the scientist sits down before the facts of nature. I know to that end I shall bring my biases, my slants, my can't-helps. I only hope that the dominance of the can't-helps will be hospitable to the impact of facts outside and if the can't-helps cannot be reshaped, at least one will strive to avoid the confusion between one's own can't helps and an iron law of God.

Gratefully yours,
Felix Frankfurter

Cambridge, Massachusetts
September 16, 1914

Dear Justice Holmes,

I have an indecisive sort of hesitancy about passing on this letter of Percy.[1] Yet, tho' it's a deeply personal utterance, I have a feeling that he would rather like to have Mrs. Holmes and you see it. In any event, the recording angel will have something to say for me.

I'm *in* [Franklin] Ford's stuff but not yet out of it. Isn't there a great heaving about him, but also a freshness of approach. But I haven't any ideas yet about his thinking which evidently he has worked out hard. You've made me pretty shy about expressing my indebtedness to you. And yet, and yet, it compels utterance. As I wander through the maze of legal dry leaves, I feel a growing sense of direction, groping yet growing, which you have awakened and furthered very decidedly. And beyond mere professional inspiration, in one's way of tackling life and making job integral with the rest of life is one of the deepest insights you have enforced in me. I bring you my gratitude in the silent use I shall make of whatever powers are mine.

Faithfully yours,
Felix Frankfurter

1. Lord Eustace Percy (1887–1958), resident of the House of Truth and member of the British Embassy staff, later became President of the Board of Education and Rector of Kings College, Newcastle. His letter to Frankfurter is missing.

Beverly Farms, Massachusetts
September 17, 1914

Dear Frankfurter,

Many thanks for your letter, which gives me the pleasure you always give, and for Percy's, which my wife and I read with deep emotion. It is very noble and makes one feel the spirit of England now. On this anniversary of Antietam 52 years ago, it warms me with the rekindled glow of the old fire. . . .

Sincerely yours,
O. W. Holmes

Cambridge, Massachusetts
September 28, 1914

Dear Justice Holmes,

I know that a good jobbist humps his back and says nothing. But this principle too cannot be pressed to its untruthfully logical extreme, and so I hope I do not forfeit my claim to earn membership in your Society if, on the day my new job begins, I too make a point—long enough to tell you with what inspiration, what patient insight and steadying courage you help to send me into this world.

Gratefully,
Felix Frankfurter

Washington, D.C.
November 27, 1914

Dear Frankfurter,

You have given as much pleasure as you have received so, as the earlier Judge Lowell said of a case of people who escaped from a scuttled ship and then libelled their boat for salvage: that account is *in equilibrio*.[1] I have read Croly's and Lippmann's new books and written to both of them.[2] I know not whether my criticisms of Croly (for what I think the superstitions as to capital whereof you and I have talked and, for looking more to the government and less to voluntary groups for the realization of personality than I should) will meet any response in his mind. Perhaps he will think it old fogey talk. I told him of my high appreciation and admiration for his deep and careful thinking he displays. My other occupations are the usual ones. After writing two decisions, I point out agreeably that I could wish this were put a little differently and that that fallacy had been avoided in the opinions of others.[3] Alas, the moment draws to an end and I must replace the action with the passive side of boredom next week. I hope all is going well with you. I hear the best accounts.

Sincerely yours,
O. W. Holmes

1. John Lowell (1824–97) of the United States District Court (first circuit) in *Price v. Sears*, Fed. Cas. #11, 416 (1877).

2. Herbert Croly, *Progressive Democracy* (New York: Macmillan, 1914); Walter Lippmann, *Drift and Mastery* (New York: M. Kennerley, 1914).

3. Holmes was probably referring to his unanimous opinions in *Willoughby v. Chicago*, 235 U.S. 45 (1914) and *Sage v. Hampe*, *Id.* at 99, 106. *Willoughby* dismissed an eminent domain dispute as being outside the Court's jurisdiction even though state courts had disagreed on the matter. *Sage* overturned a ruling of the Supreme Court of Kansas that had allowed a conveyance of Indian land that an Act of Congress forbade. Holmes wrote: "The policy involved here is the policy of the United States. It is not a matter that the States can regard or disregard at their will."

Washington, D.C.
December 24, 1914

Dear Frankfurter,

This is just a line, that I was intending to write before your card came today, to send you all our good wishes.[1] I heard someone, I forget who it was, say that he thought you were rather lonely at Cambridge. I hope not with all my heart, and I don't believe it. At all events, you know that there are a good many people in the world who love you and value your friendship very highly and you can't be alone in the world whatever you are in Cambridge. I miss you here sadly, but I have been so hard at work that I have had little time for regrets. Don't forget us.

Sincerely yours,
O. W. Holmes

1. The card referred to is missing.

Washington, D.C.
January 21, 1915

Dear Frankfurter,

Many thanks for your letter and the pamphlet.[1] I need not tell you that I hear with the utmost eagerness of all that concerns you and, if I haven't written before in answer to your other letter of Dec. 3, it is that I have been under constant pressure. This week I have written three cases, distributed two and hope to hand round the last today—and that means, as you can see, little time off the job.[2]

A glance through Cohen's piece makes me feel like an old fogey but I hope that my moderate response to the new doesn't mean ossification in old ideas so much as a general scepticism that embraces new as well as old.[3] I long ago said that continuity with the past was not a duty but only a necessity (in my speech at Langdell's dinner), meaning rather a hit at the animus of some of the historians.[4] But on the other hand, history means the study of embryology and the postulate of continuity—the bet that an unknown region will show the same principles at work that one knows, in other instances, has been the foundation of most of the discoveries and generalizations that have been made. I should have thought that the notion of organic process had led to an entirely new view of institutions. There is fashion in ideas as much as in dress and *value* now has vogue. Far be it from me to undervalue it but to the miraculous I am inaccessible, although I have no formula of necessity. I don't know anything about the universe. It may be, I should think most likely was, a spontaneity of some unimaginable sort. But as a bettabilitarian, I bet that any phenomenon stands in quantitatively fixed relations to antecedent phenomena and to that extent I am a necessitarian. There is a reaction just now for freedom, *ducibus* Bergson and W. James, but I take little stock in it. Of course, great men count but that is consistent with my view as is the organic capacity to imitate and adapt. I haven't had time yet to study the article—I dare say I should agree with most of it—but I fancied I saw a leaning toward miracle. Alas, my doubts attach to many of the shibboleths of the young—(your lot of gifted chaps). I don't believe some of the things deeply implied in the writings of Croly and Lippmann, much as I delight in them and I almost need your encouragement not to think that I am an old hulk on the sands. But as I still take a hand in the actual, I try not to be too much bullied by clever remarks from the cloister. I wish we could have a talk. For I must go to work and can write no more.

Ever sincerely yours,
O. W. Holmes

1. The letter and pamphlet referred to are missing.

2. The two distributed cases were unanimous opinions in *Duffy v. Charak*, 236 U.S. 97 (1915), and *Denver v. Home Savings Bank*, *Id.* at 101, 105. *Duffy* upheld a Massachusetts law entitling mortgagees to receive and dispose of their property but returned the case to bankruptcy court for further consideration. The *Denver* case rejected the city's claim that its certificates of indebtedness, unlike municipal bonds, did not have to be negotiable: "What is true about bonds is true about certificates of indebtedness. . . . The essence of each is that they contain a promise under the seal of the corporation, to pay a certain sum to order or to bearer." The third case was probably *United States v. Holte*, *Id.* at 140, 145, a 6–2 majority opinion which held that a woman transported in violation of the White Slave Traffic Act (1910) could be found guilty, under the U.S. Penal Code, of conspiracy with the person transporting her, "if we abandon the illusion that the woman is always the victim." Justice Joseph R. Lamar (1857–1916), with Justice William R. Day (1849–1923) concurring, dissented.

3. Morris R. Cohen, "History vs. Value," *Journal of Philosophy* 11 (1914): 701. Reprinted in Cohen, *Reason and Nature* (New York: Harcourt Brace, 1931).

4. "Learning and Science: Speech at a Dinner of the Harvard Law School Association in Honor of Professor C. C. Langdell, June 25, 1895," reprinted in Holmes, *Collected Legal Papers*, 138–40.

Cambridge, Massachusetts
January 27, 1915

Dear Justice Holmes,

I'm keenly awaiting your dissent in the Kansas case.[1] In the meantime, for the fact of dissent and the smell of your opinion, at this distance even, my thanks. I'm stirred up about the case but not at all as an onward-and-upwarder. Its effect on the industrial forces is all too problematical—it may result in extra-legal means of strengthening the unions, in educative discipline, or in an attempt to decentralize capital still more to equalize the fighting forces. As to all that, many deeper and complex factors are at work of course. But I *am* stirred up about the decision as a student of constitutional law and how she is made. You'd let me say before your fire that I thoroughly dislike the majority decision, so perhaps it won't be *lese* judiciary to say it on paper. I *was* happy when I saw you drive another spike into the *Adair* case.[2] And I like your dissenting company.[3]

Thanks ever so much for your last letter. No, Cohen isn't a miracle-worker. I *know* you'd find yourself in accord with his main outlook. I know because he does with you. As for youth, I don't believe the Gods *were* jealous when, to prove *their* youth, they sent forth our Justice.

Faithfully yours,
Felix Frankfurter

1. *Coppage v. Kansas*, 236 U.S. 1, 27 (1915). The 6–3 majority opinion by Mahlon Pitney (1858–1924) held that a Kansas statute outlawing yellow-dog contracts—agreements employers required employees to sign stating that they would not join a labor union as a condition of employment—was an interference with the freedom of both employers and employees to set the terms of their own labor. Holmes dissented: "Whether in the long run it is wise for the workingmen to enact legislation of this sort is not my concern, but I am strongly of opinion that there is nothing in the Constitution to prevent it. . . . If that belief, whether right or wrong, may be held by a reasonable man, it seems to me that it may be enforced by law in order to establish the equality of position between the parties in which liberty of contract begins."

2. In *Adair v. United States*, 208 U.S. 161, 191–92 (1908), John Marshall Harlan's (1833–1911) 6–2 majority opinion ruled unconstitutional, as a violation of liberty of contract, an act of Congress prohibiting railroads from discriminating against union workers. Holmes dissented: "I quite agree that the question what and how much good labor unions do, is one on which intelligent people may differ . . . but I could not pronounce it unwarranted if Congress should decide that to foster a strong union was for the best interest, not only of the men, but of the railroads and the country at large." McKenna dissented separately. *Adair*, although somewhat weakened by *Chicago, Burlington and Quincy Rail Road v. McGuire*, 219 U.S. 549 (1911), Justice Charles Evans Hughes's (1862–1948) unanimous opinion upholding protective legislation for workers as a legitimate use of state police power, was later reinforced by *Adkins v. Children's Hospital*, 261 U.S. 525 (1923). See below, February 14, 1923.

3. In *Coppage*, 236 U.S. 1, 42, Justice Day, joined by Hughes, wrote a dissent concluding that the Kansas law "sought, not to require one man to employ another against his will, but to put limitations upon the sacrifice of rights which one man may exact from another as a condition of employment."

Washington, D.C.
January 28, 1915

Dear Frankfurter,

You always make me proud of and on account of you—the latter in this instance because of the MS and print on the title page of your *Selection of Cas-*

es.[1] I think the selection a good scheme and one that will make the lads feel as if they were getting closer to life than in studying the scope of an *absque hoc.*[2] I felicitate and thank you.

Ever yours,
O. W. Holmes

1. Felix Frankfurter, *A Selection of Cases under the Interstate Commerce Act* (Cambridge: Harvard University Press, 1915).
2. Without this: In common law pleading, the opening words of a partial denial of an adversary's allegation.

Washington, D.C.
January 31, 1915

Dear Frankfurter,

While waiting for the haircutter at last I have read the piece by Cohen that you sent me. I got a distorted notion from my first glance and hasten to apologize and to say that I think it not only remarkable but admirable and, as you predicted, I find myself in almost absolute agreement with it. My only reserve is with reference to what is not developed, Cohen's own theory of the source, nature and validity of our judgments of value and, perhaps I should add, his aversion to the necessitarian point of view. Of course, I don't mean a *world* compelling necessity. I know nothing about the whole of things—I mean only the assumption that a phenomenon will be found to have fixed quantitative relation to antecedent phenomena. That I believe. I also believe that it has no bearing on conduct and is of little more practical importance (to a thinker) than a configuration of the void. As I wrote almost before you were born, "the mode through which the inevitable comes to pass is effort" or very nearly those words.[1] I can't stop to look them up. Of course history presupposes a set of valuations in the historian—that is why it is said that each generation must rewrite it—is why Gibbon, a great man, says little to us and F. de Coulanges in his *Origines* says relatively much—the emphasis of interest has changed.[2]

But I didn't set out to discourse, but only to recant and to thank you for giving me another real pleasure.

Yours,
O. W. Holmes

1. *Collected Legal Papers*, 305. See below, April 1, 1915.

2. Numa Denis Fustel de Coulanges (1830–99), French historian known for his devotion to the scientific method. See *Les Origenes du systeme feodal* (Paris: Hachette, 1890).

Washington, D.C.
[April 1, 1915]

[Holmes to Frankfurter]

[Top of letter missing]

This is about nothing in particular so you needn't fear that I am going to ask you to do something—the first apprehension that seizes one on getting a letter from a friend.[1] No, this is simply an explosion of amiable sentiments, to which I will add, as it just occurs to me, my hope that you received my recantation about Cohen's "History vs. Value." When I read it, instead of projecting it from within, I was delighted with it.

Wigmore has just written asking me to write something for the 10th anniversary of the *Illinois Law Review*.[2] I have written explaining the impossibility, but before I send it I think I shall try to see whether I have a few words available to express my old convictions that have been stirred up by reading Del Vecchio's *Formal Bases of Law* in Wigmore's philosophical series.[3] Of course, I don't agree with it but I fear that what is on my lips would sound blasphemous to the good orthodox of Illinois. [Section cut out here]. . . . I haven't quite made up my mind. I wish you were here to advise me. I read it to Hughes, and he said print it. That chap has got some horizons that you wouldn't suspect at first under his nonconformist conscience.[4]

Yours ever,
O. W. Holmes

1. The letter referred to is missing.

2. "Ideals and Doubts," *Illinois Law Review* 10 (1915): 1. See also, *Collected Legal Papers*, 303–307. John Henry Wigmore (1863–1943), a close friend of Holmes, was Dean of the Law School, Northwestern University.

3. Giorgio Del Vecchio, *The Formal Bases of Law* (Boston: Boston Book, 1914). While Holmes did not subscribe to Del Vecchio's neo-Kantian idealism ("consciousness constructs the universe and as the fundamental fact is entitled to fundamental reverence"), he believed that "as there are many things that I cannot help doing that the universe can, I do not venture to assume that my inabilities in the way of thought are inabilities of the universe." *Collected Legal Papers*, 304.

4. Hughes, the son of a Welsh-born, Methodist minister from upstate New York, had been Governor of New York from 1907 to 1910 when President Taft appointed him to the Supreme Court. He resigned in 1916 to run unsuccessfully for President against Woodrow Wilson. He

later served as Secretary of State under Harding and Coolidge. In 1930 he returned to the Supreme Court as Chief Justice, serving until 1941.

Washington, D.C.
April 16, 1915

Dear Frankfurter,

The first thing I did on receipt of your letter this morning was to write to Christie.[1] And subject to some further consideration whether I had better not meddle, I shall send the letter when I do this. I am too hurried to discuss the point mentioned in your former letter as to state requirements to carry below cost. But it is a class of legislation in which I am more ready to interfere than some others.

I had a very pleasant letter from Cohen and some articles of his which I shall have bound. I have on my table from the library Barbour's *Hist. of Contract in Early English Equity*, which, so far as I have looked at it, seems to back me up in matters upon which Ames criticized me—both as to a movement toward enforcing gratuitous promises in Equity and as to the early history of assumpsit.[2] I was the first to take up those subjects and I think Ames's study of detail coupled with an ever-present desire to pitch into me has rather covered up my work although I still think it touched the most vital points on the latter question. In the former, I reconstructed the fish from a scale and I am pleased to see Barbour back me up from sources then inaccessible. . . . Wigmore's enthusiastic mention led me also to run through Henderson *The Fitness of the Environment*—Conclusion: the universe is biocentric.[3] I am not so much impressed as Wigmore was—perhaps because of reading *Bridgewater Treatises* in my youth.[4] In a given world, if an organism fits the environment, of course, the environment fits the organism. But as to the possibilities of the universe, I don't care to speculate except to amuse myself with the thought of omnipotence seeking to avoid *ennui* by trying how many universes could be fitted into the same space, each internally correlated and none in any way impinging upon any other so that each is unconscious of all the rest.

Yours ever,
O.W.H.

1. The letter referred to is missing.

2. Willard T. Barbour, *The History of Contract in Early English Equity* (Oxford: Clarendon Press, 1914). Holmes's argument with James Barr Ames (1846–1910), Dean and Professor at

Harvard Law School, began in the 1880s when Ames criticized Holmes's analysis of the obligation of contracts in *The Common Law* (Boston: Little, Brown, 1881). At the heart of their disputations on complex practices such as *assumpsit* (action on breaches of contract made without seal) was Holmes's tendency to find in Teutonic procedures the basis of the common law against Ames's ascription of greater influence to Roman law. Mark DeWolfe Howe suggests that a further cause of tension was Holmes's decision in 1882 to resign his Harvard professorship, less than a year after accepting it. See Howe, *Holmes: The Proving Years*, 228–31.

3. Lawrence J. Henderson, *The Fitness of the Environment* (New York: Macmillan, 1913).

4. *The Bridgewater Treatises on the Power, Wisdom and Goodness of God as Manifested in the Creation*, 8 vols. (London: W. Pickering, 1833–36). Though animated by natural theology, these volumes were filled with scientific information.

Washington, D.C.
May 29, 1915

Dear Frankfurter,

Many thanks for your letter and the piece by Graham Wallas which of course has my sympathy.[1] This morning, after sending round my last case, (assigned to me this week, I may get others later) I have been reading with great pleasure two articles just sent to me by Cohen.[2] I shall write to him—he also is one I agree with so far as I follow him on a first reading. The language of philosophers is sometimes a little difficult, because at any given time certain phrases have acquired a significance that one who keeps only a general eye on the subject does not know. But he is a mighty good writer—indeed, you young fellows in *The New Republic* show that we can write as well in this country as anywhere and fill me with courage even though you humble me personally. Before I forget it—last summer and later on my birthday I had letters from Mrs. King that it shamed me not to acknowledge but in both she seemed to be in transit, and I knew not where to write. If you ever see her, do give her my compliments and sincere thanks. It was a great joy to see you the other day—I only wished I could have seen you more. I look forward to doing so this summer.

Ever Sincerely Yours,
O. W. Holmes

1. The letter referred to is missing; Graham Wallas (1858–1932), a leading member of the Fabian Society and a founder of the London School of Economics, stressed the importance of social psychology in the study of political theory. See *Human Nature in Politics* (London: Constable, 1908) and *The Great Society* (New York: Macmillan, 1914).

2. Morris R. Cohen wrote numerous articles and reviews in 1915. Most appeared in *The New Republic* and several were reprinted in *Law and the Social Order* (New York: Macmillan, 1933).

Washington, D.C.
May 30, 1915

Dear Frankfurter,

Ain't this paper fine? I think it is an introduction of McReynolds at all events.[1] I learned of it from him. I want to add what I forgot yesterday—that I don't know Ehrlich's *Soziologie des Recht* except that I believe I have one chapter that he sent to me.[2] I shall be sure to forget the name, but some day may write to ask you what I asked you from Washington about what.

Yours ever,
O.W.H.

I disremember what the Slocum case is about, though I guess.[3] I haven't seen Thayer's article.[4] He sent me a good one on the continuous improvement of the law of evidence.[5]

I only use this paper when I want to put on sides except now to show you what I could, if I would.

1. James C. McReynolds (1862–1946), Attorney General of the United States, 1913–14, had just completed his first year as an Associate Justice. He served on the Court until 1941.

2. Eugen Ehrlich, *Grundlegung der Soziologie des Rechts* (Munich: Duncker and Humblot, 1913), published in English as *Fundamental Principles of the Sociology of the Law* (Cambridge: Harvard University Press, 1936).

3. *Slocum v. New York Insurance Co.*, 228 U.S. 364 (1913). In a 5–4 decision by Willis Van Devanter (1859–1941), the Court held that when a jury verdict for the plaintiff has to be set aside as a matter of law, the constitutional guarantee of a jury trial means that the judge, who should have directed a jury verdict for the defendant in the first place, must order a new trial even when there is no additional evidence to be presented. Charles Evans Hughes's dissent, in which Holmes, Pitney, and Horace H. Lurton (1844–1914) joined, took a less rigid view of the linkage between the Constitution and eighteenth-century modes of procedure, thus allowing scope for reform.

4. Ezra Ripley Thayer, "John Chipman Gray (1839–1915)," *Harvard Law Review* 28 (1915): 539.

5. Thayer, "Observations on the Law of Evidence," *Michigan Law Review* 13 (1915): 355. Thayer called for more flexibility in the admission of evidence but concluded, "one must not be tempted to over estimate what rules of law can do. No system or body of rules can run itself. With a good judge the worst system will work well; with a poor one the best system will work badly."

Beverly Farms, Massachusetts
July 5, 1915

Dear Frankfurter,

At last we are here—arrived last week—and my bills having been paid and business done so far as heard from. I'm ahead of the time for the improvement of my mind and the pleasures of friendship. I was much disturbed the other day to hear that you expected to be working in New York during the summer but surely it will not prevent our seeing you here? I have looked forward to it so much. Meantime tell me again the name of the German sociologist or legal philosopher that you mentioned in the winter as one that Pound swears by and, if it be possible and convenient and the book is not too infernally large, perhaps they would lend it to me from the library?[1] It has been raining here like the devil and is now which is conducive to the practice of the virtues.

Yours ever,
O. W. Holmes

You know that my start from Washington was delayed by the death of George my messenger the morning we were to leave. A curtain caught fire and he was burned to death trying to put it out.[2]

1. See above, May 30, 1915.

2. The following notice appeared in the *Washington Post*, June 23, 1915: "George Marston, colored, 60 years old, was badly burned about the face, hands and body last night, when he attempted to extinguish fire in a lace curtain at his home, 1616 Corcoran Street Northwest, which had been ignited by a burning gas jet. His underclothing caught fire. He was treated by his family physician. The damage to the property was $25." George Marston died on June 24 at Freedman's Hospital.

Beverly Farms, Massachusetts
July 8, 1915

Dear Frankfurter,

We shall be delighted to see you Saturday, July 17 for over Sunday I hope. Leaving Sunday night would be the act of your old enemies the Philistines, but of course you will be free to do as you please when the time comes. I received the book yesterday and read the first 30 pages more or less which leave me still in doubt whether he is coming out in philosophy or confusion. I shall go on with "deliberate speed" as I have to with German, alas.[1] I hope I may keep the vol. for a few weeks until I finish it. I am scrupulous about borrowed books and am worried till I return them. One must, if (to quote a recent decision of mine), "he brings to his contract the modest intelligence of the prudent man."[2]

Ever sincerely yours,
O. W. Holmes

I reopen to say that I had read only about 20 instead of 30 Ehrlich, and that now having read 30 I am much interested and pleased. His notion of the body of the law coming from the practice inside the groups and not appearing in the *Corpus Juris* I think was more or less anticipated by Tarde, *Transformation du Droit* if I remember the title right.[3] And I am pleased to note that I have insisted more than once on the priority of contracts over any theory of contract and the struggle for life between oath-hostage and interrupted sale to lay the foundations of such a theory.

1. Holmes had used this phrase in a unanimous opinion on a tax case, *Virginia v. West Virginia*, 222 U.S. 17, 19–20 (1911): "A question like the present should be disposed of without undue delay. But a State cannot be expected to move with the celerity of a private business man; it is enough if it proceeds, in the language of English Chancery, with all deliberate speed." As an Associate Justice of the U.S. Supreme Court, Frankfurter suggested the phrase to Chief Justice Earl Warren (1891–1974) as the latter was writing the second school desegregation decision, *Brown v. Board of Education*, 349 U.S. 294, 301 (1955). Referring to the first desegregation decision, *Brown v. Board Of Education*, 347 U.S. 483 (1954), Warren ordered District Courts "to enter such orders and decrees . . . as are necessary and proper to admit to public schools on a racially nondiscriminatory basis with all deliberate speed the parties to these cases." Also, see below, May 30, 1925.

2. *Lumber Underwriters v. Rife*, 237 U.S. 605, 609 (1915). Holmes wrote the majority opinion reversing an appeals court decision that oral evidence should be admissible in considering the validity of an insurance claim. The import of an insurance policy, Holmes said, "as everyone understands, is that the document embodies the contract." White, Day, and McKenna dissented without opinion.

3. Gabriel Tarde, *Les Transformations du droit* (Paris: Alcan, 1893).

Beverly Farms, Massachusetts
August 17, 1915

Dear Frankfurter,

Your sending the letters should have been acknowledged and thanked for a long time ago but Wigmore sent me proofs and manuscript and also Vol. 2 of his *Ancient Legal Institutions* and I read them all so that not till now have I felt free from the incubus of duty.[1] It is queer how serious books transmute themselves into duty—doubly if they are connected with one's job. So long as they are, so one may be said to be taking life at first hand as they are the material on which one works. It is high time that I take it at second hand in *belles lettres* and amusement. To let myself down gently, I yesterday took Plato's *Republic* (in a transl.—I haven't yet been able to get the Greek) and found it much more interesting, I almost said amusing, than I had expected. I always like to see germs. Meantime I don't know where you are or where to return the letters. My wife read them to me while I played solitaire which blunted their edges a little but I appreciate their intelligence and high feeling. I have seen Beveridge twice—he is a near neighbour—and have found real pleasure in his spontaneity and gusto. He is writing a life of John Marshall and is full of it.[2] Most of the time I am solitary and happy in being so—I can't get Frankfurters to talk with every day.

Sincerely Yours,
O. W. Holmes

1. The letters referred to are missing. See John Henry Wigmore and Albert Kocourek, eds., *Primitive and Ancient Legal Institutions* (Boston: Little, Brown, 1915).

2. Albert J. Beveridge (1862–1927), historian and Senator from Indiana, 1899–1911, was a leading Republican progressive. He consulted frequently with Holmes about *The Life of John Marshall*, 4 vols. (Boston: Houghton, Mifflin, 1916–19).

Washington D.C.
October 11, 1915

Dear Frankfurter,

Your telegram came ahead of the Club as we were not at home this p.m. I will endeavor to communicate it at the first regular meeting.[1] The Court has opened, the President has been called upon and biz. begins on the morrow. Indeed, I this moment have read an opinion in a case that went over.[2] No more leisure after now. If you divergondate into such paths—*Elizabethan Literature* by Robertson M. P. in Home University Library, 50 cents per, which I read in the train coming on, I thought altogether admirable and the chapter on Shakespeare the best ever.[3] Otherwise it is of the vol. on the Renaissance by Edith Sichel, written with feminine liking for easy reference to things not generally known, and *me judice*, not known to her—still, not hopelessly dull.[4]

I hope you are content with your handiwork—the engagement of Brown and Dorothy Kirchwey.[5] I took it for granted that it was accomplished, before they left us although she seems not to have assented formally until later. It seemed to me all right and I gave them my blessing.

Heaven bless your labors at the school. I shall miss you here sadly.

Yours ever,
O. W. Holmes

P.S. I had a letter from Alex Aaronson forwarded to me here. He, I think, was the brother of the wonderful one and didn't see that I had anything to say. I should greet him if he came this way but I have no distinct recollection of him.[6] Tell Pound that if he was real good, he would complete my collection of all his writings known to me by sending me his epitome of lectures on jurisprudence that I saw in the hands of my new secretary today.[7]

1. The Telegram referred to is missing. The Monday P.M. Club was an open house at the Holmeses when the Supreme Court was in session.

2. Probably, *Gsell v. Insular Collector of Customs*, 239 U.S. 93 (1915), submitted on May 14, 1915, and decided on November 15, 1915, by dismissal because it was brought on a writ of error rather than an appeal.

3. John Mackinnon Robertson, *Elizabethan Literature* (New York: Holt, 1914). Number 95 in Home University Library of Modern Knowledge.

4. Edith Helen Sichel, *The Renaissance* (New York: Holt, 1914).

5. LaRue Brown (1883–1969), a Harvard Law School classmate of Frankfurter and expert on minimum wage legislation, became an active New Dealer and, after World War II, a leading figure in the Americans for Democratic Action. Dorothy Kirchwey Brown (1888–1981), daughter of child labor reformer George Kirchwey, was a distinguished civil libertarian and philanthropist. Her sister, Freda Kirchwey (1893–1976), edited *The Nation* from 1932 to 1955.

6. Alexander Aaronsohn (1888–1948), journalist and member of a famous family of Palestinian pioneers, was a founder of the Nili, a secret group that passed information to the British Army in the hope of evicting the Turks from Palestine. His *With the Turks in Palestine* (Boston: Houghton, Mifflin, 1916) was a popular account of this movement. "The wonderful one" was his brother Aaron (1876–1919), an agronomist whose discoveries of wild wheat helped to stimulate the growth of the Palestinian economy.

7. Pound's epitome was published as *Outline of Lectures on Jurisprudence* (Cambridge: Harvard University Press, 1914). Originally published in 1903.

Washington, D.C.
October 12, 1915

Dear Frankfurter,

Our letters crossed.[1] Yours curiously recalled one that I was writing this morning to an old friend of mine in England both of whose sons have been killed.[2] She had written in a nobly exalted strain and I said in the course of my answer that to trust ourselves to the infinite in some form was the lesson and achievement of life. But while I was speaking from my heart, I couldn't but remember what Carlyle said when he was told that Margaret Fuller had said (in the pretentious way that some of those people spoke): "I accept the universe."—"Gad, she'd better," quoth Carlyle.[3] The keynote to me is that we are inside the universe. Therefore, it has been able to produce (without much bellyache) consciousness—significance—beings with ideals. If the universe doesn't answer to those terms, it is because they are too small, not because we are bigger than that which produced, supports and contains us. Only the illusion that we know adequately the prime stuff—matter—

force—whatever you choose to call it and that as we see it, in the table for instance or, in a flash of lightning, it is not our equal, makes us capable of despair, and of feeling that we are Prometheus alone with the rock to which he is bound—a fool feeling based on conceit. All of which I have said before but I must repeat it whenever the question comes up. I also must repeat that every wise man is a mystic at bottom—not in the sense of unalterable communications from behind phenomena—but in that of realizing that all ends in mystery if only you put it in the right place and don't try to get it in between the interstices of phenomena as do Catholic spiritualists and W. James. But I must go and play solitaire. Many thanks for your inspiriting letter.

Yours always,
O. W. Holmes

1. The letter referred to is missing.

2. Ethel Grenfell, Lady Desborough (1867–1952) was the niece of Henry Cowper (1836–87) who had also been a close friend of Holmes. See Howe, ed., *Holmes-Laski Letters*, 323, and Novick, *Honorable Justice*, 312–13.

3. The Fuller-Carlyle exchange supposedly took place in 1846. See David Alec Wilson, *Carlyle on Cromwell and Others (1837–48)* (New York: E. P. Dutton, 1925), 346–51. Margaret Fuller (1810–50) was a transcendentalist reformer and writer.

Washington, D.C.
November 4, 1915

Dear Frankfurter,

Your book has come and brings a glow to my innards[?] though I can't read it at present.[1] I really should like to, for I felt about the Interstate Commerce Act as Francis Parker (whom you never heard of) once said about President Eliot.[2] He said, there are two forces that govern mankind that Eliot doesn't understand and therefore fears: Imagination and Humor (Don't repeat this, as Eliot is alive).

The Monday P.M. Club gathered in force for the first time last Monday and you were not forgotten but like an idiot I did forget to read your telegram I had been keeping for the purpose.

May I again approach Pound through you? I saw somewhere a reference to an article of his, "Law in Action and Law in Books," or some such title which, so far as I know, I haven't seen.[3] The title is almost in the very words, one that I thought about years ago. I haven't had time to read his article on rights but I regard the whole machinery of rights and duties as epicycles.[4] Did it ever strike you that if you want to know your rights (of person or property), you must turn to a book on torts? Books on property treat of conveyancing. I say Law in Books is merely Sibylline leaves of prophecy as to when the public force will be brought to bear on you through the courts (See *American Banana Co. v. United Fruit Co.*).[5] And a statement of rights is merely part of these prophecies—the talk about rights is what I believe the philosophers call a hypostasis of the prophecy. If you don't want to mix up law with morals etc., (as you may, *qua* philosopher, but may not *qua* lawyer), you should approach it with a cynical mind—be a bad man and say I don't care a damn about your approval or disapproval. All I want to know is what will happen (through the courts) if I do so and so—respectfully submitted.

Yours ever,
O. W. Holmes

1. Probably, *Cases under the Interstate Commerce Act*, which Frankfurter assigned in his public utilities course. See above, January 28, 1915.

2. Francis Parker (1837–1902), noted progressive educator; Charles W. Eliot (1834–1926), President of Harvard from 1869 to 1909.

3. Roscoe Pound, "Law in Books and Law in Action," *American Law Review* 44 (1910): 12.

4. Probably, Roscoe Pound, "Interests of Personality," *Harvard Law Review* 28 (1915): 343, 445. Pound viewed the emergence of legal systems and their recognition of various rights as a function of the "development" of the state.

5. *American Banana Co. v. United Fruit Co.*, 213 U.S. 347, 356–57 (1909). Holmes's unanimous opinion dismissed plaintiff's evidence of United Fruit's efforts to crush competition, including the company's suborning of the Costa Rican government, by finding these actions outside the jurisdiction of the Sherman Anti-Trust Act: "Law is a statement of the circumstances in which the public force will be brought to bear upon men through the courts. But the word commonly is confined to such prophecies or threats when addressed to persons living within the power of the courts."

Washington, D.C.
November 5, 1915

Dear Frankfurter,

What I wrote yesterday ought to have been condensed by me into a single orphic saying—A *duty/right* is the hypostasis of a prophecy. Which I hereby copyright with you.

I forget whether I said that if Pound had a copy of the article I referred to, "Law in Action and Law in Books," I should be grateful for one.

Yours,
O. W. Holmes

P.S. So, "Force" is the hypostasis of the prophecy that "bodies" will behave to each other in a certain way or, more accurately, that phenomena will have a certain sequence. It adds nothing and intelligent men of science know that it adds nothing.

O.W.H.

Cambridge, Massachusetts
November 11, 1915

Dear Justice Holmes,

I have to report a coincidence which those more hospitable to the miraculous world erect into significance. I was talking the other day with Barbour (he who wrote the study of the early law of contracts in equity) about all sorts of things, *inter alia* your theory of contracts.[1] I was led to remark that I thought it was tied up with your general attitude as to the meaning and scope of law and pulled from the shelf 213 U.S. to read to him from *American Banana v. U.S. Fruit Co.*. I then went to my room and there in the much-prized handwriting was your letter referring me to *American Banana Co. v. U.S. Fruit Co.*, 213 U.S. So I say the spiritually, mediumistically inclined, I'm sure, could build up a whole chapter to prove the undemonstrable. I was content to be tickled by the coincident without thinking God was inside of it. (I wonder if this craving to button up things that are meant to be loose, this synthesizing where the links are missing, is just sheer human gullibility or, primitive survivals of big or little gods-making or, one form of man's endless groping for explanations. Of course, that precious craving is to be nurtured at all hazards; if only they wouldn't think results come so cheaply, at so little cost of the pain of thought). Not only the reference to the case, but the matter of your letter and those concentrated P.S.s hit eager soil. I shall guard the copyright and protect your interests therein by securing for it the royalty of discriminating readers and hearers. This sounds smug but I find more and more that to move minds, truth or insight that has a sharp point is suspect and, as for scholarship—that mustn't be flavored or pungent! Well, Pound was delighted with it. All this "rights" talk always bothers me and I suspect my own competence when I find a thousand profound minds, or at least, fellows who write big books talk about them. How a big book does subordinate me! I wonder if my scepticism about most of them is the ordinary self-protection of incompetence, or inveighing what one hasn't or can't do! And yet, not wholly I'm sure. The more I see of Pound's work, the more I wish he'd liberate himself from his learning. He now has plenty of wood to make his own fire (you see how unconsciously I steal from you). But he *is* a scholar with a true scholar's disinterested generosity. I suppose "force" as a hypostasis is a direct descendant from the deification of phenomena—from deification to reification to a formula of sequence. Which reminds me of a little girl who did not know what "gravitation" was. Her teacher struggled to explain it to her. In despair, she held a book in her hand and, as she released her hand and the book descended, she said, "You see, Mary, gravitation is what makes the book fall." "It would fall anyhow," said Mary. *She* has the making of a scientist.

I wonder if you thought as well as I did of Justice Higgins' article in this month's *Harvard Law Review*?[2] It seemed to me to have all the romance of bending theories to the test of life—of trying to adjust conflicting demands to larger common interests, or at least making me know their demands through disinterested expert guidance.

Always faithfully,
F.F.

1. See above, April 16, 1915.

2. Henry Bournes Higgins, "A New Province for Law and Order: Industrial Peace through Minimum Wage and Arbitration," *Harvard Law Review* 29 (1915): 13. Higgins (1851–1929), a liberal politician and judge, was President of the Australian Court of Conciliation and Arbitration.

Washington, D.C.
November 30, 1915

Dear Frankfurter,

The book with Pound's article has come—am I to return it when read or am I to infer from its not being marked that I can keep it? In either event, I am much obliged to you. The work has begun again and I am hard at it. The principal products of leisure are a formula for Shakespeare: Song and tall talk—and the invention of a correlate to philosophy: misosophy.[1]

Yours ever,
O. W. Holmes

1. Hatred of philosophy.

Washington, D.C.
December 19, 1915

Dear Frankfurter,

Once more let me thank you for the red book over which I joyfully have accepted *dominium*, having read the article with the expected pleasure.[1] I think I agree with Pound that I should prefer to sum up my results in a connected work but I am not sure.

I put the case of the married man to my wife. She reinforced my unwillingness as it means a major interest outside his work.[2] It is true that the work is not very much but if baby has the megrims, papa won't have the freedom of mind and spirit that I like to find. So let us regard that as an undesirable alternative till you tell me that it is the only possibility which I gather is not the case.

I agree with all the good things that you say about Lamar.[3] I think he is looking forward to coming back but (strictly between ourselves) I sadly doubt it. Also, I had taken the same pleasure as you in the passage of McKenna's.[4] Did I tell you of another passage, a distinct sentence, that is delightfully distorted by taking it alone—"It is misleading to say that men and women have rights?"[5] I told him I should make it the text of a destructive sociological discourse.

Did I ever tell you of Corot the painter that I heard once that he began as a most careful draughtsman, working out every detail and came to his magisterial summaries at the end? I have thought of that in writing opinions latterly. Whether the brethren like it I don't know. Of course, the eternal effort of art, even the art of writing legal decisions, is to omit all but the essentials—"The point of contact" is the formula—the place where the boy got his fingers pinched. The rest of the machinery doesn't matter. So the Jap. master puts five dots for a hand, knowing they are in the right place and the etcher elaborates what he wants you to see and leads up to it with a few scrawls. A Merry Christmas to you. Some of the little chilluns dined here the other night. Would that you were here, but of course I am glad for you that you are not.

Yours ever,
O. W. Holmes

1. See above, November 4, 1915.

2. Beginning with the Court's 1915–16 term, Frankfurter screened prospective secretaries for Holmes. Shelton Hale (1884–1920) was eventually appointed.

3. Joseph R. Lamar served as Associate Justice of the Supreme Court from 1911 to 1916. Woodrow Wilson nominated his close advisor, Louis D. Brandeis (1856–1941), as Lamar's replacement. An acrimonious debate ensued, centering upon Brandeis's reform politics and his

Jewish faith. On June 1, 1916, the Senate confirmed Brandeis by a 47–22 vote. See A. L. Todd, *Justice on Trial: The Case of Louis D. Brandeis* (New York: McGraw-Hill, 1964).

4. The passage that Holmes and Frankfurter found so amusing probably came from *Mackenzie v. Hare*, 239 U.S. 299, 311 (1915), a unanimous opinion in which McKenna denied the suit of a woman who sought to regain citizenship and local voting rights after marrying a British subject: "The identity of husband and wife is an ancient principle of our jurisprudence. It was neither accidental nor arbitrary and worked in many instances for her protection. There has been, it is true, much relaxation of it but in its retention as in its origin it is determined by their intimate relation and unity of interests, and this relation and unity may make it of public concern in many instances to merge their identity and give dominance to the husband."

5. In *Hoke v. United States*, 227 U.S. 308, 323 (1913), McKenna's unanimous opinion upheld the White Slave Traffic Act of 1910 (Mann Act) by drawing an analogy from Congress's power to regulate interstate commerce. The sentence preceding Holmes's quote reads: "Of course it will be said that women are not articles of merchandise, but this does not affect the analogy of cases; the substance of the congressional power is the same, only the manner of its exercise must be accommodated to the difference in its objects. It is misleading to say that men and women have rights. Their rights cannot fortify or sanction their wrongs; and if they employ interstate transportation as a facility of their wrongs, it may be forbidden to them."

Washington, D.C.
December 25, 1915

Dear Frankfurter,

Another mark of your kindness has come and I thank you.[1] I hope to read it forthwith as we have a week, though an interrupted one, ahead. . . . I hope you are having a Merry Christmas and, at this point Harrison came in, and hearing that I was writing you, joined his wishes to mine.[2] It is a moment of affectionate thoughts and you get a lot of them from here.

Ever sincerely yours,
O. W. Holmes

1. The gift is unknown.

2. George L. Harrison (1887–1958), Holmes's secretary, 1913–14, served as President and then Chairman of the Board of RCA, 1941–54.

Washington D.C.
December 31, 1915

Dear Frankfurter,

Please accept my sincerest thanks for showing the letter that I return herewith.[1] It naturally moves me deeply and, if I hadn't been interrupted by a call from Richard Wigglesworth, I had some remarks that I might have made.[2] One was, how those who believe no creed become religious at a moment like this but, I suspect, more those outside than those in the trenches where, unless I am mistaken, you might find gaiety as the miasmatic mist of misery (I repeat what I said to my secretary, as it rather pleased me).

Wigglesworth was wondering whether a year here wouldn't be good for him. I was trembling all the time lest he ask to be my secretary. Between ourselves, I don't want one of my connections here and the Wigglesworths believe too much in a phraseology of conventional virtues for me to breathe freely in their company. When it was reported to me that my nephew had spoken of going to the camp at Plattsburg as an example, I told him if a son of mine talked about doing anything as an example, I would boot him out of my house.[3] I am happy to say he made himself all right with me but the incident illustrates. I remarked, incidentally, that my secretaryship was not in my hands—I don't believe you would have been likely to send him to me—but let me know the name before concluding my bargain. When you write to Christie, give my love to him. I send you every good wish and prophecy for the New Year and other years to come.

Yours ever,
O. W. Holmes

1. The letter referred to is missing.

2. Richard B. Wigglesworth (1891–1960) was Holmes's nephew; his mother was Mrs. Holmes's younger sister. He was a Republican Congressman from Massachusetts from 1928 to 1958 and also served as U.S. Ambassador to Canada, 1959–60.

3. Plattsburg (N.Y.) was a civilian military camp, organized in 1915 by a variety of voluntary groups concerned that the European conflict endangered American security.

Cambridge, Massachusetts
January 14, 1916

Dear Justice Holmes,

I suspect that the Lord has made me none too hospitably inclined to the Samuel Smith scheme of salvation—nor Arthur Hill—and I think you need have no fear that our candidates will possessive [sic] any obtrusive Christian virtues.[1]

What I really started out to say was to utter thanks for a few very pretty and pithy recent opinions of yours. *New York v. Sage* (the reservoir dam site case), *Ex parte Uppercu* and, the Denver tax increase case pleased me heartily, particularly the latter which is along lines of immediate interest.[2] I'm going into so-called Administrative Law and I'm astonished how we repeat the pious formula when the realities of modern society compel a distribution and discharge of affairs that cannot possibly fit into the formulistic scheme of separation and non-delegation of power and all that. (I think you'd be interested in *Local Government Board v. Arlidge*, 1915, A. C. 120).[3]

O! if you knew how I praise whosoever is to be praised, if any, *your* "magisterial summaries," particularly these days when I have to read opinions by the wholesale. Which reminds me, not too irrelevantly, of a very charming novel I read lately. If you read such things—it goes well, I should think, with solitaire—let me introduce to you *Herself* by Ethel Sidgwick (I believe the daughter of the Oxford prof).[4]

Always faithfully,
Felix Frankfurter

I dined with Mrs. Curtis the other day and we had a merry time.[5] I *did* and I think "we" did.

1. Samuel F. Smith (1808–95), Boston born editorial secretary of the American Baptist Missionary Union; Arthur D. Hill (1869–1947), liberal Boston lawyer, assisted Frankfurter in the selection of Holmes's secretaries and taught at Harvard Law School from 1915 to 1919.

2. All unanimous decisions. *New York v. Sage*, 239 U.S. 57, 61 (1915), reversed an appeals court decision granting a generous award to a land owner whose parcel comprised only a portion of a large public works project: "The City is not to be made to pay for any part of what it has added to the land by thus uniting it with other lots, if that union would not have been practicable or have been attempted except by the intervention of eminent domain." *Ex parte Uppercu, Id.* at 435, 440, ordered evidence produced that a lower court had sealed following an earlier suit in which petitioner was tangentially involved: "So long as the object physically exists, anyone needing it as evidence at a trial has a right to call for it." In *Bi-Metallic Investment Co. v. Colorado, Id.* at 441, Holmes upheld a state decision allowing the state board of equalization to revalue Denver's taxable property.

3. *Local Government Board v. Arlidge* (1915), Law Reports, House of Lords, Appeal Cases, 120, held that a quasi-judicial administrative body, acting under rules of conduct laid down by Parliament, could adopt procedures it deemed suitable and that the courts could not inquire whether this practice was itself just.

4. Ethel Sidgwick, *Herself* (Boston: Small, Maynard, 1912). Oxford scholar Arthur Sidgwick (1840–1920) was the author of *Introduction to Greek Prose Composition* (London: Rivingtons, 1875), a standard text with many editions.

5. Ellen Amory Curtis (1868–1952), wife of Boston attorney and yachtsman Charles Pelham Curtis (1860–1948), was an intimate friend of Holmes.

Washington, D.C.
January 17, 1916

[No Salutation]

Tip top, dear boy, tip top. All that remains is for the law schools to go ahead and justify your exhortations and verify your prophecies.[1] They have in some respects the best chances, but the generalizing mind is the thing wherein you find it. You will do your share.

Yours ever,
O.W.H.

1. In "The Law and the Law Schools," *Reports of the American Bar Association* 40 (1915): 365, Frankfurter challenged "Bar and Bench" to pressure schools to teach students, "the law as an instrument and not an end of organized humanity, . . . not as a harsh Procrustean bed into which all persons and all societies must inexorably be fitted, but as a vital agency for human betterment."

Washington, D.C.
January 28, 1916

Dear Frankfurter,

The New Republic is on my table but I am behindhand, having been frightfully busy. I note your recommendations and have already noticed marks of Laski's penetration (a far from amiable reference to things not generally known such as my article on Early English Equity).[1]

I suppose this Adler who writes in the January *Harvard Law Review*, "Labor, Cap. and Bus. at Com. Law," is the same who wrote the former article I liked.[2] It still shows the same learning but I am less impressed by this discourse. Of course, it is well to recognize that all business, for the matter of that, all life in a community has a public function, but I don't think history helps much—both because I don't believe the earlier times acted on economic theory but rather, because a gentleman didn't expect to have a damned smith refuse to shoe his horse and because no one would care a tuppence what their theories were, we think we know more about it. Also, I don't find much help in the thesis. The difficulty is to decide what is for the public good. I was tempted to touch the point in a case decided Monday, *Mt. Vernon-Woodberry Cotton Duck Co. v. Alabama Interstate Power Co.*, but decided it was more prudent to avoid controversy by simply referring to the cases that have decided that a use may be public though the immediate user is private.[3] There is a long, rather imbecile opinion in 100 Maine (if my memory is right) to the contrary.[4]

I have distributed three cases this week and, as the docket broke down, am beginning to breathe, after working rather too intensely.[5] I hope that I see a glimpse of leisure in this next month as I am up with my work.

Yours as always,
O. W. Holmes

1. The British political theorist Harold J. Laski (1893–1950) was about to be appointed instructor in history and government at Harvard. He met Holmes in the summer of 1916 and their famous correspondence ensued. Laski referred favorably to Holmes's "Early English Equity," *Law Quarterly Review* 1 (1885): 162, in a review of George E. Woodbine's *Bracton De Legibus et Consuetudinibus Angliae* (New Haven: Yale University Press, 1915) appearing in *New Republic* 3 (1915): 129.

2. Edward A. Adler, "Labor, Capital, and Business at Common Law," *Harvard Law Review* 29 (1916): 241. Adler argued that "the consistent application of intelligible principles" would rescue law from the "chaos . . . largely due to the disregard of the fundamental principle . . . that labor, capital, and business are all parts of one another, and collectively, we might almost say, are the community itself." In "Business Jurisprudence," *Harvard Law Review* 28 (1914): 135, Adler pointed out that the perplexities of regulating business derived in part from the reluctance of common law countries to recognize business law as a distinct branch of jurisprudence.

3. In *Mt. Vernon-Woodberry Cotton Duck Co. v. Alabama Interstate Power Co.*, 240 U.S. 30, 32 (1916), Holmes's unanimous opinion upheld a probate court's right to take land and determine compensation for a power project: "To gather the streams from waste and to draw from them energy, labor without brains, and so to save mankind from toil that it can be spared, is to supply what, next to intellect, is the very foundation of all our achievements and all our welfare. If that purpose is not public we should be at a loss to say what is."

4. *Brown v. Gerald*, 100 Maine 351 (1905), a unanimous decision which held that the manufacture and selling of electricity for manufacturing or mechanical purposes was not a public use for which private property could be taken against the will of the owner.

5. *Kansas City Western Railway Co. v. McAdow*, 240 U.S. 51, 55 (1916), unanimously affirmed a judgment for McAdow in an injury suit that had been appealed on the question of whether federal or state law governed the case. Holmes concluded: "The liability of the defendant does not appear to be affected." *Gast Realty Co. v. Schneider Granite Co., Id.* at 55, 59, unanimously found that a municipal ordinance governing assessments for public improvements had violated plaintiff's Fourteenth Amendment rights: "The defendant's case is not an incidental result of a rule that as a whole and on the average may be expected to work well, but an ordinance that is a farrago of irrational irregularities throughout." *Lamar v. United States, Id.* at 60, 64, unanimously rejected plaintiff's charge that his conviction for intent to defraud by impersonating a Congressman was invalid on jurisdictional as well as Constitutional grounds: "Jurisdiction is a matter of power and covers right and wrong decisions."

Washington, D.C.
January 29, 1916

Dear Frankfurter,

[Shelton] Hale it is, then. Poor Thayer's letter returned herewith.[1] I don't often get such an all round recommendation. Of course you will let him understand that I reserve the right to die or resign although at this writing I hope to do neither, the last returns from the interior being satisfactory. . . .

My thanks to you and Hill not forgetting the important rider from the madam.

Ever sincerely yours,
O. W. Holmes

1. Dean of Harvard Law School Ezra Thayer had committed suicide by drowning in the Charles River, September 16, 1915.

New York, New York
March 5, 1916

Dear Mrs. Holmes,

The Gods have willed it otherwise! I've been called home by the critical illness of my father and I don't dare hope that the crisis will be over for at least forty eight hours. So please count me out from one of the most prized pleasures I ever looked forward to or can look forward to. Yet, it all counts too deeply in my life—he does, and will you let me say, you two do—for me to be out of that Shrove Tuesday Dinner [and] all that it symbolizes. His life boxes the circle of the Great Adventure; it is one, in one's own independent venture, in joy and in loneliness of study and the silent encounter of trial.

A dinner befitting his Youth!

Gratefully,
Felix Frankfurter

New York, New York
March 6, 1916

My Justice Holmes,

The gentlest of snows is falling and I face one of those griefs that one meets somehow and is silent about.[1] That it should be in poignancy that I greet you with gratitude, that the gayer notes are just now hushed, that I should feel it unstrained to write to you—because the deepest significances are those that help sustain solitude—perhaps gives you the fullness of my affection, the lasting proof of how precious the debt of your friendship, how you help me to face life without denial of its Romance, its Mysteries, its Pains. If I shall strive tho' reason be lacking, if I shall enjoy with sceptical honesty, if I give whatever there is in me to give and leave the rest where it belongs—in all that, I shall find the spur and gratitude of loyalty to you as a dear friend, but beyond that, loyalty to all that makes my devotion incommunicable.

As one of your lads I greet you with thanksgiving.

Faithfully,
Felix Frankfurter

1. Frankfurter's father, Leopold Frankfurter, died March 6, 1916.

Washington, D.C.
March 8, 1916

Dear Frankfurter,

One cannot say much when one's friends are brought up against the great sorrows but it is some relief to the rest of us to know that we are being remembered with affectionate solicitude, as you may be sure that you are by me. If I have helped to give you courage, you have repaid it with interest and while this machine is to me, as Hamlet says, I look forward to the inspiring continuance of a friendship that has stepped in just when those of my youth have disappeared in death.[1]

Affectionately yours,
O. W. Holmes

1. I love thee best, O most
best, believe it. Adieu.
'Thine evermore, most dear lady, whilst this
machine is to him,'
Hamlet, Act II, Scene II, 122:23

Cambridge, Massachusetts
March 22, 1916

Dear Justice Holmes,

It's almost easy for me to see how death—its experience—drives people to a new acceptance of old slumbering supernatural beliefs. I can see why Charles Kingsley chose the occasion of Huxley's loss of his first-born to ask whether now Huxley does not believe in immortality and brimstone and the rest of it (Have you ever read Huxley's answer to Kingsley in Huxley's *Life and Letters*?).[1] That's an easy way out for them that can take it. For the rest of us it's a test of faith to go on without a definite haven—to go on with zest for experience in living, with readiness to make that venture of what the groping human spirit is capable of, without assurance or even hope of "reward" or return trip. Not that pins don't seem to be bowled over, not that they are not bowled—but if it were not thus, what would the test of the readiness to face life amount to, except a shallow holiday. What matters, what helps, is the community of weakness, the support of affection, whence strength comes. And so your letter coming from you matters with the depth of immediacy and of humility that all the paraphernalia of dogma and church could not have mattered, at least if one is my "kind of a hairpin."

You remember that fresh-eyed, reassuring youth Ivar Campbell? He fell at Kut-el-Amare.[2] I have a letter from his mother full of fine courage. Mesopotamia seems not so remote as it was a little while ago. Young [Alexander] Aaronsohn is with me for a few days and his tales shame some of the Arabian nights. He has to understate actualities to arouse belief. Think of him—a Palestinian, a Turkish subject and so mobilized to fight for Germany which he fears and loathes as the opponent of his spiritual longings.[3] He is thinking and when he gets to Washington, I shall send him to you. He has things to say.

To speak of less important things, I thought your opinion in the Tea Rose trade mark case was very interesting.[4] Along this line, there is lots to say that must be left unsaid. McKenna's opinions in the Trading Stamps cases pleased me much.[5] They gave me new strength in my belief in his perceptions in these constitutional questions, and it's so the fashion to sneer at him.

Always gratefully,
Felix Frankfurter

1. Leonard Huxley, *Life and Letters of T. H. Huxley* (New York: Appleton, 1900), I, 233–39. Thomas Huxley wrote, "had I lived a couple centuries earlier I could have fancied a devil scoffing at me . . . and asking me what profit it was to have stripped myself of the hopes and consolations of the mass of mankind? To which my only reply was and is—Oh devil! truth is better than much profit." Charles Kingsley (1819–75), the leader of the Christian Socialist movement in England, urged social reform through a combination of Christian doctrine and cooperative production.

2. Ivar Campbell (1889–1915), English poet and diplomat, was attached to the Embassy in Washington from 1912 to 1914. At the battle of Kut-el-Amara, the British surrendered 10,000 troops to the Turkish Army.

3. See above, October 11, 1915.

4. Justice Pitney's unanimous opinion in *Hanover Star Milling Co. v. Metcalf*, 240 U.S. 403, 425 (1916), held that a trademark protected a product only in the state or states where it was marketed. Holmes's concurring opinion qualified the point: "It is natural and very generally correct to say that trademarks acknowledge no territorial limit. But it should never be forgotten . . . that when a trademark started in one state is recognized in another it is by the authority of a new sovereignty that gives its sanction to the right."

5. In *Rast v. Van Deman and Lewis*, 240 U.S. 342 (1916), and two companion cases, *Tanner*

v. Little, *Id.* at 369, and *Pitney v. State of Washington*, *Id.* at 387, McKenna unanimously upheld the right of states to regulate and tax merchants who used profit sharing coupons and trading stamps.

Washington, D.C.
March 23, 1916

Dear Frankfurter,

Your letter moves me as well as requires my thanks . . . Of course your friend will be welcome here when he comes but kindly write his name so that I can read it. I have to say to many here that it is not enough to learn to write but is well also to learn to read when they grumble at my ms., but you have me up a stump on the name this time. I have had one or two calls from Lippmann, the last yesterday p.m., that gave me great pleasure and while I blushed to speak of what he said of me, I could tell him with sincerity how thrilled I was by his discourse on Amy Lowell and that I was *ebahi* as a little boy when he wrote politics—so ignorant am I—so knowing he.[1]

Also, I agree with you in being much pleased with McKenna's cases that you mentioned. I am hoping to read a book tomorrow as we are adjourned and I have tucked in pretty much all my ends just before beginning fun.

I trust that my remarks in the Tea Rose case received your assent. I don't know who if any disagreed with them. Hughes, I understood, agreed but thought the diversities then expounded likely to have but little importance in view of the interstate business. I dare say he was quite right but I felt a logical necessity to expound what seemed to me the accuracies of the case on the assumption made by the court that we were dealing with state affairs. The vague talk that trade marks know no state lines may so easily lead one whose life is "one altar smoke, so pure" (if my quotation is right) into damnation by reason of a false dogma held in the fastness of his brain. I must go forth to get a breath of air before dinner or I should write more.

Ever sincerely yours,
O. W. Holmes

1. In *New Republic* 7 (1916): 178, Walter Lippmann (1889–1974) critically reviewed Amy Lowell's (1874–1925) selections in *Some Imagist Poets: An Anthology* (Boston: Houghton, Mifflin, 1915): "I'm afraid that Miss Lowell calls a preoccupation with incidentals a brave attempt to be external and universal."

Cambridge, Massachusetts
March 28[?], 1916

Dear Justice Holmes,

And now Laski joins in delight over your trade mark opinion![1] I have said nothing all this time about Brandeis and the currents he has set going here because there is too much to be said for a letter. But it's connected with another matter—Arthur Hill's coming to join us. He is very eager to and Pound wants him but there is much opposition in Boston legal quarters. They didn't like his coming out for Brandeis and they still are bothered by his espousal of T. R. (I tell him that his "radicalism" is amusing and his herosism is "unearned"). They put it on professional grounds—say he lacks stability and isn't a "serious lawyer." Moorfield Storey is particularly vigorous.[2] I was wondering if you had any definite impression or beliefs as to his equipment as a lawyer? If yes, a note to Pound would help much. I don't believe Hill will be a productive scholarship—nor does he—but he has [a] stimulating, energetic mind that would rouse the student body and would be effective if he gave himself to the work completely. I'm sure he will, because his political ambitions have faded and this would give him a sense he is doing something. It's rather amusing that Hill should feel the local intensities and limitations for he rather likes to defend them.

I have such angelic intentions when I start to write—it's my pen and not my purpose that is crooked. But don't ever bother to decipher me if I don't succeed in plain writing. The friend I was speaking of is young Aaronsohn—he of Palestine.

Isn't this the year for the polonia?[3]

My devoted greetings.

Faithfully,
Felix Frankfurter

1. The following note from Laski to Frankfurter was enclosed: "That Holmes opinion is fascinating. May I keep it? It might easily result in working out zones of local productivity based on intra-state competition and the big thing is the possibility it opens up for the future. It also purifies commercial life. Don't you think that the whole theory of states-rights wants reworking in terms of the new nationalism?"

2. Moorfield Storey (1845–1929), Harvard Overseer and once secretary to Senator Charles Sumner, was President of the American Bar Association in 1916. In this capacity he organized a contingent of seven former A.B.A. Presidents to oppose Woodrow Wilson's nomination of Louis D. Brandeis as Associate Justice of the Supreme Court.

3. In the Holmeses' backyard (1720 I Street, Washington, D.C.) there was a *Paulownia tomentosa*, a flowering Chinese tree named after Anna Paulovna, daughter of Czar Paul I (1754–1801).

Washington, D.C.
April 13, 1916

Dear Frankfurter,

The *Law Review* has come, and I can't tell you how touched and charmed I am.[1] Very few things in my life have given me so much pleasure. I well know that I owe it to your constant kindness that I receive such a crowning reward, and I thank you from my heart.

Ever sincerely yours,
O. W. Holmes

1. The April 1916 issue of the *Harvard Law Review* (volume 29) was dedicated to Holmes on his seventy-fifth birthday. Frankfurter's contribution, "The Constitutional Opinions of Justice Holmes," concluded: "In their impact and sweep and fertile freshness, the opinions have been a superbly harmonious vehicle for the views they embody. It all seems so easy,—brilliant birds pulled from the magician's sleeve. It is the delusive ease of great effort and great art."

Washington, D.C.
April 29, 1916

Dear Frankfurter,

You show your usual kindness in sending me Judge Cardozo's letter.[1] I am vainer than you are and shall keep it, but if you repent and want it back, let me know. I have two little cases for tomorrow that clean me up to date and we sit only one week more.[2] I should think you would die if you kept on doing what you say you do as to the state decisions. They usually follow a lead like a flock of sheep and it is only here and there, so far as I know, that one feels a vital wiggle. But I guess you get over the ground faster than I could.

I have a theory of Aesthetics by Bendetto Croce, transl. by D. Ainslee, who thinks him one of the leaders of all time, but as yet I have read only a few pages a week.[3] Also, Miss Noyes's *Mark* which I shall read in time but not yet.[4] I notice that F.H., in *The New Republic* just come, speaks of T. Veblen as a great social analyst. I haven't read the notice (of a new book by E. L. Masters) and from the sentence wasn't sure whether it was chaff or earnest and, I haven't the book of Veblen to which he refers.[5] The book on *The Leisure Class* I did read over and thought it took 300 pages of material for about 30 and overlooked a good deal although showing talent. Ought I to read more? Sometime back I did read E. Kelly's *20th Cent. Socialism*.[6] When a man talks about the sums withdrawn by capital as one of his starting points, I wait for better days until he shall have begun to think.

Goodbye, dear lad, I must go and play solitaire after a tiring week ending, however, after conference with a heavenly drive with my wife to see the double flowering cherry trees by the basin that reflects the monument, where men fish and I want to and then to go under the railroad and down stream by the riverside and round the point and back opposite the military college by about three miles more of the trees in bloom. Spring has broke loose, today the birds sang and I was the happier for just having read your letter.

Yours ever,
O. W. Holmes

Please express to Pound my high appreciation of the honor he did me by contributing to the April *Harvard Law Review.*[7]

1. Benjamin N. Cardozo (1870–1938) of the Supreme Court of New York was Holmes's successor on the U.S. Supreme Court in 1932. Cardozo's letter said of Holmes, "The subject before one seems obscure and presto! one strikes an opinion of his, and the dark places are illumined. He is in a class all by himself." See Cardozo to Frankfurter, April 14, 1916, Box 38, folder 27, Holmes Papers.

2. *De La Rama v. De La Rama*, 241 U.S. 154, 158 (1916), a unanimous opinion dismissing a writ of error in a divorce proceeding which the Court heard originally, 201 U.S. 303 (1906), on appeal from the Supreme Court of the Philippines under the Territorial Practices Act (1874). Holmes found no reason to disturb "the local practices sanctioned in this case by the local courts" and also determined that appeal rather than writ of error remained the proper mode for requesting review. *Johnson v. Root Manufacturing Co.*, *Id.* at 160, unanimously upheld the claim of Johnson, trustee for a bankrupt construction company, that an agreement settling liens against work done for a railroad should equitably cover all enforceable liens and not give preference to any particular claim.

3. Benedetto Croce, *Aesthetic as Science of Expression and General Linguistic*, Douglas Ainslee, trans. (London: Macmillan, 1909).

4. Frances Noyes [Hart], *Mark* (New York: E. J. Clode, 1913). Holmes wrote the phrase "in time" in Greek.

5. Francis Hackett (1883–1962) was book review editor of *The New Republic.* His review of Edgar Lee Masters, *Songs and Satire* (New York: Macmillan, 1916), linked the author's poetry with Thorstein Veblen's *Theory of Business Enterprise* (New York: Scribner's, 1904) in responding to the public demand for "iconoclastic and materialistic" values. Hackett characterized Masters as "a man of forty or so, sceptical, unsentimental, unloyal, deharmonized." *New Republic* 6 (1916): 354.

6. Edmond Kelly, *Twentieth Century Socialism; What it is not; What it is; How it may come* (New York: Longmans, Green, 1910).

7. Roscoe Pound, "Equitable Relief against Defamation and Injuries to Personality," *Harvard Law Review* 29 (1916): 640.

Beverly Farms, Massachusetts
July 16, 1916

Dear Frankfurter,

This is not to tell you what pleasure your visit gave me, which you know, but to abuse your books that you have recommended and sent. Beard, *Econ. Interp. Const.* seems to have taken a lead from Patten, *Development of English Thought*—a much cleverer and more amusing book, that searches the biographies of the leaders from Hobbes to Darwin to find the *apercu* by which they broke in, system-making coming later and being less significant.[1] Beard's thesis was that holders of personalty or investment capital shaped the Constitution and dominated the ratification process, shutting out agrarian-debtor or realty interests. He finds it in some economic change—the true source as he thinks of new philosophy. Beyond the anti-thesis personalty vs. realty, I don't see much profit in Beard's minutiae. One doesn't need research to know that Washington, Hamilton et al. had the prepossessions of the comfortable classes. The disclaimed yet ever-present innuendo that they all were influenced by having some stock that would appreciate, seems to me rather unworthy trifling except that B. probably believes that economic are the only real motives wherein I think him wrong.

I haven't quite finished Sorel.[2] I suppose the war has somewhat postponed the immediacy of his reflections, but I don't get his postulates which he doesn't state. I should think he believed in the other myth—of the sums withdrawn by capital (into the clouds) and did not bear in mind what I think an obvious truth, that capital is the only field of struggle between different groups of producers. He does give a hint of different notion when he speaks of *free* labor but I can give that no meaning except less highly organized and therefore less productive labor which I hardly can reconcile with his suggestion that labor will take over the capitalist regime when it is at the height of success, but if so, there must be the same adjustments to the foreseen wants of six months or more ahead, i.e., the same withdrawals of capital as now. In short, I never yet could make out from any socialist book any rational statement of any *economic* grievance, and I think an honest leader would say to the working man, you have got all there is now and all your fights are among yourselves. Of course, it is a different matter if they say, whether we pay or not, we don't like and don't believe in upper and middle class manners and ways of thinking and want to do away with them. I should think they were wrong for reasons easy to state but I should understand it. But as I don't believe there is any wholesale economic grievance, I do not anticipate any fundamental *bouleversement* in my short time. Laski's articles show his brilliancy and are in the fashion of the day. I think myself that personality is a figure of speech, not a fact as it is of a physical organism and that one can reason from it only with caution but that needs talk which we will have next time.[3]

Ever yours,
O.W.H.

1. Charles A. Beard, *An Economic Interpretation of the Constitution of the United States* (New York: Macmillan, 1913); Simon N. Patten, *The Development of English Thought* (New York: Macmillan, 1899).

2. Georges Sorel, *Reflections on Violence* (New York: B. W. Huebsch, 1912), espoused syndicalism, a general uprising of workers resulting in government by trade unions or collectives.

3. Laski's early writing was influenced by the English historian John Neville Figgis (1866–1919), whose *Churches in the Modern State* (London: Longmans, Green, 1913) held that each group in society had a personality of its own and an inherent liberty of growth. Holmes believed that sovereign power made no concessions and, hence, that the personality of institutions and groups was superfluous. See Harold J. Laski, "The Apotheosis of the State," *New Republic* 7 (1916): 302, and Howe, ed., *Holmes-Pollock Letters*, 2:22, 25–26.

Beverly Farms, Massachusetts
August 6, 1916

Dear Frankfurter,

Do you know any good book discussing the adjustment of industrial disputes, compulsory arbitration, etc.—those dealing with concrete legislation preferred? I pass on to you a question sent to me by my secretary, Charley Poe of Seattle, which I can't answer.[1]

I believe I made to you my criticism on the chain-industry book.[2] The writer says you have got the goods and leave the price to be lumped in the general charges for the year. I can't tell whether a law is good till I have an itemized bill of the cost. I made some remarks to Laski about Figgis and his independent groups but, by his answer, infer that he did not appreciate the different point of view from which I wrote. I don't doubt the value of the groups or their independent origin, though I regard their personality as a figure of speech. I was thinking of their theoretical relation to the sovereign from a (sound) legal point of view—not of what it was desirable for the sovereign to do—but he inferred that at bottom I doubted whether life was worth living and said, wait till you see my wife. I hardly should accept the inference, and doubt if anyone could make life richer than it has been made for me, so far as it does not depend upon oneself. But I liked to hear the lad say it because it made me believe that he too had struck it rich. I hope we shall see you both down here again before the end of the summer.

I have been interrupted in my writing by a very pleasant call from Bundy and his wife, both seeming in good condition.[3] For the last few days, I have been busy paying bills but I am creeping through the *Oedipus Tyrannus* with the help of a pony and a dictionary and have been reading Verlaine.[4] Some amusing reflections I reserve till we meet as I must seal this up. I suppose you are sweating in N.Y. but as I don't know, shall send this to Cambridge, please forward.

Yours ever,
O. W. Holmes

1. Charles K. Poe (1878–1960), a descendant of Edgar Allen Poe, served as counsel for Standard Oil in Oklahoma territory before establishing his Seattle practice.
2. R. H. Tawney, *The Establishment of Minimum Rates in the Chain-Making Industry under the Trade Boards Act of 1909* (London: G. Bell, 1914).
3. Harvey H. Bundy (1888–1963) and Katherine Lawrence Bundy (1890–1983). Bundy was Holmes's Secretary (1914–15) and later served as Assistant Secretary of State (1931–33) and as special assistant to Secretary of War Henry L. Stimson during World War II.
4. French poet Paul Verlaine (1844–96).

Beverly Farms, Massachusetts
August 10, 1916

Dear Frankfurter,

It is most kind of you to give me such quick response.[1] I mail the documents to Poe at once by this mail. I can't help thinking that you, like the rest of us, believe what you want to, and are inclined to be content with the visible result. It must be paid for and paid for by the workmen. I wish if *le bon Dieu* agrees with me, He would write me letters of fire on the sky!

The Crowd has all there is
The Crowd pays for everything.

But you know all my old saws. I should write more, but I must go forth and I will post this as I go. You don't give me a N.Y. address therefore, I send as before.

Yours always,
O. W. Holmes

1. The letter referred to is missing.

Beverly Farms, Massachusetts
August 14, 1916

You still didn't give your address so I shall try a new one.

Dear Frankfurter,

The articles you sent were fully appreciated by us and were handed on to Tom Barbour, with intent to spread them further on their return.[1] At Laski's recommendation, I got Zangwill's *War for the World* and have begun it, to find that it stirs my emotions at once.[2] It seems as if an exquisite moral susceptibility were the gift of many Jews. The religious temperament moves me deeply and yet does not get the last word. I suppose therefore that it naturally would hate my type, and so explain to myself the feeling of a man whom I suppose to regard me more or less in that way. The interests of feeling and explanation are at opposite poles.

Today I am regretting not having read the papers and therefore, not knowing the issue upon which the railroad strike is threatened.[3] If it comes off, I should expect to believe that there was folly all round and wickedness somewhere—of course, recognizing that wickedness is a word by which I express my dislike for the inevitable—inevitable, if and after it happens. How I wish that you were here to expound to me. Of course, I agreed with you in what you wrote the other day about the desirability of the ends arrived at by minimum wage laws but my doubt is that until an intelligent effort is made to trace the incidence of the cost and to find out some ground more substantial than faith (which means believing what you want to) for thinking that they don't cost more than they come to, we hardly are in a position to legislate.

I also have got Wallas, *The Great Society*, one of the books you mentioned.[4] I don't know what to do in the way of getting a new subscriber for *The New Republic*. I hope the appeal is not too ominous. I can't think of anyone to whom to apply but perhaps I may—the notice was received this morning. Till our next.

Yours ever,
O. W. Holmes

1. The articles referred to are missing. Thomas Barbour (1884–1946), Holmes's friend and Beverly Farms neighbor, had a distinguished career as a comparative zoologist at Harvard.

2. Israel Zangwill, *War of the Worlds* (London: Heinemann, 1916).

3. The conflict centered upon the railroad brotherhoods' demand for an eight-hour day. Woodrow Wilson averted a strike by pressuring Congress to pass the Adamson Act (September 3, 1916), granting the eight-hour day to all railroad workers involved in interstate traffic. See Arthur Link, ed., *The Papers of Woodrow Wilson*, vol. 38 (Princeton: Princeton University Press, 1982), 101, 124–25.

4. Graham Wallas, *The Great Society* (New York: Macmillan, 1914).

Beverly Farms, Massachusetts
September 5, 1916

Dear Frankfurter,

Your last good letter deserved an immediate answer.[1] Something prevented and then I heard you were away in the country where perhaps you still are. So, this is only a friendly tweak. Laski proposed himself for a second visit and I was delighted with him more than ever, not least with the affection he showed for you. He seems to me less tinctured with the kind of belief that some of our friends seem more or less to entertain, that universal bliss can be wrought by a Presto-Change. The only thing that I will say about your remarks is that it hardly is safe to regard the available margin of increased effort by speeding up, new invention, increased acreage, etc., as an infinite resource to be drawn upon at will, like the atmosphere or the sea. I doubt if we may not discover that even the last two have their limits. But, thank Heaven, for the last day or two I have succeeded in dropping improvement either of society or my own mind and have amused myself with literature. Last night I read some of Mrs. Repplier's essays in *Countercurrents*, which, if I remember rightly, was somewhat unfavorably reviewed in *The New Republic*, but which pleased me a good deal—because she thinks *hardly*, as against the sentimental way which is more in vogue.[2] Of course, I should disagree with her in various details, but I like to see someone insist on the fact that the march of life means a rub somewhere. As they used to say about saddles in the army, one strained the man another galled the horse. I have used the image to you before.

We are beginning to think of the end of vacation. I suppose that we shall leave about the last of the month. If I can't see you here, I hope I shall in Washington and that I shall hear from you from time to time. Dear me, with what frightful swiftness time runs for the old.

Affectionately yours,
O. W. Holmes

1. The letter referred to is missing.
2. Agnes Repplier (1855–1950), Philadelphia essayist whose *Counter-currents* (Boston: Houghton, Mifflin, 1916) disdained settlement workers and pacifists.

Beverly Farms, Massachusetts
September 19, 1916

Dear Frankfurter,

Your letter of the 16th (posted yesterday) comes this morning.[1] You will be welcome any day. Telephone to me tomorrow (today you are arriving and

I suppose it would be too early to reach you). I can't wait to say a word more about Miss Repplier. I forgot that I spoke about her to you. Of course, you touch the point where she seems narrow and I don't sympathize with her and what I said was not that she thought hard, but that she thought *hardly*: i.e., with a sense of the bills to be paid and with a repudiation of the notion that universal bliss could be had by elegant conversation without being ready to fight for it. To be continued in our next.

Yours ever,
O. W. Holmes

1. The letter referred to is missing.

Washington, D.C.
November 2, 1916

Dear Frankfurter,

You have the most generous disposition to the qualities of your fellow men, it seems to me, that I know. But I was pleased myself, I remember, when on seeing that many later cases referred to Harrington and reading that, I discovered that it was *Leviathan redivivus*.[1] *Apropos* of which, I must tell you of my experience with the latter work. At the beginning of July '61, I thought that I would read it. I was walking down Beacon Street from the Athenaeum with it under my arm when, as I passed the State House, someone told me that the Governor had commissioned me in the 20th Mass. I returned the book and went up to Pittsfield recruiting, and thereafter into camp and to the war. In [1872] I took it out again. Forthwith, my wife, as now is, accepted me, and that day I read no more. Some years later, perhaps knowing how she had interfered with my spiritual improvement, she gave me the original edition, and then at last I read it with the present appreciation and, as it turned out, with future advantage.

I am hard at work. Yesterday p.m., the C.J. [Edward D. White] turned over to me a stinker in which counsel have put acres of spongy detail in their brief where it seems to me that a few brief facts to be picked from the mass are all that are material.[2] We have had, earlier, some I.C.C. cases.[3] Let me add that I revere the stomach that can digest those problems and understand their language (this means you, not the I.C.C.). As the verse says:

I cannot sing the old song
I do not know the words.

Affectionately yours,
O. W. Holmes

1. James Harrington, *The Common-wealth of Oceana* (1656); Thomas Hobbes, *Leviathan* (1651).

2. Probably *O'Neil v. Northern Colorado Irrigation Co.*, 242 U.S. 20, 26 (1916), a unanimous opinion in which Holmes held that a state law enabling water districts to assign priorities among claimants did not violate the plaintiff's Fourteenth Amendment rights: "The construction of a statute does not take a party's property without due process of law simply because it takes him by surprise and when it is too late for him to act on the construction and save his rights."

3. In *Louisville and Nashville R.R. Co. v. U.S.*, 242 U.S. 60, 74 (1916), Holmes's majority opinion rejected an Interstate Commerce Commission finding of third-party discrimination in the switching practices of two railroads within their jointly owned terminal: "It is objected that upon this view a way is opened to get beyond the reach of the statute and the Commission. But the very meaning of a line in the law is that right and wrong touch each other and that anyone may get as close to the line as he can if he keeps on the right side." Justice Pitney, with Justices Brandeis, John H. Clarke (1857–1945), and Day concurring, dissented. Also, see below, December 6, 1916.

Washington, D.C.
November 5, 1916

Dear Frankfurter,

We will await the result. Your paper is forcible and candid.[1] I will not attempt to state what I consider fundamental facts in the controversy, but will unite with you in the prayer, May the Best Man Win. I am under high pressure as usual and have just discovered, after nearly writing an old case turned over to me, that there does not remain a quorum of those who heard it so that I suppose it must be reargued or resubmitted and, for the present, my last week's labor goes for nothing. I am not particularly sorry. I understand that you do not want your article back.

Yours as ever,
O. W. Holmes

I had sent you a letter before this arrived.

1. Frankfurter's "Wilson and Roosevelt," *New Republic* 9 (1916): 3, endorsed Woodrow Wilson because Wilson's first term reform program had enacted the regulation of corporations advocated by Theodore Roosevelt's New Nationalist platform of 1912. Holmes intensely disliked Wilson and supported Republican candidate Charles Evans Hughes, who had resigned from the Supreme Court to accept the nomination. See Howe, ed., *Holmes-Pollock Letters*, 1:237, 240; Howe, ed., *Holmes-Laski Letters*, 33.

Cambridge, Massachusetts
November 16, 1916

Dear Justice Holmes,

The other night, at Mrs. Valentine's request, I read to her from the Memorial Day address and from "The Soldier's Faith."[1] It comforted her much, gave her the strength of understanding and shared faith. "The man who wrote that" she said, "knew Robert before their hands met." I'm sure that's so. No one I know lived with completer courage, with gayer sincerity and fine honesty. And he lived thus to the very last. I happened to have been with him (on my way back from our Sunday night together) when the cruel blow came, unannounced and unrecognized. He was the master of the situation throughout, all was done that could have been done—fortunately, a particularly valuable, friendly doctor was near at hand—and he was gay and gallant and concerned about others, about my missing my train to Boston, tho' much in pain, till he gently fell asleep, as he lived and as he would have wished—strength and good humor and serenity. He compels me to write and to try to live his going thus calmly. You will know when I say that the closest friend of my own years is gone. And what a fine nobility Mrs. Valentine is showing. They both felt strongly against the lachrymose way of meeting death and she lives that faith unfalteringly. He would have been proud of her radiance on his last trip—funeral they called it—as she wore a lovely purple dress he so much liked, and she gave me the privilege of riding out with her because, as she said, she wanted to be with the friends he lived with and worked with and not the family whom he liked well enough, but remotely. Altogether, courage and nobility, old as man, is new with each fresh, unique experience; and how Valentine's life—its wonderful pluck and struggle and joy—refutes those who would alter the wisdom of all ages that struggle *is* the law of life—its law and its salt.

Valentine's going has blurred out most of all else these last two weeks, at least in the doing. But you know I have not been neglectful, and least of all ungrateful. When I came, I found that photograph which has removed black, or green, envy from my heart. It now commands my room not the less so that its nearest neighbor is a picture of the most striking girl I know.[2] No, the significance is more artistic than romantic for, "she's another's lawful wedded wife." The transaction is wholly innocent. Truly, I cherish that photograph from you. As for your telegram—what can I say that isn't beyond saying? It came on a sad day for me—it came with a renewed sense of my affectionate indebtedness to you. Know this—what life may have for me of good in days to come, you are in it very deeply.

Gratefully,
F.F.

1. Robert G. Valentine, owner of the House of Truth and former U.S. Commissioner of Indian Affairs, died of a heart attack, November 14, 1916. His widow was Sophia French Valentine. Holmes's Memorial Day address (1884) and "The Soldier's Faith" (1895) are reprinted in Lerner, ed., *Mind and Faith of Holmes*, 9–16, 18–25, and Howe, ed., *Occasional Speeches*, 4–16, 73–83.

2. Probably, a photograph of Alice Duer Miller (1874–1942), poet and suffragist, who helped Frankfurter prepare Woodrow Wilson's appeal for an eight-hour day for laboring men and women. See Phillips, ed., *Frankfurter Reminisces*, 142–44.

Washington, D.C.
December 6, 1916

Dear Frankfurter,

If there weren't a lot of other reasons for affection, your constant thoughtful kindness would be enough. I need not say that I value Hand's good opinion very highly, as all I know of him and his work lead me to believe him to be one who really counts.[1] I am hard at work. I have tried to tinker an opinion so as to get a majority, and have written a little one for this week but there is a lot of stuff on hand that I must be ready to recite about on Saturday.[2] Give my love to Laski and tell him I haven't had a chance to write.

Yours ever,
O.W.H.

Pollock tells me to look at Jenks in the Nov. [*Harvard Law Review*].[3] He says mighty clever but I haven't rec'd the Rev., so haven't seen it yet.

1. Judge Learned Hand (1872–1961), Federal District Court of Southern New York, was a leading jurist and close friend of Frankfurter. An attached note from Hand to Frankfurter (December 8, 1916) reads: "Of course, if you send him whatever I write about him, it becomes very demoralizing for all three of us; especially as we shall all like it. I am surprised about suspended sentences. Can't really understand it if O.W. H. concurred." The case referred to was *Ex parte United States*, 242 U.S. 27 (1916), a U.S. Justice Department petition for a writ of mandamus against a Federal District Judge's decision not to imprison a "duly sentenced" individual. Chief Justice White wrote the unanimous opinion that temporarily stayed the writ, but held that a federal court had no inherent power, after imposing a criminal sentence, to suspend it during good behavior; to exercise this authority, the Court held, required an act of Congress establishing a probation system. Congress subsequently provided the authorization. See 18 U.S.C. 3651 (1948).

2. Holmes's next opinions, all unanimous, were announced on December 18. *Louisville and Nashville R.R. Co. v. Ohio Valley Tie Co.*, 242 U.S. 288 (1916), held that Interstate Commerce Commission hearings on damages were conclusive, i.e., further damages could not be sought through independent proceedings in court. *Illinois Central Railroad Company v. Peery*, *Id.* at 292, denied a personal injury suit under the Federal Employers' Liability Act (1908) since the accident occurred when the train was not employed in interstate commerce. *Baltimore and Ohio Railroad Co. v. Wilson*, *Id.* at 295, 298, upheld a personal injury suit under the same act against the company's claim that employee negligence should be considered since the litigation found

no violation of the Hours of Service Act (1908), which plaintiff had also invoked: "In this case there was evidence that whether technically on duty or not the plaintiff had been greatly overtaxed before the final strain of more than sixteen hours and that as a physical fact it was far from impossible that the fatigue should have been a cause proximately contributing to all that happened."

3. Edward Jenks, "English Civil law," *Harvard Law Review* 30 (1916): 1, argued that despite the social tensions of wartime traditional individual liberties were restricted infrequently compared with other western democracies.

Washington, D.C.
December 19, 1916

Dear Frankfurter,

Your letter gives the most pleasing prospects.[1] Everything sounds all right. I hope you spoke with Hill before writing because I shouldn't want to hurt his feelings. If you didn't, won't you do so (and not mention writing to me), and then let me know that it's all right. Of course Bunn must be told that I now, as always since I was 72, reserve the right to retire but, unless something unforeseen happens, I have no intention of doing so since I am as happy as ever in my work and want to do as much as the fates permit.[2] I shall be particularly glad to have a man who is sharp on the law, because once in a while I want a man who is all there right off. It is odd that yesterday, when your letter came, I had just rec'd one from Laski, mentioning the remark of a law student (I suppose): "They don't make much of Holmes in Minnesota."[3] I am so pressed (as usual) that I can't do more than say what is necessary but I am greatly pleased at the prospect and, if Hill agrees, shall be glad to have you speak to Bunn in terms of agreement.

Billy Sunday, acc. all newspapers, sometimes says pretty amusing things, amongst his horrors e.g., when you pray, pray, don't say, see you later, God.[4]

I don't quite get your view as to the tank cars—did you think the decision wrong?[5] I was inclined to agree to it. I delight to hear from you and apologize for the necessary poverty of my answer.

Affectionately yours,
O. W. Holmes

1. The letter referred to is missing.

2. Charles Bunn (1893–1964), later Professor of Law at Wisconsin, entered the U.S. Army and thus never served as Holmes's secretary. Vaughn Miller (1892–1964), a Tennessee lawyer, filled the post in 1917–18.

3. Howe, ed., *Holmes-Laski Letters*, 43–44.

4. William A. Sunday (1863–1935), popular Presbyterian evangelist and prohibitionist.

5. In *United States v. Pennsylvania R.R. Co.*, 242 U.S. 208 (1916), Justice McKenna, in a unanimous opinion, held that the Interstate Commerce Commission Act (1887) and its subsequent amendments did not include the power to compel carriers to provide oil tank cars.

Cambridge, Massachusetts
December 21, 1916

Dear Justice Holmes,

Your ample time for concern, despite your pressure, about Hill's feelings made me feel my own inconsiderateness in not telling you that I had conferred with him about Bunn and he enthusiastically concurred so that's settled at least in a world where some issues are still open.

I didn't quarrel with the Oil Tank decision.[1] It only led me to think of the large waste of trying to squeeze out of the words of a statute what legislatures did not put into them. And so, I think, it's worthwhile to give some thought towards the systematic framing of statutes and the policies back of them. The opinion in the Oil Tank Case, incidentally, again gives me much pleasure in McKenna. I can't make converts for my discovery, except those who'll give me a chance to show 'em—it's curious this tenacity of the bar's opinion that he is a weak sister! What do I care if his opinions on mining law are weak (I don't know) or his notions of contract not a la Williston.[2] He *does* seize the marrow of the big issues before the Court, and he delights eg., "words were multiplied, but was meaning changed" or, "ambushed in obscurity" or, "A friend of the Court appears in the form of a Salt Company."

After all, Billy Sunday may tickle but does not make votes. Boston may still float in rum—just at present in slush.

It's been a year where the zest of life met challenge. Perhaps I'm entitled to say—surely, more than a year ago—that you've got to pay for things, above all for the eager faith to go on. If my appetites for all the everlasting mystery we call life is as eager as ever, and perhaps more sharpened in its discrimination, if there is glory in the fight, I owe much to him whose own life is the most convincing inspiration for the glory of the struggle. From a grateful heart the affectionate wishes to Mrs. Holmes and yourself.

Felix

1. See above, December 19, 1916.
2. Samuel Williston (1861–1963), leading authority on the law of contracts, taught at Harvard Law School from 1890 to 1938.

Washington, D.C.
December 25, 1916

Dear Frankfurter,

Your letter has come and the book of moving poems and I thank you as I so often had occasion to, since the happy day when John Gray sent me a letter about you.[1] I have written to Bunn in answer to one from him so that matter is at rest. As to the eminent person you mention, as you know, I rather agree than disagree with you. He reminds me of a fragment of quartz with two or three facets crystallized and the rest amorphous. How many answer the same analogy! Except for the momentary distractions of Christmas, I am drawing a breath after weeks of mad worry—Goethe be damned. Haste often is necessary if a man is a judge and not a privy counsellor in a principality a foot square. My cases are disposed of except one just assigned to me where Brandeis and I differ. One of those that I got through on Saturday I wrote to dismiss and gathered that the majority preferred to affirm.[2] So I told them that as I understood they agreed to my reasoning, I would change the tail and when some sharp chap noted the incongruity, he would think it an oversight of the Court. This isn't as bad as the Pipe Line Cases—for the reasoning is allowed to stand, I just cutting out a few phrases that too plainly indicated the conclusion.[3] If I were talking instead of writing, I should open some other themes. As it is, and as, in spite of the prospective calm, the moment is troubled, I bid you an affectionate *au revoir*. With every good wish.

Yours ever,
O. W. Holmes

1. W. H. Davies, *Collected Poems* (New York: Knopf, 1916). Davies (1871–1940), a Welsh lyric poet, wrote of his experiences as a tramp and traveller.

2. Probably, *Minneapolis and St. Louis R.R. Co. v. Winters*, 242 U.S. 353, 356 (1917), a unanimous opinion rejecting a personal-injury suit, based upon the Federal Employers Liability Act, because the accident occurred while plaintiff was repairing an engine not engaged in interstate commerce: "An engine as such is not presumably devoted to any kind of traffic and it does not appear that this engine was destined especially to anything more definite than such business as it might be needed for."

3. In *The Pipe Lines Cases*, 234 U.S. 548 (1914) Holmes's majority opinion, reversing the decrees of the U.S. Commerce Court, held that the Hepburn amendment to the Interstate Commerce Act regulated pipeline carriers and thus applied to the Standard Oil Company. Justice McKenna dissented.

Cambridge, Massachusetts
January 12, 1917

Dear Justice Holmes,

The only justification I have for sending you these feeble words of mine about Valentine is a strong desire to send it.[1] One always dreads such things as memorial meetings, but somehow this one came off well. It wasn't funereal, it wasn't sentimentally insincere. Valentine's ruling perspective and sturdy feeling seemed to control all who spoke of him. One utterance was very profoundly eloquent. It would be hard to find two more antithetic antecedents than those of the Puritan aristocrat, Valentine, and the exiled Russian Jewish labor leader Polakoff.[2] They met when Valentine went to New York last winter to be the adviser in the Dress and Waist Industry. Polakoff was the union leader, distrustful of all "social workers." Well, Valentine completely dispelled the accumulated suspicion. As Polakoff narrated their first contact, in his broken, labial English, how class suspicion turned into understanding of Valentine's disinterestedness, his search for truth free from all bias, the audience in Faneuil Hall was moved as only the eloquence of deep sincerity and feeling can move and the world seemed less crammed, strife was subordinated. It was very fine.

I'm all eagerness to read your dissent in the Webb-Kenyon Law Case. I suppose the majority reconciles all the irreconcilables from the Original Package Cases down—the kind of thing the C.J. [Edward D. White] has such talent for doing.[3] And while I'm about law, there is a recent libel case that may amuse you. Defendant, an undertaker, distributed what purported to be his rival's cards to families afflicted with serious illness, thus: "Bear in mind our Undertaking Department. H. L. Hughes." Hughes sued, and his complaint was sustained.[4] The case reminded me of your opinion in *Peck v. Tribune Co.*[5]

Laski is doing wonders as a teacher. He took over a theologic course from a sick professor. The average attendance during the year has been 12. At Laski's second lecture there were 26 righteous listeners. He has made a deep impression here on students as well as scholars. To me he is sheer joy.

Still reverting to law—may the Lord forgive me my sins!—you might care to glance at a note in the January *Harvard Law Review*, 270 on "Municipal Liability for Tort", *apropos* our talk some time ago.[6] What a mess these cases on municipal corporation and partnership are and the partnership mess I'm not even interested in to clear up. These lads here are a constant spur. They are a good, tough lot and, when they begin to find out that you want the give-and-take of independence and not disciples, they give you fight.

You seem to me to be driven with work. But then, that's the answer to all these shallow croakers for euthanasia. Those aren't the terms of the game. How we envy you, tho', the results of your work.

Devotedly,
F.F.

1. Frankfurter enclosed a copy of his memorial remarks.

2. Sol Polakoff of the International Ladies' Garment Workers Union.

3. In *Clark Distilling Co. v. Western Maryland Railroad Co.*, 242 U.S. 311, 331 (1917), the Court, in an opinion written by Chief Justice White, upheld the Webb-Kenyon Act of 1913,

which provided federal support for state liquor control laws by exempting liquor from the immunities of interstate commerce, thereby delegating authority to those states that forbade the manufacture, sale, or possession of intoxicating liquors. White concluded that the delegation was legitimate because Congress "had considered the nature and character of our dual system of government, state and national, and instead of absolutely prohibiting, had so conformed its regulation as to produce cooperation between local and national forces of government to the end of preserving the rights of all." *Clark Distilling* was complicated by the fact that West Virginia, the state in question, recognized the right of individuals to possess liquor for personal use. Holmes and Willis Van Devanter dissented without opinion. Also, see below, January 13, 1917.

4. *Hughes v. Samuel Brothers*, 159 N.W. 589 (1916).

5. *Peck v. Tribune Co.*, 214 U.S. 185, 189 (1909), a unanimous decision upholding plaintiff's suit against a newspaper for publishing her picture in a whiskey advertisement over an endorsement by Mrs. A. Schuman, nurse. Holmes wrote: "The reason is plain. A libel is harmful on its face. If a man sees fit to publish manifestly hurtful statements concerning an individual, without other justification than exists for an advertisement or piece of news, the usual principles of tort will make him liable, if the statements are false or are true only of some one else."

6. Felix Frankfurter, "Municipal Liability for Torts," *Harvard Law Review* 30 (1917): 270.

Washington, D.C.
January 13, 1917

Dear Frankfurter,

What you say of Valentine is beautiful and moving. Like each new thing that you have done since I have known you, it brings you a little closer into my mind and heart. Even your more optimistic outlook and prophecy for human destinies than I can venture upon makes you dearer to me. I think such a speech as that makes the world better. Following your suggestion, I have just read your note on Municipal Liability for Tort.[1] I wish I had seen it a little earlier. It certainly is suggestive. Question, pp. 271, 272 whether who is to pay the cost is not important to the question whether a particular claim is part of cost (if I take the sentence rightly).[2] I think a very important distinction in a rational law as to the liability of master for servant is between the cases where he can throw the damages on the public, as in big, permanent affairs like railroads, and the isolated ones where he can't and I think the theoretical limit of recovery in the former class is the economic value of destroyed or impaired life, limb, etc. to the community.

I had just written to Laski before your letter came explaining that I didn't write the opinion on the Webb-Kenyon law as I took him to suppose and, giving a short statement of why I dissented marked "*entre nous* and Felix."[3] So, I won't repeat it. I didn't write anything and have regretted that I didn't either say a few words or shut up. I thought the law should be construed more narrowly to avoid awkward doubts and, as it seemed to me, to express its probable meaning, but I had intended not to dissent and, at the last minute was stirred to do so by dissatisfaction with the opinion—thinking, as I did, the result also wrong.

I have just read Bernard Shaw's article in a late *New Republic* with much pleasure at what seemed to me its wisdom and wit.[4] I cut it out to send to an English correspondent who is never able to see truth in any criticism of England and yet is more detached in understanding than the run. I look forward to seeing you one of these days.

Always affectionately,
O.W.H.

I am delighted at what you say of Laski.

1. See above, January 12, 1917.

2. See above, January 12, 1917. Frankfurter wrote: "And whether a particular claim is properly part of cost or not cannot depend on who is to pay the cost. For instance, damage from the negligent digging of a ditch is no more properly charged up to the ditch if it is intended for a water pipe than if it is to hold a sewer. There is then no reason in economic fairness why this particular element of cost should be singled out from others for exemption."

3. Howe, ed., *Holmes-Laski Letters*, 54: "I dissented . . . being of the opinion that the statute should not be construed to simply substitute the state for Congress in control of interstate commerce in intoxicants—i.e., to permit a state to say although the purpose of the shipment (personal consumption) is one that we permit, we forbid the shipment in interstate commerce—the unlawfulness by state law thus consisting solely in the element of interstate commerce. . . . I thought the act did not mean more than to say that if on other grounds the shipment would be illegal but for the want of power on the part of the state over interstate commerce, the fact of I.C. should not interfere."

4. In *New Republic* 9 (1917): 270, George Bernard Shaw reviewed Cecil Chesterton, *The Perils of Peace* (London: Werner, Laurie, 1916), agreeing with the author's view that the western alliance lacked fortitude: "If you go to War, you engage yourself not only to fight, but not to squeal."

Washington, D.C.
March 5, 1917

Dear Frankfurter,

The President is inaugurated and I don't think that I have caught cold from sitting out of doors to look at his back while he discoursed. It was a fine sight, a great crowd but we gave our tickets for the procession to my nephew and niece and I came home, took a drink and a snooze and just now was awakened by your as ever welcome letter.[1] Mrs. Browning?—hum—her poetry makes me think of several things—of a woman in a man's dress coat, waggly in the bottom—of a sick room and the smell of flannel—of a criticism of *Aurora Leigh* when it appeared—that Mrs. B. first worshipped her God, then her husband and now herself.[2] I think there is undeniably some genius in her but for the most part unpleasantly wrapped up. I think there is little of her that I should want to read again.

Pollock wrote to me about the *Amerika* case and I have meant to look at it but haven't.[3] Pound's discourse—*Courts*—(not the Common Law) and legislation, reprinted from the *American Political Science Review* an address of December 28, 1911, I find in my books of his pamphlets and it is excellent.[4] I wonder if that is what you refer to?

I hope that Curtis will be elected to the Constitutional Convention.[5] I think it would be hard to find another young man who united such ability, preparation, liberal candor and charming character.

Your discourse as to your own attitude in case of war seems to me to put it rightly and brings peace to my heart. But I hope, for the sake of the Law School and the Law, that it will not be necessary to make any serious break in your career. I agree, on the other hand, that now I should allow less than I did in my own case 50 years ago to the consideration of the special faculties that one may attribute to oneself as a ground for not taking the chances of war. And I only rejoice that if you have to serve, it is not likely to be in the field.

I have only 3 cases to fire off tomorrow—none of any great importance.[6] Brandeis stirred me to write a memo in a case not yet decided that I should like to read to you as, though rapidly written, I thought it put a point of view with some force.[7] I expect I shall distribute that tomorrow. And, Brandeis and I also are lying low to fall upon the enemy when a wrong decision on another point comes along as I fear it will.[8] As Peleg Chandler told me about Jere. Mason, replying to a florid argument of Choate's, he stood up about 6 feet and a half, put his foot on a chair and said, "I can't gyrate to you as my brother Choate has done, but I should like to submit a few p'ints."[9] My love to the young Alaskans.[10]

Affectionately yours,
O. W. Holmes

1. The letter referred to is missing. Holmes's nephew and niece were Edward Jackson Holmes (1873–1950) and his wife Mary Beaman Holmes (1875–1964).

2. Elizabeth Barrett Browning, *Aurora Leigh* (New York: C. S. Francis, 1857).

3. *Admiralty Commissioners v. S.S. Amerika* (1917), Law Reports, House of Lords, Appeal Cases, 38, upheld the doctrine that in a civil court an individual's death cannot be complained of as an injury.

4. Roscoe Pound, "Courts and Legislation," *American Political Science Review* 7 (1913): 359. Pound attributed the difficulties of the subject to overly detailed law making, crude legislation, lackadaisical enforcement of rules, and "absolute theories, both of law and law making, which lead both courts and legislatures to attempt too many universal rules, to attempt to stereotype the ideas of the time as law for all time."

5. Charles Pelham Curtis, Jr. (1891–1959), son of Ellen Amory Curtis, was elected to the

1917 Massachusetts Constitutional Convention. In 1924 he became the youngest Harvard graduate to be elected to the Board of Overseers. Later, he wrote *Lions Under the Throne* (Boston: Houghton, Mifflin, 1947), a clear and nontechnical summary of the workings of the U.S. Supreme Court.

6. *McDonald v. Mabee*, 243 U.S. 90 (1917), a unanimous decision reversing, as a violation of the Fourteenth Amendment, a Texas district court decision allowing an action for money, executed by a warrant appearing only in a newspaper, against a man who had left the state; *Pennsylvania Fire Insurance Co. v. Gold Issue Mining Co.*, *Id.* at 93, a unanimous decision upholding a Missouri law allowing suits involving out-of-state property against corporations licensed in the state; *The Five Per Cent Discount Cases*, *Id.* at 97, 106, reversed a U.S. Customs Court decision extending the Underwood Tariff (1913) discount on goods imported in U.S. ships to foreign shipping when treaty obligations conflicted. Holmes upheld the government's argument that in cases of conflict the discount should be suspended rather than extended: "There is a strong presumption that the literal meaning is the true one, especially against a construction that is not interpretation but perversion." Justice Day dissented.

7. This memo may have supported Chief Justice White's opinion in *Wilson v. New*, 243 U.S. 332 (1917). See below, March 27, 1917.

8. Probably, *Southern Pacific Co. v. Jensen*, 244 U.S. 205 (1917). See below, March 27, 1917.

9. Peleg Whitman Chandler (1816–89), expert on bankruptcy laws and Solicitor, City of Boston (1846–53); Jeremiah Mason (1768–1848), U.S. Senator from New Hampshire (1813–17), later Massachusetts lawyer; Rufus Choate (1799–1859), lawyer and U.S. Senator from Massachusetts (1841–45).

10. Harold and Frida Laski and their baby daughter Diana.

Washington, D.C.
March 27, 1917

Felicissime!

Or, oh, my most particular Felix (particular=special). At the moment, I lay down my pen from the necessities of a dissent on a question of state power (none of yours) in which I have endeavored to let off a few convictions and spicy thoughts.[1] The lad [Shelton Hale] thinks it doesn't go very smoothly, but for the time being I am not displeased with it. I also have finished and sent to the printer the cases assigned to me yesterday—and so, as I say, I have laid down my pen.[2] Only, however, to take it up again for a word with you. I am disturbed at the point to which you advert in the Adamson case. I told the C.J. [Edward D. White] that I went the whole unicorn as to the power of Congress and I understood that he wouldn't do more than assume, for the sake of argument, that Congress couldn't meddle when the parties agreed. But the opinion looks very much like a direct denial of power in that case.[3] I take no stock in the distinction (this is all *entre nous* of course). My impression was that Day had the most rational dissent, although I thought it manifestly wrong to say that property is [taken?] when a rate is fixed as presumptively just unless and until shown otherwise by experience.[4] If absolute certainty is the condition of Constitutional power, God help us. I hear rumors that we came near universal anarchy if the strike had gone on. I don't know, but it is getting to be time to find out what is/who are the governing powers in this country.[5]

I must write to Laski that I dreadfully (no—slightly) fear that his dialectically correct notions of sovereignty will lead him into errors of sympathy and emotion.[6] Patriotism is the demand of the territorial club for priority, and as much priority as it needs for vital purposes, over such tribal groups as the churches and trade unions. I go the whole hog for the territorial club and I don't care a damn if it interferes with some of the spontaneities of the other groups. I think the Puritans were quite right when they whipped the Quakers and if it were conceivable—as every brutality is—that we should go back a century or two, the Catholics would be quite right, if they got the power, to make you and me shut our mouths. Which, being so, I think any nation perfectly justified in thinking whether it will have them or not in its territory. If you care to show these remarks to Laski, it will save my rewriting them. I am in the most Philistine of humors. The lad here calls himself a pacifist as well as a socialist and exhibits a thin and stubborn rationality. I find myself very fond of him and even liking his society above the average of secretaries but getting devilish little juice or promise out of his asms for isms. When he talks of more rational methods, I get the blood in my eye and say that war is the ultimate rationality. Good night, dear lad, every love to you.

Affectionately yours,
O. W. Holmes

1. *Southern Pacific Co. v. Jensen*, 244 U.S. 205, 222 (1917), a 5–4 decision, written by Justice McKenna, holding that an injured stevedore could not recover under the New York Workmen's Compensation Act (1914) because recourse to state law was not a "common law remedy" that federal maritime law saved to suitors. Holmes and Pitney dissented separately with Brandeis and Clarke concurring with both. Holmes observed: "The common law is not a brooding omnipresence in the sky but the articulate voice of some sovereign or quasi-sovereign that can be identified. . . . It always is the law of some State."

2. *Lehigh Valley R.R. Co. v. United States*, 243 U.S. 444 (1917), a unanimous decision upholding an Interstate Commerce Commission suit against a railroad that was carrying freight for certain customers at less than published rates. In *Motion Picture Patents Co. v. Universal Film Co.*, *Id.* at 502, 519–20, the majority opinion, written by Justice Clarke, denied a claim for patent protection because the invention "would give to the plaintiff such a potential power for evil over an industry which must be recognized as an important element in the amusement life of the nation." Holmes, joined by McKenna and Van Devanter, dissented: "There is no predominant public interest to prevent a patented tea pot or film feeder from being kept from the public." Holmes, McKenna, and Van Devanter dissented without opinion in a companion case, *Straus v. Victor Talking Machine Co.*, *Id.* at 490.

3. *Wilson v. New*, 243 U.S. 332 (1917), a 5–4 decision upholding the Adamson Act (1916), which established an eight-hour day for railroad workers operating in interstate commerce. Chief Justice White held that, although the law amounted to wage fixing, Congress could set a temporary standard in the wartime emergency. Therefore, the case did not raise the due process issue that conservative jurists used to invalidate most wage and price fixing laws in the years before the New Deal.

4. Day wrote: "I cannot agree that constitutional rights may be sacrificed because of public necessity, nor taken away because of emergency which might result in disaster or inconvenience to public or private interests." *Id.* at 372. Pitney and Van Devanter dissented jointly. McReynolds issued a separate dissent.

5. The Adamson Act averted a nationwide rail strike and thus probably helped Woodrow Wilson gain reelection.

6. See above, July 16, 1916.

Chicago, Illinois
December 23, 1917

Noblest of Friends:

Ulysses had no more calmly exciting time than I in these industrial wayfarings.[1] I had hoped to bring you tales of romance, adventures of doubts and hopes and faith for Christmastime. Instead, we are trying to extinguish the growing fires of a volcano in the packing industry, and bring the sanity of peace where strife prevails. And we shall succeed by no miracle of genius, but just a little humor and detachment and stout sense.

How much and how often I have lighted the fires of my mind and heart in your Promethean presence, on this trip, you will never know. . . . You have given me color and warmth and wings and inspiration and not a little joyous faith. I have not hoarded you—wherever I was able to ignite a spark (and Fortune was kind), My Justice held or helped to hold the torch. The world is so very, very young, and so extensively amenable to good sense and more of life. Travelling helps put men and significances in scale. And so, you tower more than ever. All glad days to Mrs. Holmes and yourself.

Devotedly yours,
Felix Frankfurter

1. Beginning in September 1917, Frankfurter served as secretary and legal counsel for President Wilson's Mediation Commission, which attempted, with mixed success, to alleviate labor-management conflict in the copper, lumber, and meat packing industries during the war. Frankfurter attracted bitter conservative criticism for his reports criticizing management deportation of striking miners in Bisbee, Arizona, and prosecution illegalities in the murder trial of California radical labor leader Thomas J. Mooney (1885–1942). See below, December 1, 1921, and Parrish, *Frankfurter and His Times*, 81–97.

Cambridge, Massachusetts
May 18, 1918

Dear Justice Holmes,

By way of footnote to my remarks on the Child Labor Case, I hope I made clear that I do not at all regret the Court's decision nor, if I may speak with scientific respect, do I dissent.[1] I *am* troubled if the Court seeks to reconcile this decision with the McCray case.[2] But I shall doubtless be enlightened when the text of the opinion comes.

Always yours,
F.F.

1. In *Hammer v. Dagenhart*, 247 U.S. 251, 281 (1918), the Court, in an opinion written by Justice Day, ruled that the Child Labor Act of 1916, forbidding the transportation in interstate commerce of goods manufactured by firms employing children under fourteen, was unconstitutional as an infringement of the power of states to regulate employment in manufacturing activities. Holmes, with Brandeis, Clarke, and McKenna concurring, dissented: "The act does not meddle with anything belonging to the States. They may regulate their internal affairs and their domestic commerce as they like. But when they seek to send their products across the state line they are no longer within their rights." This decision was overruled by *United States v. Darby*, 312 U.S. 100 (1941).

2. *McCray v. United States*, 195 U.S. 27 (1904), sustained the Oleomargarine Act of 1886, which included a prohibitive tax on artificial coloring. Chief Justice Fuller's majority decision, to which Holmes concurred, held that the judiciary could not void an act of Congress, otherwise within its power, because of the legislative motive.

Washington, D.C.
June 15, 1918

Dear Frankfurter,

You are too kind—if I had not been hurried, I had thought to try to get Henderson's book to take with me, and I am very much obliged to you.[1] I hope, as we talked, that this is not good-bye for the summer. If you let me know beforehand, I will do my damndest to keep a room for you.

I wish you would tell Major Requin how admirable I thought his article about General Foch and that I was prevented from calling on him by the unexpected odds and ends of the finish.[2] I had not read the article through when we talked, but I did afterwards and thought it a model of good taste and encouragement. *Au revoir*—I hope.

Affectionately yours,
O. W. Holmes

1. Probably, Frankfurter's former student, Gerard Henderson (1891–1927), who had just published *The Position of Foreign Corporations in American Constitutional Law* (Cambridge: Harvard University Press, 1918).

2. Edouard J. Requin, "Our Faith in Foch," *New Republic* 15 (1918): 176. Requin (1879–1953), a strategist on the French General Staff, later commanded the Maginot Line in the sector of Nancy.

Washington, D.C.
October 14, 1918

(I don't know your military rank—so please excuse the Esq.)[1]

Dear Frankfurter,

Your departure needed no explanation. But I was intending to write to you to express my apprehension that you were running the machine too hard. This at least you ought to do—viz: to make sure of sufficient and regular meals. The temptation to let them wait is great no doubt—but you must have an eye to the long run. My exhortation no doubt is as useful as other moral advice, but it comes from affectionate solicitude, and I am sure that it is wise to have an eye to the long run—including hours of work and sleep. Whenever you feel like coming here, you are sure of welcome.

Yours ever,
O. W. Holmes

1. Frankfurter was a major in the Army reserves but refused military rank throughout the war because, he said, "As a civilian I could get into the presence of a General without saluting." See Lash, *Diaries of Frankfurter*, 20–29.

Beverly Farms, Massachusetts
September 25, 1919

Dear Frankfurter,

Your letter brings joy to my heart.[1] For I do believe, that your kindness for me has not been shaken by the sight you have had of so many impressive personalities in the old world.[2] I listened to you in wrapt wonder and also with delight to see that it had not affected the naturalness and spontaneity of your thinking and your ways. You have brought a great deal of comfort and companionship to the natural loneliness of old age and I ask nothing better than that it may continue while I last.

Affectionately yours,
O. W. Holmes

1. The letter referred to is missing. A brief note from Holmes to Frankfurter, January 11, 1919, has been omitted.

2. Frankfurter made several European trips at the behest of President Wilson's confidant, Colonel Edward M. House (1859–1938). In 1917 he accompanied the ill-fated Morgenthau Mission, which attempted to separate Turkey from the Central Powers. Frankfurter attended the Versailles Peace Conference as a member of the Zionist Organization of America delegation. In this capacity, he sought with little success to secure the recognition of Zionist claims to Palestine and to mobilize the European labor movement behind Wilson's peace plan and the League of Nations. See Parrish, *Frankfurter and His Times*, 85–87.

Washington, D.C.
November 1, 1919

Dear Frankfurter,

Your letter gave me pleasure and satisfaction to know that all is going well. But the same causes that have delayed my answer make it impossible for me to write outside the job.[1] I am too busy. Just now I am full of a tentative statement that may see light later on kindred themes to your subject but I don't yet know whether what I have written *quasi in furore*, as Saunders says, is good enough.[2] And ahead of me is a string of cases to be remediated and that drives me mad. I already had told Laski that the notion of my writing an article was no go.

Apropos of this police power for aesthetic purposes (*between ourselves*), they made me strike out of the Okla. bank case (*Noble v. Haskell* wasn't it?) a contrast with nations with whom the Minister of Fine Arts was not less important than the Sec. of the Treasury.[3]

I hope that I may see proof, if they ever reach printing the prospective collection of my earlier things—*at least of the letter on economic themes*—published in *The Cosmopolitan* or some such magazine, contrary to my intention.[4] It had misprints that nullified the sense and italics that were not mine. I must stop and go to work.

Affectionately yours,
O. W. Holmes

1. The letter referred to is missing. Holmes had been invited to give the Phi Beta Kappa oration at Harvard.

2. As if possessed. Sir Edmund Saunders (d. 1683) was the King's Bench reporter from 1666 to 1672. The "statement" is probably Holmes's dissent in *Abrams v. United States*, 250 U.S. 616 (1919). See below, November 12, 1919.

3. *Noble State Bank v. Haskell*, 219 U.S. 104 (1911), a unanimous opinion affirming the police power of the states to regulate banks by requiring them to make payments into a Depositors' Guaranty Fund. Regarding national character and the arts, Holmes's dissenting opinion in *Tyson v. Banton*, 273 U.S. 418, 447 (1927), observed: "We have not that respect for art that is one of the glories of France. But to many people the superfluous is the necessary, and it seems to me that government does not go beyond its sphere in attempting to make life livable for them." See below, March 19, 1927.

4. Holmes's original essay was published, with the responses of other well-known figures such as Charles W. Eliot, Washington Gladden, and Jack London, in Frederick Upham Adams, "Are Great Fortunes Great Dangers?" *Cosmopolitan* 40 (1906): 392. The revisions were negligible in republication as "Economic Elements," *Collected Legal Papers*, 279–82, assembled by Frankfurter and Harold Laski.

Cambridge, Massachusetts
November 12, 1919

Dear Justice Holmes,

And now I may tell you the gratitude and, may I say it, the pride I have in your dissent.[1] You speak there as you have always spoken of course. But "this time we need education in the obvious" and you lift the voice of the noble human spirit.

The times also make me especially shy about my personal happiness and yet I should be less than healthy and honest did I not say how you send me off—somehow gladder than I thought anybody, but Marion, now could make me.[2] If I came to Mrs. Holmes and you no less humble than your knight of romance in not caring a damn what anybody thought (tho' I know I can afford this gesture of indifference), knowing you would be glad and yet happy that you were happy, blame yourselves and all the good angels of mercy.

Faithfully,
F.F.

1. *Abrams v. United States*, 250 U.S. 616, 630 (1919), upheld the Sedition Act (1918) although the appellants were not protesting American involvement in World War I but had published pamphlets attacking the government's expeditionary force in Russia. The Abrams decision was written by Justice Clarke, an Ohio lawyer who served on the Supreme Court from 1916 to 1922 and later headed the League of Nations Non-Partisan Association. Holmes, joined by Brandeis, dissented: "[Our Constitution] is an experiment, as all life is an experiment. Every year if not every day we have to wager our salvation upon some prophecy based

upon imperfect knowledge. While that experiment is part of our system I think we should be eternally vigilant against attempts to check the expression of opinions that we loathe."

2. Felix Frankfurter and Marion Denman were married December 20, 1919.

Cambridge, Massachusetts
November 26, 1919

Dear Justice Holmes,

I wired you in hopes that you might do "it" for Luina would be so happy to have you be the voice of God and man.[1] I should have added that I do not, of course, want you to add to your labors or yield against your inclination. I need no such sacrifice to know how deeply we have you with us in any event.

It's always good to find someone proves what you know. Alvin Johnson has done that in this week's *New Republic* in his attempt at a quantitative study of the potentialities of revolution in this country.[2] It might interest you.

I still read and rejoice over your dissents and Pound has stolen from me when he says your paragraphs will live as long as the *Areopagitica*.

Morris Cohen is here and he and Laski and I are boxing the compass many times round the cosmos. You are the only monistic principle among us.

Affectionately,
Felix Frankfurter

1. Because of lack of legal authority, neither Holmes nor Learned Hand could perform the ceremony for Frankfurter and Marion Denman. Judge Benjamin Cardozo of New York married the couple.

2. Alvin Johnson, "Is Revolution Possible?" *New Republic* 20 (1919): 367. Johnson (1874–1971), Director of the New School for Social Research, 1923–45, believed that Revolution was unlikely but feared that management policies were frustrating workers' cooperative tendencies and thus increasing the possibility of future conflict.

Washington, D.C.
November 30, 1919

Dear Felix,

Your letter is a great relief to my mind for I can't go into the details—largely not affecting you—that made me say no. As long as you know how unwillingly I should refuse anything you asked, it is all right. Give my affectionate greetings to the beautiful one.

I have been toying with a couple of trifles in the way of cases that had a slight flavor of theory in each.[1] It has been excluded from one by some of those alert to spot such things and I have substituted some pap that would not hurt an infant's stomach. I should have thought that I struck out innocuous *enfantillages* but my prophetic soul divined rightly that the watchers of the ark would be down on me. I am hoping to get a chance to read a book—Ehrlich's *Die juristiche Logik*—this week but whether I shall I know not.[2] Every day something turns up to be done.

I read Alvin Johnson's article that you mentioned with satisfaction to see hot things so coolly and wisely measured. One point only surprised me—that he even should have believed for a moment that any economic trouble was due to the profiteers. He is an economist and I bow to his authority but, it always has seemed to me that they were another illustration of people getting blackguarded who happen to illustrate and incarnate the fundamental facts of life like Rockefeller. People damned Rockefeller when he embodied the inevitables. They didn't say, damn order of the universe or the Great Panjandrum yet it was the order of the universe that they disliked.

Brandeis told me that you said Perkins was down on my dissent.[3] And I have supposed that that would be the point of view of the conservative but, as yet, I have heard nothing of it and even the virtuous *Springfield Republican* seemed pleased with Brandeis and me. However, that is ancient history and I am thinking about other cases now. It is Sunday Evg. and I close to go to the Tavern for victuals but alas not for drink.

Affectionately yours,
O. W. Holmes

1. *Liverpool Navigation Co. v. Brooklyn Terminal*, 251 U.S. 48, 53 (1919), a unanimous decision upholding a District Court decision on a libel in admiralty that determined that the value of the tugboat, not the value of the flotilla, was the limit of the owner's liability: "The notion as applicable to a collision case seems to us to be that if you surrender the offending vessel you are free, just as it was said by a judge in the time of Edward III, 'If my dog kills your sheep and I freshly after the fact tender you the dog you are without recourse against me.'" *Chicago, Rock Island and Pacific R.R. Co. v. Cole, Id.* at 55–56, unanimously affirmed a state judgment that decisions on contributory negligence may be left to the jury in all cases without violating the Fourteenth Amendment: "It is said that legislation cannot change the standard of conduct, which is matter of law in its nature into matter of fact, and this may be conceded; but the material element in the constitutional enactment is not that it called contributory negligence fact but that it left it wholly to the jury."

2. Eugen Ehrlich, *Die juristische Logik* (Tubingen: Mohr, 1918), one of the principal statements of sociological jurisprudence.

3. Thomas Nelson Perkins (1870–1937), counsel to the Harvard Corporation and spokesman of conservative Overseers who wanted to fire Frankfurter, Zechariah Chafee (1885–1957), and Harold Laski for their advocacy of free speech and worker's rights during the Red Scare. In Laski's case, the Overseers succeeded. See Kramnick and Sheerman, *Laski*, 122–50.

Washington, D.C.
December 4, 1919

Dear Frankfurter,

Your correspondence with Perkins seems to me to illustrate what I often say in conference: that you never can decide a case by general propositions—each of you could admit all that the other said, except his conclusion.[1] What the conclusion should be in this particular case, I am too ignorant to judge. I can't imagine that anyone would object to publicly maintaining the wisdom of letting the Russians stew in their own juice unless the public counsel were mixed with sympathies the expression of which, at this time of course, means a fight. The time for going into a fight each must judge for himself. I think you are too level-headed to be looking for martyrdom. Martyrs I suspect generally are damned fools (how Garrison would hammer that proposition with his wooden mallet and Phillips slice it with his scymitar—both to the personal discredit of the utterer) but the nasty little truth bug still lives in the sentence. That is about all I can say. You both talk well in your letters and I don't know which judgment was right, though of course I like your feeling.

Affectionately yours,
O. W. Holmes

December 5. P.S. I do think there is another aspect to be considered. Of course, I believe in academic freedom but, on the other hand, it is to be remembered that a professor's conduct may affect the good will of the institution to which he belongs. It may turn aside gifts that otherwise would have come to it or students that it would like to have. I don't think a man would do his whole duty if he merely indulged his spontaneity even in a case where he had opinions that required courage to state and that he thought it desirable to make known. He must weigh this harm that he may do his employer while he takes his employer's pay. Suppose, for instance, that you know that if, while a professor, you presided over the meeting, you would cause a rich old bird to knock out a legacy of a million to this college. I don't think you would have a right to do it. I think it would be a question between resignation and silence. This doesn't in the remotest degree mean that I think you are wrong in the particular case—as I said, I can't judge—and each particular case must be judged by itself.

1. On Armistice Day, 1919, Frankfurter had presided at a Faneuil Hall rally urging the Wilson administration to recognize the Soviet Union. Perkins rebuked him and a sharp exchange of letters ensued. See Parrish, *Frankfurter and His Times*, 120–23.

Washington, D.C.
December 21, 1919

Dear Frankfurter,

Sunrise and morning star
And one clear call for me
For I must see the barber ere I lunch
And must go out at three

I may not have got Tennyson's words exactly but the facts are substantially accurate and I snatch the moment before the barber comes.[1] I didn't think that there was any danger that you would misinterpret my last letter as implying a criticism which was far from my thoughts, so I did not hurry.

Hasn't *The New Republic* been a little dyspeptic the last two numbers? Various gents like Rhodes and Untermeyer seemed to catch it and I thought Francis Hackett was not in his most amiable mood in his discourse about not disturbing the young man's faith.[2] But don't repeat it, for it may have been I, as I have been coughing at night which is not good for the temper.

There is little doing to report. I am hung up on the two cases that I have, for Pitney and others to have a whack at me—but one I don't care about and the other is pretty safe.[3] I suppose that after tomorrow's conference and adjournment I shall get a couple more with plenty of time to do them in.[4] A good deal of time was taken during the week in arguing the Post Office Division Cases—whether the [Postmaster General] was warranted in dividing the weighing for 90 days by 105, or should divide by 90—to get the average daily mail—not thrilling.

At odd minutes, but not this last week, I have been laboriously extracting the kernel from Ehrlich, *Der juristische Logik* but the dictionary, like the nut picker, gives slow results. His general ideas are not novelties but his account of the development of the law on the continent is instructive and the book seems to me excellent with something of the German need to state everything. I remember how *Fliegende Blatter* used to amuse me by the way in which it took you by the two ears and shoved your nose into a job.[5] It didn't want any misunderstanding. How different from the French assumption that you twig the innuendo even of a silence. If I get time during the adjournment, I shall finish him.

I have suffered really a great loss in the closing of the print shop opposite the British Embassy. It was my weekly resort and Dayton was a very pleasant man to boss it. But it didn't pay, it seems, after the war stopped—rather curious, that—seeing that, as I understand, he had done well until then. As you see, I have nothing but the casual to tell, except to wish you and the dear and beautiful Luina a Merry Christmas which I do with all my heart.

Affectionately yours,
O. W. Holmes

On the deportation of aliens, the [*New Republic*] ought to remember that the decisions have gone very far in giving to government a right to do as it damn chooses.[6] I speak from ancient memory.

1. Sunset and evening star,
And one clear call for me!
And may there be no moaning of the bar,
When I put out to sea
Crossing the Bar, I

2. *New Republic* 21 (1919): 81–84, included critical reviews, by Charles A. Beard of James F. Rhodes, *History of the United States, 1877–1896* (New York: Macmillan, 1919), and by Alvin Johnson of Louis Untermeyer, *Including Horace* (New York: Harcourt, Brace and Howe, 1919), as well as Hackett's article questioning the value of unreflective patriotism.

3. *Birge-Forbes Co. v. Heye*, 251 U.S. 317, 323 (1920), a unanimous decision affirming the suit of Heye, a German cotton broker, against a Texas exporting firm: "The plaintiff had got his judgment before war was declared, and the defendant, the petitioner, had delayed the collection of it by taking the case up"; *The Mail Divisor Cases, Id.* at 326, 329, a majority opinion, denying a suit by railroad companies against the Postmaster General for changing the method of calculating the weight of mail: "From the beginning of the Government the Postmaster General, as the head of a great business enterprise, always has been entrusted . . . with a wide discretion concerning what contracts he should make." Day and Van Devanter dissented.

4. *Rex v. United States*, 251 U.S. 382 (1920), a unanimous opinion rejecting a petition to reinstate an 1866 claim against the Ute Indians on the basis of recent legislation removing the defense of alienage—the contention that the tribe was not hostile though a depredating band from the tribe was—as a ground for dismissal. Holmes affirmed the judgment of the Court of Claims that the suit was invalid because it was not dismissed for alienage when originally brought. In *Silverthorne Lumber Co. v. United States, Id.* at 385, 392, Holmes's majority opinion extended the exclusionary rule to corporations by upholding the company's right, under the Fourth Amendment, to withhold incriminating documents that had been illegally obtained in an earlier search: "The essence of a provision forbidding the acquisition of evidence in a certain way is that not merely evidence so acquired shall not be used before the court but that it shall not be used at all." White and Pitney dissented.

5. *Fliegende Blatter*, a weekly humor magazine, published in Munich, 1844–1944.

6. On December 19, 1919, the Wilson administration deported to the Soviet Union 249 alien "radicals" including Emma Goldman (1869–1940) and Alexander Berkman (1870–1936). See *New Republic* 21 (1919): 37.

Washington, D.C.
January 15, 1920

Dear Felix,

Your letter is as welcome and as difficult to read as ever.[1] However, "Use every man after his desert, and who should escape whipping"—the profane have found fault with my handwriting. . . . I get letters (*apropos* of booze) telling me that the last chance out is to upset the Amendment or, as I notice lawyers, presumably retained, prefer to say—the so-called amendment—but I don't borrow trouble till I get to it. I was very sorry to miss you both the other day but it couldn't be helped. My love to the beautiful one. I will try to maintain that you are as bad as ever as you request.

Affectionately yours,
O. W. Holmes

1. The letter referred to is missing.

Washington, D.C.
January 28, 1920

Dear Frankfurter,

This is to answer the letter received this evening, as this morning's was to answer the telegram received in the morning.[1] I should be glad and obliged if you would think about the lad for me, for next year. I think it would not be bad to take Laski and Hill into your councils, as you probably would, not that I imagine the result would be changed.

Affectionately yours,
O. W. Holmes

I read with delight about when the Big Four met in *The New Republic*.[2]

1. The letter and telegram referred to are missing; Holmes's note has been omitted.
2. John Maynard Keynes, "When the Big Four Met," *New Republic* 21 (1919): 103, blamed the failure of the Paris Peace Conference on Woodrow Wilson's stubbornness.

Washington, D.C.
February 11, 1920

Dear F.F.,

Your nomination of Day Kimball gives me much pleasure both from what you write and what my secretary says.[1] I hope he will accept, subject to my right to die or resign, which I have mentioned since I was 70 but which I intend to do my best to avoid.

As soon as I got your letter and one from Laski (both yesterday) I wrote to him. I heard, almost at the same time that I heard of the *Lampoon*, that it had been a boomerang and had caused many to take his side but I hesitated to write until I heard more as I could not know how he was feeling.[2] It is disgusting that so serious a scholar and thinker as he should be subject to the trampling of swine. I think that the influence of Figgis' writing quite *alio intuitu* has not been altogether for the best and has made the pluralistic business rather more of a hobby than it deserves to be, but everything that Laski writes is a contribution and whether he overemphasizes one side or not can or, at least, should be met only by reasoning as cool as his and it will take masters to do it. Who is the editor of the *Transcript* and why did he want to attack L. (to say nothing of the dirty mode)?[3]

I glanced over, for I did not really read it, our young Kimball's exposition as to Free Speech and got the impression he had "bit off a little more, etc." Perhaps I shall hear his views one day! I hope so.

I hope you like your contracts in restraint of trade—it seems to me another place where courts and legislatures have drooled.[4]

Affectionately yours,
O. W. Holmes

1. The letter referred to is missing. Day Kimball (1893–1955) later became a British citizen and served on the Supreme Court of Bermuda.

2. The entire issue of the *Harvard Lampoon*, January 16, 1920, was devoted to "Philip Catiline Laski . . . Senator for Semetia." An "Auto Biographia Laskivia" stated, "My favorite color is orange because it is both red and yellow." The *Lampoon* was edited by Edward A. Bacon (1897–1968), who became a Milwaukee banker and Republican national committeeman.

3. The *Boston Evening Transcript*, January 16, 1920, defended the *Lampoon* by arguing that Laski had the right of free speech and "that right belongs too to the Harvard student, and in greater degree even, to a group of Harvard students such as the Lampoon represents." The *Transcript* was edited by George S. Mandrell (1867–1934).

4. The reference is unclear but may refer to one of the cases discussed below, March 10, 1920.

Washington, D.C.
February 17, 1920

Dear Frankfurter,

Many thanks for your letter and the piece by Stanley Hall laying out Sir Oliver Lodge in so comforting a way.[1] I was glad incidentally to see that he treats telepathy in almost the same terms as spiritualism. I had noticed that seemingly sane and fairly level headed writers sometimes treated that with respect. And, as everything in this world is a question of fact, I had wondered whether it made a better show than I could believe short of the most compulsory evidence.

You make me a little anxious about Laski. I hate to think that the poor chap should have suffered from such a paltry attack. But I know how it is. Years ago I said to Arthur Sedgwick, why is it that while we don't mind the attacks of fools, their praise sets us up? And he made the witty answer—because it's true. But later self observation has shown me that I mind the attacks more than the praise. And the reason is that we find it so easy to think ill of ourselves that when anyone suggests it, we say perhaps at least he's right. I hear rumors that Laski is preparing to leave for England. Of course, I know that he would like a place there, say at Oxford but I have heard nothing from him that looks like any present arrangement. As I think he is a little unwilling to speak of the matter to me, I mention the matter, *entre nous*, to you. I should miss him dreadfully.

Another thing that I don't want to mention to him—I have just finished his wife's and his translation of Duguit.[2] This is the second book of Duguit that I have read and I get mighty little nourishment from him. He seems to show a sad lack of analytical power in all his talk about sovereignty.

I don't know what you mean about Croly on Lincoln—it has escaped me.[3] As to why Christianity originally got possession of the Western world, I refer you to Renan, S. Reinach and many others.[4] That does not seem to me wonderful. As the feller said, seeing Niagara Falls—what's to hinder? As to its persistence, whatever atmosphere men are brought up in persists. Their first impressions largely determine what they revere and love or hate. Very few are dispassionate or rational on such matters. You don't wonder that Mahometanism persists or Bouddhism. Your wonder as to Christianity is based (I suspect) on an exaggerated notion of the difference between the run of us and the run of them. Of course, too, the prevailing religion is backed up by the great vested interests etc., and many, I suspect Croly as well as English landholders, have an unconscious sag towards what they, perhaps also unconsciously, perceive to be their interests or a help to the accomplishment of what they want. Think not, young feller, that because you or I may flatter ourselves that we are detached (perhaps wrongly), most men are or ever pretend to be. I am delighted to infer that Kimball will come to me.

Affectionately yours,
O. W. Holmes

1. The letter referred to is missing. G. Stanley Hall (1846–1924), psychologist and President of Clark University, criticized the British educator and spiritist Sir Oliver Lodge (1851–1940), who was lecturing in Boston on life after death. Spiritism, said Hall, "is the last stronghold of superstition in the world, the common enemy of science and religion." See *Boston Herald*, February 12, 1920.

2. Leon Duguit, *Law in the Modern State* (New York: B. W. Huebsch, 1919).

3. Herbert Croly, "The Paradox of Lincoln," *New Republic* 21 (1920): 350, likened Lincoln's statesmanship to "the words and actions of Jesus."

4. Ernest Renan, *The History of the Origins of Christianity*, 7 vols. (London: Mathison, 1890); Solomon Reinach, *Orpheus: A General History of Religions* (New York: G. P. Putnam's, 1909).

Washington, D.C.
March 10, 1920

Dear Frankfurter,

I agree with you as to the steel trust but, as I said to Brandeis, I couldn't change my vote (to use the odious phrase that is in use with us) because I thought that a majority of the Court, if the other two could have taken part, would be the other way.[1] As to the opinion, I did not attempt suggestions that would have been of little use. I also was disappointed that the *Colgate* case was not applied.[2]

I wrote to your wife last night, thanking her for her charming letter and asking her to tell you how moved I was by what you wrote. It is a wonderful thing for an old fellow to find that he is not lonely when pretty much all of his contemporaries and early friends have gone.

Affectionately yours,
O. W. Holmes

1. Frankfurter's letter is missing. In *United States v. United States Steel Corp.*, 251 U.S. 417, 451 (1920), McKenna's 4–3 majority opinion, in which Holmes concurred, rejected the government's antitrust suit: "The corporation is undoubtably of impressive size and it takes an effort of resolution not to be affected by it or to exaggerate its influence. But we must adhere to the law and the law does not make mere size an offence or the existence of unexpected power an offence." Day, with Pitney and Clarke concurring, dissented. Brandeis and McReynolds took no part in the case.

2. *United States v. Colgate and Co.*, 250 U.S. 300, 307 (1919), a unanimous decision by Justice McReynolds dismissing a suit brought under the Sherman Act (1890): "In the absence of any purpose to create or maintain a monopoly, the act does not restrict the long recognized right of trader or manufacturer engaged in an entirely private business, freely to exercise his own independent discretion as to parties with whom he will deal."

Washington, D.C.
April 12, 1920

Dear Frankfurter,

Your telegram this morning is the first news that I have of the invitation from Harvard, but it's no go. I have refused everything—the Law School, the Alumni and all the rest—and the reason holds doubly good for this, both that I have refused the others and that I haven't the time and energy to spare.[1] One can't say anything worth saying without paying for it—cash, in my case—and I haven't the cash. One is never sure that one is not yielding to indolence and timidity, for I certainly am timid as to anything not done but *voila vous etes*.

The other day Laski adverted to something of Wigmore's and previously, Wigmore had intimated in a letter that something of his would appear, as I inferred, *apropos* of or suggested by the *Abrams* case.[2] Do you know of any such matters? I have seen nothing from his hand for a long time except the letter above mentioned. If you do know of such a piece, please let me know what and where it is as I always want to see what Wigmore says.

I hope you both are well. My wife has had a cold that has kept her to her room for over a week. The doctor says, the common cold of commerce but I wish she seemed stronger. Her right hand woman is also down and has been in bed about the same time. I keep well, coughing a little at night after talking with anyone but that is an old friend.

Affectionately yours,
O. W. Holmes

1. The telegram referred to is missing. The invitation from Harvard was probably a request for a commencement address.

2. John H. Wigmore, "Abrams v. United States: Freedom of Speech and Freedom of Thuggery in War-Time and Peace-Time," *Illinois Law Review* 14 (1920): 539: "In a period when the fate of the civilized world hung in the balance, how could the Minority Opinion interpret law and conduct in such a way as to let loose men who were doing their hardest to paralyze the supreme war efforts of our country?"

Rochester, New York
April 19, 1920

Dear Justice Holmes,

I'm in this typically colorless American city—esthetics is certainly not one of their wants—on a very interesting labor litigation. About half a dozen of Law School men, some contemporary with me, some younger, are having a grand time defending an injunction suit along industrial and economic lines and away from the arid "legal rights" assumptions of a Pitney in the *Hitchman* case.[1] The defendants are an organization of some two hundred thousand, led by Sidney Hillman, the most constructive-minded labor leader I know.[2] I'm in the case as a volunteer because I'm interested in having some pet ideas accepted by the courts. The case will very likely go up to the N.Y. Court of Appeals and we shall try to have that court, upon a different record, refuse to accept the lead of the *Hitchman* case.[3] I can't help telling you that *the* most helpful "law" in this whole field is still your paper on "Privilege, Malice and Intent."[4] Our whole brief is constructed around your analysis and, fortunately, the New York cases have largely accepted that analysis. But judges continue to indulge "the illusion of mathematical certainty" and to think they are, like a silkworm, unfolding "law" from the legal cocoon when in fact they are but translating their own unconscious economic prejudices or assumptions. The *Hitchman* case is a striking demonstration of the truth of this observation. It's great fun to go into the laboratory of the courts and try to secure acceptance of closer lucubrations.

Which takes me to Wigmore. The poor man has not yet come out of his uniform and thinks the War is still on. So he has let a perfect diatribe against your *Abrams* opinion in the April *Illinois Law Review*—the same number that contains a measured but enthusiastic analysis of your opinion.[5] I'm rather sad about Wigmore—it's the kind of recklessness that he not infrequently manifests. It's none the less saddening that a mind like his should be so violent and so tempestuous. All through the war he was hell-bent, and humorless beyond words but I had hoped the "militaristic" virus would wear off. It hasn't. You'll be interested in a paper on the Abrams case by my colleague Chafee in the forthcoming *Harvard Law Review*.[6]

The clash between "fear" and "faith" is a pretty far-reaching one in personalities and the reactions to the present distempers of the world furnish constant illustrations. For instance, our Attorney General, Palmer, sees spooks and "Bolshevists" everywhere—and thereby helps not a little to create them.[7] The enclosed little editorial from the *N.Y. World* speaks a good deal of sense, as I see it. Some of your brethren are fear traders and their distilled fear they call "constitutional law." I thank all the gods there be that you're on that Bench!

I do hope the spring is bringing Mrs. Holmes her strength. Luina—who is here—and I are sending our affectionate greetings.

Devotedly,
F.F.

P.S. Have you seen Henry James' *Letters*? I've read a few and they have made me a bit impatient. He is rather catholic in his criticism. Everybody is a [?]—

Tolstoi, Stevenson, Meredith, complaining about Meredith's obscurities and needless speculative psychologizing, as tho' the author of *The Golden Bowl* were not Henry James.[8] His letters made me wonder how generous and wide James' critical faculties really were. I had always felt that, in his own field, he was a shallow Meredith, but his letters reveal a less genial personality than I had supposed without disclosing greater depths. However, I shall read more of them to become "judicial" but he has touched me in some of my favorites, especially Meredith.

Alas, we shall lose Laski from this side—I shall miss him very hard, but for him it's the thing to do.[9]

1. *Hitchman Coal and Coke Co. v. Mitchell*, 245 U.S. 229, 274 (1917). Mahlon Pitney's majority opinion reversed a Circuit Court of Appeals ruling and upheld a District Court decision granting the Hitchman company an injunction against the United Mine Workers. The Hitchman employees had already signed a "yellow dog" contract which conceded that they had the right to join a union but went on to stipulate that they could not remain with the company if they did so. Brandeis's dissent, joined by Clarke and Holmes, supported the Appeals Court decision: "When this suit was filed, no right of plaintiff had been infringed and there was no reasonable ground to believe that any of its rights would be interfered with." The "Law School men" included Emory Buckner, Gerard Henderson, Robert Szold (1889–1977), Max Lowenthal (1888–1971), as well as the labor economist Leo Wolman (1890–1961).

2. Sidney Hillman (1887–1946), President of Amalgamated Clothing Workers of America (ACWA) and a major power in organized labor and Democratic party politics in the 1930s and 1940s. For a discussion of his role in this case see Steve Fraser, *Labor Will Rule: Sidney Hillman and the Rise of American Labor* (New York: Macmillan, 1991), 162–66.

3. *Michaels v. Hillman*, 183 N.Y. Supp. 197 (1920). The Michaels, Stern company's injunction was upheld and the ACWA had to pay damages. However, the Court denied the company's suit to disband the union as an illegal conspiracy. Frankfurter urged Hillman not to appeal but instead to bargain for the reinstatement of some employees and the dropping of damage charges. This tactic succeeded. See Parrish, *Frankfurter and His Times*, 124–25.

4. In "Privilege, Malice and Intent," *Harvard Law Review* 8 (1894): 1, 9, Holmes abandoned his belief that judges enforced an external or objective standard in deciding cases. By acknowledging private loyalties and the inevitability that their decisions would usurp the legislative function, however, judges were even more obliged to exercise restraint in allowing individuals and organizations latitude to pursue competitive activities, even though these could harm others: "The time has gone by when the law is only an unconscious embodiment of the common will. It has become a conscious reaction upon itself of organized society knowingly seeking to determine its own destinies." Horwitz, *Transformation of American Law*, 130–37, portrays Holmes shifting his ideas in response to the increasingly bitter struggles between labor and capital: "Economic and social struggle undermined and eroded all efforts to find clear external bright-light boundaries between right and wrong. Compared to the prevailing judicial theory of rights, this approach permitted much greater scope for economic struggle, especially for labor unions, since it required a finding of actual intent or malice. Since most legal restrictions on labor unions derived from a conception of absolute property rights, Holmes deserves to be seen as the preeminent figure in dismantling the system of legal thought based on absolute rights."

5. See *Illinois Law Review* 14 (1920): 601, 607, a note by Chicago attorney Louis G. Cald-

well (1891–1951): "Those who still have faith in our Bill of Rights are saved from pessimism by the courageous voice in our Supreme Court."

6. Zechariah Chafee, Jr., "A Contemporary State Trial—The United States versus Jacob Abrams et al," *Harvard Law Review* 30 (1920): 747. Chafee, a foremost civil libertarian, concluded, "The whole proceeding from start to finish has been a disgrace to our law, and none the less a disgrace because our highest court felt powerless to wipe it out." See also Polenberg, *Fighting Faiths*, 272–84.

7. A. Mitchell Palmer (1872–1936), Attorney General of the United States, 1919–21, and main force behind the Red Scare.

8. Percy Lubbock, ed., *The Letters of Henry James*, 2 vols. (London: Macmillan, 1920). Of George Meredith, James wrote: "The fantastic and mannered in him were as nothing, I think, to the intimately sane and straight; just as the artist was nothing to the good citizen and the liberalised bourgeois." See Vol. II, 266.

9. Harold Laski had accepted a professorship at the London School of Economics.

Washington, D.C.
April 25, 1920

Dear Frankfurter,

Your letter was a joy to me, as always. I am so glad to see your importance gaining increased recognition. I got Wigmore's piece after you told me where it was and glanced over it on the bench but came to the conclusion that it wasn't reasoning but emotion. He certainly got the military sting good and hard—he was a damned sight more a soldier than I ever was and I shouldn't be surprised to hear him tell me that I didn't understand patriotism as I inferred that he thought I didn't understand the emergencies of war.[1] He seems only less dogmatic than Zane.[2] Absolute beliefs are a rum thing. I always wonder at a man who takes himself seriously all the time. I was repeating to Hand yesterday my old chestnut that a gentleman couldn't be a philosopher or a philosopher a gentleman. For a gentleman postulates himself as an ultimate over against the universe. I said to Hand that I thought that the sin against the Holy Ghost. Thought afterwards that if one were out for trouble with a paradox, one might put it: The sin against the Holy Ghost is self respect. I have been surprised at some of Wigmore's *pronunciamentos* before but I remember noting how tremendously military his bearing was, in uniform.

Yes, Indeed, we shall miss Laski—both for suggestion and affection but I am glad he has the opportunity. Your brief I shall hang on to against a possible articulation of my own, which it may help in a case that has hung here a good while.[3] I shall send this to Cambridge, not knowing whether you have finished with Rochester.

My wife isn't able to go out yet but is better. I grieve to think that she will miss the second great show here—the double flowering cherry trees along the river in their perfection now. After conference yesterday, Clarke, Van Devanter and I hookied off to see them, leaving Brandeis who intended to go out canoeing in spite of wind with Mrs. B. on the Pot'omack, as our English friends say. Laski put me up to an edition of Malthus that I wanted and got. He has the eye for a book that my wife has for a flower. It will be part of your duties to give me reasonable information as to books to be read this summer. Please give my love to Luina.

Affectionately yours,
O. W. Holmes

1. During World War I, Wigmore was a colonel on the staff of the Provost Marshal General.

2. John M. Zane (1863–1937), a Chicago lawyer, had criticized Holmes's ideas in "A Legal Heresy," *Illinois Law Review* 13 (1919): 431. See below, February 9, 1922.

3. The case was probably *Fort Smith and Western R.R. Co. v. Mills*, 253 U.S. 206 (1920), which was argued December 13, 1917, and decided June 20, 1920. See below, May 20, 1920.

Cambridge, Massachusetts
May 15, 1920

Dear Justice Holmes,

I miss my guess if Mrs. Holmes doesn't like the enclosed sketch tho' she may find the appreciation of G.B.S. too dithyrambic.[1]

After two weeks trial at Rochester, I realize more than ever how the law fools itself when it's concealing policy behind arid discussion of rights. I hope you will read William Hard's article in *The New Republic* for May 19th and you'll see what I mean.[2]

I found a batch of opinions awaiting but above all your migratory bird opinion.[3] It's one of the finest pearls you've ever cut—I wish I could say in words the exhilaration that opinion gave me. Really it's a thrilling piece.

I'm sorry Pound bothered you about me. There is absolutely no occasion for concern. I'm here as long as I want to stay and whether I have a named or nameless chair doesn't matter. The simple truth is that Nelson Perkins and I live in a different world.[4] He is prudent and "practical"—I must be free or feel free and do my work with a sense of zest. His inclinations are generous and tolerant but he hasn't the guts to act on them. In a word, he is a tribal creature. We all are, of course, but his is the narrow tribe of Beacon Hill and State Street—you know it well. It doesn't bother me in the slightest and my personal relations with Perkins are pleasant enough.

For the rest, I have a fine time with the boys at the Law School and, I'm venturesome to think, they with me. Spring is here at last and the year's work is drawing to a close. We're going abroad for the summer but I do hope we'll have a glimpse of you at Beverly before your next year's work begins. Luina sends her best.

Devotedly,
F.F.

1. The enclosure is missing.

2. William Hard, "The Eyes of the Law on Labor," *New Republic* 22 (1920): 372, criticized the refusal of Rochester trial judge Adolph J. Rodenbeck (1864–1960) to admit sociological evidence: "The Amalgamated is being tried for its life, and, really, its life cannot get into the court room."

3. *Missouri v. Holland*, 252 U.S. 416, 433 (1920), a 7–2 decision upholding the Migratory Bird Treaty Act of 1918 between the United States and Great Britain as a legitimate extension of federal authority over a matter traditionally left to the states: "When we are dealing with words that also are a constituent act, like the Constitution of the United States, we must realize that they have called into life a being the development of which could not have been foreseen completely by the most gifted of its begetters. It was enough for them to realize or to hope that they had created an organism; it has taken a century and has cost their successors much sweat and blood to prove that they created a nation. The case before us must be considered in the light of our whole experience and not merely in that of what was said a hundred years ago." Van Devanter and Pitney dissented without opinion.

4. See above, November 30, 1919, and December 4, 1919. Perkins and the conservative Overseers were pressuring Dean Pound to fire Frankfurter.

Washington, D.C.
May 20, 1920

Dear Frankfurter,

Such a good and cheering letter from you. I *guess* that your feeling and attitude is nearer to things as they are than Pound's who (I hope) is a little over anxious and suspicious. I need not say that I am pleased and elated that you think well of the Migratory Bird case.

I had a letter from Laski this a.m. to which I gave the right of way for an answer as it had some business in it about the prospective book of my essays, etc.[1] I have just finished up my work substantially, subject to possibly being called in to relieve some overburdened one as to which I mean to call on the C.J. this p.m. The only thing I have on hand is a scrap of a case of the kind as to which Devens, when we worked in the same room in Boston, would say, Go forth little tit-man? teat man?, and all the powers of sophistry shall not prevail against thee.[2] In this case, sophistry will not be tempted to try, I expect. But this is strictly private as *non constat* that I am not big with constitutional *pronunciamentos* upon mighty themes.

I tried to enliven my discourse on Monday in another dissent from McReynolds (5 to 4) on Workmen's Compensation in admiralty cases by saying that so far as I know, the fathers of the Constitution approved strong drink (as against the C.J.'s notion that special principles apply in liquor cases).[3] Today, I get an anonymous letter saying that A. Lincoln would have had his Bible and ask in God before he said such a thing, but then A.L. was a great man. What a queer lot the anonymous would be if you could get them in a room—perhaps it would take Boston Common.

I note that I am to read Hard's[?] article when I have finished this. I started a while ago on Harrington's *Oceana*, 1656, but as it has waited 250 years, it can wait a little longer.[4] It is wonderful how hard it is to get two consecutive hours of reading. As I write, boy scouts come in for five dollars and other buzzle flies are around my nose. I hope what you suggest for next summer may come true, but I don't venture to make plans in advance now.

Affectionately yours,
O. W. Holmes

Homage to fair Luina.

1. Holmes, *Collected Legal Papers*.

2. Charles Devens (1820–1891), Associate Justice of the Massachusetts Supreme Court, 1873–77, 1881–91, and Attorney General of the United States, 1877–81. The case may have been *Fort Smith and Western R.R. Co. v. Mills*, 253 U.S. 206, 209 (1920), a unanimous decision upholding a wage agreement negotiated by a receiver at a rate below the minimum stipulated by the Adamson Act (1916): "We must accept the allegations of the bill and assume that the men were not merely negatively refraining from demands under the act but, presumably appreciating the situation, desired to keep on as they were. To break up such a bargain would be at least as unjust and impolitic and not at all within the ends that the Adamson Law had in view." Although concurring, Justices Day, McReynolds, Pitney, and Van Devanter reiterated their minority opinions, expressed in *Wilson v. New*, 243 U.S. 332 (1917), that the Adamson Act violated property rights. See above, March 27, 1917.

3. *Knickerbocker Ice Co. v. Stewart*, 253 U.S. 149, 169 (1920), extended the *Jensen* ruling, 244 U.S. 205 (1917), by holding that Congress's express authorization that state workmen's compensation laws could be applied in maritime cases violated uniform application of federal law. Noting the Court's readiness to defer to state law in prohibition cases involving interstate commerce, Holmes, with Brandeis, Clarke, and Pitney concurring, dissented: "When institutions are established for ends within the power of the States and not for any purpose of affecting the law of the United States, I take it to be an admitted power of Congress to provide that the law of the United States shall conform as nearly as may be to what for the time being exists." See above, January 12, 1917, and March 27, 1917.

4. James Harrington, *The Common-wealth of Oceana* (1656). See above, November 2, 1916.

Washington, D.C.
May 27, 1920

Dear Frankfurter,

Tawney's pamphlet will be posted to you with this in separate envelope.[1] I thank you for sending it and much hope I shall see him. My primary reflection is, as I wrote to Landau this morning, that I deplore exquisiteness, intellect, style and high moral purpose when I see them united![2] But I have no doubt but he gives the existing atmosphere (that books like his help to create) which must be accepted and dealt with as a fact. I will not recur to my old hobbies as I began to in a letter to you that I started last night. It is plain enough that he says nothing and, it seems to me, hardly thinks of some things that I regard as obvious and fundamental. You know well enough what they are. I only will say a word of what I may call capital in gross—the kind Tawney objects to. I wonder if it does not express the subordination of the particular profession to the public interest which may be disagreeable but has to be faced, that capital moving here and there in search of gain, so far as managed by intelligent prophets (and if not intelligent, they will lose it), leaves the profession and goes elsewhere when it sees a greater profit in another place. In other words, adjusts labor to the expected equilibrium of social demands 6 months or a year from now. Well, the pamphlet is a noble little work and I am not sure, if I were God, that I should not promptly exterminate the author—loving him better than most that I allowed to survive. The messenger enters—adieu—my love to you.

Yours ever,
O. W. Holmes

1. R. H. Tawney, *The Acquisitive Society* (New York: Harcourt, Brace, 1920), 180, called for the functional organization of society, to be accomplished by government limiting profits and facilitating the transfer of industry to salaried managers accountable "to the community for whom production is carried on."

2. Lloyd H. Landau (1894–1957), Holmes's Secretary, 1918–19, was an attorney with the New York firm of Root, Clark, Buckner and Ballantine, which became Dewey, Ballantine, Bushby, Palmer and Wood.

Washington, D.C.
May 31, 1920

Dear Frankfurter,

The criticism is a keen one and hits something that I often have noticed—that everyone must have noticed—the opposite of what Bill Hunt (his painter) said to me about old Shaw after he had painted him—that if he were alone with a stable boy, he would find a common human basis on which to talk to him.[1] James confined himself to a world of taste and excluded everything else or pretty nearly did so. He could be human and generous. He was hurt while young trying to stop a runaway horse. His piece about the Belgians coming into Rye was full of real feeling.[2] He was an Irishman, qualified with the observing, critical, slightly adverse eye under the social enthusiasm. But I can't go on. My table is not empty but the fight between Texas and Oklahoma furnishes innumerable pamphlets and now I must off to Arlington and return to work.[3]

Affectionately yours,
O.W.H.

1. William Morris Hunt's (1824–79) portrait of Lemuel Shaw (1781–1861), Chief Justice of the Massachusetts Supreme Court from 1830 to 1860, hangs in the Essex County Court House in Salem.

2. Of the procession of Belgian refugees arriving in the Sussex town in late September, 1914, Henry James wrote. "It was swift and eager, in the autumn darkness and under the flare of a single lamp—with no vociferation and, but for a woman's, scarce a sound save the shuffle of mounting feet and the thick-drawn breath of emotion." Quoted in Leon Edel, *Henry James, The Master: 1910–1916* (Philadelphia: Lippincott, 1972), 514.

3. *Oklahoma v. Texas*, 253 U.S. 465 (1920), a border dispute involving oil and gas wells. As intervenor, the U.S. government administered the property through a receiver. The Court's order unanimously ratified the receiver's report and provided for adjudication of the boundary.

Beverly Farms, Massachusetts
June 22, 1920

Dear Frankfurter,

Your line of *au revoir* came just before we started for Boston (on the 16th) getting here Saturday evening.[1] I don't so much envy you as I should if I were younger and, if so many of my friends in England were not dead or sad, but still I am not free from malevolence at the way you slip into all the sights![2] But I will be magnanimous and wish you a good time. We have had some stormy weather and one isn't in very comfortable condition on leaving Washington in the heat, but the country is adorable. Our rhododendrons were (and are) in bloom. The lilacs had not quite finished blossoming as we came down by automobile and the parched fever of the metrolopus [sic] had disappeared. The process of improving the mind begins slowly, as always. I play a lot of solitaire in the first days. I suppose it is sort of automatic rest. I am, however, reading a book that Laski mentioned,

Cole, *Social Theory* which for the first 80 pages does not seem to get very far from the obvious.[3] I am hoping to disagree with him later.

I see that Harvey pitches into the Court, following what I think the bad example of the Chief Justice and McKenna, for not giving reasons for their conclusions as to the 18th amendment.[4] There were good reasons for not giving them, but personally I think that the validity of the amendment needed none. The attack seems to me like what I said about so called great cases in the *Northern Securities* matter—bringing hydraulic pressure to bear upon first principles to see if they couldn't be made doubtful.[5] There was a lot of money and they took a sporting chance. But of course the decision opens vistas. And, although it seemed to me plain, it appeared that there could be a difference of opinion about the meaning of the "concurrent" power given to Congress and the States. How remote all this twaddle will seem to you when you get this! But one has to write about the material one has. The poor Chief was heroic this term but dreadfully hampered and my last news was that the operation on his eyes must be postponed to the autumn. He seemed very sad as we said goodbye. McKenna was on the train coming up and very pleasant, as usual. Van Devanter also showed a deal of grit. He was suffering badly from lumbago etc., but put through the 18th amendment and the main burden, shared by Pitney, of the private war between Texas, Oklahoma and the U.S.[6] Pitney also looked worn, but it seemed a relief to him to lay his opinions on one side and do this business.

My worst trouble now is that my trunk with my checkbooks and some clothes has not arrived but I hope for it today. And so I finish my futile gossip. I have as near a vacuum ahead as a not very tired judge could wish and when you appear, burgeoning with actualities, I shall hope to counter with some nice point of theory. The only interest of a fact is that it leads to a theory and the only good of a theory is that it sums up facts. So, as with Hegel, they sit in one another's laps in a circle and don't fall. My love to Luina.

Affectionately yours,
O. W. Holmes

1. The letter referred to is missing.

2. Frankfurter was touring Europe for the summer. Three brief postcards from Frankfurter and a note from Holmes have been omitted.

3. G. D. H. Cole, *Social Theory* (London: Methuen, 1920), promoted "guild socialism," or a gradual transition to public ownership of industry by unions and workers cooperatives.

4. "The Passing of State Rights," *Harvey's Weekly* (June 19, 1920): 10. George B. Harvey (1864–1928), editor of the *North American Review*, began *Harvey's* in 1918 to criticize Woodrow Wilson and promote Republican candidates. In 1920 he was instrumental in securing the nomination and Presidency for Warren G. Harding. Justice Van Devanter's majority opinion in *National Prohibition Cases*, 253 U.S. 350, 406 (1920), upheld the Eighteenth Amendment as a legitimate exercise of the Congressional power to amend the Constitution. He fur-

ther ruled that the Volstead Act, which enforced prohibition, did not, as the plaintiff state governments claimed, violate the Constitution by granting states joint powers of enforcement; rather, the legislation granted concurrent power that did no more than supplement federal enforcement power. States were not required to approve the Volstead Act, nor could they pass legislation intended to thwart the law or the Eighteenth Amendment. Chief Justice White and Justice McReynolds wrote separate concurring opinions. Justices Clarke and McKenna dissented separately with McKenna contending sardonically that the Eighteenth Amendment required the passage of enabling legislation by Congress and state legislatures: "The conviction of the evils of intemperance—the eager and ardent sentiment that impelled the Amendment—will impel its execution through Congress and the States."

5. In *Northern Securities Co. v. United States*, 193 U.S. 197, 400–1 (1904), the Court ruled 5–4, on a suit in equity, that the railroad holding company organized by James J. Hill and E. H. Harriman was an unlawful combination within the meaning of the Sherman Anti-Trust Act (1890). Holmes's dissent contended that a criminal charge, for example, conspiracy in restraint of trade, had not been proved and that the Court had responded instead to popular fear of big business, which he described as "some accident of immediate overwhelming interest which appeals to the feeling and distorts the judgment. These immediate interests exercise a kind of hydraulic pressure which makes what previously was clear seem doubtful, and before which even well settled principles of law will bend."

6. See above, May 31, 1920.

Washington, D.C.
October 24, 1920

Dear Frankfurter,

This is only a line of greeting without particular object. I am at the pause between preparation and reciting at tomorrow's conference at 10:45 a.m., hateful hour. Also, I have a little case—whether it will go or not I don't know. As originally written, it had a tiny pair of testicles but the scruples of my brethren have caused their removal and it sings in a very soft voice now, but whether I shall be told to let it be heard remains to be seen.[1] I presume the caution was wise as even Brandeis, who passed the original, told me he had misgivings. I don't see a great deal of him outside the daily meetings but I get great comfort from his intellectual companionship and wise talk.

It has been pretty steady work so far, especially because of the unusual mass of *certioraris* at the beginning of the term. It is thought that many of the bar don't believe that we all give personal attention to everyone. If they heard the talk at conference, they would be convinced that we did. We have had some interesting cases. Those on the Lever Act, as amended, led me to read an excellent, if somewhat verbose, discussion by George H. Earle, Jr. that was distributed by Hughes in connection with his attack. It is called, *Does Price Fixing Destroy Liberty?*[2]

Except that, no books except what my wife reads to me pending solitaire. She read extracts from James Huneker's recollections—one item tickled me.[3] A friend speaking of the performance of a songstress the night before said, it was (ob)*scene* but not heard. I hope things are going well with you. My compliments to Mrs. Luina.

Yours as ever,
O. W. Holmes

1. In *Western Union Telegraph Co. v. Speight*, 254 U.S. 17 (1920), Holmes's unanimous opinion held that the company's policy of sending some intrastate messages in interstate traffic, which had resulted in a suit over a delayed message, did not evade state law. See Howe, ed., *Holmes-Laski Letters*, 287.

2. George H. Earle, *Does Price Fixing Destroy Liberty?* (Philadelphia: n.p., 1920). In *United States v. Cohen Grocery Co.*, 255 U.S. 81 (1921), the Court, in a unanimous opinion written by Chief Justice White, declared unconstitutional a section of the Lever [Food Control] Act of 1917. Former Associate Justice Charles Evans Hughes represented defendants in two related cases, *Tedrow v. Lewis and Son Co., Id.* at 98, and *Kinnane v. Detroit Creamery Co., Id.* at 102. The Court did not deny the government's right to fix prices in wartime but found that the statute set no adequate standards for "unreasonable" prices and hence violated the Fifth and Sixth Amendments.

3. James G. Huneker, *Painted Veils* (New York: Boni and Liveright, 1920).

Washington, D. C.
November 1, 1920

Dear Frankfurter,

A line of thanks for your as usual delightful letter and a protest as to concurrent.[1] Between ourselves—oh no—if I remember rightly, it was expressed in the opinion, I never had a doubt that the word meant simply that both powers should have jurisdiction, as in *Wedding v. Meyler*, that either or both could pass laws in aid of the Constitution, not that both must concur in a specific law. I forget what Clarke said, but it raised no qualms in my mind.[2]

I have a free week ahead with the dentist to mark the point. In 15 minutes I start for him with the promise of other visits to follow. As to books, I feel as if I ought to read some damned thing that you or Laski would recommend but, luckily barring what you mention in your letter, I don't know what it would be. And I may settle down into literature. I have some thoughts on rereading Faust (part 1). I don't have the conveniences at Beverly. Also, I couldn't do better than reread the admirable volume I got from Cohen, Tourtoulon, *Principes Philosophiques de l'Hist. du Droit.*[3] Do you know it? A little too much system but a scepticism that comes home to me. I suppose the omnivorous Pound at least can recite on it. The time approaches I must be off. Homage to Mrs. Luina.

Affectionately yours,
O. W. Holmes

1. The letter referred to is missing. The Court argued extensively over the meaning of "concurrent" powers of enforcement under the Eighteenth Amendment in *National Prohibition Cases*, 253 U.S. 350 (1920).

2. *Wedding v. Meyler*, 192 U.S. 573 (1904), a unanimous opinion, written by Holmes, giving Ohio and Indiana concurrent jurisdiction over the Ohio River. McKenna's dissent in *National Prohibition Cases*, 253 U.S. at 392, cited Holmes and stressed the necessity of Congress and the States passing concurrent prohibition legislation. Clarke's dissent, *Id.* at 408, agreed: "The conclusions of the Court . . . by rendering the Volstead Act of Congress paramount to state laws, necessarily deprive the States of all power to enact legislation in conflict with it, and construe the Amendment precisely as if the word 'concurrent' were not in it."

3. Pierre de Tourtoulon, *Les Principes philosophiques de l'histoire du droit* (Paris: F. Alcan, 1908). Morris R. Cohen wrote the preface for the translation, *Philosophy in the Development of the Law* (New York: Macmillan, 1922).

Cambridge, Massachusetts
November 22, 1920

Dear Justice Holmes,

It's a dreary Monday morning—rain and sleet and snow, the bedraggled vanguard of winter—but lo! great joy fills my room, radiance and valor and wisdom, as I open to find your book and a gift from you.[1] I *am* happy to have it, from you and a most precious collection it is. As I page the book I realize that *most* of it I know by heart and yet, and yet how new and exhilarating it all is, how stirring to mind and what ferment to one's own meager effort. I thank you deeply. I'm not an autograph hunter—I rather priggishly disdain that frailty of men. But in your case, I *do* want it and so I shall send the book for your signature.

Have you seen Pollock's pages on the Abrams case in October *Law Quarterly*?[2] For once I can convey also Luina's devotion.

Felix F.

1. Holmes, *Collected Legal Papers*, had been edited by Harold Laski.

2. Sir Frederick Pollock's note, *Law Quarterly Review* 36 (1920): 333, ridiculed Abrams's belief that the Bolshevik government was a republic, but added, "I am not prepared to regard such belief as in itself a criminal offence, or to abandon the elementary rule of justice that every case must be tried and determined according to what is laid and proved."

Washington, D.C.
December 19, 1920

Dear Frankfurter,

At last there comes a moment in which I can answer your welcome (as ever) letter.[1] It is true, as you surmise, that I have been in a storm of work and a week ago thought that the case I had would take me through the approaching adjournment if not through the summer vacation. But I distributed it on Thursday and seem to have a majority though I know not whether it will go on the morrow. I am in the same condition as to an earlier one, which has elicited a memorandum *contra*, though I believe it still keeps the prevailing number. These two are all I have to date.[2]

As to your recommendation of reading—well possibly, while I play solitaire, my wife may comply but in the little time that I have, I keep pretty close to books bearing on my general drift. I *have* read and with the usual pleasure Santayana's volume, *Character etc. in the U.S.* (a wonderfully keen appreciation of W. James in it).[3] In the main, I have had no time to read anything but records. I have received W. James's *Letters* which stir many old emotions in me, though I haven't read them—only opened here and there.[4] Kimball (my secretary) wants me to reread W.J.'s *Pragmatism* that we may jaw. He has extracted more subtile significances than I remembered. By the by, I find him thoroughly delightful and A 1. He does his work promptly and incisively and his companionship is as pleasant as they make 'em.

I don't know exactly what you had in mind in saying that you should await word from me before naming a lad for next year. Of course, my chances grow more shaky year by year but though warned long ago that old men couldn't trust their judgment, they have to even if that judgment is that they will not trust it. It seems to me that the work comes at least as easy as ever and that I haven't fallen off yet. Therefore, unless something busts or some sudden decline supervenes, I shall keep on and want a secretary. I shall hate to part with Kimball, but I wouldn't advise a young man to stay more than a year even if he wanted to. So have me in mind, and if you can find another as clever, presentable and companionable as D.K., I shall indeed be blessed. My Homage to Luina.

Affectionately yours,
O.W.H.

1. The letter referred to is missing.

2. In *Erie Railroad Co. v. Public Utility Commission*, 254 U.S. 394 (1921), Holmes's majority opinion upheld the right of the state to regulate grade crossings. White, McReynolds, and Van Devanter dissented. In *Southern Pacific Co. v. Berkshire*, *Id.* at 415, he found the railroad without liability in the death of a man who was killed by the arm of a mail bag that

had been installed according to U.S. Post Office regulations. Clarke, Day, and Pitney dissented.

3. George Santayana, *Character and Opinion in the United States* (New York: Scribner's, 1920), 64–96. Santayana wrote: "I think it is important to remember, if we are not to misunderstand William James, that his radical empiricism and pragmatism were in his own mind only methods; his doctrine, if he may be said to have one, was agnosticism and just because he was agnostic (feeling instinctively that beliefs and opinions, if they had any objective beyond themselves, could never be sure they had attained it), he seemed in one sense so favourable to credulity."

4. *The Letters of William James*, 2 vols. (Boston: Atlantic Monthly, 1920). These letters were edited by James's son, Henry James (1879–1947).

Washington, D.C.
December 22, 1920

Private

Dear F.F.,

Your letter came this evening and I must send a line at once, between most of a day spent on an opinion, the greater part of the time being spent in trying to find things in the record, and going out against my will at 8:45 p.m. for a little birthday party.[1] I must, I say, not that your kindness needs instantaneous response. I have come to rely upon it but to reject with horror the notion that charges of the usual kind that the war was Morgan's War or the like can be false statements within the statute.[2] My way of putting it is that they are on their face comments on and inferences from public facts, not professing to embody private information but only judgments such as everyone is put to form. I didn't agree with Brandeis first, that this wasn't a war statute—it was passed and applied in time of war.[3] It was none of the defendant's business whether it would or would not be applied in time of peace, or would or would not be repealed then. The principle of the first case I wrote here, *Otis v. Parker*, applies *me judice*.[4] [Second,] I don't think the principle of taking possession of the subject matter, applied in [interstate commerce] applies or can apply to a matter that the states may deal with by their general powers unless they run across something that necessarily excludes them.[5] Their meddling with I.C. is only permissive. They have the same right to deal with this general subject that they have with murder. I thought there was great force in the argument that the defendants had rights as citizens of the U.S. though I wasn't prepared to dissent on that ground. I disagreed, however, with most that McKenna said, especially, again, that you could stop free speech by a general law because it might be unlawfully interfered with. I think the 14th Amendment was not set up in the record if my memory is right. That is all that I can say off hand, but I had to say so much.

Affectionately yours,
O.W.H.

1. The letter referred to is missing.

2. *Gilbert v. Minnesota*, 254 U.S. 325 (1920), a 7–2 decision upholding a Minnesota law prohibiting teaching or advocacy against wartime conscription. McKenna wrote the opinion, which held that states have an active duty to cooperate with the national government in the prosecution of war on the home front. Holmes concurred only in the result. Brandeis and White dissented.

3. Brandeis's dissent, *Id.* at 334, pointed out that the law was intended to apply in peace as well as war. The grounds of his dissent were threefold: that Congress had preempted the field; that to speak freely on national issues was a privilege of citizenship; and that freedom of speech was a liberty protected by the Fourteenth Amendment. Chief Justice White's dissent argued only that Congress had the exclusive legislative power.

4. In *Otis v. Parker*, 187 U.S. 606, 608 (1903), Holmes's majority opinion held that a California law forbidding margin sales was constitutional and not a deprivation of property under the Fourteenth Amendment: "While the courts must exercise a judgement of their own, it by no means is true that every law is void which may seem to the judges who pass upon it excessive, unsuited to its ostensible end, or based upon conceptions of morality with which they disagree."

5. This issue was discussed in the *Gilbert* case. See U.S. Supreme Court Reports. *Cases and Points* (1920), "Brief of Plaintiff in Error," 20: "The policy underlying the exclusiveness of congressional power arises from the necessity of uniformity. If the states had been left free to enact regulations of interstate commerce, there could have been endless confusion and conflict, a result clearly seen by the framers of the Constitution."

Boston, Massachusetts
January 14, 1921

Dear Justice Holmes,

That's a particularly fine opinion of yours in the Erie Railroad grade-crossings case.[1] Strange how these things need to be said again and again and how you drive them home with ever-fresh pungency and perspective. And even three see not the light!

The Clayton Act case must have seemed a familiar rehash of *Vegelahn v. Guntner* and *Plant v. Woods* issues though here there was a new phase.[2] To be sure, Congress *was* dishonest in the Clayton Act, and both Congress and the Presbyterian Pope (alas! what a feeble Pope he, that dwells in the White House now, is) handed "Labor" a gold-brick. And yet, and yet for the Court to say that all those words mean nothing. It needed no prophet to foretell the result and yet, it *is* a strong dose. I speak, of course, purely *qua* lawyer.

So far as the social consequences go, the decision might well teach Messrs. Gompers et al. a few things!

O how I would like to stretch my legs before your fire and listen to you. I sometimes wonder just how you ever came out of this part of the world. The answer is you came out of it! I wrote this because I had to and now goodnight.

F.F.

1. *Erie Railroad v. Public Utility Commission*, 254 U.S. 394, 410 (1921). Holmes's majority opinion found that state police power was implicitly reserved in the original land grant to the railroad, thus compelling it to obey the agency's orders: "Grade crossings call for a necessary adjustment of two conflicting interests—that of the public using the streets and that of the railroads and the public using them. Generically the streets represent the more important interest of the two."

2. *Duplex Co. v. Deering*, 254 U.S. 443, 488 (1921), a New York case in which Justice Pitney's majority opinion held that the prohibition against labor injunctions in the Clayton Antitrust Act (1914) did not protect unions engaged in a secondary boycott. Brandeis's dissent, joined by Clarke and Holmes, argued that the conflict was "not for judges to determine. . . . This is the function of the legislature which, while limiting individual and group rights of aggression and defense, may substitute processes of justice for the more primitive method of trial by combat." Holmes's Massachusetts Supreme Court dissents, *Vegelahn v. Guntner*, 167 Mass. 92 (1896), and *Plant v. Woods*, 176 Mass. 492 (1900), supported labor's right to pursue its own ends by peaceful picketing even though the results might injure the interests of capital.

Washington, D.C.
January 20, 1921

Dear Frankfurter,

How many times your kind words have given me courage in despondency! I thank you often in my heart. The Clayton Act case was the one though that most stirred me in this batch. I thought Brandeis's opinion admirable and, although I had some misgivings as to what the New York Court would have said, to which if necessary there might have been further answers, I agreed with it joyfully or rather, sadly because of the small adherence it secured. I have been much driven this week and therefore write but this line before going to my evening game of solitaire.

Yours ever,
O. W. Holmes

Cambridge, Massachusetts
January 26, 1921

Dear Justice Holmes,

Morris Cohen constantly tells me that I expect too much from reason. But just because its range is so limited, I want to make it go as far as possible. And so I have been curious to try to pierce below the surface of Pitney's opinion in the Clayton Act case. Why did he decide as he decide—why does he live in a world into which, apparently, your "Privilege, Malice and Intent," with all its implications, has never intruded[?][1] I tried to answer that question and if you glance over an editorial in *The New Republic* for January 26, you will see that what answer I could make you furnished.[2]

And I have been further struck with the want of correlation on the part of judges—as of other mortals—of cases that intrinsically call for a common questioning. Thus, my old discovery McKenna writes about the validity of the forfeiture of an innocent auto for carrying guilty "firewater" and never a glimpse to his dissenting opinion last year, in the Arizona Liability cases, which insisted that "no liability without fault" was an immutable principle handed to Moses at Sinai![3] It ceases to be immutable in a revenue case and if practice is contrariwise! I thought that seldom can the ego show greater self-denial than some of your concurrences without comment. But then, you *do* manage to say your say. And how permanently and vividly you have said it. I was rereading your essays the other day—some of them for the 'steenth time—and it's like the beauty of familiar cliff and waters. Partly, you make one feel "what's the use of my own poor puny effort." But not for long—that's *not* the strongest effect. You delight, deeply, and spur to effort. You little know what it means to have you *there*.

Affectionately,
F.F.

1. Holmes, "Privilege, Malice and Intent," *Harvard Law Review* 8 (1894): 1. See above, April 22, 1920.

2. "The 'Law' and Labor," *New Republic* 25 (1921): 245. Frankfurter contended that the Court had refused to recognize "the matrix of the industrial struggle" but also that organized labor was ill-equipped to influence the passage of protective laws: "The Duplex decision demonstrates anew labor's need for expert assistance. . . . There is a need of a general staff to do continuous thinking for labor, trained writers and speakers to interpret needs and the methods of labor to the general public."

3. In *Goldsmith Grant Co. v. United States*, 254 U.S. 505 (1921), McKenna's majority opinion upheld a law permitting seizure of conveyances used in removing goods with the intent to defraud the government of taxes, notwithstanding the fact that the vehicle's owner "was without notice of the forbidden use." Justice McReynolds dissented without opinion. In *Arizona Employers' Liability Cases*, 250 U.S. 400, 436 (1919), McKenna, joined by White, Van Devanter, and McReynolds, dissented from Justice Pitney's majority opinion, which upheld a state

liability law mandating employer contributions irrespective of fault. McKenna wrote: "It seems to me to be of the very foundation of right—of the essence of liberty as it is of morals—to be free from liability if one is free from fault." Holmes concurred with the majority in both cases but wrote an opinion only in the *Arizona* case, *Id.* at 433: "It is said that the pain cannot be shifted to another. Neither can the loss of a leg. But one can be paid for as well as the other. . . . It is said that liability is unlimited, but this is not true. It is limited to a conscientious valuation of the loss suffered."

Washington, D.C.
January 30, 1921

Dear F.F.,

Of course I liked your article but I am bound to admit that to anyone who allowed his personal preferences to affect his judgment there was strong case for holding the Clayton Act to be a piece of legislative humbug—intended to sound promising and to do nothing. It seems to me, however, that although it was not an unlikely conjecture that that was what was meant, we were bound to assume the contrary and could not assume the contrary without coming to Brandeis's conclusions. But I don't think it a case for treating the majority opinion as bending the obvious to their wishes. I don't mean that you do, but perhaps there is a slight tendency that way. As I believe I said before, if the lawfulness of the effort apart from Statute should be tested by the law of New York, I think it pretty doubtful whether the Court of Appeals would hold this O.K. but I thought Brandeis entitled to take the benefit of the doubt and, if necessary, in view of the wrong (as I think) decision as to the right of U.S. Courts, to decide the common law of a state for themselves. I should, if necessary, interpret the lawfulness referred to as meaning lawfulness as our court might interpret the common law when no statute intervened. I went and go the whole hog with Brandeis but I am not inclined to be severe on the opposite view, even while I think it a public misfortune.

I expect to fire off two little cases tomorrow and to start the February recess with a clean slate except what may be assigned to me Monday or Tuesday.[1] So I have hopes to civilize up a bit, and am open to suggestions about reading although I have some things on my table entitled to the right of way. I hope all is well with you, as I infer.

Affectionately yours,
O. W. Holmes

I have written to Cohen—College of The City of New York. I hope it will reach him expressing my gratification at his notice of my book in the [*New Republic*].[2]

1. *Alaska Fish Co. v. Fish*, 255 U.S. 44, 48 (1921), a unanimous opinion upholding a tax on herring by the Alaskan territorial government: "If Alaska deems it for its welfare to discourage the destruction of herring for manure and to preserve them for food for man or for salmon, and to that end imposes a greater tax upon that part of the plaintiff's industry than upon similar use of other fish or of the offal of salmon, it can hardly be said to be contravening a Constitution that has known protective tariffs for a hundred years." *Stark Bros. Co. v. Stark*, *Id.* at 50, unanimously upheld an appeals decision limiting damages in a trademark infringement suit.

2. *New Republic* 25 (1921): 295. Of *Collected Legal Papers*, Cohen wrote: "It is easier for a professional philosopher to take Justice Holmes at his word and to discuss his book in the pale medium of abstract thought. But the wise reader will turn to the book itself for a concrete realization of the author's contention that to think great thoughts one must have a heroic soul."

Washington, D.C.
February 5, 1921

Dear Frankfurter,

Just a line to say that I meant no more with regard to your critique than that I thought there was perhaps a slight atmosphere of blame.[1] The piece as a whole gave me real pleasure and if it is a harbinger of labor's recognizing that it cannot transcend science and that the expert not only in law but elsewhere cannot be neglected without kicking against the pricks, I rejoice indeed. Probably I have told you with what a shudder I read in *Le Feu* (Barbusse) that the truth is simple which means follow your prejudices and off hand judgments and don't mind what students say.[2] It appeared to me a war cry of Down to Hell and I was the more pained by it that I had seen something similar in some speculative French book—I forget what, now.

I have circulated my only opinion and it is coming back approved. I may get one more after today's conferences but I don't see how I can fail to have some leisure. I have paid my income tax—the exclusion of our salary made an amazing difference.[3] I have had my throat painted with Argyrol and, except possible engagement with the dentist, my ends are all tucked in and I begin to think of culture with no very definite program. I am looking into Leslie Scott's book on *The Case of Requisition—DeKeyser's Royal Hotel Ltd. v. The King* which seems to have established the wholesome doctrine that the king must pay if he takes.[4] It is rather amusing to view the elaborate search for precedents in the ancient records. One likes that British attitude of respect for the past even if one doesn't feel it very strongly. I read N. Matthews' brochure on the Roman Law as to Valuation with the impression, as I wrote to him, that the comments of the writer would be enough to convince me of what I long have believed, that our system of law was far more developed and more profound.[5] I hope that all is going well with you. My love to the Missus.

Affectionately yours,
O. W. Holmes

1. See above, January 26, 1921.

2. Henri Barbusse, *Le Feu* (Paris: E. Flammarion, 1916), published in the United States as *Under Fire: The Story of a Squad* (New York: E. P. Dutton, 1917), a graphic portrait of World War I trench warfare. Barbusse (1874–1935) also wrote *Stalin: A New World Seen Through One Man* (New York: Macmillan, 1935).

3. In *Evans v. Gore*, 253 U.S. 245, 265 (1920), the majority opinion, written by Justice Van Devanter, held that a Federal tax upon the salary of a U.S. District judge violated Article III, Section 1, of the Constitution, which states that judicial compensation should not be diminished during a judge's continuance in office. Holmes, joined by Brandeis, dissented: "I see nothing in the purpose of this clause of the Constitution to indicate that the judges were to be a privileged class, free from bearing their share of the cost of the institutions upon which their well being if not their life depends."

4. Leslie F. Scott and Alfred Hildesley, *The Case of Requisition: In re a Petition of Right of De Keyser's Royal Hotel* (Oxford: Clarendon Press, 1920), a study of a 1919 Appeals Court case in which the government's property taking, citing the Defence of the Realm Act (1914), was denied on the ground that it violated the Magna Carta.

5. Nathan Matthews, "The Valuation of Property in the Roman Law," *Harvard Law Review* 34 (1920–21): 229. Matthews (1854–1927) served as Mayor of Boston, 1891–95.

Washington, D.C.
February 16, 1921

Dear Frankfurter,

Apropos of Curtis, one difficulty has occurred to us.[1] Will he be able to go up and down stairs? My library is up, rather a steep flight, as you know. I hope this may not be a bar but I feared to leave it unmentioned. Your visit was an unmixed delight to us.

Yours,
O. W. Holmes

1. Laurence Curtis (1893–1989), Holmes's secretary, 1921–22, lost a leg in an airplane training accident in World War I. Later he became active in Massachusetts Republican politics and served as state treasurer, 1946–48, and in Congress, 1952–62.

Cambridge, Massachusetts
March 16, 1921

Dear Justice Holmes,

You glowed through your warm words and at this distance we rejoiced all the happy day.[1] You can hardly realize what an exciting day it was for us.

What a "Magisterial" opinion you wrote in the *Milwaukee Leader* case.[2] You said it all in the few, pungent sentences. The more I studied the case—I discussed it with my seminar in Administrative Law—the less I can comprehend the seven. I see "Great Causes" are on.

Always,
F.F.

1. An exchange of letters around Holmes's birthday on March 8 has been omitted.

2. *Milwaukee Publishing Co. v. Burleson*, 255 U.S. 407, 437 (1921). Justice Clarke's 7–2 opinion upheld the Postmaster General's use of the Espionage Act (1917) and other postal laws to revoke the mailing privileges of the *Milwaukee Leader*, a newspaper critical of U.S. war policy. Brandeis and Holmes dissented separately. Holmes wrote: "The United States may give up the Post Office when it sees fit, but while it carries it on the use of the mails is almost as much a part of free speech as the right to use our tongues, and it would take very strong language to convince me that Congress ever intended to give such a practically despotic power to any one man."

Cambridge, Massachusetts
March [?], 1921

Dear Justice Holmes,

I have a letter from Redlich full of *Begeisterung* about his visits with you.[1] His is a fertile mind and a far-flung spirit and you fired him as nothing and no one has done in the country. "The crown of all has been Justice Holmes." Think of the silly hang-over of the war that makes of Redlich still an "alien enemy."

You will agree, I think, that Strachey's opening chapter in the *New Republic* in his *Victoria* was an "elegant commencer."[2] The fellow wields a rapier pen and he has the beguiling atmosphere of innocence.

You were generous to send us such a charming Easter greetings. The ground is breaking even here and the birds are bursting. And soon the summer'll be. I have an ambition to see your old rock at Beverly one of these days with Luina. She had such a treasured visit with Mrs. Holmes during her last trip. She was full of it for days.

Affectionately,
F.F.

1. Josef Redlich (1869–1936), Professor of Public Law at the University of Vienna and, later, at Harvard Law School, was an expert on English government.

2. Lytton Strachey's *Queen Victoria* (London: Chatto and Winders, 1921) was partially serialized in *New Republic* 26, beginning March 30, 1921.

Washington, D.C.
April 16, 1921

Dear Frankfurter,

The distractions of the job have kept me silent too long, though I haven't much to tell. I expect on Monday to fire off an interesting case if not delayed by the dissent and unless I am turned to dissenter by some change that I do not expect.[1] Also, I had a long final call from the delightful Redlich who talked brilliantly. He is flattering but seems to me essentially sincere. It is a joy to meet a man who is on the hair trigger for ideas.

Let me ask two questions. Do you know Ehrlich's address?[2] Have you seen anywhere any notice of me by Hough?[3] Wickersham said the other day that he—I am confident that I get the name right—had written a notice of my book, as I understood it [Wickersham] said, in the *Harvard Law Review* but that must be a mistake.[4] I think so highly of Hough that I should value it if he has said a kind word. I had a letter from Laski which said, what very probably he told you, that on his visit to Lady Astor you seemed to be the only man who had got hooks into her from these parts.[5] I find it easy to believe. I wrote the other day to Harcourt, Brace and Howe for 4 copies of my book and was told that they sold out the first edition and were delayed by a strike at the printing office in getting out a new one. I always have wanted to send a copy to Ehrlich but haven't known how to direct. Redlich said he would find out but that is uncertain. In any event, I must wait till the new edition is out.

Of course, I have no time for reading, but I have read one book that seems to me great, Herman Melville's *Moby Dick*—an account of sperm whaling with a story. I remember him dimly as a neighbor of ours at Pittsfield. A reader might think he got too much pork for a shilling but I would hardly give up a word of it. That cuss took life at first hand and, in spite of my formulas, the book is as living today as in 1851 when it came out. I fancy that that was too much a period of polite conversation for Melville's savage actualities to please as much as they now do me. Your letters of course gave me great pleasure as they always do. This is an inadequate return.

Affectionately yours,
O. W. Holmes

My compliments to Luina.

1. In *Block v. Hirsh*, 256 U.S. 135, 158 (1921), Holmes's 5–4 decision reversed a Court of Appeals decision and grudgingly upheld a congressional rent control law for the District of Columbia: "It is enough that we are not warranted in saying that legislation that has been resorted to for the same purpose all over the world, is futile or has no reasonable relation to the relief sought." McKenna's dissent, *Id.* at 161, employed an argument often used by conservative jurists: "If such exercise of government be legal, what exercise of government is illegal? Houses are a necessary of life, but other things are as necessary. May they too be taken from the direction of their owners and disposed of by government?" See Alexander M. Bickel and Benno C. Schmidt, Jr., *History of the Supreme Court of the United States: The Judiciary and Responsible Government, 1910–21* (New York: Macmillan, 1984), 527–31.

2. On Eugen Ehrlich (1862–1922), Professor of Roman Law at the University of Czernowitz, see above, May 30, 1915, and November 30, 1915.

3. Charles Merrill Hough (1858–1927), judge of the U.S. Circuit Court of Appeals for the Second Circuit, reviewed *Collected Legal Papers* in the *Columbia Law Review* 21 (1921): 296. See below, April 18, 1921, and April 20, 1921.

4. George W. Wickersham (1858–1936), Attorney General of the United States from 1909 to 1913, later headed President Hoover's National Commission on Law Observance and Enforcement (1929).

5. Viscountess Nancy Astor (1879–1964), Virginia-born suffragist and Member of Parliament.

Cambridge, Massachusetts
April 18, 1921

Dear Justice Holmes,

I see by the *Transcript* you wrote the rent law opinion and I'm looking forward to reading it with the most eager relish.[1] And I also see that according to McKenna you struck at "the very root" this time not only of our Constitution, but at "civilization" itself. It was a close shave, wasn't it? All of which makes me wonder more and more about that "due process" clause. Of course, a Court composed of Holmes and Brandeis and Learned Hand and Cardozo makes the question an easy one: the due process clause does serve as an articulate expression of age-old experience. But one has no business to assume in the run of life our Court will have dominantly such a membership and the question then becomes a balancing of gains and costs. And I must say I increasingly have me doots. Not the least of the things that weigh with me is the weakening of the responsibility of our legislators and of our public opinion, or rather, the failure to build up a responsible public opinion. We expect our Courts to do it all.

Ehrlich is somewhere in Switzerland but I'm sure anything sent him c/o Dr. Solomon Frankfurter, University of Vienna, Vienna, Austria will duly reach him (that's an uncle of mine, who is Librarian of the University and knows him).[2] Hough wrote a sprightly piece about you in the March *Co-*

lumbia Law Review. I wrote him (he is an old, kind friend of mine from N.Y. days) that after reading his piece, I could not but recall that his attitude towards you was John Sterling's towards Carlyle, "agreeing in all things except opinion."[3] Hough is a brusque, military, brave soul with drastic limitations but a sturdy honesty and devotion. He replied that he felt better now that he got something off his chest and his "little buzzing" will hardly bother one who "if not the greatest lawyer, certainly the greatest personality in the English speaking law world for a generation."

There is one man I am *most* anxious to have you know as he is most anxious to see you. That's Judge Cardozo of the N.Y. Court of Appeals. I don't know what you think, but he is to me one of the judges I count on the fingers of one hand. And he is an altogether lovely personality—a very reticent and sensitive man who deals sanely and bravely with realities.

I must get hold of Melville's book. Are you reading Strachey's *Queen Victoria*? Isn't his picture of Melbourne and the Queen fascinating? Do you happen to know whether Lord Dannisburgh, in *Diana*, was meant for Melbourne?[4] Also, and quite differently, do you happen to know anything about the new Lord Chief Justice, Sir A. T. Lawrence?[5] His judicial output gives a neutral tint. I wish much for a jaw with you.

Always my fondest,
Affectionately,
F.F.

1. *Boston Evening Transcript*, April 18, 1921. See above, April 16, 1921.
2. Solomon Frankfurter (1856–1941), brother of Felix Frankfurter's father, Leopold, was briefly imprisoned by the Nazis in 1938. He died just before he was to have emigrated to America.
3. John Sterling (1806–44), author and romantic poet.
4. The relationship between Lord Dannisburgh and Diana Warwick in George Meredith's *Diana of the Crossways* (London: Constable, 1909) is generally assumed to be drawn from the liaison of William Lamb, second Viscount Melbourne (1779–1848), who was Prime Minister, 1834 and 1835–41, and the social reformer Caroline Norton, Lady Airlie (1808–77). See James O. Hoge and Clarke Olney, eds., *The Letters of Caroline Norton to Lord Melbourne* (Columbus: Ohio State University Press, 1974).
5. Alfred Tristam Lawrence (1843–1936) served as Lord Chief Justice from 1921 to 1922.

Washington, D.C.
April 20, 1921

Dear Frankfurter,

Many thanks for your letter and the quick reply to my inquiries. Although I do not know as much of Cardozo as you do, all that I have read of his writing leads me to agree with you. You feel the edge of his blade cutting and not merely sliding down the lines of least resistance. He certainly is a razor and not a kitchen knife. I hope that I shall meet him before I die.

Of course, your doubt as to the effect of leaving fundamental responsibilities to this Court in weakening the sense of responsibility in the legislators is classic and serious. The best defence I ever heard came from Brandeis many years ago—that constitutional restrictions enable a man to sleep at night and know that he won't be robbed before morning—which, in days of legislative activity and general scheming, otherwise he scarcely would feel sure about. I am afraid McKenna thinks that security at an end. Have you ever noticed his frequent recurrences to where are you going to draw the line?—a mode of argument that to my mind shows a failure to recognize the fundamental fact that, I think I may say, all questions are ultimately questions of degree. But a Catholic perhaps does not look favorably upon so Darwinian a view. I think he was very much disturbed by the decision. I doubt if the Chief [Edward White] was so much but am not sure. Van Devanter in spots is a very stout conservative and I think McReynolds is generally for holding a pretty tight rein. I was content with my statement and made no changes after receiving the dissent although it criticised the opinion as such, which I think bad form.

I have written a case this week from which I expect McKenna will dissent again, (on wholly different matters) but which I think clear.[1] I will wait, indeed must, about Ehrlich until I can get my book. At present, I have only my own copy. Hough certainly is a personality himself. You always feel a discernible individual at work when he speaks—which is hardly the case with most—with any but a very few.

Curtis called yesterday—the next year Secretary. I speak of next year nowadays with bated breath. My wife and I both liked him at once. The Curtis physiognomy came back as familiar as the lines of a worn shilling. He is all right, and a whiff of old Boston. Time to go to Court. I shut up.

Affectionately yours,
O. W. Holmes

1. *Nickel v. Cole*, 256 U.S. 222 (1921), a 7–1 decision upholding a Nevada transfer tax law against the claim of trustees under a will made after the law was passed but before it became effective. McKenna dissented without opinion while Clarke took no part in the case.

Cambridge, Massachusetts
April 25, 1921

Dear Justice Holmes,

Do let me say what I feel now that I've read your *Block v. Hirsh*—that you never wrote any opinion in the grander manner, with more easy and muscular power. It's *all* there and one (even one who knows your works as sedulously as I do) wonders how you've put it all there in such few strokes. And I suspect if I knew how long or how briefly the actual writing took, I'd be still more dazed. You will forgive me for saying these things, for you will admit I do not often articulate my admiration. I am surprised that you got Pitney to concur. There is, of course, a good deal of the hard reasoning lawyer in him and he couldn't swallow, I suppose, the naive absolutes of McKenna. The latter certainly baffles predictability. For again and again he has written to prove the empirical character of questions under the "due process" and yet here he writes like Cardinal O'Connell talks about "axioms."[1] I give it up but I am glad you persuaded Pitney and Day (who used to see pretty straight in these matters) over the hurdles.

Curtis came back quite happy over his visit. I'm glad Mrs. Holmes and you liked him. He *is* likeable. You won't find him the keen (the narrow) blade that Kimball is but there is more temperament for you.

I have a request, now that you spoke so warmly of Cardozo's work. He is a *very* shy and self-distrustful man, a rarely beautiful character. If opportunity ever offers for you to drop him a line to say that you'll hope he'll call if he ever finds himself in Washington, it would, I'm sure, bring him deep joy. Spring is here and I suppose the Japanese cherries are out. I envy you this sight. Luina sends her devoted greetings.

Affectionately,
F.F.

1. William Henry Cardinal O'Connell (1859–1944), Archbishop of the See of Boston.

Cambridge, Massachusetts
April 26, 1921

Dear Justice Holmes,

The enclosed is from the *London Nation* and it may interest you.[1] One of my closest friends here and colleague, Manley Hudson, is to be in Washington for some international law meetings and he is particularly eager to have talk with you, about nothing in particular, and possibly also see Mrs.

Holmes for he has heard some of the wonders that Luina and I brought back; or, rather, he has felt all the ebullient spirit which our visit gave us.[2]

They were truly wondrous days—those impacts so rare and so abiding. I shall not say more but you gave us preciousness forever. You sent me back with a vivified and re-invigorated sense of the unrelenting struggle that is life, if a fellow puts whatever qualities he has to the test, and a new sense of the romance of it all. I more than ever want to bring out whatever stuff may be in me, as exquisitely and as fine a piece of work as I can chisel and more than ever "selfishness" and "altruism" are silly irrelevances. Yes, "the bird is on the wing!" It was a high joy to see those two dear young people we left at 1720.

Devotedly,
F.F.

1. The clipping is missing.
2. Manley O. Hudson (1886–1960) taught international law at Harvard, 1921–54, and served as a judge on the Permanent Court of International Justice from 1936 to 1946. He edited the *Journal of International Law*, *World Court Reports*, and *International Legislation*, a nine-volume compilation of 670 multilateral treaties signed between 1919 and 1945.

Washington, D.C.
April 30, 1921

Dear Frankfurter,

Once more thanks for your letter of April 25 *apropos* of *Block v. Hirsh* and Cardozo. My only hesitation is about writing to him from the clear sky. The Lord knows that I should be proud to see him in this house if he ever came to Washington. Perhaps I may overcome my doubt.

Your Hudson called this p.m. and we jawed from 3 to 5. I had the usual apprehension afterwards of having talked chestnuts and egotisms—which is another egotism—to bother with misgivings. At all events, I found him a delightful man who seems to live in atmosphere and not to be a bird in a cage. I should think the boys would find him to be another stimulating one. Certainly I did and I wish I could get more of his views. If he comes again, I will undertake to be silent and drink in all that he will tell.

McKenna, as you say, is unpredictable—a few days ago he was saying to me that all in life is a question of circumstances and added, that really was the rationale of your decision in the rent case. He has intimations that perhaps come out oftener in his talk than in his opinions, but he has them. He dissented last Monday in a case of little interest (I know not why) and yet afterward he said that the point of my decision was that it didn't infringe constitutional private rights if the judges of a state court talked like damned fools.[1]

I have another case that I suppose will go on Monday but again of little general interest.[2] Brandeis has a good one that I hope will go.[3]

Affectionately yours,
O. W. Holmes

Compliments to Madame Luina.

1. *Nickel v. Cole*, 256 U.S. 222 (1921). See above, April 20, 1921.

2. *St. Louis–San Francisco R.R. Co. v. Middlekamp*, 256 U.S. 226 (1921), a unanimous decision upholding a Missouri franchise tax on the percentage of the corporation's capital employed in the state.

3. Justice Brandeis did not issue an opinion until June 1, 1921, when he delivered seven.

Cambridge, Massachusetts
May 2, 1921

Dear Justice Holmes,

Of course I did not mean to have you write to Cardozo out of the clear sky. I thought that one of these days when the review of one of his opinions is before you, a handle would be afforded.

Hudson came back all aglow, "lit up" with excitement about his visit to you. He *is* a stimulating fellow to the men—curious-minded and thorough, at once quizzical and venturesome. He is a bit lonely, tho', or rather, needs the infusion that [do] so many men wanting in vital robustness. And he got it from you in rich measure.

I hope your conscience does not coerce you to think you must read Bryce's two new vols. on *Democracies*.[1] They are not so dull as he is—will you forgive this arrogance—but they *are* pretty superficial and unpenetrating. *Per Contra*, Graham Wallas's new vol., *Social Heritage*, at least comes to grips with some real issues of modern society even tho', as the school boys say, "he doesn't get anywhere."[2] But then I'm not as demanding as Laski is that a political thinker should make "plain the pathway from a part to the whole of things, which is the test of the eternal men like Plato and Hobbes and Hegel." *Did* they? Wallas is a little vol. that you may want to read this summer. I'm rejoicing in *Moby Dick*. You discovered him for me. Soon another work year will have been over. My respectful greetings to Mrs. Holmes.

Always faithfully,
F.F.

1. James Bryce, *Modern Democracies*, 2 vols. (New York: Macmillan, 1921).
2. Graham Wallas, *Our Social Heritage* (New Haven: Yale University Press, 1921).

Cambridge, Massachusetts
May 20, 1921

Dear Justice Holmes,

Naturally, I have been thinking of the break for you in an association of nearly twenty years.[1] A strong personality and a most kindly one, as I myself experienced on a few occasions—one always felt in the C.J. how the outsider also feels strongly quiet and thorough gallantry in the C.J.'s going. And I can also realize, a bit, how Lane's going must have moved you.[2] He always was a romantic figure and he gloriously remained so unto the last: warm, driving, accepting curiosity dominated him. To revert to the C.J., it was characteristic that his last opinion—at least the last I have seen—should have been his vigorous nationalist dissent in the Newberry case.[3] I have often thought that the Chief's response to the motion of the bar on Mr. Justice Lamar's death—the comments on a fellow Southerner, with a kindred outlook on life—were rather self-revelatory, as I suppose appraisal of other men's lives is bound to be, unconsciously, autobiographic.[4]

The year is soon over and at last sun and spring are out, here, to stay. We shall be around, Luina and I, through most of [the] time and both of us hope much that some day it may be allowed us to come out to Beverly Farms, just for a few hours at least.

I saw Tom Barbour the other day at an Einstein lecture.[5] I don't undertake to recite on it, but Einstein himself is beautifully clear.

Always devotedly,
Felix Frankfurter

1. Chief Justice Edward D. White died on May 19. Former President William Howard Taft was confirmed as his successor on June 30.

2. Franklin K. Lane (1864–1921) had served on the Interstate Commerce Commission and, from 1913 to 1921, as Secretary of the Interior.

3. In *Newberry v. United States*, 256 U.S. 232 (1921), Justice McReynolds's decision found that the section of the Federal Corrupt Practices Act (1911) limiting campaign contributions was inapplicable to primary elections. The case resulted from the 1918 Michigan primary election for the U.S. Senate in which the automobile tycoon Henry Ford (1863–1947) sought both Republican and Democratic nominations but lost the Republican primary to Truman H. Newberry (1864–1945), a wealthy businessman who had served as Secretary of the Navy under Theodore Roosevelt. In the general election Newberry narrowly defeated Ford, who demanded a recount and a congressional investigation. In November 1919, the Justice Depart-

ment indicted Newberry for campaign spending violations; he was convicted and sentenced to two years in the Leavenworth penitentiary but on the advice of his attorney, Charles Evans Hughes, appealed to the Supreme Court. Following the decision, the Senate voted to seat Newberry but only for the balance of the 1922 congressional session. Faced with the prospect of additional investigation, Newberry resigned his seat. White's dissent, *Id.* at 267–68, asserted Congress's right to legislate, but concurred with the majority that the statute had been misapplied and that Newberry was entitled to a new trial without prejudice: "I find it impossible to say that the admitted power of Congress to control and regulate the election of Senators does not embrace as appropriate to that power, the authority to regulate the primary held under state authority." Holmes, concurring with the majority, wrote no opinion. See Bickel and Schmidt, *The Judiciary and Responsible Government*, 969–82.

4. 241 U.S. xvi (1916). White wrote of Lamar: "Too young to have been a participant in the Civil War, he was yet old enough to have appreciated the anguish of that appalling conflict, the multitude of noble lives on both sides which were forever stilled, the homes made desolate, the fields wasted, and the blight of a destroyed society and of nearly all the prosperity which came, at least, in one section, as a result of that struggle."

5. Albert Einstein (1879–1955) visited the United States in April and May to explain his theory of relativity and to raise money for Hebrew University in Jerusalem.

Washington, D.C.
May 21, 1921

Dear Frankfurter,

The ceremonies are over and I have gone back to plain clothes and circulating a little opinion. I almost wonder that we pay attention to orators. They seem such an old story to me and then with a strong vitality, like the late Chief, one doesn't believe he is dead, for a good while, but expect to see him come round the corner. His death hardly is to be regretted apart from the personal loss because he could not have got much further pleasure out of life—pain and indignities had too strong a hold. Lane I knew familiarly rather than well. I always was told that he was a great figure in the I.C.C. (Brandeis seemed to think not so in the cabinet). Anyone could see his marked ability. I had a charming letter from him not too long before his death but rather rung my heart as I thought he was conscious that the end might be near. In our own case, not withstanding what I said above, one understands what Dr. Henry Bigelow said to me (when as I inferred and in fact he was contemplating it): Death is the biggest thing there is.[1]

I thought of you when I wrote two of the decisions I fired off last Monday.[2] I got so excited in the effort to concentrate that it almost upset me for a little. The one about retreating to the wall, *Brown v. U.S.*, I took from the C.J. and I fear will disgust Beale who wrote a good article on the history but upheld the classic doctrine.[3] The one I have just sent out is a trifle that I took from one of the other [Justices]. I should think it might be the last but I shudder when I think of possibilities.

Of course I look forward to seeing you both but attempt no arrangements as yet. I expect now that feeling of empty anxiety and wonder what duty it is that I have omitted or what frightful mistake committed that marks the cessation of efforts. I have had one or two good talks with Brandeis. They always rejoice me.

Affectionately yours,
O.W.H.

1. Henry J. Bigelow (1818–90), surgeon, pioneer in the use of anaesthesia and author of *Medical Education in America* (Cambridge: Welch, Bigelow, 1871).

2. *Brown v. United States*, 256 U.S. 335, 343 (1921). Brown killed Hermes, who had threatened him on federal property, and was convicted of second degree murder. The Appeals Court upheld the decision but Holmes's majority opinion reversed by holding that a man threatened with "immediate danger of death or grievous bodily harm" could stand his ground and kill his assailant without being guilty of murder. Clarke and Pitney dissented without opinion. *American Bank and Trust Co. v. Federal Reserve Bank, Id.* at 350, 359, unanimously rejected an attempt by the Federal Reserve to force several country banks to join the Federal system by demanding over-the-counter payments for checks: "The policy of the Federal Reserve Banks is governed by the policy of the United States with regard to them and to these relatively feeble competitors. We do not need aid from the debates upon the statute under which the Reserve Banks exist to assume that the United States did not intend by that statute to sanction this sort of warfare upon legitimate creations of the States."

3. Joseph Henry Beale, Jr. (1861–1943), was Professor of Law at Harvard. His article, "Retreat from a Murderous Assault," *Harvard Law Review* 16 (1903): 567, concluded: "The interests of the state alone are to be regarded in justifying crime; and those interests require that one man should live rather than that another should stand his ground in a private conflict."

Cambridge, Massachusetts
May 25, 1921

Dear Justice Holmes,

I'm all excited by your two "little" cases, *Brown v. U.S.* and the *Federal Reserve* case.[1] "Superb" was Pound's exclamation as I read parts to him. Of course it's all in your "Path of the Law" (an endless storehouse for me) but the beauty of the new applications and the incisively new formulation—"Ossify into rules"—how much of obstructive law that sweeps away![2] And the Reserve Bank case gives guidance to the dynamic growth, the conflict of social policies we call "torts." Thank you.

Always devotedly,
F.F.

1. See above, May 21, 1921.
2. In "The Path of the Law," *Harvard Law Review* 10 (1897): 457, Holmes argued, contrary to the traditional interpretation including his own in *The Common Law*, that in the modern age the law dealt with torts apart from duties or customs to be followed irrespective of context. Applying this view in *Brown v. U.S.*, 256 U.S. at 343, Holmes referred to the effect of early legal decisions mandating retreat from murderous assault: "Concrete cases or illustrations stated in the early law in conditions very different from the present . . . have had a tendency to ossify into specific rules without much regard for reason. . . . Rationally the failure to retreat is a circumstance to be considered with all the others in order to determine whether the defendant went further than he was justified in doing; not a categorical proof of guilt."

Hadlyme, Connecticut
July 24, 1921

Dear Justice Holmes,

The enclosed *causerie* on Melville will interest you.[1] There is considerable ferment, both here and abroad, about him; what do you suppose accounts for this revival of interest? And that makes me ask you to what you attribute the growing new interest in philosophy? Of course, the everlasting enigmas remain both enigmas and everlasting. But I do think there is absorption in ultimate speculations. The curiosities Einstein aroused are partly due to the mystifications he provoked. But beyond that, don't you agree there is much more philosophic speculation than there was, say, in the decade following the great scientific era, following Darwin et al? Partly, I'm led to think, the disillusionments about mere "science" following the Great War, partly the stimulation towards mystical (and misty) brooding following wide-spread experience with the puzzles of life may account for what, in my ignorance, I take for a new outpour of philosophizing. How, by the way, did Haldane pan out . . . ?[2]

I'm also sending you a small paper by Prof. Tufts (please return it at your *entire* leisure) which shows anew how "mistrust" in dealing with concrete problems gropes towards what conscious reason fashions.[3] I suspect you will have many an illustration of the clash between conscious exploring to determine "policy" and unconscious, uncritical inclination during the regime of Taft C.J. I just wonder—apart from all else—how he will acquire necessary new habits of hard, sedentary work, to which he has been a stranger for many years. All of which makes me more than ever grateful that we have you to give the pace no matter who is C.J. I think I told you that even you seldom gave me such thrills as towards the end of last term in the case of "retreating to the wall" showing how mere history must not forever be encysted into law, and, in the succession tax case (what is "direct" taxation), giving a rapier thrust to sterile "logic" divorced from history![4]

We are here on the Connecticut, not having the grandeur and chorus of your ocean and countryside, yet with a very lovely view of the Connecticut River and cozy hills. Luina and I send our fondest.

Faithfully yours,
F.F.

1. The enclosure is missing.

2. Richard Burdon Viscount Haldane, *The Reign of Relativity* (New Haven: Yale University Press, 1921), a popular explanation of Einstein's work.

3. James H. Tufts, "The Legal and Social Philosophy of Mr. Justice Holmes," *American Bar Association Journal* 7 (1921): 359, an appreciative review of *Collected Legal Papers* that linked Holmes's ideas to the philosophy of pragmatism espoused by William James.

4. In *New York Trust v. Eisner*, 256 U.S. 345, 349 (1921), Holmes's unanimous opinion upheld a federal estate tax by noting that such levies were traditionally regarded as indirect taxes and thus were not unconstitutional or unapportioned direct taxes: "A page of history is worth a volume of logic."

Beverly Farms, Massachusetts
July 25; 1921

Dear Frankfurter,

Many thanks for Tufts' interesting pamphlet and more for the letter that tells me where you are. I had been hoping to hear from you. You raise interesting questions. As to Melville, I wrote to the Cambridge bookbinder that I had no recollections beyond a shadowy figure. With regard to philosophy, I didn't know that anything was happening but if it is, I should suppose the fundamental explanation to be the increasing realization that Darwin had not exhausted the question of variations and that, as was pointed out long ago, the physicists before they know it are talking metaphysics. Hence, Bergson on the one side and Haldane, via Einstein and Hegel, on the other. Haldane's book led me to read the most diabolical work in existence, Hegel's *Logic*, translated by Wallace.[1] There is so much of what seems to me charlatan word juggling to effect the transition from the timeless processes of logic to the movement of the world and life in time, and so to create the universe out of nothing. No go *me judice*. But he had a good deal of the future in his head and profound insights. I doubtfully believe him great. Shaw's *Back to Methuselah*, which I think a failure, shows the tendency you observe but riles me by bringing literary gifts to aid a dogmatic attitude to which, so far as I can see, he is not entitled.[2] I saw the same disgusting thing in a quotation from Ruskin in a good book, Greeks and Barbarians, that I am reading. He says—and affirms his statement to be deliberate—that the condition of Adam Smith's mind was damned.[3] I think he had better have kept a civil tongue to better men than himself.

Just now I am finishing two vols. on *The Medieval Mind* (H. O. Taylor) which I think in every way delightful and admirable.[4] When I finish it I think I may take up Homer again. Greeks and Barbarians made me realize that I had not read what I have in former years maybe fully enough. Hitherto, I have got more of the palish pleasure of the classics from the tragedians. Last summer I reread *Prometheus Bound* with great gusto. Taylor makes me want to read some of the medieval men, but I expect that I shall restrain such peccant humors. In short, I soon shall be a field fallow for planting and trust to the birds for seed. I have no prophecies but await events as to the new C.J. His experience ought to be valuable. Love to you both.

Affectionately yours,
O. W. Holmes

I don't know whether, as I hope, you burn my letters. I hate the notion of anything concerning me becoming public except what I write for publication.

H.

1. William Wallace, transl., *The Logic of Hegel* (Oxford: Clarendon Press, 1892).
2. George Bernard Shaw, *Back to Methuselah* (London: Constable, 1921).
3. Most of Ruskin's references to Adam Smith appear in *Fors Clavigera: Letters to the Workmen and Labourers of Great Britain (1871–1884)*. The following passage, written in 1876, is representative: "You are living in the midst of the most perfectly miscreant crowd that ever blasphemed creation. Not with the old snap-finger blasphemy of the wantonly profane, but the deliberate blasphemy of Adam Smith: 'Thou shalt hate the Lord thy God, damn His laws, and covet thy neighbour's goods.'" See, E. T. Cook and Alexander Wedderburn, eds., *The Works of John Ruskin*, vol. 28 (London: George Allen, 1907), 764.
4. Henry Osborn Taylor, *The Medieval Mind*, 2 vols. (London: Macmillan, 1911).

Beverly Farms, Massachusetts
August 9, 1921

Dear Frankfurter,

Why is it that people in writing what presumably is an address make it absolutely illegible? It is a common trick, but I was about to say that I would follow the print and send to Cambridge, when previous knowledge and a magnifying glass convinced me that what looked like Hademelon must still mean Hadlyme, Conn.

What you say of and from Croly is very cheering but I am remote from the world and have been continuing the philosophical debauch of which I think I mentioned the earlier stages.[1] I have been reading Aristotle's *Metaphysics* (in a translation). It is wonderful—one does not realize it—how, a good deal even to this day, he has made the world think in his terms. The book is a queer mixture of profound insight and laborious discussions of sophisms not worth following, to which the short answer is pooh! One is led to believe that he a good deal shaped the Christian conception of good and that he is the remote cause of Hegel's chip-chop about Being—I think I have told you before of my surprise at discovering that he, not John Adams or Quesnay, was the originator of "government of laws and not of men." I am thinking of sending for Plato's *Timaeus* and, with or without that, adieu to those themes. It bores me to extinction to read books that interest only from their place in the history of thought, whereas Laski would gollup them down with gusto. Possibly, I may take a short turn at Homer—*not* in a translation—but that also is a mitigated joy. I am trying to improve my mind and civilize up so as to be able to meet the new and the old in October. These are the "short and simple scandals of the poor."[2]

Affectionately yours,
O.W.H.

1. The letter referred to is missing.
2. Finley Peter Dunne, *Mr. Dooley's Opinions* (New York: R. H. Russell, 1901), 122: "No wan cares to hear what Hogan calls: 'th' short an' simple scandals iv th' poor.'"

Beverly Farms, Massachusetts
August 19, 1921

Dear Frankfurter,

Many thanks for the passage and indeed the whole notice of Croce whose *Aesthetic* I read in the English translation years ago—a big chap.[1] But by the blessing of the Lord, I am through with philosophy for the moment, having wound up after Aristotle's *Metaphysics* with Plato's *Timaeus* including a really remarkable introduction by the English editor and translator.[2] It is eminently a case where you have to make an effort and seek instruction if you want to follow Croce's directions and reproduce even faintly Plato's real thought. I did it very imperfectly but I got my money's worth. If you take him externally, as Aristotle seems to have done more or less, construct the universe out of God, chaos and triangles, it seems a waste of time.

Now I am relaxing into amusement. I am finishing *The Story of a Style* by

W. Bayard Hale—*apropos* of Wilson—a lot of just criticism that was the cause of my reading the book, in aid of my previous belief on the ground of reading a few fragments that Wilson was far from the admirable writer that he had been called.[3] But Hale seems not to be the calm critic but to hate the man and to be out for blood, without much regard to justice. Enough remains, however, to gratify the malevolent impulses. Then I have a book I bought in town the day before yesterday: Van Gennep, *La Formation des Legendes*—which seems entertaining; Laski's new book—essays most of which I have read I imagine, but just arrived and not yet examined; and a life of Adam Smith by Haldane left here by Beveridge to prove that Haldane had written the book which I doubted.[4] So I have food for two or three days ahead. We read *The Rescue* last summer.[5] It has the gifts you mention, but my recollection is that, all said and done, I didn't care much for either heroine or hero. I think Beveridge did a pretty big thing in his *Life of Marshall* although Marshall's gifts are not those that most move me. I think I should stand by what I said from the bench in Massachusetts a good many years ago.[6]

Why wasn't the English offer all that the Irish reasonably could ask?[7]

Yours ever,
O. W. Holmes

1. See above, April 29, 1916.

2. Cambridge scholar Richard Dacre Archer-Hind (1849–1910), *Translations into Greek Verse and Prose* (Cambridge: University Press, 1905).

3. William Bayard Hale, *The Story of a Style* (New York: B. W. Huebsch, 1921). Hale (1869–1924), an Indiana born clergyman and journalist, wrote a campaign biography of Woodrow Wilson and enjoyed great success as a wartime correspondent for the *New York World* and the *New York Times*. His intrigues on behalf of the Kaiser, however, led to disgrace. He died in Munich.

4. Arnold Van Gennep, *La Formation des legendes* (Paris: E. Flammarion, 1910); Harold D. Laski, *The Foundations of Sovereignty* (New York: Harcourt, Brace, 1921); Richard Burdon Viscount Haldane, *Life of Adam Smith* (London: W. Scott, 1887).

5. Joseph Conrad, *The Rescue* (Garden City, N.Y.: Doubleday, Page, 1920).

6. Responding to a motion of the Massachusetts Supreme Judicial Court to adjourn in honor of the centenary of John Marshall's assumption of the Chief Justiceship, Holmes questioned whether Marshall was an "originator of transforming thought," but added that "his might, his justice and his wisdom" made him the representative figure of American law. See *Collected Legal Papers*, 266–71.

7. By 1921 British efforts to defeat Irish Republican forces (Sinn Fein) had foundered. Negotiations produced the Anglo-Irish agreement (December 6, 1921), which accorded dominion status to the twenty-six counties of the Irish Free State and left the six counties of Ulster under British rule.

Beverly Farms, Massachusetts
August 30, 1921

Dear Frankfurter,

Many thanks for your letter and enclosures.[1] I had not seen the notice by Tufts and should like to know when you next write what the publication is in which it appears.[2] I can't quite make it out. I have seen several notices since I have been here—a superlative one in the *Illinois Law Review*, signed A.K., I suppose Kocourek—also equally amiable in the *Iowa Law Bulletin and Weekly Review*.[3] Of course, there were a lot before I left Washington. My wife says, "Ask him to send one every other day." But I have been much surprised and a little worried by the outpouring. Pride goeth before a fall and whenever anything sets me up, I expect very shortly to get taken down. I was impressed too yesterday by what Beveridge told me about a crack Japanese who had been ambassador everywhere . . . resigning at 60 "to meditate." I don't yield to the impression, because if meditating means thinking about the meaning of life, I don't think I should add much to what I think now and if it means simply a quasi-hypnotized contemplation, that is not my temperament and it seems to me better to produce all that one can until warned of waning powers. But I tremble.

For a few days past I have been idle and, as I said to my wife, drumming on a bubble of emptiness. After finishing with Plato's *Timaeus*, I left philosophy. I am through Laski's book except one or two that I had read before—one by my friend Einstein, not the mathematician, on *Tudor Ideals* and some legal stuff and now am thinking of Homer—interrupted by a bothery bit of business that will call me to town.[4] Laski's first essay, which I suppose is new, struck me as masterly.[5] I was worried by a request to review it from the [New York] *Evening Post*. The letter spoke of the notices of L.'s books as unsatisfactory. I had supposed that they had been much praised. So I was distracted between the duties of affection and the consciousness that I didn't understand what practical changes Laski desired well enough to write without study coupled with the need and desire for leisure. I declined because I couldn't believe that Laski needed any boost from me to be appreciated by those that count. A man who doesn't read the newspapers doesn't know the signs of the times, and perhaps I am not entitled to be sceptical as to the great changes L. anticipates. My instinctive expectation is: fundamental talk—some readjustments of detail and then much as before. What the Hell is the use of being 80 if one can't be an old fogey?

I quite agree with you as to Pound's piece—admirable and flabbergasting for its learning.[6] My future Secretary had an article, stimulated by you, in the same number, and sent it to me.[7] As to due process of law, I never supposed that I had any particular influence on the Court or that any change was likely with the present membership. I should think you let yourself in for a dull job.[8] My homage to Luina.

Affectionately yours,
O. W. Holmes

1. The letter referred to is missing.
2. See above, July 24, 1921.
3. Two reviews of *Collected Legal Papers* by Albert Kocourek in *Illinois Law Review* 16 (1921): 1156 and Edwin W. Patterson in *Iowa Law Bulletin* 6 (1921): 250. See below, September 1, 1921.
4. Lewis David Einstein, *Tudor Ideals* (New York: Harcourt, Brace, 1921). Einstein (1877–1967), a scholar and diplomat who served as U.S. Minister to Czechoslovakia from 1921 to 1930, had an extensive correspondence with Holmes. See Peabody, ed., *Holmes-Einstein Letters*.
5. "The Foundations of Sovereignty," in *The Foundations of Sovereignty and Other Essays*, 1–29.
6. Roscoe Pound, "The Maxims of Equity," *Harvard Law Review* 34 (1921): 809.
7. Laurence Curtis, "Judicial Review of Commission," *Id.* at 862.
8. Frankfurter was beginning to write "Twenty Years of Mr. Justice Holmes' Constitutional Opinions," *Harvard Law Review* 36 (1923): 909.

Hadlyme, Connecticut
September 1, 1921

Dear Justice Holmes,

Tufts' review appeared in the *Journal of the American Bar Association* (the official organ of that body). I'm glad you noticed the review in the *Iowa Law Review*. It was written by a pet pupil of mine, E. W. Patterson, who is now a professor out here.[1] And did you see the review by Prof. Philbrick of Northwestern (I think) in *The Freeman*?[2] It was one of the most understanding that I have seen.

When I read Luina your expression of concern over the "outpouring" evoked by the essays, says she, in her innocence, "Why doesn't he realize what he is and what he means to men." Whereupon, I tried to explain to her how thorogoing your scepticism and how deep your humility.

As to Laski's latest, you are right not to worry. Of course, to us, there is nothing more stirring than your "well done." I know what it means to Laski. But certainly he would dread to think you felt any drive to review and you touch the root of the matter when you say he need fear no want of appreciation from those that count. I don't know whether I told you that Croly reports Laski as the happiest man he met in London—he is in the environment that he loves and engaged in all the activities that so rejoice him.

I should think a good many who haven't your sprightly excuse of years have become increasingly sceptical of vast changes coming suddenly, or even very quickly to pass. For myself, I have never been less allured by the magic of phrases or formulas or dogma (whether Marxian or Mallockian) answering to the intractable complexities of the world.[3] I think, tho', there is some deep monistic craving that leads men to find the key to existence in one patent Yale lock be it "socialism" or Hoover's "individualism" (the latter has been just as dogmatic that the economics he was brought up on is *the* thing, as Lenin is—or was!—dogmatic, it's the damnation of all things). That's why it doesn't seem sufficient, for instance, for some people to see great possibilities in the cooperative movement—they must at once fly to the absurdity that the cooperative movement will render "needless the State" (whatever that may mean). For myself, I see social-economic development along many roads—some industries (like railroads) state-owned, some cooperatively conducted, some regulated, some left wholly to free adventure and uncurbed enterprise. Which is what, to my thinking, is a purely practical problem, depending on time, place and circumstances. But I find that kind of outlook doesn't please either my "radical" friends, nor my conservative ones—man wants dogma! I have some things to say of Ireland but "continued in our next."

F.F.

1. A review of *Collected Legal Papers* by Edwin W. Patterson (1889–1965), Professor of Law at Columbia, 1922–57, in *Iowa Law Bulletin* 6 (1921): 250: "Here lie the typical expressions of his manifold personality: his scholarship, his shrewd common sense, his graceful yet vigorous style."

2. Francis S. Philbrick, "A Genial Sceptic," *The Freeman* (June 29, 1921): 378. Philbrick acknowledged Holmes's impact on constitutional law but criticized his social philosophy: "He is a reformist by conviction and intent, but by the constraint of other convictions and of qualities of temperament he is an inertionist. His economic opinions fall short of even moderate liberalism."

3. English social philosopher William Hurrell Mallock (1849–1923). Mallock's autobiography, *Memoirs of Life and Literature* (London: Chapman and Hall, 1920), and other writings, most notably *Social Equality* (London: R. Bentley, 1882), opposed all theories favoring a wider distribution of wealth.

Beverly Farms, Massachusetts
September 3, 1921

Dear Frankfurter,

A most kind and delightful letter from you. I think we are in substantial agreement as to the general outlook. Of course, such views don't please either extreme. If a memory from boyhood is correct, Macaulay in his *History* has some sensible remarks about those who were called Trimmers and probably I have told you how after *Vegelahn v. Guntner* a labor man came up to me expansive and I said, you wait—you'll hate me like Hell the next time, of which I had some slight verification when I dissented in the *Northern Securities* Case.[1] Walter The Tinman—a Bill Hunt in hardware—said to my wife: when a man goes to Washington there are influences.

I have made a discovery or rather, verified what I knew long ago. There are little corners of ignorance that bother one for years. Two hours attention clears them up and gives one a stupidly postponed peace. This applies especially to the classics. Sallust always has been merely a name to me. I found a translation among my books and although translations are no good for poets and a poor substitute always, yet for a second class person they do well enough. I read his account of Catiline in an hour or two and the mystery is gone. If I had the Latin, I would verify the bright spots, but that is a secondary matter. I may remark incidentally that he made me wonder whether Catiline represented an abortive popular movement against the plutocrats of the time. Our knowledge comes from Cicero who was the opposing power and Sallust who was on the same side. Sallust says that Catiline got all the criminals of the world together but one can't but notice that he also says that not a follower of Catiline's would yield to offers of pardon and reward, and peach, and ultimately they all died in their tracks. I guess if we could have all the facts, the case would seem mixed and very probably, taking the difference between their thinking and ours, we shouldn't care very much for either.

Apart from the usual making out of checks at the beginning of the month, and some little trust business that I have handed over to others so far as possible, I still am idle—fooling around with *belles lettres* scraplets. On the 6th an Englishwoman, introduced by Laski, comes to luncheon, 13th–15th the Bryces, 28th start for Washington. It seems as if the vacation began and ended today. My homage to Luina—would that I could believe her words.

Yours as ever,
O.W.H.

I reopen my letter to say a word on Philbrick's notice which I received a few days ago. He says, "whatever that may mean" when I say that I don't think you can do much by tinkering with property without taking in hand life. I meant what I suppose he would think horrible—restricting propagation by the undesirables and putting to death infants that didn't pass the examination, etc. etc. I don't know enough to say that I want it but I think it the condition of intelligent socialism. Also, he thinks I consider only whether men eat. I think that unintelligent criticism. If statistics showed that the amounts withdrawn for the luxuries of the few w[ere] insignificant and that the crowd now had all there was, I should think it followed that the crowd had all the possibilities of leisure and all the rest that there were. If those possibilities should be distributed differently, it seems to me that the only way to do it is to produce a change of social desires, so that less of certain products and more of certain others will be called for, etc. etc. I won't go on but I suspect that Mr. Philbrick believes in some ism, I don't know exactly what, and speaks from the tacit assumptions that I shouldn't believe. I do assume that he shows himself a superior man by what he writes.

H.

1. See above, June 22, 1920, and January 14, 1921.

Beverly Farms, Massachusetts
September 9, 1921

Dear Frankfurter,

The 21st will be too late to see you here as we expect to go to Boston on the 24th but probably we can ask you to dine with us at the Touraine. Let us postpone this date until a little later. I write the moment I read your letter to say at once that I hope you will use all your influence against the notion of increasing our number, which is, in my opinion, the worst of mistakes.[1] It would not help us in any way. We dispose of all the cases that are argued except in instances of differences of opinion or where the Justice to whom the case is assigned makes a delay of a sort that numbers will not help. The trouble is not with disposing of the cases but with getting them before us. No more cases would be argued before 10 or 11 JJ. than are before 9. I am not the man to give advice as to cutting down the jurisdiction, but several of the others could. I have no doubt that some further limitation could be made. I think that it was a great improvement to cut down the D.C. to substitute applications for *certiorari* for a writ of error as of course in certain state cases and to send Porto Rico to the First Circuit.[2] I cannot put too strongly my conviction that the increase of number would be a fatal mistake and I am so near the end of my work that I believe my judgment is free from personal bias if that should be suspected. I know that the late Chief held the same opinion, and I should be surprised if all the justices did not agree. The suggestion has been defeated heretofore.

As to Ireland, no doubt there have been plenty of wrongs in the past but I don't see how England could let her become an independent country.

I forgot until I had closed my last letter to ask who Professor Philbrick is.[3] I suppose I should blush not to know. I am so anxious that the Bar Association should not take what I think not only a mistaken step but one that would threaten the very life of the Court that I send this off bang! without further delay. I have got a book or two suggested by Laski to fill my last moments here.

Affectionately yours,
O. W. Holmes

1. The letter referred to is missing. Representative Charles H. Brand (D-Ga.) had introduced a bill to authorize the President to appoint additional Judges to the Supreme Court. It never came to a vote. See *Congressional Record* (April 14, 1921), Vol. 61, part 1, 290.

2. An article by Chief Justice Taft, "Adequate Machinery for Judicial Business," *American Bar Association Journal* (1921): 453, outlined these changes and urged expansion of district court judgeships.

3. Francis S. Philbrick (1876–1970?) taught law at the University of Illinois and the University of Pennsylvania. He also edited the laws of Illinois and Indiana and was the author of *The Rise of the West, 1754–1830* (New York: Harper, 1965).

Washington, D.C.
November 6, 1921

Dear Frankfurter,

Hand's review in the *Quarterly* that you sent to my wife naturally gratified and also touched me.[1] I was feeling a little down and it set me up. I return it in separate parcel herewith.

I fire off two cases tomorrow—nothing very much—but one of them drove me into temporary madness from the want of adequate references to the documents etc. involved.[2] I have recovered. I think that I shall not march in the procession this week, out of deference to the reputed dangers of exposure to the old, although I feel as if I were shirking. I think the Chief is taking hold well. All good messages to your Missus.

Affectionately yours,
O. W. Holmes

I have been thinking how a slight change of focus upsets all our values. It was suggested by a passage in *Alice in Wonderland*. How conceivable it is that in 50 years what we all quote and chuckle over will seem perfectly flat—and so of more serious matters.

1. Learned Hand's review of *Collected Legal Papers* in *Political Science Quarterly* 36 (1921): 528, remarked: "They say the soul of Rabelais roams the earth gathering spirits for the Abbey

of Theleme, those who are gay, nimble, courteous, feat, witty, amorous, simple, courtly, kind, pleasing, happy, genial, wise, humble, tolerant, joyous. Now the initiated tell us that among these there is none he has more certainly chosen than the captain of Antietam, young then and young now."

2. *Marine Railroad and Coal Co. v. United States*, 257 U.S. 47 (1921), unanimously rejected the railroad's claim and occupation of government land along the Potomac notwithstanding the adverse effect of a government landfill. *Springfield Gas and Electric Co. v. Springfield*, *Id.* at 66, 70, unanimously upheld the Illinois Public Utilities Act (1913), which allowed municipally owned electric plants to sell electricity to private customers while subjecting competing private corporations to regulation of their rates by public commission: "The conduct of which the plaintiff complains is not extortion but, on the contrary, charging rates that draw the plaintiff's customers away."

Cambridge, Massachusetts
November 22, 1921

Dear Justice Holmes,

I cannot begin to tell you how much your opinion in *Springfield Gas Co. v. Springfield* pleases me.[1] It deals a body blow to that obscurantist ghost of a distinction between "the private and public" capacities of municipalities. I happen to teach the law of municipal corporations and nothing wearies my soul more than to have cases go off on those phrases about "private" vs. "public" functions. For instance in *Heim v. McCall*, McKenna points out that "counsel have not given us a sure test of when action by a city is governmental and when proprietary"; and yet, in *Los Angeles v. Los Angeles Gas Corp.* the distinction is taken as settled and made for the decision in the case.[2]

And so I throw my hat up at your latest and not the least because you abstain from all citations, and decide in a straightforward way. It's like coming into sunshine and fresh air again.

Always devotedly,
F.F.

1. See above, November 6, 1921

2. *Heim v. McCall*, 239 U.S. 175 (1915); *Los Angeles v. Los Angeles Gas Corp.*, 251 U.S. 32, 40 (1919). Both of these McKenna opinions were unanimous. Holmes concurred without opinion. *Heim* upheld a New York labor law enabling the state to specify American citizenship and state residency as preferential qualifications for employment on public works projects. The *Los Angeles* case used the Fourteenth Amendment to restrict the city's taking of municipally chartered lighting systems in order to extend its own: "What the grant was at its inception, it remained and was not subject to be displaced by some other system, even that of the city, without compensation to the corporation for the rights appropriated."

Washington, D.C.
November 26, 1921

Good old Frankfurter, you fortify my ancient doubts. I wrote a dissent in *Mount Hope Cemetery v. Boston*, decided not to deliver it and repented my decision in later years.[1] I don't now as the dissent would have been inadequate but my doubts have remained, with the consciousness that I haven't studied the question to the bottom.

I was on the verge of writing to you. Christie gave me the impression that someone or ones were trying to make out that you caused our government to induce the Canadian Government to release Trotsky when they had him by the leg.[2] Whether foresight of the part he was to play is imputed to you, I don't know. Is there anything in it or has it blown over? And why do people want to bother you in the first place? Tell me for I do not quite understand. I do not take it that you have a burning faith in any ism. Is it the mere fact that you regard all hypotheses as possible or rather don't regard the postulates of the status quo as entitled to pass unquestioned or have you been getting in with some crowd that even I should not sympathize with or has nothing particular happened?

Also—this is a distinct and unconnected matter—I forget what I have written to you about my letters, but if you have not burned them, I should feel easier if you would assure me that none of them should be published after my death. I print what I want printed and write to you with a feeling of absolute freedom which could not be if there were such a possibility. Also, I am not proud of my epistolary performances. They often come from a languid pen and are written, so to speak, in dressing gown and slippers.

Yours as ever,
O.W.H.

1. *Mount Hope Cemetery v. Boston*, 158 Mass. 509 (1893), a unanimous decision written by Justice Charles Allen (1827–1913), held that the Massachusetts legislature could not transfer a municipally owned cemetery to the newly created Mount Hope corporation without compensation to the city, since the municipality held the property in a proprietary, not a governmental capacity.

2. In April 1917 Leon Trotsky and his family, returning to Russia from exile in America, were detained in a Nova Scotian camp for German POWs. Under pressure from the Petrograd Soviet, the Russian Provisional Government protested and, after a month's delay, the Canadian government allowed him to proceed. Frankfurter was undoubtedly aware of this incident but there is no evidence of his direct involvement. See Frederick C. Giffen, "Leon Trotsky in New York City," *New York History* 49 (1968): 391, and William Rodney, "Broken Promises: Trotsky in Canada," *Queen's Quarterly* 74 (1967): 649.

Cambridge, Massachusetts
December 1, 1921

My Precious Friend,

Luina and I were deeply moved by your last letter—the generous concern for me, your confidence in me. It goes to the very heart of me and is one of those rare gifts that will abide forever. *Imprimis* be entirely at ease. Nothing *is* happening to me, and nothing will (bold as that sounds). Only time is needlessly wasted. Otherwise, I'm not ruffled in the least, partly, I suspect, because of my buoyant vitality, partly because men's foolishness does not too much surprise me.

You can also be entirely sure that I have not "been getting in" with *any* crowd. You know my "crowd," so far as I have any—men like Croly, Brandeis, yourself (if I may classify you so vulgarly). *The* point is that I haven't any crowd. That's why Max Eastman in his *Liberator* (or *Masses*) calls me "bourgeois" and Fred Fish thinks me "dangerous."[1] I verily believe I'm an occasional target because I worship no sacred cow, and because I do regard it the business of the mind to inquire altho' neither advocating nor expecting any sudden or upsetting changes and loving what America means passionately. The specific occasion—and the source of most of this silly feeling against me—is my share in the Mooney case. You may recall that I was connected with a commission appointed by President Wilson, during the war, to look into industrial difficulties, and *inter alia*, the Mooney case.[2] People don't reason about that case; there are hot partisans on both sides. The enclosed report constitutes my offending. But it let loose all the passions of fear, hysteria and ignorance. The result is I'm a "Bolshevik," "anarchist," etc. (I can't help recalling that Story J. was thundered against as an "agrarian"!!). Roosevelt was led to write fiercely about the Mooney case in a private letter to me, which resulted in correspondence between us. *After his death*, his letter to me—without my reply—was widely published, and anonymously circulated. William Roscoe Thayer prints it in his life of Roosevelt and I shouldn't be a bit surprised (he was violent during and after the war) if he first gave it out.[3] But that has been a recurring source of attack against me. T.R. stood on the stern ground that "murder is murder" without stopping to consider that the essence of the matter is to *prove* crime according to the processes of law, even if the accused is the scum of the earth. And I verily believe that Luina isn't merely a biased wife when she says, "*you* really care deeply about law, no matter whom it hits or favors." For I've been shocked at the number and the eminence of people who shrug their shoulders about the Mooney case by saying, "He is a bad egg." For instance, (*entre nous*) the Archbishop of San Francisco told me in his own palace that

"Mooney was tried in atmosphere of guilt" but he wouldn't say so publicly because, "Mooney is a bad man." I have no "ism" as you well know but I do cling hard to the theory and practice of the processes of law as the method for dealing with conflicting pressures.

The latest phase involves Beck, the Solicitor General, who pleasantly suggests the Trotzky business etc., etc. Beck wrote what I regarded an unpardonable perversion of the Mooney situation and I replied to him, all in *The New Republic*. He returns to the attack at length.[4] Of course, I had as much to do with Trotzky as you did. I can't recall even having heard his name until he came into power. So here you have the whole story and you can be *entirely* at ease about me. It's not to be wondered at that after an upheaval such as the war and its aftermath, reason is not wholly enthroned, tho' it is a bit surprising that some of the most "educated" are the least self-possessed. But then, their "education" is a very small part of them.

As to your letters, of course any wish of yours is sacred to me. So far as I am concerned what you write me—and you can hardly realize what letters from you mean—is buried. I do hope you will let me talk to you about your general attitude towards your correspondence when next we meet.

Have you seen Pound's little volume on *The Spirit of the Common Law*, his Dartmouth lectures and familiar matter to you?[5] His Yale lectures will interest you still more—they ought to be out in the spring.[6]

Just a closing word about "public" and "private" aspects of municipal corporations. I'm greatly relieved by what you say of your doubts as to the *Mt. Hope Cemetery* case. I have never been able to go that case and never been happy about my doubts because of your concurrence. I shall hereafter remember that it does not always follow that where the vote lies there the head lies too!

Affectionately yours,
F.F.

1. The radical Max Eastman (1883–1969) later became an editor for *Reader's Digest*. Frederick P. Fish (1855–1930) was a Boston patent lawyer and, from 1901 to 1907, President of American Telephone and Telegraph Co.

2. On the Mooney case, see above, December 23, 1917, and Parrish, *Frankfurter and His Times*, 87–101. Frankfurter's review uncovered numerous illegalities in the prosecution's case and recommended a new trial. California Governor William D. Stephens (1859–1944) ignored the recommendation but did commute Mooney's sentence to life imprisonment. Twenty years later Mooney was pardoned.

3. William Roscoe Thayer, *Theodore Roosevelt: An Intimate Biography* (Boston: Houghton, Mifflin, 1919), 440–41. Thayer (1859–1923), a Harvard Overseer, for many years edited the Harvard Graduate Magazine.

4. On the dispute between Frankfurter and U.S. Solicitor General James M. Beck (1861–1936) see *New Republic* 28 (1921): 189, 218; *Id.* 29 (1922): 212.

5. Roscoe Pound, *The Spirit of the Common Law* (Boston: Marshall Jones, 1921).

6. Roscoe Pound, *An Introduction to the Philosophy of Law* (New Haven: Yale University Press, 1922).

Washington, D.C.
December 6, 1921

Dear Frankfurter,

Pouf—the sword dance is danced and I think I have kept off the blades in a case just sent to the printer—so now I turn to my unduly delayed answer as to Benjamin.[1] I am in your hands and if you say yes, I doubt not that I shall be happy subject of course to the standing order that I am under no honorary obligation not to die or resign although, as heretofore, I have no wish or premeditation to do either.

Your other, later letter delights me. I didn't suppose there was any real cause for anxiety but wanted a word of assurance. I have been so busy that I haven't yet read the report you enclosed but will anon. I was delighted at the labor decision of the C.J. yesterday and though, of course, there were details as to which I should go farther, I was so content to get what we got that I didn't think it wise to say any qualifying words.[2] I think it removed one ball from some recent decisions of the Court. I would fain say more but must go to Court.

Affectionately yours,
O. W. Holmes

1. Robert M. Benjamin (1896–1966), an expert in administrative law, served as Holmes's secretary, 1922–23.

2. In *American Steel Foundries v. Tri-City Trades Council*, 257 U.S. 184 (1921), Taft's 8–1 decision ruled that courts could not, under the Clayton Anti-Trust Act, enjoin persuasion through peaceful picketing, though the number of pickets could be limited to avoid intimidation. Justice Clarke dissented.

Washington, D.C.
December 23, 1921

Dear Frankfurter,

A thousand thanks for your kind expressions and wishes which you know are fully reciprocated. The *Truax* case disappointed me after the C.J. had so successfully stifled competition the week before in the *Tricity* matter or whatever it was called.[1] I am thinking thoughts.

I have a case this week that, if it goes through, I think you will like—at least in the matter of form.[2] The substance you might not care much for. Brandeis has returned it with praise but no one else yet.

I have been chuckling since Monday with some devil talk I let off to an unknown female at our At Home. I told her abuses were the parents of the exquisite which disappeared from this country with wine—that you couldn't have a society like that of Greece except on some sort of slavery—and that I loathed most of the things that I decided in favor of. If she had been a newspaper reporter, which for all I knew or know she might have been, what headlines were possible as to cynicism in high places. But as I said to Wigmore yesterday, a paradox takes the scum off your mind.

One has more heart to wish a Merry Christmas this year than one has had for many years past.

Affectionately,
O.W.H.

1. In *Truax v. Corrigan*, 257 U.S. 312, 344 (1921), Taft, speaking for the 5–4 majority, held that a state statute depriving courts of jurisdiction to halt picketing by injunction was unconstitutional under the due process clause of the Fourteenth Amendment. In dissent, Holmes wrote: "There is nothing that I more deprecate than the use of the Fourteenth Amendment beyond the absolute compulsion of its words to prevent the making of social experiments that an important part of the community desires, in the insulated chambers afforded by the several States, even though the experiments may be futile or even noxious to me and to those whose judgments I most respect." Brandeis dissented separately. Pitney, with Clarke concurring, also dissented. See Novick, *Honorable Justice*, 350, 477, and White, *Justice Oliver Wendell Holmes*, 397–99.

2. *The Western Maid*, 257 U.S. 419, 432 (1922), a 5–3 decision forbidding suits against the government for vessels involved in collisions while engaged in public service: "We must realize that however ancient may be the traditions of maritime law, however diverse the sources from which it has been drawn, it derives its whole and only power in this country from its having been accepted and adopted by the United States. There is no mystic over-law to which even the United States must bow." McKenna, with Day and Clarke concurring, dissented. McReynolds took no part in the case.

Washington, D.C.
January 4, 1922

Dear Frankfurter,

Yesterday I fired off a dissent concurred in by Brandeis and McKenna as to unfair competition and an opinion as to lien on government ships after they get into private hands which last rather pleased me and greatly disturbed

McKenna judging by his jeremiad, concurred in by Day and Clarke, talking as if we overruled cases.[1] We overrule nothing but talk. On the other hand, he seemed pleased by the dissent which I was surprised at his agreeing to. All good wishes to you and Luina.

Affectionately yours,
O. W. Holmes

1. *Federal Trade Commission v. Beech-Nut Co.*, 257 U.S. 441, 457 (1922), a 5–4 decision, written by Justice Day, upholding the commission's authority to enjoin the company from refusing to sell to dealers who disregarded the company's suggested resale prices. Holmes, with Brandeis and McKenna concurring and McReynolds dissenting separately, dissented: "I cannot see how it is unfair competition to say to those to whom the respondent sells, and to the world, you can have my goods only on the terms that I propose, when the existence of any competition in dealing with them depends upon the respondent's will. I see no wrong in so doing, and if I did I should not think it a wrong within the possible scope of the word unfair." On *The Western Maid*, *Id.* at 419, see above, December 23, 1921.

Cambridge, Massachusetts
January 7, 1922

Dear Justice Holmes,

I have just read your ex-Government ships opinion with excitement. It tickled me all over. You know, of course, the great stimulus you are to many of us in our work—for me, none greater. But you are also a source of despair. What can we creeping worms do, and what good is it, when you toss off (I know it isn't quite tossed off) an opinion that illumines so much so brilliantly in a few pages.

Always gratefully yours,
F.F.

Washington, D.C.
February 9, 1922

Dear Frankfurter,

This is about nothing in particular except to thank you for what you say about Lepaulle.[1] He excited my sympathy as presenting rather strikingly the eternal difficulty when young men with large and high ideals encounter, not without rebellion, the dull and mean details. It is a question partly of circumstances no doubt but more of how much fire they have in their belly, whether they can burn the details into crystal.

Your Dr. Schindler took a cup of tea with me in my library yesterday afternoon.[2] I was feeling pretty tired and he is not an aggressive talker. So I didn't know whether he got his money's worth but it went off pleasantly. As our waitress has just left rather suddenly and we are taverners for the moment, I didn't ask him to dine.

My cases are all written and agreed to by everybody except that in one Clarke may dissent.[3] And I have embodied in a short dissent my views on fraud orders.[4] Whether in view of the decisions it will be worthwhile to publish them I still hesitate and await the conference (this of course strictly between ourselves).

There are applications for rehearing in the cases as to United States ships that I wrote—citing Laski, Pound et al. and rather patronizing me on a theme that I venture to believe I have considered more than the lawyers.[5] At the argument they seemed to think that no one not familiar with navigation could master the mysteries of the personification of the ship. I also ventured to believe that I knew as much about the history of the matter as any of them. Some time ago, to my amusement, Zane said that anyone who thought *Kawananakoa v. Polybank* was right had better give up thought of being a lawyer which is hard on an old man who can't begin over again.[6] So far as I know, Zane, who wiped the German jurists off the slate and exterminated Hobbes, Bentham and Austin, has kept dark as to the truth that is to take their place. It is a great gift to know that you are right.

I am hoping D.V. for a little culture. I have a book Brandeis lent me about *Pausanias* and that delightful man Nevinson's *Essays in Freedom and Rebellion*.[7] Laski brought us together and I liked him so much. He was here, as probably you know, for the *Manchester Guardian*. But first a little business and the dentist to which (former) I now turn.

Affectionately yours,
O. W. Holmes

1. Pierre G. Lepaulle (1893–1979), a graduate student at Harvard Law School, became Professor of Law at the University of Paris.

2. Rudolf Schindler (1888–1968), a German physician who migrated to the United States in 1934.

3. *Gooch v. Oregon Short Line R.R. Co.*, 258 U.S. 22, 24, 32 (1922), a 5–3 decision that denied plaintiff's suit to recover from injuries suffered in a train accident because he did not file a written claim within thirty days as his railroad pass stipulated: "We perceive nothing in the form of the notice to invalidate the requirement." Clarke, joined by Taft and McKenna, noting that the Cummins Amendment (1915) to the Interstate Commerce Act provided a ninety-day period to file property claims, concluded: "The rule is a novel and cunning device to defeat the normal liability of carriers and should not be made a favorite of the courts."

4. *Leach v. Carlile*, 258 U.S. 138, 140–41 (1922), a 7–2 decision, written by Clarke, upholding the authority of the Postmaster General to determine the possible fraudulence of

pharmaceutical advertising and to prohibit the delivery of mail to the offending advertiser. Holmes and Brandeis dissented. Holmes, adverting to the rights of correspondents, wrote: "I do not suppose that anyone would say that the freedom of written speech is less protected by the First Amendment than the freedom of spoken words. Therefore I cannot understand by what authority Congress undertakes to authorize anyone to determine in advance, on the grounds before us, that certain words shall not be uttered."

5. See above, December 23, 1921. Plaintiff's counsel cited Laski's "Responsibility of the State in England," *Harvard Law Review* 32 (1919): 447, to contend that the principles of sovereign immunity should not be taken as sacrosanct.

6. In *Kawananakoa v. Polybank*, 205 U.S. 349, 353 (1907), Holmes's unanimous opinion held that the territory of Hawaii was not a necessary party to a suit resulting from a foreclosure on land owned in part by the government: "A sovereign is exempt from suit not because of any formal conception or obsolete theory, but on the logical and practical ground that there can be no legal right as against the authority that makes the law on which the right depends." John M. Zane chastised Holmes's decision for supporting "the atrocious German theory of law and justice which has desolated much of the world" in "A Legal Heresy," *Illinois Law Review* 13 (1918): 431.

7. James G. Frazer, *Pausanias and Other Greek Sketches* (New York: Macmillan, 1900); Henry W. Nevinson, *Essays in Freedom and Rebellion* (New Haven: Yale University Press, 1921).

Washington, D.C.
February 20, 1922

Dear Frankfurter,

You put a painful question to me about Hohfeld because he always blew my horn and naturally I would say nothing to belittle his value.[1] Furthermore, his analyses and criticisms, so far as I examined them, were generally pretty sound, and I don't doubt that his work makes for the side of accurate thinking. Which being said, I must admit, as once I wrote to Kocourek, who has done further refining in the same direction, that I saw but limited advantage in the elaboration of cycles and epicycles.[2] Like the rules of logic or good manners or painting, they may help to make an insight articulate once in awhile, but the idea of bothering oneself with all that hocus-pocus for daily purpose seems to me superfluous. You don't learn to reason, or behave, or paint, in that way. A man of accurate thoughts will have avoided the pitfalls without the guides. I remember Cook(?) or whoever it was that postmortemed Hohfeld undertook to say that I had fallen into one and I thought I showed, on the contrary, I had consciously avoided it but I forget particulars.[3]

No Keynes for me just now—Brandeis has just put me on to a book about Crete and I am absorbed. After that I have some odds and ends, and there are dames to be called on and written to and only this week before we begin again. I have some cases and probably a dissent to fire off. One of the cases has a half page that seems obvious but that required thought to state.[4] I wondered if anyone would notice it and Brandeis did, as I hoped, but I am making too much of it by so much talk. A little point on the relation of state law to the Constitution. I read Pound's book [*The Spirit of the Common Law*] the other day and, although I was more aware of breadth and learning than of poignant personal reaction, I thought it would be a great influence for good if generally read.

Anon I must titivate for the Attorney General's dinner.

Yours as ever,
O.W.H.

When next you write, tell me if Laski did not leave Harvard College of his own choice. I came across the belief that he was compelled or requested to leave and that Lowell no longer stood by him.

1. Yale Law School Professor Wesley N. Hohfeld (1879–1918), stressed the study of "jural relations" in legal education. His principal contention was that the law was clarified by precise definition of terms, especially by understanding the logical interrelations of right, duty, privilege, and immunity, rather than by providing students with the contextual information of the social sciences.

2. For a debate on this subject see, Albert Kocourek, "The Hohfeld System," *Illinois Law Review* 15 (1920): 24, and "Various Definitions of Jural Relations," *Columbia Law Review* 20 (1920): 394; Arthur L. Corbin, "Jural Relations and their Classification," *Yale Law Journal* 30 (1921): 226. See also, Horwitz, *Transformation of American Law*, 152–56.

3. Walter W. Cook (1873–1943), Professor of Law at Chicago, Yale and Columbia, edited Hohfeld's *Fundamental Legal Conceptions* (New Haven: Yale University Press, 1919).

4. In *Burrill v. Locomobile Co.*, 258 U.S. 34, 39 (1922), Holmes's unanimous decision upheld a state law that substituted a suit against the state for one against the collector of taxes as the remedy to recover taxes that had been held unconstitutional by the Supreme Court: "Congress has made no provision that governs the liability in this case and therefore has left it to the law of the State where the wrong is done."

Washington, D.C.
March 28, 1922

Dear F.F.,

Many thanks for the enclosed and other kindnesses.[1] I have been and still am in a scrabble though I have sent the corrected proof of my only case to the printer. Other cases to be examined further, *certioraris* and motions and almost a million letters and books.

Little of interest in my doings. A decision cutting down the turntable cases to a somewhat stricter statement, with a larmoyant dissent by Clarke,

C.J. [Taft] and Day acceding.[2] Also an opinion in an opium case when written by me convinced the majority of the opposite view so McReynolds, Brandeis and I appear as dissenters.[3] I didn't care much about it, but the result seemed to me queer. Any tendency to a swelled head is quickly corrected here.

You asked me about Peckham.[4] I used to say his major premise was God damn it, meaning thereby that emotional predilections somewhat governed him on social themes. A good man, faithful, of real feeling and a master of Anglo Saxon interjections.

I stepped out of a cloud of biting mosquitos for a word of freedom with you. Now I go back to the swamp.

Affectionately,
O.W.H.

1. The letter referred to is missing.

2. In *United Zinc and Chemical Co. v. Britt*, 258 U.S. 268, 276, 279 (1922), Holmes held that the company was not liable for the death of two children who trespassed on the company's land and were killed by going into an innocuous appearing but poisoned pool of water. He wrote: "It is suggested that the roads across the place were invitations. A road is not an invitation to leave it elsewhere than at its end." Clarke retorted: "The facts, as stated, make it very clear that in the view most unfavorable to the plaintiffs below there might be a difference of opinion between candid men as to, whether the pool was so located that the owners of the land should have anticipated that children might frequent its vicinity, whether its appearance and character rendered it attractive to childish instinct so as to make it a temptation to children of tender years, and whether, therefore, it was culpable negligence to maintain it in that location, unprotected and without warning as to its poisonous condition." The turntable cases, *Railroad Co. v. Strout*, 17 Wallace 657 (1874), and *Union Pacific Railway Co. v. McDonald*, 152 U.S. 262 (1894), had upheld corporate liability because the companies had knowingly maintained dangerous equipment. United Zinc pleaded ignorance of the poisoned pool. See White, *Justice Oliver Wendell Holmes*, 381–84.

3. *United States v. Behrman*, 258 U.S. 280, 290 (1922), written by Justice Day, construed the Narcotic Drug Act (1914) to incriminate a physician who wrote narcotic prescriptions for a known addict in amounts several thousand times a single dosage. Holmes's dissent agreed with the District Court ruling which had quashed the indictment because the physician had given the prescriptions "in the regular course of his practice and in good faith." He concluded: "It seems to me wrong to construe the statute as creating a crime in this way without a word of warning. Of course the facts alleged suggest an indictment in a different form, but the Government preferred to trust to a strained interpretation of the law rather than to a finding of a jury upon the facts."

4. Rufus Peckham (1838–1909), Associate Justice of the U.S. Supreme Court, 1895 to 1909.

Washington, D.C.
April 10, 1922

Dear Frankfurter,

D.V. we will have jaw together anon. Meantime I have been below par and there have been domestic hitches. I doubt not that you will feed with us, but until my wife hears from people she had written to before your letter came she is tied.

I forget why *certiorari* was granted in the case of the poisoned pool, perhaps because some of us wanted to qualify the turntables. I will talk but not write about the Kansas law, and I will look at [1922] 1 A.C.[1]

I missed last Saturday's conference which hasn't happened often to me, but the doctor gave me relief and pleasure by saying it was an attack of asthma. That accounts for various things that looked ominous but didn't seem to find organic justification. I stayed at home, forgot responsibility and had a divine day—dozing and dawdling over *Cytherea* and Radcliffe's *Fishing from the Earliest Times*.[2] Adorable expenditure of learning on who first mentioned the artificial fly or the jointed rod—which comes first, hook, spear or net? And a thousand other things—a truly delightful gossip of arcana.

I fired off my two cases today—nothing much, and drove with my wife to see the double cherries beginning to open and the magnolias gone mad, and am none the worse—just a little pale.[3]

Affectionately,
O.W.H.

1. The letter referred to is missing. In *Howat v. Kansas*, 258 U.S. 181 (1922), Chief Justice Taft's unanimous opinion ruled that a labor leader's sentence for contempt, stemming from a ruling of a state Court of Industrial Relations empowered to order binding arbitration in public interest industries, did not raise a federal question of depriving defendant of his rights. The case referred to in [1922] 1 A.C. cannot be identified.

2. *Cythereia: or, New Poems upon Love and Intrigue* (1723); William Radcliffe, *Fishing from the Earliest Times* (New York: Dutton, 1921)

3. *Forbes Boat Line v. Board of Commissioners*, 258 U.S. 338, 340 (1922), unanimously supported the company's claim to recover canal tolls unlawfully collected and rejected a state law validating retroactive collection: "Defendant owed the plaintiff a definite sum of money that it had extorted from the plaintiff without right." *White Oak Co. v. Boston Canal Co., Id.* at 341, unanimously found both parties at fault for the grounding and ruin of the steamer Bay Port in the Cape Cod Canal.

Washington, D.C.
May 4, 1922

Dear Frankfurter,

Criminal Justice in Cleveland has just arrived and of course I have at once read your preface beyond which I am not likely to go for the present.[1] I congratulate you with all my heart. It seems to me a model. It expresses the scientific spirit with perfection and puts it with restrained and admirable force. If the book answers to the preface it is a type of what seems to me of all things the most needed, and I am proud and happy that you have been a directing mind in it.

I have been so busy that I have not answered one or two letters from you, notwithstanding the pleasure they gave, as always.[2] However, I am now free for the last chore I have on hand—to make up my mind out of a wilderness of documents and briefs longer than the Bible where the line of the South Bank of the Red River is and also various business details that have been awaiting leisure.[3] If I ever get through them and have any money left after receiving my D.C. tax bill, I mean to visit the print department of the Congressional Library and, if they have some duplicates to dispose of that I want, to add some little thing to my slender collection, and after that to read a book—first, I think Francis Hackett's *Story of the Irish Nation*.[4] He wrote to me a charming letter when he left *The New Republic*. I was sorry that it had to be.

The only case I had to write is on no burning theme.[5] I think the C.J.'s opinion as to commission merchants and dealers in stock yards is fine.[6] It has a sort of march, like the movement of interstate commerce that it describes. I am considering whether to come in on another good one that has not yet gone. As probably I have said before, he is most pleasant to work with. I have a note from Brandeis that perhaps he may go to Kentucky today. Otherwise, I want a jaw with him, which he foreshadows.

My asthma and coughing are rather better but the weather is rainy which interferes with my plans. My wife said she had a very nice letter from your wife this morning. And now to work.

Affectionately yours,
O. W. Holmes

1. Felix Frankfurter and Roscoe Pound, eds., *Criminal Justice in Cleveland* (Cleveland: The Cleveland Foundation, 1922).

2. The letters referred to are missing.

3. *Oklahoma v. Texas*, 258 U.S. 574 (1922), a suit in equity with the United States as intervenor, in which Van Devanter, for the unanimous Court, settled certain boundary claims but left undetermined the exact location of the Red River's South Bank.

4. Francis Hackett, *Story of the Irish Nation* (New York: Century, 1922).

5. In *Sloan Shipyards v. U.S. Fleet Corp.*, 258 U.S. 549, 567 (1922), Holmes's majority opinion held that the government's Fleet Corporation, which constructed, purchased, and requisitioned vessels during the War, was liable for suits, the powers conveyed by Acts of Congress notwithstanding: "The sovereign properly so called is superior to suit for reasons that often have been explained. But the general rule is that any person within the jurisdiction always is amenable to the law." Taft, with Clarke and Van Devanter concurring, dissented.

6. In *Stafford v. Wallace*, 258 U.S. 495 (1922), Chief Justice Taft's majority opinion upheld the power of Congress, under the Commerce Clause, to regulate the Chicago Stockyards. McReynolds dissented without opinion.

Cambridge, Massachusetts
May 16, 1922

Dear Justice Holmes,

I cannot possibly convey to you what a word of professional commendation from you means to me. In all literalness, to have you touch me with your sword gives me more to go on than anything else that my work can possibly evoke. And, therefore, you moved me to the very bottom of my heart by what you say of the enterprise and the promise embodied in the Cleveland volume. Of course I need not add that the work of detail was almost wholly that of others. I profoundly share your conviction—you uttered it decades ago—as to the need of quantitative aims in studying our social institutions instead of generalized talk. I am about to embark on the planning and partial direction of studies of some of our administrative agencies ("executive justice" Pound summarily calls it) such as the Post Office, and the Immigration Administration.[1]

I am eagerly awaiting the Child Labor Opinion.[2] The Court's unanimity certainly surprises me. Of course the C.J. is right in saying that everyone knows the law was meant to prevent child labor and not to tax it; but, wasn't the same thing true of the oleomargarine tax?[3] However, the news accounts of yesterday's opinion are very early and I shall wait and see.

There is a review of Laski's book by F.P. in the April *Law Quarterly Review* you may have seen. Certainly it ought to make Laski feel proud to have evoked so ample a comment from Pollock. There is one rather curious point—F.P.'s criticism of Laski as unduly influenced by Ames.[4] I wonder what he means?

The year of work is soon up, for you and me. It has been a particularly swift one and one that has brought me much joy in my work.

Always devotedly,
F.F.

1. These studies never materialized. For Frankfurter's positive view of administrative solutions to legal conflicts, see Felix Frankfurter, *Mr. Justice Holmes and the Supreme Court* (Cambridge: Harvard University Press, 1938), 45–73.

2. Following the Court's decision in *Hammer v. Dagenhart*, 247 U.S. 251 (1918), which declared unconstitutional the first federal Child Labor Act, Congress passed a second act that relied upon a prohibitive tax instead of a ban on the products of child labor in interstate commerce. In *The Child Labor Tax Case* (*Bailey v. Drexel Furniture Co.*), 259 U.S. 20 (1922), Chief Justice Taft's 8–1 majority opinion ruled the second law unconstitutional as well. The Court held that Congress was not trying to raise revenue but rather was seeking to employ regulatory powers reserved to the States. Clarke dissented without opinion. In concurring with the majority, Holmes, who dissented in *Hammer*, wrote no opinion. See above, May 18, 1918. In considering alternatives in the aftermath of the *Bailey* decision, Frankfurter rejected a Constitutional amendment as impractical and endorsed Herbert Hoover's call for renewed action in the states, particularly by newly enfranchised women's groups: "If the women will it, not only would child labor be prohibited by paper legislation but the enforcement of such laws, and an environment fit for children to be born into and to grow up in, will quickly become the possession of every State in the Union." See "Child Labor and the Court," *New Republic* 31 (1922): 348.

3. *McCray v. United States*, 195 U.S. 27 (1904). The aim of this tax was to prevent the sale of oleomargarine colored to look like butter.

4. Frederick Pollock's review of Laski's *Foundations of Sovereignty*, *Law Quarterly Review* 38 (1922): 242, criticized James Barr Ames and, implicitly, Roscoe Pound, for encouraging Laski's belief that sovereignty was divisible between church and state. Holmes agreed with Pollock. See above, April 16, 1915, and July 16, 1916.

Washington, D.C.
May 25, 1922

Dear Frankfurter,

Many thanks for your notes and the recommendations of books to which I shall attend.[1] They were just what I wanted. *Between ourselves* as to the transportation of liquor, the sentence ending, "but are of opinion that the letter is too strong in this case," was followed by the words "for the spirit sought to be introduced" but as one J. thought them better omitted, and I rather agreed, I struck them out.[2] I had some extra cases but got through them all last week—5 opinions between Sunday morning and Thursday luncheon, written, printed and distributed which was putting high pressure.[3]

Now I have the kind of leisure that means thinking up odds and ends to be attended to before leaving. I mean to try to get one of the three books you named to take on the train. I doubt if I shall have any more writing to do.

Affectionately yours,
O. W. Holmes

1. The notes referred to are missing.

2. In *Grogan v. Walker and Sons*, 259 U.S. 80, 89, 94 (1922), Holmes's 6–3 decision observed: "The Eighteenth Amendment meant a great revolution in the policy of this country, and presumably and obviously meant to upset a good many things on as well as off the statute book. It did not confine itself in any meticulous way to the use of intoxicants in this country. It forbade export for beverage purposes elsewhere." McKenna's dissent, joined by Day and Clarke, cited trade treaty obligations and rejoined: "There is appeal in the declaration. It presents the attractive spectacle of a people too animated for reform to hesitate to make it as broad as the universe of humanity. One feels almost ashamed to utter a doubt of such a noble and moral cosmopolitanism, but the facts of the world must be adduced and what they dictate."

3. All unanimous opinions. In *Morrisdate Coal Co. v. United States*, 259 U.S. 188, and *Pine Hill Coal Co. v. United States*, *Id.* at 191, Holmes sustained provisions of the Lever Act (1917), which fixed prices during the war, against claims that Government purchases and regulations amounted to uncompensated takings. In *Santa Fe Pacific v. Fall*, *Id.* at 197, Holmes upheld the railroad's equity suit against Secretary of the Interior Albert B. Fall (1861–1944) for invalidating a legislatively sanctioned exchange of coal lands two years after the fact when the land selected by the company had increased in value. *Federal Baseball Club v. National League*, *Id.* at 200, 208–9, rejected defendant's claim that the American League and National League conspired to monopolize the baseball business in violation of the interstate commerce clauses of the Sherman Anti-Trust Act (1890): "The business is giving exhibitions of base ball, which are purely state affairs. It is true that, in order to attain for these exhibitions the great popularity that they have achieved, competitions must be arranged between clubs from different cities and States. But the fact that in order to give the exhibitions the Leagues must induce free persons to cross state lines and must arrange and pay for their doing so is not enough to change the character of the business. . . . The transport is a mere incident, not the essential thing. That to which it is incident, the exhibition, although made for money would not be called trade or commerce in the commonly accepted use of those words." *Mutual Life Insurance Co. v. Liebing*, *Id.* at 209, 214 upheld defendant's claim for survivor's benefits under the terms of Missouri law, where the policy was issued, against the action of the company, which had canceled the policy for an unpaid loan that was taken out in New York: "In whichever way regarded the facts lead to the same conclusion, and although the circumstances may present some temptation to seek a different one by ingenuity, the Constitution and the first principles of legal thinking allow the law of the place where a contract is made to determine the validity and the consequences of the act."

Brookline, Massachusetts
July 22, 1922

Dear F.F.,

A line at least shall answer your delightful letter though I can't write.[1] Things have gone well, but when you are in the trap you learn that to get out is a long slow job. The whole thing is serious and you can't treat it lightly. Of course I have done nothing except read a few books. That's all I can say. I'm in the middle of a taxing trial, doing pretty well, absorbed in the egotism of the sickroom but still able to recognize a fellow man. My love to your partner.

Affectionately,
O.W.H.

1. The letter referred to is missing. Holmes spent most of the summer in Corey Hill Hospital where he was operated upon for removal of the prostate.

Chatham, Massachusetts
August 23, 1922

Dear Justice Holmes,

It's such a joy to address you again at Beverly Farms! It must have been a stiff road over which you had to travel and you have covered it with such an abiding lift for us all.

Redlich was here the other day—ran over for a few hours from Williamstown where he is lecturing—and he asked me to tell you how deeply he rejoices that all went well. He has sparkling eyes, the sparkle of meditation, and all their light shone in them as he spoke of you: "He is the great master of all of us." Redlich is an increasingly rich vein to strike—he is saturated with experience of life as well as of books. So much of the talk about Europe, and the Great War's consequences, is by men who only discovered Europe yesterday. When Redlich speaks, one feels how deep and gnarled the roots of history are—with him it all imperceptibly runs back to '48 and that to the Napoleonic Wars, and that to the rest of nationalities and the Reformation, and that to the Holy Roman Empire, etc., etc., etc. When a scholarly European says we're not historically-minded, he has a deal of meaning behind it.

It's a joy to see Brandeis as we see him here—playful, simple, affectionate. What caricatures people who do not know him make of him! And how truly "conservative" he is with the conservatism of the man of insight who knows that "continuity with the past is not a duty but a necessity."

And we talk much of you, always with a new gladness of heart.

Faithfully yours,
F.F.

Beverly Farms, Massachusetts
August 24, 1922

Dear Frankfurter,

Talk about putting heart into people—your letters always put heart into me, but I can't reply in kind yet. I am recovered surgically but I realize by my weakness that I have been through a pretty severe pull and that it will take time before I am good for much except to lollup around on beds and couches. I have a pretty long list of books read in the hospital—largely drool—and now I have fallen back on the Bard—and am reading the plays of W. Shakespeare and little else. Most of them strike me as heavy bodies, carried up to the sky by two or three electric sentences. I should, as now minded, blaspheme against the greater part of the *Mid-Summer Nights Dream* and a good slice of *Romeo and Juliet* in the middle of which I now am. I am no prude but the bawdy talk is a bore and the chipchop of Euphues even in the love passages is the likes.[1] Well I go forth for a short hour's morning drive and will post this line of thanks to you. Homage to Luina and my love to Brandeis.

Affectionately yours,
O. W. Holmes

1. Euphues: bombast or high flown language, from John Lyly, *Anatomy of Wit* (1578), a compendium of affected jargon from the Elizabethan court.

Beverly Farms, Massachusetts
September 11, 1922

Dear Frankfurter,

Many thanks for the chance to read the admirable *Prologue to American History* returned by this mail.[1] Morison seems to be a new star in literature. I am getting on well—slowly gaining strength and doing nothing. If we were together, I should jaw about Shakespeare. He makes me think of Turner.[2]

Yours ever,
O.W.H.

1. Harvard historian Samuel Eliot Morison (1887–1976) gave this lecture at Oxford where he was Harmsworth Professor from 1922 to 1925.

2. British landscape painter J. M. W. Turner (1775–1851). "The bard makes word fugues about life rather than pictures it, often with questionable regard to dramatic fitness," Holmes wrote Pollock, September 4, 1922. See Howe, ed., *Holmes-Pollock Letters*, 2:100–103.

Washington, D.C.
October 20, 1922

Dear F.F.,

All communications from you are welcome. The last, your book [*Criminal Justice in Cleveland*], makes me regret that I can't try to learn something about the subject by reading it. But what with having to live at the Powhatan and drive to my house and not being excessively strong, I find I can do nothing but work and gasp. I had an opinion last Monday that was like the New England Primer and would have sounded like drool hadn't the judicious Secretary [Robert M. Benjamin] told me to cut out a chunk.[1] For Monday (unless held up by the C.J.), I have a case that I am not ashamed of although the custodians of propriety won't let me speak of the petty larcenies of the police power.[2] I am just working along. I think not too hard but hard enough and shall be glad of the adjournment to get a breath.

Homage to Luina.

Yours always,
O. W. Holmes

1. *Knights v. Jackson*, 260 U.S. 12 (1922), a unanimous decision upholding a Massachusetts Supreme Judicial Court ruling that distributions of the state income tax to local schools did not violate the property rights of nonbeneficiaries under the Fourteenth Amendment.

2. *Jackman v. Rosenbaum Co.*, 260 U.S. 22, 32 (1922), also a unanimous decision in which Holmes upheld a Pennsylvania statute, based upon custom, permitting an adjoining owner to destroy an old party wall and build a new one without incurring liability for incidental damages under the Fourteenth Amendment: "In a case involving local history as this does, we should be slow to overrule the decision of the Courts steeped in the local tradition, even if we saw reasons for doubting it, which in this case we do not."

Washington, D.C.
November 2, 1922

Dear F.F.,

Your selection sounds promising including its assumption that I shall survive the buffets of another year.[1] At present I am shut up with a cold at the top of the Powhatan. If one must be shut up there couldn't easily be a better place for I see all the Kingdom of the earth from our rooms. But I have been sorry not only for myself but for Benjamin that there should have been a month of dust and confusion while that damned elevator goes in. I believe it has nearly completed its entrance now. Benjamin is excellent. He saved me from drool by advising me to cut out two sentences in that first case. He is always a careful critic and has shaken me from my dogmatic slumber on the doctrine of election. The only other case that has come out yet, on party walls in Pittsburgh, they wouldn't let me speak of being driven to rely upon the petty larcenies of the police power. . . . I didn't see any harm in it though I felt sure that someone would.[2]

Pitney will be a real loss but I don't expect to see him again.[3] Of course I don't say so publicly though I think a bill has been introduced to enable him to retire. And so farewell. I am a worm of little value till this cold departs.

Yours as ever,
O.W.H.

1. Frankfurter selected James M. Nicely (1899–1964) as Holmes's Secretary for 1923–24. Nicely later served as a trustee of the Carnegie Endowment for Peace and as treasurer of the Ford Foundation.

2. See above, October 20, 1922.

3. Mahlon Pitney retired at the end of the year and was replaced by Edward T. Sanford (1865–1930) of the Federal District Court for Tennessee.

Cambridge, Massachusetts
November 10, 1922

Dear Justice Holmes,

I have just read your opinion in the Pittsburgh party wall case and it's like drinking the erstwhile fizz water. I did not realize that you had left yourself anything new and vivid to say about the Fourteenth Amendment, or even that your old views could be put with new pungency. But you've done the trick again and this opinion is as fresh and pungent as *Otis v. Parker*.[1] What a sparkling fountain it draws from!

It pleases me much that you find Benjamin so useful and pleasant. He is a good lad.

The elections have come and gone and the world rolls on.[2] It *is* a tough old world.

Luina sends her devoted greetings to both of you. And so do I.

F.F.

1. See above, December 22, 1920.

2. In the Congressional election of 1922 Albert J. Beveridge, Holmes's friend and summer neighbor, was defeated in the Indiana Senate race. Massachusetts Senator Henry Cabot Lodge barely retained his seat but Republicans won thirteen of sixteen Massachusetts House districts.

Washington, D.C.
November 27, 1922

Dear Frankfurter,

Many thanks for late favors. I have been in a scrabble and have found it hard to write. Two cases held up yesterday at conference—one that I don't care much about has the majority so far but Brandeis will write considerations contra.[1] The other, which I think has God's truth about the police power, seemed to provoke hesitations in pretty much everyone.[2] I didn't grasp very well the varying difficulties and said I would put my head under my wing and sleep until someone wrote. This morning I have two awaiting me and as soon as I have finished this apology for silence shall fall upon them. I rather think less troublesome than last week's.

I have had nothing lately. F. Pollock says that Masefield on Shakespeare in the Home Library Series is fine.[3] Warren's book on the Supreme Court I have finished since getting down here and think it very able and interesting and instructive.[4]

At last we have got into this house and I go up and down in the elevator. I think I get stronger gradually but still am rather weak in the joints. I don't go anywhere—treating myself as still an invalid. Some kindly intentioned friends here said why don't you resign and take a rest. I say I don't want to rest but to keep going until I falter. I want to produce and judicial opinions have been my outlet so long that it is too late to change. Now to work.

My compliments to Luina.

Affectionately yours,
O.W.H.

1. *Portsmouth Harbor Land and Hotel Co. v. United States*, 260 U.S. 327, 330 (1922), a 7–2 decision upholding appellant's claim that the Government had taken their land without compensation by establishing a naval battery nearby and firing over it: "As the United States built the fort and put in the guns and the men, there is a little natural unwillingness to find lack of authority to do the acts even if the possible legal consequences were unforeseen. If the acts amounted to a taking, without assertion of an adverse right, a contract would be implied whether it was thought of or not." Brandeis, with Sutherland concurring, dissented.

2. *Pennsylvania Coal Company v. Mahon*, 260 U.S. 393, 413–16, 422 (1922). See above, xxiii–xxv. Holmes's majority opinion overturned a Pennsylvania law that prohibited mining beneath improved lands. Noting that the company's land title predated the statute and specifically reserved the right to mine without regard to surface damage, Holmes allowed that "property may be regulated to a certain extent" but found that the law went "too far" and took property without compensation: "The question at bottom is upon whom the loss of the changes desired should fall. So far as private persons or communities have seen fit to take the risk of acquiring only surface rights, we cannot see that the fact that their risk has become a danger warrants the giving to them greater rights than they bought." Brandeis's dissent supported the law as a measure promoting public safety, and rejected the argument that "recip-

rocal advantage" must be shown, "unless it be the advantage of living and doing business in a civilized community." See Baker, *Justice from Beacon Hill*, 567–69; White, *Justice Oliver Wendell Holmes*, 401–403.

3. John Masefield, *William Shakespeare* (London: Oxford, 1911).

4. Charles Warren, *The Supreme Court in United States History* (Boston: Little, Brown, 1922).

Washington, D.C.
December 8, 1922

Dear Frankfurter,

Will you please give the within to your mother as I do not know her address.[1] As I see her telegram is from Cambridge I do not put on a stamp. I can't tell you how pleased and moved I was by the joint letter and the roses that came this morning. I answered by a joint letter addressed to Judge Morton on the outside and to all on the inside.[2]

I got things on Monday better than I expected and have only one case which will go unless Brandeis dissents.[3] I forgot to ask him if he was going to write but shall learn on Monday morning. I have a lot of stuff to study but hope to be able to recite on Monday. It makes me tremble to have these kind expressions for fear I shall in some way fail to come up to them before I go up to the day of Judgment.

Affectionately yours,
O. W. Holmes

1. Enclosed was a brief note thanking Felix Frankfurter's mother for remembering Holmes's twentieth anniversary on the Supreme Court.

2. James M. Morton (1869–1940), U.S. District Judge for Massachusetts.

3. *Pennsylvania Coal v. Mahon*, 260 U.S. 393 (1922). See above, November 27, 1922.

Washington, D.C.
December 22, 1922

Dear Frankfurter,

The very generous notice of my anniversary in *The New Republic* renewed the terrors of which I have written to you before but of course went to my heart.[1] I do not know whether to recognize your friendly hand in the actual writing or not—that you are in some way responsible for it I hardly can doubt. Such a thing cannot but make one happy and feel as if the long day's task had not been in vain. Thanks would be out of place for what one hopes is a sincere statement, but it is proper at least to say that I am deeply moved. The terror is not only that one may fall down but that when people go to the top of the hill, the next stop seems to come down again. I shall hope not to see a reaction although this morning I received an anonymous letter to the effect that we were all prohibitionists and knaves. This bears to you my appreciation and every Christmas wish.

Affectionately yours,
O. W. Holmes

Please give my love to Luina.

1. *New Republic* 33 (1922): 84.

Washington, D.C.
February 14, 1923

Dear Frankfurter,

It is delightful to hear from you again.[1] I thought that perhaps you were frozen off by agreement with Brandeis and *The New Republic* in the case of the underground coal support and not willing to say so.[2] That would be a great mistake (I mean, to feel shy on that account) although I have not seen the slightest reason to doubt the decision, but only to regret that I didn't bring out more clearly the distinction between the rights of the public generally and their rights in respect of being in a particular place where they have no right to be at all except so far as they have paid for it.

I have been driven and harassed by a swarm of mosquitoes but I have today struck a moment of calm (having paid my income tax) and Pound's book has come just as I was longing for it.[3] I have read a chapter already with high appreciation and so confidently expect to admire it that I don't write to Pound until I have finished the volume.

I heard that you were coming on to argue a case?[4] I have written an introduction for Wigmore—the last outside job this old gent will ever do.[5] Also, I have just sent round an opinion in a Porto Rico case that gives me a mild titillation.[6]

I had a brief interval earlier and reread Spinoza's *Ethics* and then the clouds closed round me again. You perceive the shaky touch (intellectual touch) of a just intermitted tension.

Yours as ever,
O. W. Holmes

1. The letter referred to is missing.

2. *New Republic* 33 (1923): 136. Also, see above, November 27, 1922.

3. Roscoe Pound, *Interpretations of Legal History* (New York: Macmillan, 1923).

4. Frankfurter was appellant's counsel in *Adkins v. Children's Hospital*, 261 U.S. 525, 570 (1923), a 5–3 decision, written by Justice George Sutherland (1862–1942), finding unconstitutional a Washington, D.C., law setting a minimum wage for women because it violated the Fifth Amendment's guarantee of liberty of contract. Holmes dissented: "This statute does not compel anybody to pay anything. It simply forbids employment at rates below those fixed as the minimum requirement for health and right living." Chief Justice Taft, with Sanford concurring, also dissented. Justice Brandeis excused himself because his daughter Elizabeth (1896–1984) served on the Minimum Wage Board. The decision was specifically overruled by *West Coast Hotel v. Parrish*, 300 U.S. 379 (1937). See Baker, *Justice from Beacon Hill*, 575–80.

5. Introduction to John H. Wigmore and Albert Kocourek, eds., *The Rational Basis of Legal Institutions* (New York: Macmillan, 1923), xxxi: "For the most part men believe what they want to. . . . But reason means truth and those who are not governed by it take the chances that some day the sunken fact will rip the bottom out of their boat."

6. *Diaz v. Gonzales*, 261 U.S. 102, 106 (1923), a unanimous decision upholding a ruling of the Puerto Rican Supreme Court to allow a parent to sell land, including the interest of a minor child. Noting that the decision was derived from a different legal system, Holmes concluded: "Our appellate jurisdiction is not given for the purpose of remodelling the Spanish American law according to common law conceptions except so far as that law has to bend to the expressed will of the United States."

Washington, D.C.
April 2, 1923

Dear Frankfurter,

The Interpretation of Statutes, 1st 1/2 14th Century was sent to you this morning.[1] I read it with pleasure and I hope some profit. I felt with this writer as with the conspiracy man in the same series an indefinable evidence of unfamiliarity with the law as a practical thing—therefore left me doubting whether anything in particular had been proved except the fidelity of Mr. Plucknett's study and his familiarity with the lingo of real actions mostly forgotten by us.[2] But nothing would be difficult if it weren't for the damned words that people use.

Affectionately yours,
O.W.H.

1. Theodore F. T. Plucknett, *Statutes and Their Interpretation in the Fourteenth Century* (Cambridge: University Press, 1923).

2. Percy Henry Winfield, *The History of Conspiracy and Abuse of Legal Procedure* (Cambridge: University Press, 1921). Cambridge Studies in Legal History was edited by Harold D. Hazeltine (1871–1960), an American-born legal scholar who taught at Cambridge.

Washington, D.C.
April 13, 1923

Dear Frankfurter,

Thanks for your letter. I was surprised at the results—which I had guessed would be either an even division or in your favor.[1]

Winfield forwarded your letter of introduction and I wrote to him at the Law School hoping that he would dine with us while here.[2] I have this morning received a letter from Laski in high spirits. He says he has declined to run for Parliament, I should think wisely. I trust that you were not discouraged personally by losing the case. Evidently no one could have brought about a different decision.

Affectionately yours,
O. W. Holmes

1. The letter referred to is missing. On the *Adkins* decision, see above, February 14, 1923.
2. Percy Winfield (1878–1953), Professor of Law at Cambridge University, was lecturing at Harvard in 1923.

Washington, D.C.
April 21, 1923

Dear F.F.,

Your Winfield has come and gone and we liked him very much. He and I "parcourired the universe" as a girl once said to me, twisted the tail of the Cosmos and generally had an A 1 evening together if he liked it as much as I did. I have rather a neat little case for Monday/tomorrow—if the C.J. [William H. Taft] is well enough to agree as I have no doubt he will.[1]

Yours ever,
O.W.H.

1. *Spaulding and Bros. v. Edwards*, 262 U.S. 66 (1923), a unanimous decision holding that an attempt by the Internal Revenue Service to tax goods consigned for export was a violation of Article I, section 9 of the Constitution, which imposed various limitations upon congressional powers, including the power to tax.

Washington, D.C.
June 6, 1923

Dear Frankfurter,

Many thanks for your encouragement in my all but solitude. As to teaching the young, you will find that I said little and that cautiously and was willing to agree with the Court as to the fool law against German alone.[1] I agree with you as to Brandeis' performance—I thought it very fine.[2] I think perhaps I take it a little more skeptically than he does. It has its arbitrary side as when he won't recognize any change in the value of money—but it was a noble piece of work.

Yours,
O.W.H.

1. The letter referred to is missing. In *Meyer v. Nebraska*, 262 U.S. 390 (1923), the Court held that state statutes forbidding modern foreign language instruction of children who had not passed the eighth grade violated the liberty guaranteed by the Fourteenth Amendment. Holmes, joined by Sutherland, expressed his dissent in a companion case, *Bartels v. Iowa*, *Id.* at 404, 412, decided on the basis of *Meyer*: "Youth is the time when familiarity with a language is established and if there are sections in the State where a child would hear only Polish or French or German spoken at home I am not prepared to say that it is unreasonable to provide that in his early years he shall hear and speak only English at school." Holmes and Sutherland agreed with the Court's ruling in another companion case, *Bohning v. Ohio*, *Id.* at 404, because the legislation singled out the teaching of German for prohibition. See White, *Justice Oliver Wendell Holmes*, 438–39.

2. *Atlantic Coast Line v. Daughton*, 262 U.S. 413 (1923), a unanimous decision upholding a tax on a railroad's net income from property valuated within one state although the property was also used in interstate commerce.

Beverly Farms, Massachusetts
June 26, 1923

Dear F.F.,

Your letter greeted me on arrival here, Saturday, but I have been feeling a little pale and have postponed answering a day or two.[1] The journey in tired us both very much and the hot weather in Washington and here took it out of me.

I am not bothering about improving my mind—but bought Sainte Beuve's *Causeries*, the whole lot, for amusement, instruction thrown in.[2] He is instructive in his reverence for the exquisite. By a queer coincidence, a day or two later a letter from Laski told me that he had just bought the same. So I am going to try to sit still and idle. We both did absolutely nothing from Tuesday A.M. to Sat. P.M. at the Touraine but lolluped about, slept and ate. I haven't loafed so for years and mean to now. I suppose my work was more of an effort than I realized. This doctor said it was a miracle that I was able to do it. But while I feel the advances of old age, I do not want to give in until I have some warning that my work is not up to the mark. Damn—I should like to keep on the go.

But I won't undertake to write at length now.

Affectionately yours,
O. W. Holmes

1. The letter referred to is missing.
2. Charles-Augustin Saint-Beuve, *Causeries du lundi*, 15 vols. (Paris: Garnier, 1852–62).

Beverly Farms, Massachusetts
July 3, 1923

Dear Frankfurter,

Curtis told me on Sunday of your article in the *Harvard Law Review* and said he would send it to me but I haven't received it yet.[1] I waited until I should which naturally I am impatient to do but I must say at once how overwhelmed I am by your kindness—for I know that you are kind in it, you have given me great joy and pride.

I wasn't very well when I got here but I am on my pins again, trying to strengthen them—for as yet I have walked but little. As in the late months then to the earlier days of Benjamin (an admirably considerate and satisfactory Secretary), I am not trying to improve my mind, but loitering in literature—Saint Beuve's *Causeries*—as I believe I told you. I don't expect to go anywhere or do anything except eat, sleep, walk a little, read a little, and try—a doubtful venture, to get back some bodily elasticity. I hope that you will have or are having a real vacation.

Affectionately yours,
O. W. Holmes

1. Felix Frankfurter, "Twenty Years of Mr. Justice Holmes' Constitutional Opinions," *Harvard Law Review* 36 (1923): 909, 919. Frankfurter's analysis, relying heavily upon exerpts from Holmes's opinions, is consistent with the adulatory tone of his letters, for example: "Assuredly Mr. Justice Holmes did not bring to the Court the gifts of a lawyer who had been immersed in great affairs, and yet his work is in the school of statesmanship. He is philosopher become king. Where others are guided through experience of life he is led by the humility of the philosopher and the imagination of the poet."

Chatham, Massachusetts
July 8, 1923

Dear Justice Holmes,

I quote the following paragraph from a letter which has just come from Judge Cardozo—even the very pleasant things he politely says about me, according to Wigmore's doctrine of "integration": "I have your delightful article on Holmes. Great I have long known him to be, but an article such as yours brings out in high relief the gnomic quality of his greatness. Marshall, Story and all the rest of them together never produced a tithe of such quotable things. Whenever I feel dull and wish to brighten up what I say, I look to him for light and aid. You have talked about him charmingly. The comment is worthy of the text."

Yours always,
F.F.

Beverly Farms, Massachusetts
July 8, 1923

Dear Frankfurter,

It is beautiful and bully—to quote either the late General Whittier or Bill James, I forget which of those disparates used the phrase.[1] Of course, again I am gratified and grateful. I infer that you really have begun your vacation and that Chatham is your address. I was very sorry not to see you as we paused in Boston but my wife and I were both so exhausted by the journey, the heat and the antecedents that we weren't up to asking anyone to come to us.

I have glanced at Pound's article following yours and from a flying shot should not think it was one of his greater contributions—but I shall try it again sitting perhaps with a different result.[2] I infer from what you say that Wigmore's book with my little introduction is out. I haven't yet seen it and, though I kept a few copies, felt bound not to send it to anyone until the volume appeared. Stupidly, I forgot to bring my copies along. It was a burden to have the galley proof of the work to come piling in just when I was busiest—but in the next adjournment I did the needful and then said solemnly: Never again.

I had a letter from Nicely (the next Secretary) which pleased me. I told him in reply that I reserved the right to die or resign—but, although advice has not been wanting to get out before I made some discreditable failure, I intend to try another winter unless the doctor should surprise me by saying: No. I agree with Dicey and other wise people that it is well to stop before you have to—but I want to get all I can out of myself up to the danger point.[3] I think you agree with me? I send you both every good wish and especially that you may enjoy a well earned rest.

Affectionately yours,
O. W. Holmes

1. Charles A. Whittier (1840–1908) was one of Holmes's closest comrades during the Civil War.

2. Roscoe Pound, "The Theory of Judicial Decision" (part 3), *Harvard Law Review* 36 (1923): 940.

3. Albert Venn Dicey (1835–1922), Professor of Law at Oxford, met Holmes on a trip to Boston in 1870. In 1898 he visited Harvard Law School where he delivered *Lectures on the Relation between Law and Public Opinion in England during the Nineteenth Century* (New York: Macmillan, 1905).

Beverly Farms, Massachusetts
July 12, 1923

Dear Frankfurter,

Many thanks for the sight of Nagel's letter, returned herewith.[1] Think not, my son, to introduce me to Marcel Proust. I read *Du Cote de Chez Swann* soon after it came out and another of the series.[2] It had but a limited success with me—but just before I left Washington, I reread it with a good deal of emotion. It stirred all the feelings of my own youth. The steps leading from Montgomery Place, now Bosworth Street, to Province Street represent the past as well as the ruins of a chateau and are part of an infancy that presented itself to my memory as framed in the old—the folios in my father's study—its darkness—a black little Rembrandt that hung in the corner all helped—from the attic I could look down to the harbor. There was something in the roof as one saw it from the window that made me feel at home when I lunched in King's Bench Walk and looked out on the tiles. I might go on, but in short all the background and all the vague yearning of those days came back with feeling as I read. But now, as I told you, I am pleasantly skipping from one person to another in Saint Beuve and make notes on the backs of envelopes, that presumably I lose, of books to be read. So long as one has one's eyes, leisure offers entertainment enough.

Please remember me to the young Brandeis and bid him prepare to earn the living of his elders—though as I said, I don't mean to leave until I have some further warning that I had better. I have just received a typewritten report on the U.S. Coal Commission.[3] Brandeis would be deep in it at once. I turn to Sainte Beuve. Homage to Luina.

Affectionately yours,
O.W.H.

1. The letter referred to is missing. Charles Nagel (1849–1940) was Secretary of Commerce from 1909 to 1913. He was married to Fannie Brandeis (1851–1890), sister of Louis D. Brandeis.

2. Marcel Proust, *Du Cote de Chez Swann* (Paris: B. Grasset, 1919).

3. The U.S. Coal Commission, appointed by President Harding and chaired by mining engineer John Hays Hammond (1855–1936), issued its first report in 1923.

Beverly Farms, Massachusetts
July 29, 1923

Dear Frankfurter,

This is but a line to say that I hope all is going well with you and Luina. I am idling as I foretold. Six volumes of Sainte Beuve and one or two trifling tales are all that I have to show for my time. I daresay that you as we have been having some cold weather whereas Laski says they have not in England. A little earlier letter from Ireland complained of cold there. Laski talks of *Pride and Prejudice* as the perfect novel. I am going to get it and reread it. My last attack upon Miss Austen, I blush to say, bored me.

Did I ever mention a young Chinaman, Mr. Wu, now in Berlin, who writes to me from time to time?[1] Pound says he means to get him a scholarship. I wish that he might get it in time for me to see him—but that, I fear, hardly will be—but I didn't begin this letter with this in mind and I mention it with no practical intent. The youth seems remarkable but I think at present has been too much occupied with the abstractions that he naturally turns to while with Stammler.[2] Stammler is intent upon the forms of thoughts. I don't much care for them, as infinite meditation upon a pint pot will not give me a gill of beer.

Affectionately yours,
O.W.H.

1. John C. H. Wu (1899–1986), Chinese jurist and friend of Holmes, received his J.D. from the University of Michigan. His letters to Holmes, published originally in the *T'ien Hsia Monthly* (October 1935), were reprinted in Harry Clair Shriver, ed., *Justice Oliver Wendell Holmes, His Book Notices and Uncollected Letters and Papers* (New York: Central, 1936). When the Communists triumphed in 1949, Wu and his family moved to the United States. He taught at Seton Hall Law School, retiring to Taiwan in 1967. Following his death, an abbreviated ver-

sion of his correspondence was published in *Law Quadrangle Notes* [University of Michigan Law School] 31 (1987): 14.

2. Wu was studying law in Berlin under neo-Kantian philosopher Rudolf Stammler (1865–1938).

Beverly Farms, Massachusetts
August 29, 1923

Dear Frankfurter,

Your letter is most welcome on general principles and for specific themes that I take up.[1] I am glad to know what you tell of Littell, as his retirement sounded like a loss.[2] He is such a delightful writer. Also, I wonder what has become of Francis Hackett.[3] I have seen but not read Shirley's book.[4] By the by I have a full report of the case sent by D. Webster to my grandfather Holmes and a report of his agreement sent by him to grandfather Jackson. Don't undervalue Story—he did so much to make the law fluent. Of course he was a politician and I always have supposed that his appointment was political without knowing much about it. Harcourt I always saw when I went to England.[5] The first time, before his marriage to Miss Motley, he had me at a big dinner where were Froude and other illustrious at Camden Hill and I expected to hear brilliant conversation—but understood little—as is usual everywhere with outsiders so much of the talk is local and momentary—"Did you hear what Bob Lowe said last night?" etc. After dinner he took me over to Lady Airlie where I saw the famous Mrs. Norton.[6] I don't see any great difference between the English civilized man and ours—but rather they have so many more of them and then their civilization is all focused in London whereas ours is scattered.

After volume 10 of Sainte Beuve I have turned this week for a change to Carlyle's *French Revolution*—eloquent—grotesque—with insights—but too much about the meeting of two eternities and the explosion of his—too much gravy.[7] Still, he tells the story in an interesting way. I am in the last volume. He tells it *de haut en bas*[8] as if he were recording the outbreaks of dangerous monkeys. Altogether I am far from the time when I once thought this the book I would ask for on a desert island if I could have but one—a question hard to answer now. Could you answer it? Bar the Bible, Iliad or Odyssey? A book on Analytic Geometry? Perhaps a dictionary if many volumes counted as one book or the folio Shakespeare. I dunno, not Dante and I can think of no one book on philosophy though once I might have said Lotze—*Microcosmus*.[9] I think the traces of last summer have almost—not quite—disappeared and altogether I am in pretty good shape as I infer that you are.

Yours always,
O. W. Holmes

1. The letter referred to is missing.

2. Philip Littell (1868–1943) wrote the column "Books and Things" for *The New Republic* from 1914 to 1923.

3. After leaving *The New Republic* in 1922, Hackett became a popular historian and free-lance writer. His best known work, *What "Mein Kampf" Means to America* (New York: Reynal & Hitchcock, 1941), attacked the appeasement policy of the 1930s.

4. John M. Shirley, *The Dartmouth College Causes and the Supreme Court of the United States* (St. Louis: G. I. Jones, 1877).

5. Sir William George Granville Venables Vernon Harcourt (1827–1904) was a Liberal statesman and twice Chancellor of the Exchequer during Gladstone's ministries. He resigned when Rosebery's Liberal Imperialism gained control of party policy. In 1876 he married the widow Mrs. J. P. Elizabeth Ives, daughter of historian and diplomat John Lothrop Motley (1814–77) who was a close friend of Holmes's father.

6. James Anthony Froude (1818–94) was a historian and author of biographies of Caesar and Erasmus. Robert Lowe (1811–92), Viscount Sherbrooke, was a Liberal in his early career but later opposed Lord Russell's Liberal Reform Bill of 1866. On Mrs. Norton, see above, April 18, 1921.

7. Thomas Carlyle, *The French Revolution* (New York: Harper, 1848).

8. From top to bottom.

9. Hermann Lotze, *Microcosmus: An Essay Concerning Man and His Relation to the World*, 2 vols. (New York: Scribner and Welford, 1885).

Beverly Farms, Massachusetts
September 9, 1923

Dear Frankfurter,

Your letter in turn leads me to one or two remarks and I steal a few moments from Arthur Hill whom I hear discoursing to my wife downstairs, to write what I can in the circumstances.[1] I think I omitted perhaps the most important fact that makes the civilization of the old world superior to ours—that there they learn history and even aesthetics through their eyes as they walk the streets. They get them from infancy and all the time. The idea doesn't need development.

Second—I didn't realize when you spoke of reading the old cases in our reports that you were at work on your prospective book.[2] *Tracte virtute puer.*[3] I am very glad. I long have wished that you would concentrate on such a task and I don't doubt that you will do honor to yourself and the law.

Third—let me timidly suggest caution in the use of the word statesmanship with regard to judges. Of course, it is true that considerations of the same class come before their minds that have to be or ought to be the motives of legislators, but the word suggests a more political way of thinking than is desirable and also has become slightly *banal.* I didn't think the late Chief Justice shone most when he was political.[4] A statesman would consider whether it was wise to bring to the mind of Congress what it might do in this or that direction—but it seems to me wrong to modify or delay a decision upon such grounds. When economic views affect judicial action I should prefer to give such action a different name from that which I should apply to the course of Wilson or Lodge.

[Fourth]—The dictionary for the desert island could not be so considerable a work as the Oxford one—it would not have to be one volume I think—but the point would be the new words that you didn't know. My old partner Munroe once triumphed over me on a bet (without money, a Baptist) that I shouldn't know I forget what large fraction of the first twelve words in Worcester.[5] I must stop untimely—and walk with Hill but I will post this. My grateful homage to Luina for her charming suggestion on this theme. I have lots more to talk about but wait for better days. I write more legibly than you. [Sketch of man thumbing his nose].

Affectionately yours,
O.W.H.

1. The letter referred to is missing.

2. Felix Frankfurter and James M. Landis, *The Business of the Supreme Court* (New York: Macmillan, 1928).

3. Work hard, lad.

4. Edward D. White, Chief Justice from 1910 to 1921, frequently sought compromise during case conferences.

5. William Adams Munroe (1843–1905) was Holmes's law partner, 1872–82. James Emerson Worcester (1784–1865), American lexicographer, published the *Dictionary of the American Language* in 1860.

Beverly Farms, Massachusetts
September 20, 1923

Dear Frankfurter,

Much to my disappointment I am afraid that we shall not see you as we pass through Boston. The fatigue of going on is so great that we must dine alone the evening before leaving and the day is filled with necessary chores. It sounds silly, almost, but we have to spare ourselves more than I should have believed two years ago. No matter—you and I are philosophers and to a certain extent can transcend time and space. Perhaps I shall see you in Washington. The vacation has gone by with the swiftness brought by the routine of age. I have little to show for it—a dozen volumes of Sainte Beuve, Carlyle's *French Revolution*, C. S. Peirce's *Chance, Love and Logic* (philosophy—tabooed had it not been sent to me—but for the moment restoring an edge to my mind) and various stories are all that I recall as I write.[1] But I think I am stronger and the reminiscences of last summer seem nearly gone.

I shall jump into work up to my ears and I shall be curious to see whether I feel good for yet another year, after this. As I was saying to somebody lately, my judgement is resigned but my instincts are not. Well, good men like you will carry on the work and it does not bother me to think of it all being engulfed in the Cosmos. The Cosmos wanted it done whether with ulterior purposes or not I believe to be beyond our speculation and I bow my head.

Affectionately yours,
O. W. Holmes

1. Charles Sanders Peirce, *Chance, Love and Logic*, Morris Cohen, ed. (New York: Harcourt, Brace & Co., 1923). Peirce (1839–1914) had been a member of the Metaphysical Club (1870) which at various times included Holmes as well as Henry and William James, historians Henry Adams (1838–1918) and John Fiske (1842–1901), legal scholar Nicholas St. John Green (1830–76), and philosopher Chauncy Wright (1830–75).

Washington, D.C.
October 11, 1923

Dear Frankfurter,

You will get no good from me this time. I have been working like an Ethiopian brother ever since I got here of a Thursday morning. The first day I stopped only for breakfast and dirty as a pig (said to be naturally a cleanly animal) cleaned up, unpacked and fell on the *certioraris*. There has been no let up. Two decisions written this week and, my wife thinks in consequence, a brisk cold just beginning.[1] So I can only send you my love. Everything has been pleasant and we are getting on well.

Affectionately yours,
O. W. Holmes

1. Both unanimous opinions. In *Frese v. Chicago, Burlington & Quincy Railroad Company*, 263 U.S. 1 (1923), Holmes found that the family of an engineer killed in a train accident could

not recover because the engineer himself was legally responsible for the accident under the Federal Employers' Liability Act (1908). In *United States v. Walter*, *Id.* at 15, a criminal case involving fraudulent claims against the United States and a Washington, D.C., corporation in which the United States owned all the stock, Holmes affirmed the power of the federal government to protect its property, even property held indirectly through a corporation.

Washington, D.C.
October 29, 1923

Dear Frankfurter,

Your letter is cheering.[1] I also am happy—my work done and two weeks ahead! No mighty questions yet though I must talk with Brandeis as to a possible dissent.[2] A dame with a three syllable name that I have forgotten spoke to me last night at the Powhatan to tell us that you are well and happy. I think she said you were with her last summer, but I blush to say that I didn't remember her. She spoke familiarly of the days of the House of Truth. Evidently, you are very high in her books, but I can tell no more. This morning brings a copy of a letter saying that Kaneko's house in Tokio was burned and his daughter killed.[3] I must write to him at once but I dread it.

When I get a chance to take up Pound's *Readings in Roman Law*, Second Edition, Part I—(are there more? This is all I have), I am interested to note that while the Romans and, I may add, their commentators take up real legal questions, the analysis generally is rudimentary and I think it ridiculous to speak (not that Pound does for a moment) as if the Roman law were comparable with ours for the theoretic development.[4] I read the first chapter in Buckland's *Textbook* having the impression that Pound had praised it—but found it rather dull and saw no reason why I should go on.[5] If I wanted to freshen up, which I don't, I would reread Girard, or some other of the many I have fruitlessly perused in the past.[6] I think putting young men who are studying our law also to the Roman is the greatest humbug outside the domain of legally recognized fraud. Though I dare say that Pound would make it pay if I could attend his lectures. Adieu.

Affectionately yours,
O. W. Holmes

1. The letter referred to is missing.

2. *Craig v. Hecht*, 263 U.S. 255, 281–82 (1923). Justice McReynolds's 6–2 majority opinion held that a District Judge's order jailing the author of libelous criticisms of the judge for contempt could not be reviewed in *habeas corpus* proceedings. Holmes's dissent, with Brandeis concurring, concluded that *habeas corpus* was an appropriate remedy: "A man cannot be summarily laid by the heels because his words may make public feeling more unfavorable in case

the judge should be asked to act at some later date, any more than he can for exciting public feeling against a judge for what he already has done." Justice Sutherland took no part in the case.

3. Count Kentaro Kaneko (1853–1942), Japanese statesman, established a lifelong friendship with Holmes when he was a student at Harvard in 1872. His home was destroyed and his daughter killed in the earthquake of September 1, 1923.

4. Roscoe Pound, *Readings in Roman Law* (Lincoln, Neb.: Jacob North, 1906).

5. William Warwick Buckland (1859–1946) was Regius Professor of Civil Law at Cambridge. His *A Textbook of Roman Law from Augustus to Justinian* (Cambridge: University Press, 1921) received the Ames Prize from Harvard Law School.

6. Paul Frederic Girard, *Manuel Elementaire de Droit Romain* (Paris: A. Rousseau, 1896).

Cambridge, Massachusetts
November 4, 1923

Dear Justice Holmes,

Your "stream of products" has begun to flow again: the first opinion has come. It's not the most exciting question (the suability of collectors of customs) but we *do* "live by symbols" and I got a new thrill, all over again, from your writings.[1] For it drove me to rereading to Luina some bits of your speeches.

And I greet you!

The work here is going nicely. The School will soon be fit subject for restraint under the Sherman law if size be the test. We have a thousand students, tho' we are ruthless in weeding them out.[2]

Your year ought to be exciting—what with all the "furroners," but above all the interesting series of questions that are before the Court this Term.[3]

Always faithfully yours,
F.F.

1. *American Railway Express v. Levee*, 263 U.S. 19, 21 (1923). Writing for a unanimous Court, Holmes upheld a federal law limiting damages in interstate commerce over and against the decisions of state courts: "The law of the United States can not be evaded by the forms of local practice."

2. Frankfurter objected to the increasing size of the Harvard Law School. See Parrish, *Frankfurter and His Times*, 150–53.

3. "Furroners" refers to the recently appointed Associate Justices: Pierce Butler (1866–1939), Edward T. Sanford and George Sutherland.

Washington, D.C.
December 15, 1923

Dear Frankfurter,

Many thanks for your continued kindness. Leach sounds all right but I feel the uncertainties of my life and destinies so much that he should be warned with special caution that I reserve the right to die or resign.[1] I don't want to do either and don't mean to unless circumstances change. So far I feel the old gusto of life and find the work as easy as ever. But I can't tell how long this will continue. I watch pretty carefully for any indication of falling off and/or of dissatisfaction or opinion that I am falling off and hang on.

I was pleased that the case of the *Glassblowers v. U.S.* went through.[2] Some grumbling but no dissent expressed. The Solicitor General presented it as a most flagrant and iniquitous case and quoted Shakespeare inaccurately unless my memory of the bard is very wrong.[3] I have but one case on hand that is written and agreed to except by one not heard from.[4]

The foreground at present is occupied by the dentist—then some little business and then I don't see why there shouldn't be some effort to improve the mind. I have just read *Ariel, ou La Vie du Shelley* (from Learned Hand) with as much pleasure as one can feel from reading of blunders and mistakes.[5] It made me feel a little like reading about the Civil War—which I hate to do. Also, Volume I of Ferrero's *Greatness and Decline of Rome*—suggestive but I read no more of that—a cloudy appreciation of atmosphere in which the causal relations are too unquantified for an outsider to feel any confidence.[6] It was the same objection that I feel to all literary histories (as distinguished from histories of Law, Philosophy or Economics). I know there are things I ought to read but I can't think what. Just as I feel as if there were duties that I ought to perform but can't name them.

Brandeis sent me a devilish good opinion this morning and W. Lippmann made a mighty agreeable call the other evening.[7] He dined with us.

I expect my young Chinese friend Mr. Wu to come to the Cosmos Club on the 20th. You never have spoken of him I think. I don't go out, and when I talk it makes me cough but otherwise I am well. My compliments to the Madam.

Affectionately yours,
O. W. Holmes

1. W. Barton Leach (1900–71), Story Professor of Law at Harvard Law School from 1929 to 1969, was Holmes's secretary, 1924–25.

2. *National Association of Window Glass Manufacturers v. United States*, 263 U.S. 403, 412 (1923). Holmes's unanimous opinion held that an agreement between the manufacturers and a union did not violate the Sherman Anti-Trust Law: "The defendants contend with a good

deal of force that it is absurd to speak of their arrangements as possibly having any effect upon commerce among the States, when manufacturers of this kind obviously are not able to do more than struggle to survive a little longer before they disappear, as human effort always disappears when it is not needed to direct the force that can be got more cheaply from water or coal."

3. James Montgomery Beck was Solicitor General from 1921 to 1925. In presenting the government's case, Beck argued that the agreement between the manufacturers and the glass-blowers union had "cribbed, cabined and confined" workers who did not belong to the union. MacBeth, hearing of the escape of Fleance, the son of Banquo, following his father's murder, cried out: "But now I am cabin'd, cribb'd, confin'd, bound in to saucy doubts and fears." *MacBeth*, Act III, scene iv: 24.

4. *Queen Insurance Company of America v. Globe & Rutgers Fire Insurance Company*, 263 U.S. 487 (1924), or *New York v. Jersawit, Id.* at 493. Both were unanimous opinions delivered on January 7, 1924. In *Queen Insurance*, Holmes resisted a claim for stringent interpretation of "warlike operations" regarding a loss due to a collision between friendly ships. *Jersawit* found bankruptcy a valid reason for limiting a state tax on domestic corporations.

5. Andre Maurois, *Ariel, ou La Vie de Shelley* (Paris: B. Grasset, 1923).

6. Guglielmo Ferrero, *The Greatness and Decline of Rome*, 5 vols. (New York: G. P. Putnam's Sons, 1907–1909)

7. Brandeis's opinion may have been *United States v. Illinois Central Railroad*, 263 U.S. 515 (1924), a unanimous ruling upholding the rate-setting powers of the Interstate Commerce Commission, or *Peoria and Pekin Union Railway Company v. United States, Id.* at 528, also unanimous, which restrained the I.C.C. from issuing orders "without notice or hearing."

Washington, D.C.
December 29, 1923

Dear F.F.,

A happy New Year to you both and thanks for your card.

I have had a mirage of leisure while travelling through a desert of duty and dentist, but at the end of the journey I find the end of the rainbow and am having a blissful day or two without obvious neglect of something that I ought to do. Before it came, I (spurred by Laski) read Toqueville's *Ancient Regime* with great admiration and delight, Ruskin's *Seven Lamps of Architecture* with much less, and a little earlier listened to the Secretary of Labor's book—(beginning with iron puddling) with unmitigated pleasure.[1] He must be an adult male I should think. What know you? Now I have leisure's own book, Aubrey's *Brief Lives, 1669–1696*, 2 volumes, Clarendon Press: led to it by *The New Republic* (Phil Littell, wasn't it?).[2] It is long since I have bought anything that so well repaid buying. He was a friend of Hobbes and tells of him more at length than of others. Usually each gets a page or two—and such lots of people you like to hear of. Always with the smack of the contemporary.

The only tasks I have on my mind are to decide whether I will send 9 cents postage to Beverly Farms for something that I am sure not to want—and to collect a check for $1.29 proceeds of auction. But down to yesterday afternoon the time was spoiled by having to be dentified and fearing always that the tooth would break off. But 'tis o'er.

Wu's visit to me gave great pleasure. He came up to all I hoped in intelligence, feeling and judgment. So far as I could be sure that I penetrated, and I didn't think there were any oriental disguises to penetrate.

Mrs. Meyer sent me her book on Chinese Art etc., which I instantly read with great interest.[3] I couldn't help doubting whether her superlatives weren't like those of the Hegelians, the Catholics, and others who having got into a faith see everything in its terms and never can get out. I should like and yet fear to talk with her. But I am going nowhere—not even to the White House with the others on New Years Day.

I trust that all is well with you.

Affectionately yours,
O. W. Holmes

1. James J. Davis, *The Iron Puddler: My Life in the Rolling Mills and What Came of It* (Indianapolis: Bobbs-Merrill, 1922). Davis (1873–1947), Secretary of Labor, 1921–29, served in the U.S. Senate (R-Pa.) from 1932 to 1944.

2. John Aubrey, *Brief Lives, Chiefly of Contemporaries, Set Down by John Aubrey between the Years 1669 and 1696*, 2 vols. (Oxford: Clarendon, 1898).

3. Agnes Elizabeth Ernst Meyer, *Chinese Painting as Reflected in the Thought and Act of Li Lung-mien, 1070–1106* (New York: Duffield, 1923).

Cambridge, Massachusetts
January 25, 1924

Dear Justice Holmes,

I have been following the interchangeable mileage litigation with particular interest, and I rejoice over your decision.[1] Apart from its merits I'm tickled to pieces by the way you did it. It's a gem of an opinion e.g. "The statute naturally enough carried with it more or less mirage of fulfilling the hope that gave it rise." Your pen is certainly dipped in innocent poison!

Wu and I have met, and I'm greatly delighted with him. He is a very charming fellow—warm and vivid, with an intense vitality for things of the mind. We had a merry go about our hero—he insisting the poet turned jurist, I adhering to the philosopher become King.

Things go very happily at the School—I feel, fond illusion, that I'm "imparting ferment" to some of these lads.

Faithfully yours,
F.F.

1. *United States, Interstate Commerce Commission, National Council of Traveling Salesmen's Associations v. New York Central Railroad*, 263 U.S. 603, 610 (1924). Congress, through an amendment to the I.C.C. Act, had directed the Commission to require railroads to issue interchangeable mileage or scrip coupon tickets at "just and reasonable rates." Speaking for a unanimous Court, Holmes found that the Commission's enabling order was inconsistent with the actual wording of the law and therefore voided the order: "Coming as it did from the agitation [by traveling salesmen] for this form of reduced fares, the statute naturally enough carried with it more or less mirage of fulfilling the hope that gave it rise, but in fact it required a determination of what was just and reasonable exactly as in any other case arising under the Interstate Commerce Act."

Washington D.C.
January 26, 1924

Dear Frankfurter,

Your letter comes at a happy moment and makes me happier. I have no doubt that you are imparting ferment to those who are capable of it, and I send you my felicitations and blessing. Naturally I am pleased at your approval of my opinion. The last three Sundays have been fierce. Difficult cases to write. The last Sunday was broken in upon so that my opinion wasn't ready till Wednesday, but I think it is pretty well put, if right, as I hope.[1] The lads have all agreed to it. That leaves me with all my work done up to now. I expect we shall have a hard day today at our conference—as I foresee differences at least in one case—and there will be copious jaw.[2]

Anticipations of leisure always are disappointed but I can't help looking for it in the approaching adjournment, and with no dentist to cloud the horizon there will be the question of what to read. I am rather blank, and yet know that a lot of books are waiting if only I could think what they were. Knopf sent me *The Old and the New Germany* but I shrink a little because it is not my line.[3] A bolder man would be through it while I was vacillating. I have told you I think of the pleasures I got from Aubrey's *Brief Lives*, of the last half of the 17th century. If one resolutely laid improvement aside and sought amusement it might be easy.

I was beginning to be anxious about Wu as I haven't heard for some time, but probably his silence was consideration for the fact that I was hard driven.

I think he is a dear. I advised him to read Tocqueville's *Ancien Regime*—on the ground that those who teach us to believe general propositions are only less reliable than those who encourage us to make them.[4] I hope all is well with Pound. Brandeis is in good shape—we generally go home together. He insists on coming to my door and I express fears to trust him to get back across the street. The conferences are long and tiring but amiable. No one gets angry nowadays. My homage to your lady. It is time for me to prepare.

Yours ever,
O. W. Holmes

1. *Electric Boat Company v. United States*, 263 U.S. 621, 629 (1924), a unanimous opinion denying a patent suit over a steam generator for a torpedo after a rival company had used a similar device to gain a government contract: "The Government is not estopped to show that its contract applied only within narrow limits. . . . The claimant was thought by the Government to have failed in its undertaking, and therefore its device was laid aside."

2. Holmes was probably referring to *The Chicago Junction Case*, 264 U.S. 258 (1924), which had been argued on January 24. The Court divided 6–3, with Brandeis writing for the majority. Sutherland, with McReynolds and Sanford concurring, dissented. See below, February 16, 1924.

3. John Firman Coar, *The Old and the New Germany* (New York: Knopf, 1924).

4. Alexis de Tocqueville, *Ancien Regime* (Paris: Michel Levy, 1856).

Washington D.C.
February 16, 1924

Dear Frankfurter,

It delights me at both ends that you and Wu have taken to each other. Also, I believe you sent me Santayana's *Unknowable*, which needs a second reading.[1] His general way of thinking and mine have much in common—but he has a damned patronising way of presenting himself—reserving the right to a strictly private smile as if he also is an illusion. I have used my too limited leisure in reading Rousseau's *Confessions*—amazing that a book can be as interesting after 150 years as when it was written—a martyr of free speech—too naif to know that he was and crazy enough to think that he was a victim of plots and spies.[2]

Also, somewhat laboriously, *Faust*, part 1.[3] Is not simple pathos rarer in literature than high tragedy? Nothing could be more perfect in that way than every word of Margaret's. The rest of it seems to me rather a motley farrago—with profound and beautiful things of course. I don't think I like Goethe greatly. He sat as a statue with a star on his breast for the universal wise man. He understood poetry but not philosophy. It was not his to explain. So he said all theory is gray. I feel more kindly to the ragamuffin Rousseau little as I should be likely to believe any of his views.

Our conference is over. We sit on Monday. I have only two opinions and decided not to dissent from a case of Brandeis' in which it is not the result but the way of reaching it that I thought wrong.[4] When the opinion is delivered perchance I will tell you more. I am with him in some dissents.[5] He has written a rattling good one. I shouldn't mind idling a week longer but I have cleared my table for action and am ready.

Affectionately yours,
O. W. Holmes

1. George Santayana, *The Unknowable* (Oxford: Clarendon, 1923).

2. Jean-Jacques Rousseau, *Confessions* (1782).

3. Johann Wolfgang von Goethe, *Faust* (1790).

4. In *The Chicago Junction Case*, 264 U.S. 258, 266 (1924), Brandeis found that competitors of the New York Central railroad had shown "serious disadvantage, prejudice and loss of traffic" and thus could bring suit to block an order of the Interstate Commerce Commission allowing the sale of two terminal lines to the N.Y.C. Justice Sutherland dissented, with Justices McReynolds and Sanford concurring.

5. The dissents, both written by Brandeis with Holmes concurring, were *Texas Transportation Co. v. New Orleans*, 264 U.S. 150, 157 (1924) and *Washington v. Dawson and Co.*, *Id.* at 219, 238. *Texas Transportation*, written by Sutherland, denied a municipality the right to levy a license tax on a business that the Court determined was engaged primarily in interstate commerce. Brandeis, noting that the company was essentially an agent of businesses engaged in interstate commerce, dissented: "The New Orleans tax is obviously not laid upon property moving in interstate commerce. Nor does it, like a gross receipts tax, lay a burden upon every transaction. It is simply a tax upon one of the instrumentalities of interstate commerce." *Washington*, written by McReynolds, cited the narrow scope of federal jurisdiction in maritime law as interpreted in *South Pacific v. Jensen*, 244 U.S. 205 (1917), to rule unconstitutional a subsequent act of Congress facilitating maritime injury suits in state courts. Brandeis responded: "*Stare decisis* is ordinarily a wise rule of action. But it is not a universal, inexorable demand." On Holmes's dissent in *Jensen*, see above, March 27, 1917.

Washington, D.C.
March 3, 1924

Dear Frankfurter,

A thousand thanks to you and your dear wife for the remembrance that met me on my return today. I do not turn the corner until Saturday but as I hope to live till then, the sweet reminder will not have been in vain.

Things are going on quietly enough. Brandeis fired off an opinion this morning that in form I thought wrong but as I didn't object to the result—indeed, thought it probably right—I suppressed some observations that I printed.[1] I am hung up for McKenna to make up his mind whether my opinion is to be the Court's or a dissent.[2] This week's opinion goes to the printer tomorrow morning. I think that I rarely have passed a day in which I got so little from the discourse of the bar as today. Better luck I hope tomorrow.

I had a good call last week from Meiklejohn and Hamilton—both I think friends of yours. To my chagrin I got so interested that I forgot to offer them tea—and I talked too much—but they are dears.[3]

The working of time is like judicial legislation—interstitial—but one becomes aware of it from six months to six months. But I have got my burial lot and have no great anxieties—so I thankfully potter along with what I still am allowed to do.

I need not repeat how grateful I am for your ever generous friendship.

Affectionately yours,
O. W. Holmes

1. *The Chicago Junction Case*, 264 U.S. 258 (1924). See above, February 16, 1924.

2. *Western Union Telegraph Co. v. Czizek*, 264 U.S. 281 (1924). Holmes's majority opinion found that the liability of the telegraph company was limited, despite its role in a significant financial loss, because Czizek had not arranged for a repeat telegram to confirm correct transmission of the crucial message. McKenna dissented without opinion.

3. Alexander Meiklejohn (1872–1964), Kantian philosopher and progressive educator, had been President of Amherst College from 1912 to 1923 when he was fired for alienating both the faculty and the trustees. Walton Hale Hamilton (1881–1958) taught economics at Amherst from 1915 to 1923. He was deeply influenced by Thorstein Veblen and the British Fabians. After leaving Amherst, Hamilton taught law and economics at Yale.

Washington, D.C.
March 21, 1924

Dear Frankfurter,

Again my thanks for your kind words. As to Hough's piece—I was tickled with his two lines from the song (wondering if the quotation was right: *as* wot he said . . .).[1] As to the rest, I wondered if he supposed I didn't know or in anyway was bothered by *The China* which I wrote about in *The Common Law* before Hough was grown up.[2] I suspected him of thinking that I didn't recognize the possibility of the ship being bound when the owner was not. In short, I thought I saw farther into the matter than he did. For though to my regret I don't know the practical side of admiralty, or patents, or mines, or business or of anything to speak of, I think I do understand the fundamentals of legal theory better than most of the specialists who stand ready to bully me. I deny that I search for epigrams. I write too rapidly to stop for phrases—and I certainly do not consciously skip over a difficulty. Hough's chaff naturally made me pause to see if he had caught me doing unconsciously. To that extent I took it with a serious face, otherwise with a smile. He has been kind in speech to me on occasion, but I think there is something in my way of writing that irritates him. Not angrily—perhaps because he is an epigrammatist himself. I quoted one of his in a late opinion.[3]

Last Monday I uttered a cry from my heart against the wholesale demand of one of the commissions for free leave to call for all the papers of a corporation engaged in interstate commerce.[4] We are losing our respect for the fundamental guarantees I fear. This week I have another interesting case in which I shall have difficulty in bringing the brethren to accept what Brandeis and I want to get them to—although Brandeis differs from me on a less important point.[5] I think I may be able to get in a conciliatory phrase or two that will satisfy them but I can't tell yet.

Now I am a man of leisure—an hour with prints yesterday. Sedgwick's *Life of Marcus Aurelius* today after Laski: fine introduction to the *Vindiciae contra tyrranos* and Lao Tzu from Wu.[6] I expect to suffer from a vacant mind.

Affectionately yours,
O. W. Holmes

1. Charles Merrill Hough was an authority on admiralty law. His article, "Admiralty Jurisdiction—of Late Years," *Harvard Law Review* 37 (1924): 529, criticized Holmes's opinion in *The Western Maid*, 257 U.S. 419 (1922). The song, as remembered by Hough, went: "It ain't so much as wot 'e said./As the narsty w'y 'e said it."

2. *The China*, 7 Wallace 53 (1868), adjudicated the collision of two vessels in New York Harbor. *The China*, a British vessel, had complied with a statute that required the hiring of a licensed pilot to guide a ship from harbor. However, the Court, in an opinion by Justice Noah H. Swayne (1804–84), found the ship liable for torts even though the result was wholly due to the pilot's negligence. Holmes linked this case to the ancient common law practice of finding inanimate things liable, especially ships in admiralty cases: "The ship is the only security available in dealing with foreigners, and rather than send one's own citizens to search for a remedy abroad in strange courts, it is easy to seize the vessel and satisfy the claim at home, leaving the foreign owners to get their indemnity as they may be able." See Holmes, *The Common Law*, 24–28.

3. In *Queen Insurance*, 263 U.S. 487, 491 (1924), Holmes cited but then rejected as inapplicable Hough's epigram, "Commerce existed only as an adjustment to war," in denying an insurance claim that cited "warlike conditions" as a reason to avoid paying damages. See above, December 15, 1923.

4. *Federal Trade Commission v. American Tobacco Company*, 264 U.S. 298, 305–306 (1924). Holmes, writing for a unanimous Court, concluded that access to the papers of a corporation engaged in interstate commerce must be confined to documents relevant to the inquiry or complaint before the Federal Trade Commission: "Anyone who respects the spirit as well as the letter of the Fourth Amendment would be loath to believe that Congress intended to au-

thorize one of its subordinate agencies to sweep all our traditions into the fire, and to direct fishing expeditions into private papers on the possibility that they may disclose evidence of crime."

5. Probably *Prestonettes, Inc. v. Coty*, 264 U.S. 359, 368 (1924), argued on February 18–19 and decided April 7. Coty, a French citizen, sued to restrain the use of registered trademarks by an American company that repackaged the French perfumes and powders for sale in the United States. Finding for the company, Holmes said that the trademark "does not confer a right to prohibit the use of the word or words. It is not a copyright. . . . A trademark only gives the right to prohibit the use of it so far as to protect the owner's good will against the sale of another's product as his." McReynolds dissented without opinion.

6. Henry Dwight Sedgwick, *Marcus Aurelius* (New Haven: Yale University Press, 1921); Harold J. Laski, ed., *A Defence of Liberty against Tyrants* (London: G. Bell, 1924), published originally as *Vindiciae contra Tyrannos* (1579). Laski argued that the Huguenot scholar Philippe Duplessis-Mornay (1549–1629) rather than the diplomat Hubert Languet (1518–79) was the author; Lao Tzu, Chinese philosopher of the sixth century B.C., is generally regarded as the founder of Taoism.

Washington, D.C.
March 29, 1924

Dear F.F.,

(I wanted to see if I could imitate the admirable monogram with which you sign—it is a failure.) A moment before the simoon breaks upon me, for my prophetic soul expects a stinker from the Chief—to be written in the next days.[1] The Conference is over! I came home headachy and tired and stretched me out and slept like a log till awakened by the advent of your letter. I know neither of the books you mention but am tempted by Muirhead if I get the chance to read it.[2] I am rather cheerful as my two cases—in both of which I expected to be turned down—have a majority and unless the unexpected happens will not be held back for someone to write contra.

I have had a two or three days turn at the classics—perhaps induced by Sedgwick's *Life of M. Aurelius*. I found a volume of Seneca and turned over the pages for a few hours. I think that is all I want of him, but he and a little Plutarch make me realize anew how much the developed doctrine of the Christian Church must have owed to the educated Roman and Greek thought of the times. I read a comedy of Plautus with surprise at the ease of the Latin and without ditto at the rudimentary character of the fun. Then thinking of the day of judgment I read a book of Tacitus: Histoire—there is a man who can write—every sentence as potent as vitriol. He is one of the exceptions to the rule that I at last have the courage to lay down: The literature of the past is a bore. The exceptions are:

1) when you are studying it and the interest is not in it but in your thoughts about it.
2) when you are humbugged—as in G. Murray's *Euripides*—and your pleasure comes from what is not in Euripides.[3]
3) when by exceptional study you have adapted yourself to an alien environment.

I am not talking of excerpts and passages. I mean works taken straight ahead. Even a thing that I admire as much as I always have the *Prometheus Bound* of Aeschylus is not a pleasure to read—except lines here and there but only in its aftershadow. Dante—the greatest sensation I ever had in a literary way—is hard sledging a good deal of the time, When I take Homer I don't enjoy him by the slice but only with a nutpicker laboriously gutting slender pages. Having freed my heart by blasphemy, I send you my blessing and shut up.

Yours as ever,
O.W.H.

1. Simoon: a hot, dry violent wind laden with dust from Asian and African deserts.
2. James Muirhead (1831–89), Professor of Law at the University of Edinburgh and author of *Historical Introduction to the Private Law of Rome*, (Edinburgh: A. and C. Black, 1886).
3. Gilbert Murray, *Euripides and His Age* (New York: H. Holt, 1913).

Washington, D.C.
May 28, 1924

Dear Frankfurter,

What you say about Wu goes to my heart. His letter announcing his departure took me by surprise and was so vague as to dates that I didn't trust a letter but telegraphed to him.[1] I hope he got my wire. He certainly is an unusual and very dear lad and I feel for his anxieties on his return. As usual you put some heart into me. I haven't been very well for the past week though I am pretty fairly up now—and have been thinking rather gloomily that so far as I recall I haven't done anything this term particularly worth remembering.

I am too languid to write at length but don't misunderstand me as feeling any worse. This is normal at the end of a term. Most of my ends are tucked in and my work is done with no extrinsic worries to speak of. I long to see you—but hardly shall expect to when I get to Boston. We are so tired by the journey that I shall try to keep quiet while there, though I may have to attend to a bit of business with Palfrey.[2] Here it is rain, rain, rain—and one of my troubles, coughing, is not helped by it.

My love to you both.

Affectionately yours,
O. W. Holmes

1. On April 5, Wu had written to Holmes: "I shall return to the land of my birth by the middle of June. . . . China is on the eve of a tremendous Revolution, not political, but intellectual and spiritual. A Renaissance! This century is going to witness a rebirth of this oldest nation of the world, a child born of the wedlock between East and West. I shall play my part in that glorious movement, and you may be sure that the seed you have sown will bring forth rich harvest in a distant land." See Michigan Law School, *Law Quadrangle Notes* 31 (1987): 17.

2. John Gorham Palfrey (1875–1945), Boston lawyer, was Holmes's attorney, close friend, and executor of his will.

Cambridge, Massachusetts
June 7, 1924

Dear Justice Holmes,

Yes—Wu did get your wire in good time and he danced a philosophical dance of joy over it.

The present occupant of the White House is not one of my heroes (no man could be whose great stunt, in his father's eye, was that as a boy he got most sap out of a tree!) but last Monday he was the instrument of a very gracious event, and to a good many of us, a very happy one. The camera caught a very warm glimpse of you and you looked as though you were at the beginning, not at the end of a term.[1]

We are at present like Olympians here—deciding the fate of young men.

Always devotedly,
F.F.

1. On June 3, 1924, Holmes received the Roosevelt Memorial Association's gold medal for service from President Coolidge.

Beverly Farms, Massachusetts
July 27, 1924

Dear Frankfurter,

As often happens, just as I had been thinking how long it was since there had been any communications between us and that I certainly should write to you, your article comes.[1] I received and read it today (barring the appendix!) and think it a first class piece of work for which you deserve congratulation and praise.

And now, how go things with you? I am gradually soaking in vacation, and have got so far that I can really feel the joy of life. Subject to the natural melancholy of old age. I am no longer oppressed at every moment by the thought that I ought to be doing something—I don't know what. I take a two hour motor drive nearly every morning and almost without *arriere pensee* renew my delight in the rocks and ever changing sea and the windswept downs that you remember. The first month now happily finished was not without a task; for besides some business I had to read with a dictionary O. Spengler, *Der Untergang des Abendlandes* (volume 1), sent to me by Cohen.[2] It well repaid me by the stimulus it gave—and none the less that I happily disbelieved half of what he said. At odd moments I finished what I had left of Sainte Beuve's *Causeries*. Now I have brought from Boston Thucydides (with a translation)—the last of my Day of Judgment books (for I read enough of Tacitus for examination purposes last winter)—and *La Guerre et la Paix*—but these will keep and nothing worries or hurries me and I am feeling well.[3] I even feel more cheerful about my last winter's work. On glancing at it here and there I don't see but it was up to the mark, and if it wasn't interesting I think it was due to the cases rather than to me. I hope you can give as comfortable account of yourself and if you are near the venerable Brandeis, of him also. I miss you.

Affectionately yours,
O. W. Holmes

1. Felix Frankfurter and James M. Landis, "Power of Congress over Procedure in Criminal Contempts in 'Inferior' Federal Courts—A Study in Separation of Powers," *Harvard Law Review* 37 (1924): 1010.

2. Oswald Spengler, *Der Untergang des Abendlandes* (Munchen: C. H. Beck, 1918). Published in English as *The Decline of the West* (London: G. Allen, 1922).

3. Thucydides, *History of the Peloponnesian War*, trans. Richard Crawley (New York: Dutton, 1910); Leo Tolstoy, *La Guerre et la paix*, 3 vols. (Paris: Hachette, 1918).

Beverly Farms, Massachusetts
July 31, 1924

Dear Frankfurter,

A word at once in answer as to August 15–19.[1] Of course I want to see you. The only "only" is to try to let me know beforehand as the time approaches or arrives because it seems as if one or two of the very few engagements that I have for the summer would fall in that neighborhood, and I should want to get you without the damper of other visitors. When I finished Spengler I felt repaid by his suggestiveness, but I concluded that if he had made a philosophy for Germany, as he aspired to, he had not made one for me. I think he gets a good deal further away from the landscape than Turner did, but he makes a vivid and striking picture.[2] Now I am on Thucydides whose Greek with the Loeb translation to give me the lead I don't find hard.[3] It is the last, I believe, of my Day of Judgment books. I wrote one decision with a map on a Spanish title and I believe had to correct my map. I believe all you say about Brandeis. Give him my love.

Affectionately yours,
O.W.H.

1. The letter referred to is missing.
2. The English Impressionist J. M. W. Turner.
3. See above, July 7, 1924.

Beverly Farms, Massachusetts
September 25, 1924

Dear Frankfurter,

Many thanks for the verses which I read last night to the Hales and made them laugh consumedly—and from Mrs. Holmes for the charming photograph.[1] It was good to see you both—and good to have this vision of one of you. I hope the sight may be repeated in Washington. Our trunks have gone and for the next day or two we shall be on a hand bag basis—the most independent moment of the year. I am hoping for three days of happy idleness—then solitude with such rest as may be in town for 48 hours and then the plunge.

Affectionately yours,
O. W. Holmes

I not only hope but expect that you will have a happy term.

1. The verse has not been identified. Mr. and Mrs. Richard Walden Hale. Richard Hale (1871–1943), lawyer and founder of the Boston firm of Hale and Dorr, was a close friend of Holmes and a principal source for Catherine Drinker Bowen (1897–1973) when she was writing *Yankee from Olympus*.

Washington, D.C.
December 9, 1924

Dear Frankfurter,

It was a great pleasure, as always, to get your letter.[1] Things seem to be going well with both of us. Yesterday was the anniversary of my taking my seat. I fired off my weekly cases and this morning distribute a tuppeny little chap for this week.[2] I remember that Devens when we sat writing at the same table and he had finished a little one, would say: Go forth little titman and not all the powers of sophistry shall prevail against thee.[3] I was delighted about Charley Curtis but even as I write the news comes of Pitney's death.[4] I suppose it was a relief to all, but it gives one a touch of sadness. At first he aggravated me but as time went on I learned to appreciate more and more his faithful, serious devotion to his job, his great industry and, helped in this as in other things by Brandeis, his intellectual honesty. It is hard to get a man as good as he was, whatever reserves one may make in superlatives.

Of course I am reading nothing to speak of except cases when we sit, but I have been making up for not reading the newspaper by a book unattractive in appearance and title which nonetheless to me is golden. *These Eventful Years*, published by the Encyclopedia Britannica Company, and having articles on the war, the campaign, the countries concerned, economics, politics and in the end science, literature, music, art—all, as far as I have got (well into Volume 2), by the most illustrious and competent men.[5] I have been thrilled.

Laski writes that he draws near to the end of his book—what a fiend of achievement that chap is.[6] I always fear that he is running the machine too hard—but he comes up smiling and I hope that he and his wife, who I don't doubt keeps an eye on him about it, know better than my apprehensions. How comes on your magnum opus?

I must go to work. Best wishes. In a week I look forward to more leisure.

Affectionately yours,
O. W. Holmes

My homage to Luina.

1. The letter referred to is missing.

2. Probably *United States v. Weissman*, 266 U.S. 377, 379 (1924), a unanimous opinion denying the Government's attempt to expand the right of review in the Criminal Appeals Act (1907) after a judge had ordered a directed verdict for dismissal because the indictment failed to charge an offense: "If directing the verdict was wrong it certainly was not beyond the jurisdiction of the Court. The jury was there and the prisoner before them, and so far as jurisdiction is concerned it did not matter whether evidence had been put in or not."

3. Charles Devens, Holmes's colleague on the Supreme Judicial Court of Massachusetts and Attorney General of the United States in the Hayes administration.

4. Charles P. Curtis, Jr., had become the youngest person ever to be elected to the Harvard Corporation.

5. *These Eventful Years*, 2 vols. (New York: Encyclopedia Britannica, 1924).

6. Harold J. Laski, *A Grammar of Politics* (London: G. Allen & Unwin, 1925).

Washington, D.C.
January 6, 1925

Dear Frankfurter,

Thanks for your letter which warms my heart.[1] I have been shut up with lumbago these two days and so did not witness McKenna's *adieux* of yesterday.[2] He leaves affectionate memories behind him. Also I had to ask the Chief to see my solitary decision.[3] It has no legal interest but I think is well put in a matter of frightful importance—or that would be such unless McKenna, who has political shrewdness, is right in saying that nothing will happen and that a *modus vivendi* will be reached. It took some starch out of me to write it.

Denby called and I was horrified at first at the notion that he had been offered the place before I had been consulted but he soon put me right as to that.[4] I took to him. I like the cut of his jib and we jawed for a space. I told him that I reserved the right to die or resign and stipulated that he was neither married nor engaged. I would not have taken Leach had I known earlier that he was married but he is a good worker and his wife does not interfere—indeed, is pleasant—but I want a free man, and one who may be a contribution to society.[5] I think Denby will fill the bill if I am still here with a bill to fill. I have spent the day reading *certioraris* so I send you both my love and shut up. I had a delightful glimpse of Cohen.

Affectionately yours,
O. W. Holmes

1. The letter referred to is missing.

2. Justice McKenna retired and was replaced by Attorney General Harlan Fiske Stone (1872–1946). Stone became Chief Justice in 1941.

3. *Sanitary District of Chicago v. United States*, 266 U.S. 405, 425 (1925), contested federal

restrictions on the volume of water that Chicago could take from Lake Michigan for sanitation purposes. Holmes's unanimous opinion declared that the power of the federal government to remove obstructions to commerce was superior to that of the states to provide for the welfare of their inhabitants: "This is not a controversy between equals. The United States is asserting its sovereign power to regulate commerce and to control the navigable waters within its jurisdiction."

4. Charles Denby, Jr. (1901–82), son of U.S. envoy to China Charles Denby (1861–1938), was Holmes's secretary for the October 1925 term.

5. W. Barton Leach, Holmes's secretary in 1924–25.

Cambridge, Massachusetts
January 7, 1925

Dear Justice Holmes,

I have paid no attention thus far to newspaper talk about your resignation but tonight's *Transcript* has a "story" which has the pretense of "authority."[1] I still take no stock in it, but cannot withhold saying the following: If you are at all thinking about it and are influenced by the quality of your judicial output, then I am entitled to speak, for your opinions are among the very few subjects on which I feel my study justifies a judgment. I am wholly uninfluenced by any personal devotion, for my devotion would lead me to be very strict and scientific in my appraisal. I say without hesitation that your opinions this term show the same eye for the jugular, the same powerful deftness in striking it as of old. I hope that this does not sound arrogant—I certainly feel very humbly in writing. For myself and talking with others fit to judge I discern nothing but unabated powers.

Faithfully yours,
F.F.

1. *Boston Evening Transcript*, January 7, 1925: "A report, accepted in high official circles as authentic, was circulated today that Oliver Wendell Holmes of Boston will resign as an Associate Justice of the Supreme Court of the United States. . . . His probable retirement has accentuated the discussion now reaching fever heat over appointment and patronage."

Washington, D.C.
January 10, 1925

Dear Frankfurter,

It is 6:30 p.m. and I am but a few minutes back from the conference so I shan't write long. I wonder who the S.O.B.s are that start such yarns. I have given no intimation of any intent to retire nor have I any such intent. As Fuller used to say, I am not to be paragraphed out of my office.[1] Between ourselves, do you suppose that such items are started by malice aforethought in the interest of a succession? I have heard of one or two who would consent to fill a blank here.[2] I hope that you have indicated or will to the next year secretary that I shall hope to have him in good time. I thank you for writing and your ever kind thoughts.

Affectionately yours,
O. W. Holmes

My letter is private but of course you are free to deny authoritatively if anyone speaks of the matter.

1. Melville Weston Fuller (1833–1910), Chief Justice of the Supreme Court, 1888–1910.

2. Holmes suspected Arthur Prentice Rugg (1862–1938), Chief Justice of the Supreme Judicial Court of Massachusetts and, like President Coolidge, an alumnus of Amherst College, of plotting for his seat. Writing to Sir Frederick Pollock, he said of Rugg: "He is a friend, I think a classmate of the President, and recently was at the White House, but didn't call on me. . . . Rugg is a respectable, hard-working, rather long-winded man who, I believe, has made his own way very creditably, but from the talk of the bar and what I have read of his writing I should think not the equal of his predecessor [Marcus Perrin] Knowlton who in his day was most anxious for my appointment and showed it with a naivete that made me smile." See Howe, ed., *Holmes-Pollock Letters*, 2:161.

Washington, D.C.
January 22, 1925

Dear F.F.,

Many thanks for your Cardozo's letter which went to my heart and which I shall keep by your leave.[1] Only such things make me wonder whether I hadn't better stop before something makes them talk otherwise.

Item. I wonder that we hear nothing from Wu. A letter from China the other day referred to him but I haven't had a word.[2]

Weren't you glad of L. Hand's promotion—too long delayed?[3] I have just had to deal with an admirable opinion by him of which I have said in mine, if the boys don't change it, "after a discussion that leaves nothing to be added."[4] But as the case is not decided yet this is *entre nous*.

Affectionately yours,
O.W.H.

This has been and is a week of high pressure as perhaps my handwriting shows.

1. Cardozo had written: "Your visit a few weeks ago was welcome not only for the pleasure of seeing you and talking with you, but also for the good news you brought with you that the greatest judge in the world does not intend to resign. I thought I detected in the newspapers the signs of an effort to create a hostile atmosphere." Cardozo to Frankfurter, January 15, 1925, Box 1, folder 6, Cardozo Papers, Harvard Law School Library.

2. Wu must have soon written Holmes a despondent letter for, on January 27, Holmes responded: "I imagine that you are at the time of life when the staying power of your enthusiasm will be most tried. For me at least there came moments when faith wavered." Shriver, ed., *Uncollected Letters*, 272.

3. Learned Hand was promoted to the United States Circuit Court of Appeals (2nd Circuit) in 1924. He served as Senior Judge of that Court from 1939 to 1951 and continued sitting in cases until his death in 1961.

4. *Direction der Disconto-Gesellschaft v. United States Steel Corporation*, 300 Fed. 741 (1924); 267 U.S. 22, 28 (1925). Agreeing with Hand's decision, Holmes's unanimous opinion found that an English corporation serving as Public Trustee had, during World War I, legitimately seized and claimed ownership of stock certificates issued by a New Jersey corporation to a German corporation: "The question who is owner of the paper depends upon the law of the place where the paper is."

Cambridge, Massachusetts
January 25, 1925

Dear Justice Holmes,

If you have time I hope you will look at the recent opinion of Sargant J. (one of the best of the present English judges) in *Reynolds v. Shipping Federation* (1924), 1 ch. 28 (particularly p. 39, top) and see how thoroughly your theory of torts has become the bone and marrow of the current law.[1] Again and again in studying a particular subject I find that, if you have dealt with it, it's been dealt with.

Faithfully yours,
F.F.

1. Sir Charles Henry Sargant (1856–1942), appointed to the High Court in 1913 and the Court of Appeals in 1923, was most highly regarded for his work in chancery. *Reynolds v. Shipping Federation*, 1 ch. 28 (1924), asked whether an agreement allowing the Shipping Federa-

tion to hire only members of the National Union constituted an invasion of the plaintiff's *prima facie* right to seek and obtain employment. Sargant ruled against the plaintiff, observing that the agreement sought to advance the interests of employers and employees alike by securing or maintaining the advantages of collective bargaining. The agreement, he concluded, did not target particular individuals, but merely operated to exclude those individuals who did not possess a qualification—membership in the National Union—which was within the reach of anyone who desired employment.

Washington D.C.
March 8, 1925

Dear F. and L.,

Your kind remembrance makes my birthday happier but I do not need flowers or letters to make me realize the constancy of a friendship that has added so much to the joy and constancy with which I keep on. You have encouraged me when I needed encouragement. If I have counted for you, it hardly can repay what I owe.

Ever sincerely yours,
O. W. Holmes

Washington, D.C.
May 2, 1925

Dear Frankfurter,

The book (Bertrand Russell) came and although I have hardly known which way to turn I have found time to read it with great pleasure and I thank you heartily.[1] I agree with almost every word of it only I think he is a sentimentalist about war and doesn't truly state the motives of those who encourage others to take part in one. Also I think he has a mystic respect for the criticism of the Cosmos by man which I regard as unfounded. They all seem to me like damning the weather—merely indicating that the individual does not like it and to that extent is ill adjusted.

We draw to the end. I am in good shape and shall see at our conference today whether my two cases, all I have, can get through.[2] Then with what is assigned to me tonight and anything that I possibly may take from some other I shall have unloaded my burden. Of course we don't get to Beverly for about a month and a half but I may be able to seek some improvement before that time. We had a delightful visit from L. Hand on Thursday. I only wish that I might also have seen Cardozo. Hand hits me where I live.

I am dreadfully behind with letters and especially I have delayed a week in writing to Laski. I hope to do it tomorrow. The dentist adds to my complexities. My homage to Luina.

Affectionately yours,
O. W. Holmes

1. Bertrand Russell, *What I Believe* (New York: E. P. Dutton, 1925).

2. Probably *Colorado v. Toll*, 268 U.S. 228, 231 (1925), and *Lewellyn v. Frick*, *Id.* at 238, 252, both unanimous opinions. In *Colorado v. Toll*, the State challenged the exclusive power of the superintendent of the Rocky Mountain National Park to grant permission to use roads located within the park but constructed by the State prior to the park's creation. Holmes found that the legislation creating the park made "no attempt to give exclusive jurisdiction to the United States, but on the contrary the rights of the State over the road are left unaffected." He concluded that Colorado was entitled to try the question of the jurisdiction of the superintendent of roads. In *Lewellyn v. Frick*, Holmes ruled that the federal government's suit to include insurance policies in the estate taxes of the steel magnate Henry Clay Frick (1849–1919) was a violation of due process and would "impose an unexpected liability that if known might have induced those concerned to avoid it and use their money in other ways." See also *Frick v. Pennsylvania*, 268 U.S. 473 (1925).

Washington, D.C.
May 22, 1925

Dear Frankfurter,

Again you and your colleague are to be congratulated on a solid and suggestive piece of work.[1] It seems to me very stimulating to mind and hopes, though not without producing a possible apprehension of the effect of your regional associations upon the general bond. I feel happier about my country as I read it. I am now a gent of leisure. Perhaps you saw the report that I was to resign in the spring and that Brandeis had just returned from a sanatorium—one as true as the other.[2] Does anyone want a Massachusetts vacancy?

Yours as ever,
O. W. Holmes

1. Felix Frankfurter and James M. Landis, "The Compact Clause of the Constitution—A Study of Interstate Adjustments," *Yale Law Journal* 34 (1925): 685, 729, argued that states should address regional concerns by devising compacts among themselves, as provided for in Article VI of the Constitution, rather than awaiting federal regulation or judicial intervention: "The overwhelming difficulties confronting modern society must not be at the mercy of the false antithesis embodied in the shibboleths 'States-Rights' and 'National Supremacy.' We must not deny ourselves new or unfamiliar modes in realizing national ideals."

2. See above, January 10, 1925.

Washington, D.C.
May 30, 1925

Dear Frankfurter,

A few days ago I had a letter from Wu who is full of his schemes of a Law Institute and with it plans of a kindred which he asked me to send to you.[1] Such things convey little to me and my one injunction is that whatever else you do, you don't return them to me. I propose to forward them to you with all deliberate speed when I can get somebody to do them up. Wu's letter worried me for although he didn't ask me to do anything, I feared that he expected me to be up and doing and I am writing to him that I can do nothing except grunt with sympathy. He is a wonderfully dear young fellow, and I hope he isn't going into his dream prematurely. It does disturb me mightily.

Last Saturday I was indiscreet enough to express a notion about a Porto Rico case, which sent it to me to write, and as we had somewhere round 35 *certioraris* this week has not been idle.[2] I don't see that anything more can be added now. I am rather pleased with my share in the term's work. I have had some interesting cases and got off a few things I was glad to say and this work has come easy. I was apprehensive a few times that my opinions were shorter than Brandeis inwardly approved though he didn't say so but if, as I meant to, I hit the nail on the head I am content.

Ever sincerely yours,
O. W. Holmes

1. Wu never carried out his plan for a Law Institute which he was going to name after Holmes. See Shriver, ed., *Uncollected Letters*, 277–79.

2. In *Cami v. Central Victoria*, 268 U.S. 469 (1925), Holmes, speaking for a unanimous Court, declared that a tax on manufactured sugar imposed by the city of Carolina, Puerto Rico, was unconstitutional because it violated the limits on taxation established in the Puerto Rican Acts of 1914 and 1920.

Beverly Farms, Massachusetts
June 14, 1925

Dear Frankfurter,

From hell to here is a good deal of a change. It was completed last night and I am slowly resuming normalcy. I gave an expiring kick on the last day (Brandeis was with me) in favor of the right to drool on the part of believers in the proletarian dictatorship—only a page—please read it.[1] Now I am vacuous and mean to remain so for a time though on Laski's recommendation I asked them to send me Sainte-Beuve's *Port Royal* from the Athenaeum and am disappointed that it is not here.[2]

I don't think I ever knew such trying weather as we had in Washington. The only relief was dining on the roof of the Powhatan and seeing the darkness come on and the electric sparks come out over a vast landscape. To breathe living air is still a joy. Perhaps after a season of being simply an animal I shall have an idea once more. Homage to the lady.

Yours as ever,
O. W. Holmes

1. *Gitlow v. New York*, 268 U.S. 652, 673 (1925). Justice Sanford's majority opinion upheld the prison sentence of Benjamin Gitlow (1891–1965) for violating the criminal anarchy statute of the New York Criminal Code by advocating Communist revolution and authoring and distributing *The Left Wing Manifesto*. Holmes, returning to the issues he raised in *Abrams v. United States*, 250 U.S. 616 (1919), found "no present danger of an attempt to overthrow." He concluded: "If in the long run the beliefs expressed in proletarian dictatorship are destined to be accepted by the dominant forces of the community, the only meaning of free speech is that they should be given their chance and have their way." The *Gitlow* majority opinion represented an important milestone in the incorporation of the Bill of Rights into the Fourteenth Amendment by assuming that the First Amendment was incorporated. Benjamin Gitlow was pardoned by New York Governor Alfred E. Smith (1873–1944) after serving three years of a five- to ten-year sentence.

2. Charles-Augustin Sainte-Beuve, *Port Royal*, 5 vols. (Paris: L. Hachette, 1840–59).

Ithaca, New York
June 30, 1925

Dear Justice Holmes,

I wonder if you can happen on the July number of the *Yale Review* in which Cardozo has a paper on "Law and Literature."[1] It's a sprightly and discerning essay in which he pays you his well-known devotion. It led a lawyer friend of mine to "take a diversity" and to urge on Cardozo that while what you wrote was literature, it was not desirable "judicial exposition"—his desideratum in opinions. To which Cardozo replied as follows:

"I wrote the article for laymen rather than for lawyers or future judges. I was thinking as I wrote more of literary joys than of expository virtues. But I doubt whether I should be willing to change if my aim were something different. After all, one judges best from one's own experience. Thus judging, I find that I gain more from Holmes than from any one else, alive or dead. Pick up his opinions haphazard, even the early ones in Massachusetts, one finds them studded with sentences that illumine the dark places. I find no equal inspiration anywhere. I find that I am a bit distrustful of the development of law by exposition. Too often the exposition has the dangers of a code. I am satisfied for my part with illuminating suggestion."

To all of which I say, if I may, Amen! I have been reading Rait's volume on Dicey and with much delight. Dicey is an admiration—has been ever since I read his *Law and Public Opinion* as a law student, and he wears very well through his letters and diary.[2] I had not realized before that you and he were as intimate as his biographer indicates.

I am here for the month of July doing some summer law teaching. It's a new experience and it's a lovely spot for the venture. The student body is a mixed job lot and makes me appreciate, as never before, what Ames meant when he said, "The glory of the Harvard Law School is its student body." And for the first time I have females in the class—even so, the world is not going to the bowwows, nor is anything particular happening to them. Some are good, some are bad—strangely like boys.

I'm beginning Keyserling's *Travel Diary*—you, I assume, have long since read it.[3] Good days to you.

Always devotedly,
F.F.

1. Benjamin Cardozo, "Law and Literature," *Yale Review* 14 (1925): 699, 706. Among several references to Holmes is the following: "The sluggard unable to keep pace with the swiftness of his thought will say that he is hard to follow. If that is so, it is only for the reason that he is walking with a giant's stride."

2. Robert S. Rait, *Memorials of Albert Venn Dicey* (London: Macmillan, 1925).

3. Hermann Keyserling, *Travel Diary of a Philosopher* (New York: Harcourt, Brace, 1925).

Beverly Farms, Massachusetts
July 2, 1925

Dear Frankfurter,

Many thanks for your letter. I have not seen Cardozo's article as I don't get the law periodicals here. I should like and perhaps shall when I get to Washington. I couldn't get the two vital words of the criticism. What I should say generally is that I assume that I am writing for those skilled in the art and that long-winded developments of the obvious seem to me as out of place in an opinion as elsewhere. I am deeply gratified by what Cardozo says. It is the final reward of one's labors when such men as he and you say well done. This is absolutely true. I care more for it than for office or for any other success.

I am trying to be at leisure but find it hard at this moment because of drawing checks and a thousand mosquito bites and always because even the employments of leisure translate themselves into duties. Laski put me on to Sainte Beuve's *Port Royal*, 5 volumes. I don't quite see why though I have become more familiar with Pascal. But one asks oneself why should I become familiar with thoughts that I don't believe and that are not important to my lines of activity—not even, I venture to think, to one's general philosophy of life. However it is good to have a *piece de resistance*. I have read three volumes or close to it. As Sly says in *Taming of the Shrew*, "A most good play/would 'twere done."[1] (I think this the best thing in the drama but commentators have thought that Sly's talk was unworthy of Shakespeare and must be attributed to another hand.) Do you recommend Doughty's *Arabia* of which you spoke some time ago?[2] I am told that it was published at $17.50 and hardly want to pay that for a pig in a poke. I don't promise to get it even if you say yes. Meantime I get lovely drives and toddle round a very little.

Yours as ever,
O. W. Holmes

1. "'Tis a very excellent piece of work, madam lady: would 'twere done!" *Taming of the Shrew*, Act I: scene 1 (258–59).
2. Charles Montagu Doughty, *Travels in Arabia Desert* (New York: Boni and Liveright, 1925). Originally published in 1888.

Beverly Farms, Massachusetts
July 17, 1925

Dear Frankfurter,

Forgive this stinking paper and forgive me if I write only a word of thanks for your kindnesses. I have received and read Cardozo's article and the reviews of H. Adams—the latter returned by this mail—with the pleasure that you expected.[1] Cardozo would make me proud if I didn't think pride the most unphilosophical of emotional sins. The other seems to be delicately searching. But I am distracted by 1000 *petit soins* that require my attention and can't write at length. I have finished *Port Royal*—thank the Lord—not without profit, the greater for what Laski writes about it. And various other books demand my attention, especially Beveridge's book in typewriting—the same care about detail and the same power of telling a story as in his Marshall.[2] One volume, *Post Mortem*, by a doctor opens a promising vein to account for the actions of historic characters by medical facts.[3] He says Henry VIII had the pox and Joan of Arc suffered from suppressed menses.

That's as far as I've got. I can write no more—not on account of books but domestic details.

Affectionately yours,
O. W. Holmes

1. Henry Adams, *Democracy: An American Novel* (New York: Henry Holt, 1925), was published anonymously in 1880. Adams was confirmed as the author in 1923. Among the reviews was Edmund Wilson's (1895–1972), *New Republic* 44 (1925): 203, which linked Adams with Henry James, concluding: "We are inclined to feel that, in guarding their prejudices and principles so jealously, James and Adams eventually became prigs."

2. Beveridge was at work on a four volume biography of Abraham Lincoln. Two volumes were published posthumously as *Abraham Lincoln, 1809–1858* (Boston: Houghton Mifflin, 1928).

3. Charles MacLaurin, *Post Mortem* (New York: George H. Doran, 1922).

Beverly Farms, Massachusetts
July 30, 1925

Dear Frankfurter,

If there has been no letter of thanks for your last solid and interesting study of the business of our Constitution *peccari*.[1] I read it I hope with profit, certainly with pleasure and with the desire to see the rest. But after the task that Laski set me in *Port Royal* came his own book only finished a day or two ago.[2] It disturbs me a little to know what to say although I wrote some qualifications when I had got half through. I don't believe I ever read so definite, learned and able a working out of socialist schemes but the trouble is that I don't believe them. I don't agree with the premises as to human rights etc. I think the passion for equality is more likely to be a noxious humbug than an inspiration. I appreciate his insight in recognizing the necessity for world organization as a condition of success but I don't believe that it will come anytime I need bother about and if, as he predicts, the alternative is the ruin of civilization, I fear for the future. But prophecies are shaky things and I still sleep o'nights. I fully recognize that my feelings may mean that I am finished and lag superfluous. It makes me wonder if I do not but my feelings remain although I can't doubt that some sort of great change will come within an appreciable time from the exhaustion of present resources. Laski without definitely facing it seems to me to fall into the dramatic way of thinking that I have talked about so long. I don't believe that any change in the ownership and distribution of *our present* resources could make much difference—a question of quantity. As to the improvement that would come with a different regime I think speculation not very convincing. The world has been promised bliss before now by constitution makers. I don't want to say unpleasant things to a friend, and of course Laski didn't expect me to agree, but I don't quite know what to say.

Also I have had chapters of Beveridge on Lincoln which I think will show the gradual emergence of a figure out of the clay in a way that it hasn't been done before. And now, I am free for a little literature and amusement. *Port Royal* led me to read Lemaitre on Racine and I have sent for Racine that I may read some of his plays in the light of Lemaitre's beautiful exposition.[3] He makes me feel as if I could see the great man in a way that I never have. I have read a little Pascal with new pleasure and mean now to read the second part of *Don Quixote* although Fitzgerald writes as if it could be appreciated only in the Spanish.[4]

I had a short line from that dear Wu the other day in which he seemed like Archimedes to be pursuing his thought undisturbed by external noises and the shooting of some students. I do hope he will be able to keep on. I get occasional letters from people who haven't found out that I am behind the times and there was a drawing of and somewhat blunted interview with me in the June *Century*. But these merely remind me of a remote world which I hope will not become real to me again before October.[5] Meantime I take a daily drive, snooze a little, read a little—not much, as you see—and am very well. I hope the same is true for you and that you now are about to begin on idleness. My homage to Luina.

Affectionately yours,
O. W. Holmes

1. Felix Frankfurter and James M. Landis, "The Business of the Supreme Court of the United States: A Study in the Federal Judicial System," *Harvard Law Review* 38 (1925): 1005, focused on the early history of the federal judicial system, especially the judiciary acts which required Supreme Court justices to ride circuit.
2. Laski, *A Grammar of Politics*.
3. Jules Lemaitre, *Jean Racine* (Paris: Calmann-Levy, 1905).
4. In 1866 the scholar Edward Fitzgerald (1809–83) wrote: "I do not believe that *Don Quixote* can be translated into English: the Gravity and Stateliness of the Spanish Language is, in this case, part of the Subject." See Alfred M. Terhune and Annabelle B. Terhune, eds., *The Letters of Edward Fitzgerald*, vol. 2 (Princeton: Princeton University Press, 1980), 605.
5. W. Tittle, "Glimpses of Interesting Americans," *Century* 110 (1925): 181.

Beverly Farms, Massachusetts
August 1, 1925

Dear Frankfurter,

The enclosed is sent to you by order of Laski. It is of the old fashioned slashing kind—to be expected in view of what the notice says that Keyserling says of the English, but while I don't take it too seriously it sufficiently accords with my guess for me to feel exonerated from getting the work.[1] I am reading Racine for a day or two in the light of Lemaitre. I can see a good deal but far from enough to put Racine among the five great poets of the world with Faguet.[2] I wrote to you a day or two ago. I don't know where you are etc.! Sent to Law School.

Affectionately,
O.W.H.

1. The enclosed article is missing. On Keyserling, see above, June 30, 1925.

2. Emile Faquet (1847–1916), critic and literary historian. See *Histoire de la literature francaise*, 2 vols (Paris: Plon-Nourrit, 1900), and *Histoire de la poesie francaise de la renaissance au romantisme* (Paris: Boivin, 1923).

Beverly Farms, Massachusetts
August 11, 1925

Dear Frankfurter,

Your letter came this evening.[1] I know Gay Head and Martha's Vineyard. Just after I was appointed Judge (in Massachusetts), Shattuck, my wife and I landed there in our sailing and I hesitated to go ashore at the place because of a sign forbidding it and I thought it unbecoming that a Judge of the Supreme Judicial Court should be had up before a Justice of the Peace.[2] But that was not the first or the last time that I saw these regions. Impressive as I remember them also I was interested to see among the names on the sign *L'Homme Dieu*—pronounced I believe lummeydew.

I grieve over what you say of Keyserling and Doughty as I don't want to be bothered with either of them. The notice of Keyserling was sent to you by order of Laski who sent it to me. I wrote to him that it seems an old fashioned British slashing article. I didn't believe it except as an excuse. I infer that you are likely to agree with Laski more than I do about his book but of course I don't know conditions in England! After I read him I studied Racine a few days and then reread the second part of *Don Quixote* with surprise to see how much comes from him and more specifically from Motteux's translation—a vivid piece of English.[3] I thought I saw its influence upon Scott and found the original of Mrs. Nickelby—and what I had supposed modern phrases like "Take it from me," "My name is———" (cheeses or champagne or whatever one is going to choose).

Just now I am finishing rereading Pascal: *Provinciales*—easier than *Don Quixote*—although the questions may not interest the writing and the dialectic are so modern and pungent.[4] From time to time Beveridge and Lincoln—I don't want any damned longwinded duties and so still hope to avoid Keyserling. I blush not to know about Becker whom Laski mentioned as one of the two leading American historians—what has he written?[5] I am glad you put the fear of God into Cornell. I wish I knew more about Cuthbert Pound than I do.[6]

Yours ever,
O.W.H.

1. The letter referred to is missing.
2. George Otis Shattuck (1829–97) was Holmes's law partner. See *Proceedings of the Massachusetts Historical Society* (2nd series) 14 (1900): 367.
3. Miguel de Cervantes, *The History of the Ingenious Gentleman, Don Quixote of La Mancha*, 4 vols., Peter A. Motteux, trans, (Edinburgh: J. Grant, 1902).
4. Blaise Pascal, *Provinciales* (1657).
5. By 1925 Cornell historian Carl Lotus Becker (1873–1945) had published *The Eve of Revolution* (New Haven: Yale University Press, 1918) and *The Declaration of Independence* (New York: Harcourt, Brace, 1921).
6. Cuthbert Winfred Pound (1864–1935), judge of the New York Court of Appeals from 1915 to 1934, had been professor of law at Cornell, 1895–1904. He was unrelated to Roscoe Pound.

Beverly Farms, Massachusetts
August 15, 1925

Dear Frankfurter,

Many thanks for the notice of Laski's book returned herewith. It seems just minded, and I should think would not displease him unless to see them take the child of his bowels so easily.[1] I don't think you will let me in for Keyserling but Heaven knows. I have finished the *Provinciales* and *The Constant Nymph* and am thinking of renewing my acquaintance with *Pilgrim's Progress*![2] Also I am expecting daily another installment from Beveridge. I await the Becker with some eagerness. But speaking for this day only I am feeling rather flabby in mind and doubt if I shall do anything more profitable than take a drive.

Yours as ever,
O.W.H.

1. The notice is missing.
2. Margaret Kennedy, *The Constant Nymph* (Garden City: Doubleday, Page, 1925).

Beverly Farms, Massachusetts
September 1, 1925

Dear Frankfurter,

Many, many thanks for Becker's *Declaration of Independence*. I received it the day before yesterday and finished it yesterday with much interest and satisfaction. Otherwise I am reading the *Odyssey* at odd moments. When I consider that their notion of a happy day was to eat flesh and drink wine all day long, I can believe Clark (who married my cousin Mary) that beasts in captivity live twice as long as when free and have a better time.[1] Their food is sure and they have no enemies to fear. He says the great Washington lions have lost their teeth from age and would starve at once in the wilds. I am as quiet as possible and have no divine discontent at present. I had a sensation last week in the bronze statue just put up at the head of Gloucester Harbor close to the water where the children strew flowers every year. On the pedestal is "They that go down to the sea in ships" and the figure is a sailor on a rolling deck, at the wheel, with eyes intent.[2] It moved me slightly. It embodies all who ever died on the Banks.

Also I see living figures—throngs of men and half naked women on the beaches of Swampscott and Lynn. Evidently the time draws nearer when it will be well to go to work again.

Yours as ever,
O.W.H.

1. Austin H. Clark (1880–1954) and Mary Wendell Upham (1880?-1931) were married in 1906. Clark was a biologist at the Smithsonian from 1908 to 1950. He published 600 scientific articles and a number of books, including *Animals of Land and Sea* (New York: D. Van Nostrand, 1925).

2. The sculptor was Leonard Craske (1882–1950), a Bostonian who had been born in England.

Beverly Farms, Massachusetts
September 6, 1925

Dear Frankfurter,

Returned herein is the notice of Laski which it rejoiced me to see. I rather think that you and I substantially agree in our notions of public policy—your letter indicates it.[1] But at present I am thinking about the *Odyssey*. I am at the 22d book and have got one suitor killed. If I didn't have other things to do including many letters to write I should finish it today or tomorrow but I am delayed. I have more pleasure in it than I expected. Yesterday afternoon I saw some whippet races and a rose garden. I bet you don't know what a whippet is—a very small quasi-greyhound with no ideas except to run. All quiet and well here. If we could jaw we would jaw but I must shut up.

Affectionately yours,
O.W.H.

1. The letter referred to is missing.

Washington, D.C.
October 11, 1925

This is an appeal—oh no—I have two sheets of paper before me; one for my case to be written, one for Frankfurter. This is for him.

Dear Frankfurter,

There has been a storm of work and still is so I must be brief. I thank you for both your notes.[1] How unfailing has been your encouragement. I start cheerful and hope you do. But I tell you we have been at it. Sixty *certioraris* to pass on yesterday besides submitted and argued cases and outside matters. The conference lasts from 12 to about 7. A good night's sleep repaired damage for me, but I have a case to write,[2] fifty *certioraris* to examine, some cases postponed for fuller examination and what the week may bring forth—not to speak of books to be acknowledged and letters to be answered. I am two weeks in arrear to Laski. Of course nothing read since arrival except cases. I fear all the culture accumulated in vacation will melt like a lump of sugar.

Brandeis no doubt you saw before he came on. He seems all right though not gay. But I get my impression from coming home together after a day in court. I didn't like to have the Chief sit so long, but he knows his own powers better than I do. Sutherland was better than he was at the end of last term and the others I think are all well. This is our news. I hope yours is as good. With this bulletin I must turn to the opinion *in gremio legis*.[3]

Yours as ever,
O.W.H.

1. The notes referred to are missing.

2. In *Druggan v. Anderson*, 269 U.S. 36, 39 (1925), Holmes concluded for a unanimous Court that Congress had the power to legislate in anticipation of the enforcement of the Prohibition Amendment: "The grant of power to Congress is a present grant and . . . no reason has been suggested why the Constitution may not give Congress a present power to enact laws

intended to carry out constitutional provisions for the future when the time comes for them to take effect."

3. In the bosom of the law.

Washington, D.C.
December 3, 1925

Dear Frankfurter,

Many thanks for your letter.[1] You make me a little anxious about your knees as you are vague though encouraging.[2] I shall assume that the matter is not serious. Of course Brandeis did good jobs in the cases you mention.[3] He is not only very able but he is the most thorough of men. If I wanted to be epigrammatic I should say that he always desires to know all that can be known about a case whereas I am afraid that I wish to know as little as I can safely go on. He loves facts and I hate them except as the necessary peg to hang generalizations on. Think not that I don't appreciate the power that his knowledge gives him. The perfect critters must eat hay as well as oats.

I am glad you like the foreign exchange case.[4] It seemed to me that two drops of theory were the proper dose.

I must scrabble off to court and this p.m. Mr. and Mrs. Zimmern come to tea.[5] Tomorrow Lepaulle dines here—unusual distractions for this solitary. I suppose you go to a hospital (*not* an 'ospital) for your operation. It isn't bad—*crede experto*, with all good wishes.

Yours ever,
O.W.H.

1. The letter referred to is missing.

2. In November Frankfurter underwent minor surgery on his knees.

3. Probably *Edwards v. Douglas*, 269 U.S. 204 (1925), a 5–4 opinion upholding a broad definition of the government's right to tax individuals under the Revenue Act of 1917, and *Louisville & Nashville Railroad v. Sloss-Sheffield Steel & Iron Co.*, *Id.* at 217, an 8–1 decision affirming a ruling of the Interstate Commerce Commission against a railroad's exorbitant freight charge.

4. In *Hicks v. Guinness*, 269 U.S. 71, 80 (1925), Holmes, writing for a unanimous Court, ruled that a debt owed by a German firm to an American creditor at the outbreak of World War I had to be repaid with interest in American dollars: "The debt was due to an American creditor and was to be paid in the United States. When the contract was broken by a failure to pay, the American firm had a claim here, not for the debt, but, at its option, for damages in dollars."

5. Sir Alfred Zimmern (1879–1957), who taught international relations at Oxford, was the author of *The Greek Commonwealth* (Oxford: Clarendon Press, 1911).

Washington, D.C.
December 11, 1925

Dear F. F.,

Brandeis had told me that all was going well with you but I am very glad to hear it from you. Don't you find mitigations to the hospital? Or didn't you if, as seems probable, you have left it. All goes serenely here. I have just returned from a walk with Denby, a most companionable as well as intelligent chap. If I live to have another one, I make it a condition that he, like Denby, should be a contribution to Washington Society as well as know a little law and be able to keep my simple accounts. It has come to be expected of me and makes a difference to me in these days when I go nowhere and see hardly anyone.

In solitaire hours I am listening to *Arrowsmith*. When it began it seemed rather a squalid business and I didn't see why I should be interested in the photograph of a man who didn't interest me. But as it goes on, it carries me more and more—the old scientific man (Brandeis says the late Dr. Loeb) is really moving and I am coming to think of Upton Sinclair (or Sinclair Lewis whichever the author it) as a good deal of a bird though I don't know that I should like to be he.[1]

We have had some cases on which I find myself more able to doubt than Brandeis, and well argued. I shall be glad to breathe freely again for a week or two. Let me hear soon that you are all right.

Yours ever,
O.W.H.

1. Jacques Loeb (1859–1924), the famous pathologist of the Rockefeller Institute, served as the model for Max Gottlieb in Sinclair Lewis's *Arrowsmith* (New York: Harcourt, Brace, 1925).

Washington, D.C.
December 17, 1925

Dear F.F.,

It is joyful to hear such a good account as you give of yourself.[1] I'm glad too that the hospital experience interested you as it did me even if it bored. As to *Arrowsmith*, I had all your prejudices, probably in more violent form, and the first quarter or more of the book didn't diminish them. But the book is like the life—emerging from, I won't say the mud, but at least from the hopelessly uninteresting common to interest and distinction.

My work is done except to study further on one postponed case but leisure is always tomorrow not today.[2] Your Miss Sergeant has just called and was very pleasant but I did most of the talking without intending to be swinish and after an hour and a half I let her go as more than that tires me out.[3] I don't know what I am going to do if the leisure really comes. I have no quintessential book that would exactly fill the bill. If you know one, speak quick. But a recommendation short of an article of the creed is not enough. I would rather cut a coupon than read a dull book.

My blessings on you—don't be in too much of a hurry to get well. By the by, Lepaulle was here some days ago and was very pleasant and intelligent. This p.m. Morgan (J.H.), condemned by Laski for his book on Morley but known and liked by me of old, sends me an introductory chapter to a book by another, G. Robinson, on *Public Authorities and Legal Liability*, this chapter being separately printed for private circulation and dedicated to me.[4] I shall be like Bill Hunt's description of the casting of the colossal statue of Bavaria. They got a great pot of molten iron and put it in a pipe and they blowed and they blowed and they blowed till one said, "Look out, Bill or by God she'll bust," and then they went up and sat in the nose.[5] This chapter is called "Remedies against the Crown." Now I end as I started to on the last page.

Affectionately yours,
O.W.H.

Your letter has no other address so I must send to the Law School.

1. The letter referred to is missing.

2. *United States v. Robbins*, 269 U.S. 315, 326 (1926). Holmes's majority opinion upheld a California law that income from community property was returnable and taxable to the husband. He agreed with the law's premise that the wife's claim of vested rights in half the property was "mere expectancy" while living with her husband. Sutherland dissented without opinion.

3. Elizabeth Shepley Sergeant (1881–1965) interviewed Holmes for her essay "Justice Touched with Fire," which appeared first in the *New Republic* 49 (1925): 59, and subsequently in her volume *Fire under the Andes* (New York: Knopf, 1927).

4. John Hartmann Morgan, *John Viscount Morley* (Boston: Houghton, Mifflin, 1924); Edward Robinson, *Public Authorities and Legal Liabilities* (London: University of London, 1925).

5. The Boston artist William Morris Hunt studied at the Dusseldorf Academy in 1845 where he observed and may have helped to cast Ludwig Schwanthaler's statute of Bavaria, a sixty-foot Teutonic amazon weighing seven-and-a-half tons.

Washington, D.C.
December 29, 1925

My dear F.F.,

A thousand thanks for your remembrance.[1] I haven't had time to read the book yet, being *in medio Science and the Modern World* sent by Walter Lippmann.[2] I shall hope to get into it this week—it looks pleasant and no task. *Modern Science* is worth reading but I don't expect to see my general point of view affected as far as I've got. I have sent a telephone message to Mr. Gates and shall hope to see him as I left a large choice of times.[3] Every good wish for the New Year and may we have a jaw.

Affectionately yours,
O. W. Holmes

1. The gift is unknown.

2. Alfred North Whitehead, *Science and the Modern World* (New York: Macmillan, 1925).

3. Sylvester Gates, an Oxford graduate, was a special student at Harvard Law School, 1925–26.

Washington, D.C.
January 7, 1926

My dear Frankfurter,

. . . Talking with Brandeis the other day, who knows more about it than I do, I was delighted to hear his opinion that you had exercised a very great influence in the realm of administrative law and that many publications owed their stimulus to you. Few things could give me so much pleasure. All is going well here. Brandeis has written an opinion involving tremendous work, which I hope may carry conviction, though I fear I try not to bother about age, though it worries me a little.[1]

Affectionately yours,
O.W.H.

I was told the other day that I was a vulgarian to omit the my before dear in beginning a letter. I have thought it as more familiar and intimate but am trying to conform though the recollection came late as you may detect by scrutiny.

1. Probably *Texas & Pacific Railway v. Gulf, Colorado & Santa Fe Railroad*, 270 U.S. 266 (1926). Brandeis wrote for the majority; McReynolds dissented. The suit was based on a provision in the Transportation Act of 1920 enjoining the construction of an extension of a railroad line without first obtaining a certificate of public convenience and necessity from the Interstate Commerce Commission. The question raised was whether the tracks that had been

added were an extension as defined by the law. Brandeis concluded that they were and that the Gulf railroad had violated the law by failing to obtain the requisite permission.

Washington, D.C.
January 27, 1926

My dear Frankfurter,

May you and Mr. Corcoran pardon my delay.[1] I have been so busy that I have neglected everything except the shop. I accept your nomination. Of course Mr. Corcoran will appreciate the increasing chance that death or resignation may cut his career here short. But at present I seem to be in unusually good condition and as you know I hope to keep on so long as I don't seem to myself to be falling off and remain able to do the work. I merely reserve my rights to the above alternatives. Your account sounds very attractive.

Ever sincerely yours,
O. W. Holmes

1. Thomas Gardiner Corcoran (1900–81) was Holmes's secretary for the October 1926 Term. Together with Benjamin V. Cohen (1894–1983), another one of Frankfurter's Law School "boys," the ebullient Corcoran played a key role in drafting New Deal legislation including the Securities Act (1933), the Federal Housing Act (1933), and the Fair Labor Standards Act (1938). In later years, "Tommy the Cork" became the ultimate Washington insider and corporate lobbyist.

Washington, D.C.
February 19, 1926

My dear Frankfurter,

Your letter brings the customary gleam when I am especially glad to have it—for after lolopping about in the house with a cold I have got out only to fall into the hands of the dentist who takes the freedom out of every day.[1] However, I have been spurred by the fiend in the shape of Brandeis into sending two dissents to the printer—that is they will go tomorrow morning. One merely a few words backing him up in a tremendous piece of research in which I think he has smashed the majority view.[2] The other deprecating the application of the XIV Amendment to some state legislation that I think we had better leave alone.[3] That has brought a little gaiety and more fatigue to the day and I slept like a log for an hour before the evening meal.

It gave me quite as much pleasure as it can have given them to see the lads you mention—Gates and Smellie.[4] I haven't seen the *Law Quarterly* but am glad of what you tell me.[5] I did not get as much illumination as I should have from Whitehead's Lowell Lectures.[6] It takes so long to learn a new language, but I envy you your philosophic seances with your two—Cohen and him.

I can but this line for the moment but send my good wish to you both.

Yours as ever,

O.W.H.

1. The letter referred to is missing.

2. *Weaver v. Palmer Brothers*, 270 U.S. 402, 416 (1926). The majority opinion, written by Justice Butler, relied on the due process clause of the Fourteenth Amendment in overturning a Pennsylvania law prohibiting the use of unsterilized "shoddy" as filling material for bedding. Holmes, with Brandeis and Stone concurring, dissented: "If the Legislature of Pennsylvania was of opinion that disease is likely to be spread by the use of unsterilized shoddy in comfortables I do not suppose that the Court would pronounce the opinion so manifestly absurd that it could not be acted upon. . . . I think that we are pressing the Fourteenth Amendment too far." Holmes's dissent echoed his reasoning in *Lochner v. New York*, 198 U.S. 45 (1905). In both cases he deferred to the judgment of legislators and their determination of a need to regulate business practices that threatened the health and safety of groups within society.

3. *Schlesinger v. Wisconsin*, 270 U.S. 230, 241–42 (1925). McReynolds's majority opinion found unconstitutional, under the Fourteenth Amendment, a law presuming that gifts made *inter vivos* within six years of death were intended to escape estate taxes. Holmes, with Brandeis and Stone concurring, dissented: "The law allows a penumbra to be embraced that goes beyond the outline of its object in order that the object may be secured. . . . I think that with the States as with Congress when the means are not prohibited and are calculated to effect the object we ought not to inquire into the degree of the necessity for resorting to them."

4. Kingsley Bryce Speakman Smellie (1897–1987) was a political scientist at the London School of Economics. During the 1925–26 academic year, he was at Harvard Law School on a Rockefeller scholarship..

5. In a "Note" on *Gitlow*, *Law Quarterly* 42 (1926): 14, Pollock commented favorably on Holmes's dissent and, referring also to *Schenck v. United States*, 249 U.S. 47 (1919), and *Abrams*, added: "Much of the bitter feeling which these cases have engendered in the United States is due to the manner in which the trials were conducted . . . and to the length of the sentences."

6. On Whitehead, see above, December 15, 1925.

Cambridge, Massachusetts
March 8, 1926

My Justice,

Again the 8th of March is here—one of the two or three Matterhorn days of my calendar. I greet you and rejoice over the anniversary with all the freshness and contagious creativeness of your powers—as one does who brings deep devotion. It's a great world that contains you—and one's own life is zestful and full of impulse when good fortune has made you a part of it.

Affectionately,
F.F.

Washington, D.C.
March 27, 1926

My dear Frankfurter,

The combined exigencies of work and endless letters, coupled this week with a cold that shut me up for a day or two, have kept my pen more silent to you than my thoughts. But I could think of no one but you as likely to have written the beautiful article for *The New Republic* that left me at the moment dumb.[1] It moved me greatly even while it added a new terror to keeping on, for fear of losing such a jewel. If I am wrong as to the writing I still am sure that in some way your ever true friendship is behind it. I have not had time yet to read your latest article in the *Harvard Law Review* but hope to soon.[2]

Affectionately yours,
O. W. Holmes

1. "Mr. Justice Holmes," *New Republic* 46 (1926): 88.

2. Felix Frankfurter, "The Business of the Supreme Court of the United States: A Study in the Federal Judicial System; Pt. IV Federal Courts of Specialized Jurisdiction," *Harvard Law Review* 39 (1926): 587, examined the legislative history of the Customs Court, the short-lived Commerce Court, and the unsuccessful proposal for a Patent Court.

Cambridge, Massachusetts
April 7, 1926

My dear Justice Holmes,

I am indeed happy if my little piece in the N.R. brought you pleasure. I wrote from head and heart but only intimations of a meagre pen. Your recent opinions make me feel as though you are just beginning a fresh chapter. I have already written you the zest evoked by your patent case and now comes that spirited opinion in the Chile Copper case.[1] I do think that Learned Hand this time clearly went off the track and you showed him the true path in an unforgettable manner.

These have been gay days with Laski. He is in superb form and talk is endless. I'm not surprised that he finds deep roots here. The range and vigor of his friendships among Harvard faculty invigorates one's sense of the fellowship of scholars. It also proves the brilliance and power of his personality.

Always yours,
F.F.

1. *Alexander Milburn Co. v. Davis-Bournonville Co.*, 270 U.S. 390, 402 (1926). The case resulted from patents having been issued to two individuals for what amounted to the same invention. Writing for a unanimous Court, Holmes emphasized that the "fundamental rule" regarding patents is that "the patentee must be the first inventor." In *Edwards v. Chile Copper Co., Id.* at 452, Holmes's unanimous decision found that a tax imposed on domestic corporations was also applicable to a foreign corporation organized for the purpose of holding the stock of a domestic corporation.

Cambridge, Massachusetts
May 18, 1926

My dear Justice,

I have often ventured to say to my colleagues that all the modern tendencies in legal writing—"sociological jurisprudence," "the functional approach" and the rest of the jargonic language are indicated, if not expressed, in your essays of forty or so years ago. Again and again law review articles prove my thesis. A paper in the May *Harvard Law Review* does it again—Edgerton's on "Relation of Mental States to Negligence."[1] He elaborates and refines and spells out what is in *The Common Law*, and, he frankly say so. Yes, much of our labor these days is bringing bricks to the building of the structures for which you long ago sketched the blueprints.

I have latterly been deep in a piece of toilsome but exhilarating research, which took me into Stuart legislation and Colonial laws.[2] We haven't begun even a history of the American law that lies buried in old colonial records. I wish "100% Americanism" would take that form of patriotism—to tell adequately the history of our institutions.

Aren't the English a great people—the way they took and settled the great strike?[3] I take it your work is soon over and one will see you soon at Beverly Farms.

Always devotedly,
F.F.

1. Henry W. Edgerton, "Relation of Mental States to Negligence," *Harvard Law Review* 39 (1926): 849, challenged the assertion that "negligence is a state of mind" and argued for Holmes's definition of negligence as conduct.

2. Felix Frankfurter and Thomas G. Corcoran, "Petty Federal Offenses and the Constitutional Guaranty of Trial by Jury," *Harvard Law Review* 39 (1926): 917, 980, explored "the extent to which the Constitution compels Congress to provide jury trial in the enforcement of federal penal laws." Citing both English and American colonial records, the authors concluded: "In subjecting certain conduct to the summary procedure of magistrates, unguarded by the popular element, there was an exercise of moral judgment dividing behavior into serious affairs and minor misdeeds. The gravity of danger to the community from the misconduct largely guided the moral judgment. . . . These general tendencies, both in England and in the colonies, represent the history absorbed by the Constitution."

3. The British General Strike, called by the Trade Union Congress, lasted from May 3 to May 12 although the coal dispute, which was its origin, continued until November when the miners settled for much less than they had been offered in April. The chief hardliners were Prime Minister Stanley Baldwin and Chancellor of the Exchequer Winston Churchill.

Washington, D.C.
May 21, 1926

My dear Frankfurter,

Ever does the sight of your friendly fist give me a throb of pleasure and you are pretty sure to happen in with a cheering remark when I am a little down. Not that I mind very much whether I am up or down, as I don't think it important. When one begins to think sadly what does indicating a line of thought amount to—people will go to and fro over it without remembering you. It is well to recall that this is universal. Malthus ran a rapier through the vitals of humbugs a century and a quarter ago, and one still meets them walking happily in the streets not knowing that they are dead. The thing is to do it. Not to have people say that you have done it. Only unless they do say it one can't be sure that one isn't a fool. I sometimes repeat to myself: Oh Lord, be merciful to me, a fool.

I am glancing through a book that someone, I know not who, sent to me: *Understanding our Children*, Frederick Pierce.[1] I came last night on a passage about the superiority complex that made me wonder whether my father, who certainly taught me a great deal and did me a great deal of good, didn't also do me some harm by drooling over the physical shortcomings of himself and his son and by some other sardonic criticisms. At least he made it difficult for his son to be conceited. Within limits no doubt it is good for a child to be brought down to actualities with a bump.

The loveliness and languor of the Washington spring are on us in force. I take drives and read other gents' opinions and the other day in honor of

Wu I read Stammler's *Theory of Justice*.[2] Wu's appendix I thought superlatively good and I was touched by his reverence for a great man. But the work itself seemed to me gnawing condemned boards into sawdust. I don't think Kant improved the golden rule and this seemed to me pedagogical variations on Kant. Of course I am not fair but I do not believe that man necessarily is an end himself as I have expounded heretofore. I think morals are the superior politenesses that absorb the shock of force but I don't think them the cosmic ultimate, or even the human. But this is between ourselves as such a proposition unexplained would be caviare to the general.[3] I should not shrink from avowing the opinions with adequate explanation which you don't need. I hate to speak harshly of Stammler whom I willingly believe to have greatness in him but I not only disagreed with his book but found it very dull. If you know better, correct me.

I am interested to hear of your studies without a very clear idea as to what they are (in early American case law).

Apropos of the English way of taking things—I had a letter this morning from the middle of the strike which, after mentioned one thing and another, says, "So we are all very grumpy"—the homely moderateness of which pleased me.

I look forward to seeing you one of these days. Kindly remain alive. Even my haircutter has died and I grow more and more solitary.

Affectionately yours,
O. W. Holmes

1. Frederick Pierce, *Understanding Our Children* (New York: Dutton, 1926), 83. Pierce (1878–1963) wrote: "In my observation, conceit is nearly always one of the characteristics of the child who has been too much dominated, and who is trying to react aggressively against the domination."

2. Rudolf Stammler, *Theory of Justice* (New York: Macmillan, 1925).

3. "The play, I remember, pleas'd not the million;/'twas caviare to the general." *Hamlet*, Act II: scene 2 (456).

Beverly Farms, Massachusetts
July 10, 1926

My dear F.F.,

(How I hate that 'My' and how I yielded to a criticism that I don't believe!) Many thanks for the papers returned herewith.[1] I get pleasure from the statistics and rapture from P.L.[2] Who else could be so subtile in such adorably surprising English? Almost it persuades me (it would altogether if I had the book here instead of in Washington) to reread *Swann's Way*—this time in English after twice in French. But I must finish Delcareuil, *Histoire de droit francais au 1789*, which I hope I am not keeping too long from the Law School.[3] I am a little worried as I've only read about a third of the book. I hardly think it pays me at my age and preoccupations, though I sometimes spot a fact to be noted, and although it gives me glee to see him deny every favorite German thesis.

Beveridge this p.m. brought me in another chapter of his Lincoln and I have agreed to reread a former one that I criticised but that is a short job. As soon as may be I mean to read some novels. It was as great a pleasure to me as it can have been to you, to see you the other day. I was sorry about the hurry at the end and thought myself stupid at not making you wait for the next train. I inferred that you caught yours and also that you tried to telephone to me *in transitu* but had to leave before I got to the telephone. Time rushes by, so much more swiftly with old age. My wife came in just here and I read to her P.L. to her equal delight. She at once says we will send for *Swann's Way* and so we will. I should like to jaw with you for other hours. My love to your wife and regrets at having missed her.

Affectionately yours,
O. W. Holmes

1. The letter referred to is missing.
2. Possibly the literary critic Philip Littell.
3. Joseph Declareuil, *Histoire Generale du droit francais* (Paris: Librairie de la Societe du Recueil, 1925).

Beverly Farms, Massachusetts
August 9, 1926

Dear Frankfurter,

You are quite right I think. I feel the same uncomfortable sense of interposing a slight barrier by the "My." I shall keep it for English friends for evidently it is a shibboleth there. I see no sense in the criticism of the abbreviated form.

I have launched curses at Laski for having put me on the Declareuil but that is finished and done with while another recommendation of his Hoffding, *History of Modern Philosophy*, is giving me much pleasure and making up.[1] *Nize Baby* made me laugh consumedly.[2] Thus all goes happily on.

Yours as ever,
O.W.H.

1. Harald Hoffding, *A History of Modern Philosophy*, 2 vols. (London: Macmillan, 1924). Hoffding (1843–1931), Danish philosopher and historian of philosophy, taught at the University of Copenhagen from 1883 to 1915. Drawing upon Comte and Spencer, he emphasized the science and methods of Galileo and Newton in tracing the development of epistemology.

2. Milton Gross, *Nize Baby* (New York: Doran, 1926), a comedy about life in a New York apartment building.

Beverly Farms, Massachusetts
September 23, 1926

Dear Frankfurter,

Alas, I fear it is too late. Tomorrow is my last day here and the general nervous excitement of a transit does not suit the peaceful jaw that I should so much like to have with you. Perhaps you will turn up in Washington. I have heard no word from my secretary [Thomas C. Corcoran] that is to be but I presume that I may have told him to be on hand on Friday, October 1 at 11 a.m., neither before nor after. I don't know his address. . . . It was a great joy to see you and I hope to live to do it more than once again. Affectionate remembrances to you both.

Yours as ever,
O. W. Holmes

Washington, D.C.
November 6, 1926

Dear Frankfurter,

Your letter cheers me up just as I was wondering whether all the things that an old man not in love with himself must wonder from time to time.[1] However, I have struck leisure now, have paid my tax bills in full and still am solvent, and this afternoon read a little book, which hasn't happened before, since I got home and found over 200 *certioraris* to be considered. Yesterday and today, my wife not wanting to go out, I took the lad to the Soldiers Home, the Adams tomb in Rock Creek Cemetery, Arlington, in an effort to find the turf under which I shall lie before long, and up the river across Chain Bridge into the beautiful Virginia upland there. He is a most pleasant companion and also does his work in A 1 style.

The book I read was Vinogradoff's *Custom and Right*, which seems to me learned and interesting and not too good for human nature's daily food which pleased me, as I was led to send for it by the dogmatic pronunciamento of the great John M. Zane who deigned for the first time to praise.[2] I suspected his praise was heightened by the wish to belittle others not named but I thought including Pound. The attitude of disdain, considered very chic in Balzac and later French books, is almost the only one which I thoroughly despise. Perhaps however it shows sincerity of nature to be able to believe in oneself wholly, *sans arriere pensee*. Now I think I shall read Wallas, *The Art of Thought*, though the preliminary synopsis hardly seems dazzling.[3]

I have one case on the date for valuing the mark in a case versus the Alien Property custodian and a German debtor which I have written without reference to cases on pure principle, which so far as I know has not been considered.[4] Sutherland is writing a dissent and thinks the English cases are all the other way as also, I believe, the reason of the thing. I really am interested—he may change the majority as to which I don't care much but I am keen to see his answer to what seems to me unanswerable. I have no doubt that a good showing can be made against my view on the cases and perhaps he will reveal to me a chasm in what seems to be solid ground.

I am glad that all goes well with you. I hope that it will until we meet again.

Affectionately yours,
O. W. Holmes

The lad is working for you in his leisure hours. I imagine working hard.

1. The letter referred to is missing.

2. Paul Vinogradoff (1854–1925) was a Russian born legal historian who became Professor of Jurisprudence at Oxford in 1903, succeeding Frederick Pollock. Vinogradoff's *Custom and Right* (Cambridge: Harvard University Press, 1925) was favorably reviewed by John M. Zane in *Yale Law Journal* 35 (1926): 1026. After criticizing all efforts to write a general philosophy of the law and insisting on the need for a factual comparative approach, Zane found Vinogradoff's work "stimulating. . . . Like all good books, it suggests more than it says. The best thing about it is that when one of those gentlemen who is seeking to avoid thought and work sits down with his note book to copy out some hard and fast rule, he will be baffled."

3. Graham Wallas, *The Art of Thought* (New York: Harcourt, Brace, 1926).

4. *Deutsche Bank Filiale Nurnberg v. Humphrey*, 272 U.S. 517, 519, 522 (1926), asked whether an American citizen should be paid the dollar value of money he had deposited and had attempted to withdraw from a German bank in 1915 or the depreciated value of a later date. Holmes's majority opinion found for the bank: "An obligation in terms of the currency of a country takes the risk of currency fluctuations and whether creditor or debtor profits by the change the law takes no account of." Sutherland, with Butler, McReynolds and Sanford concurring, wrote the dissent: "A simple debt payable in marks and an obligation to deliver goods in Germany stand on the same footing. In either case, the injured party is entitled to have in the money of this country the value of what he would have obtained if the contract had been performed at the stipulated time."

Washington, D.C.
November 23, 1926

My dear Frankfurter,

Imprimis many thanks for Pound's address.[1] I read it with delight and admiration. But that is not what I am writing about now. Wu has written to me and thinks his spiritual salvation requires a visit to this country (I should think he must have overworked from his account). Preferably he wants to come to Harvard to be near to you and Pound and, I think I may add, to be within reach of me. He wants to stay two years and get $3000 or $4000 a year. I was terrified but Corcoran (delightful chap) speaks so confidently of its feasibility that I dare to write.[2] I should not like to promise to contribute much but I should hope to be able to do something. Wu suggests a temporary lectureship on The Psychology of Judicial Thinking—3 hours a week. I think the lad is precious and worth doing much for to give him a chance. If you see the way, or hope, why not write to him—at any rate, at your convenience, send me a line.

I had a case today on the time when the value of the Mark should be taken which in my opinion is rather a test of legal thinking.[3] Sutherland, McReynolds, Butler and Sanford dissent.

Affectionately yours,
O.W.H.

1. The letter referred to is missing.

2. This plan did not materialize because Wu accepted an appointment on the Shanghai Provisional Court in 1927.

3. See above, November 6, 1926.

Cambridge, Massachusetts
November 26, 1926

Dear Justice Holmes,

Your letter has just come and I hasten to write a line about Wu. Of course, I agree with you about him and Pound holds him in no less esteem. I doubt very much, however, whether a place at the Law School could be made for him, even though the money were found by Wu's friends. We ought to have such a lecturer on the Psychology of Judicial Thinking but most of the brethren would, I'm afraid, shy at the suggestion. They would suspect that it wasn't sufficiently downright "law." (To be sure, we now have Redlich giving a seminar in "comparative public law": that's "highbrow," but differently highbrow.[1] I'm giving the views of men who want to go a bit slow in improving on the past). But I'll make soundings. There may, however, be a chance for such a lectureship in the Department of Philosophy and thus, in the face of some well-known constitutional opinions, that which cannot be done directly may, perhaps, be done indirectly. I shall probe and report later—it may take a little time. For myself, I'd bring Wu here as quickly as I could get him.

I'm perfectly delighted that Corcoran is giving satisfaction. I'm not surprised—he is one of the most delightful and sweetest lads I've ever had.

Last Monday and Tuesday your Court handed down an interesting batch. I await the opinions with much interest. The mark valuation issue is the sort of question that tests legal thinking.[2] Some A.G. judge went astray on it and I should expect it to serve as a litmus paper for some of your brethren. I was pleased with your emphasis of the power of dismissal of the Massachusetts daylight saving statute.[3]

When next you make for a philosophic book may I suggest General Smuts' recent volume with its strange title of "Holism."[4]

Always devotedly,
F.F.

1. Josef Redlich (1869–1936), formerly a law professor at the University of Vienna, taught Comparative Public Law at Harvard from 1926 to 1935.

2. See above, November 6, 1926.

3. *Massachusetts State Grange v. Benton*, 272 U.S. 525, 527 (1926). Holmes's unanimous opinion refused to grant an injunction to prevent enforcement of the Daylight Savings Acts of Massachusetts: "The important rule, which we desire to emphasize, [is] that no injunction ought to issue against officers of a State clothed with authority to enforce the law in question, unless in a case reasonably free from doubt and when necessary to prevent great and irreparable injury."

4. General Jan Smuts, *Holism and Evolution* (New York: Macmillan, 1926). Smuts (1870–1950), South African military hero, statesman, and philosopher, was a leading supporter of the League of Nations. He was also sympathetic to Zionism, urging support for the Balfour Declaration, and later contributed to the draft of the United Nations Charter.

Cambridge, Massachusetts
December 6, 1926

Dear Justice Holmes,

The November 23 batch of opinions has come and with them two of yours that give me great delight. The mark-dollar case does divide the sheep from the goats![1] Your analysis of the governing principles ought to lift the fog that hangs over the cases on this subject. Not as neat a problem, but even more important issues were raised in the Daylight Saving Law Case and I am particularly glad that you underscored the considerations of restraint that ought to guide Federal Courts in enjoining State Officers.[2] I must confess to surprise that you concurred even in the result of the Indianapolis Water Company case—I assume you thought it might as well be cleaned up by your Court.[3] I can't help feeling that the disposition of these valuation cases on the complicated "facts," throws a terrible burden on the Supreme Court.

I hope that you found Miss Sergeant's piece not too much to your distaste.[4] I think that she did a very creditable job considering how new the materials of the law and judicial work were to her.

Always devotedly,
F.F.

1. On *Deutsche Bank*, see above, November 6, 1926.
2. On *Massachusetts Grange*, see above, November 26, 1926.
3. *McCardle v. Indianapolis Water Company*, 272 U.S. 400, 420 (1926). Butler delivered the majority opinion; Holmes concurred in the result. Brandeis, with Stone concurring, dissented. The Court examined the facts of this case—the value of the property used, probable earnings, operating expenses, and the amount required to constitute just compensation in the Court's application of the Fourteenth Amendment—to determine whether the Public Service Commission's denial of higher water rates or the District Court enjoinment was legitimate. Conceding that the facts were "not as specific as good practice requires," Butler nevertheless concluded that, "As the litigation would be prolonged considerably if the case were remanded for further findings, we have examined the record to determine whether the facts proved justify the [District] Court's conclusion . . . and we are satisfied that the decree is right." Brandeis wanted the case remanded with an order to apply relevant "rules" for determining value.
4. "Oliver Wendell Holmes," *New Republic* 49 (1926): 59.

Washington, D.C.
December 8, 1926

Dear Frankfurter,

Many thanks for your letter. I am delighted that you take the same view that I do in the Marks Case as I agree with you that it is a question of thinking accurately what law founds and limits the obligations.[1] In the Water case I didn't agree with Brandeis as to the judge having taken reproduction value simpliciter as his ground though my opinion had to be collected from the interstices of his discourse.[2] It isn't fresh in my mind, but that was my starting point.

I thought Miss Sergeant's piece was a wonder of care in collecting facts and so kind that it made me blush.[3] I have written to her to make two or three of her anecdotes more accurate. A man came and photographed me for her book on the darkest of days, but he thought he had got a good one. Last Monday and next Monday contributions are small stuff but as always interest me in the effort to give the thing a good shape.[4] I hope that all goes well with you and that your investigations of Boston don't take you from your regular job.[5]

Affectionately yours,
O. W. Holmes

I have written to Wu that your letter to me was not encouraging but that it did not yet exclude possibility in the philosophical department, but that if he doesn't get what he wanted it might be just the needed trial of the fire in his belly. I am afraid that he tends a little too much to easy philosophizing rather than the accumulation of raw material on which to do hard work but I don't know.

1. See above, November 6, 1926.
2. See above, December 6, 1926.
3. *Id.*
4. *Murphy v. United States*, 272 U.S. 630 (1926). Holmes's unanimous opinion upheld an enforcement provision of the National Prohibition Act allowing the government to proceed in equity, having failed to secure a criminal conviction, in order to enjoin occupancy of a "nuisance," i.e., a place manufacturing, storing or selling liquor. In *United States v. Storrs*, 272 U.S. 652, 654 (1926), Holmes, again speaking for a unanimous Court, dismissed a writ of error involving the distinction between a plea in abatement and a plea in bar: "The question is less what [a plea of abatement] is called than what it is. . . . [I]t cannot be that a plea filed a week earlier is what it purports to be, and in its character is, but a week later becomes a plea in bar because of the extrinsic circumstance that the statute of limitations has run."
5. Frankfurter had assumed the directorship of the Harvard Survey on Crime and Law in Boston, a sequel to his 1922 Cleveland study. Though never completed, several volumes of the Harvard survey were published, most notably, Sheldon Glueck and Eleanor T. Glueck, *One Thousand Delinquents: Their Treatment by Court and Clinic* (Cambridge: Harvard University Press, 1934).

Washington, D.C.
March 3, 1927

Dear Frankfurter,

Your letters always make me thankful.[1] I write but a line in reply because I am pretty "full up." I am glad that you like old Malthus, or at least to infer that you do.[2] I knew about Wu and should suppose that that would put his haste to come to this country at rest for a time. I was delighted at his having the kind of experience that he will get. The secretary—a dear fellow—has spoken to me about your coming here. There is no time when I could not give you dinner and the evening but next week I rather fear that I shall be more pressed than usual and I shall be glad if it could be a little later. But you are always welcome, as you know.

Affectionately yours,
O. W. Holmes

1. The letter referred to is missing.

2. Thomas Robert Malthus (1777–1834), English economist and moral philosopher, was best known for his "law" postulating, on the basis of demographic study, that population increases at a faster rate than its means of subsistence and, unless checked by moral restraint or disaster (war, famine, or disease), results in economic and social decline. Holmes was rereading Malthus as he prepared his decision in *Buck v. Bell*, 274 U.S. 200 (1927). See below, May 14, 1927.

Washington, D.C.
March 18, 1927

My dear Frankfurter,

Again I thank you and this time not only for your letter but for your book which I have read and which moves me much.[1] My knowledge of the case comes wholly from this source. It leaves me with a suspicion that the evidence against the defendants could be stated more strongly but with painful impressions that seem hard to remove. Is there not a motion still pending? Naturally I don't want to express any opinions at present beyond saying that I appreciate the self sacrifice and devotion to justice that led you to write the book.

Affectionately yours,
O. W. Holmes

1. The letter referred to is missing. Frankfurter's book, *The Case of Sacco and Vanzetti: A Critical Analysis for Lawyers and Laymen* (Boston: Little, Brown, 1927), was an expanded version of his article appearing in *Atlantic Monthly* 139 (1927): 409. Frankfurter described the collective hysteria that had characterized Boston during the Red Scare, reviewed the evidence presented against the two Italian anarchists, and sharply criticized the conduct of the prosecutor, Frederick Katzmann (1875–1953), and the judge, Webster Thayer (1857–1933): "The prosecutor systematically played on the feelings of the jury by exploiting the unpatriotic and despised beliefs of Sacco and Vanzetti, and the judge allowed him thus to divert and pervert the jury's mind." *The Case of Sacco and Vanzetti*, 46.

Cambridge, Massachusetts
March 19, 1927

Dear Justice Holmes,

And now that I have read the full text of your ticket scalping dissent (*Tyson* case) I am moved to rejoice over your new declaration of independence of all those sterile "apologies" which "police power" and "affected with public interest" cover.[1] You have never written a more illuminating opinion on Due Process and I throw my hat into the air for it.

Always,
F.F.

1. *Tyson and Brothers v. Banton*, 273 U.S. 418, 446 (1927). The 5–4 majority opinion, written by Justice Sutherland, found a New York consumer protection law forbidding the sale of tickets for more than fifty cents above printed price to be a deprivation of property without due process under the Fourteenth Amendment. Holmes dissented: "A state legislature can do whatever it sees fit to do unless it is restrained by some express prohibition in the Constitution of the United States or of the State, and that Courts should be careful not to extend such prohibitions beyond their obvious meaning by reading into them conceptions of public policy that the particular Court may happen to entertain. . . . The truth seems to me to be that, subject to compensation when compensation is due, the legislature may forbid or restrict any business when it has a sufficient force of public opinion behind it." Brandeis concurred with Holmes's opinion. Stone dissented separately with Holmes and Brandeis concurring. Sanford dissented separately.

Washington, D.C.
May 14, 1927

Dear Frankfurter,

A good opening discourse for what I suppose may be a fertile field.[1] I always tremble a little as I approach these regions which seem like those where the old maps bore the inscriptions *hic sunt leones*—but the bold adventurer is likely to find more asses than lions. That thought is the only comfort for one who like me finds every special line of practice a new mystery. However one keeps on exploring with what heart one may. I think my cases this term have been of rather a high average of interest e.g., the Virginia Sterilizing Act.[2] I hope that all goes well with you.

My homage to Luina.

Yours ever,
O. W. Holmes

1. The letter is missing and hence the reference is unclear.
2. In *Buck v. Bell*, 274 U.S. 200, 207 (1927), Holmes's majority opinion sustained the con-

stitutionality of Virginia's sterilization statute: "It is better for all the world, if instead of waiting to execute degenerate offspring for crime, or to let them starve for their imbecility, society can prevent those who are manifestly unfit from continuing their kind. The principle that sustains compulsory vaccination is broad enough to cover cutting the Fallopian tubes. . . . Three generations of imbeciles are enough." Justice Butler dissented without opinion. After sterilization, Carrie Buck (1906–83) was discharged from the Virginia Colony for Epileptics and Feebleminded. Twice married—her first husband died—she sang in the Methodist Church choir and cared for neighbors and an elderly relative. Her daughter lived eight years and was considered "very bright" by her teachers. See Baker, *Justice from Beacon Hill*, 603.

Cambridge, Massachusetts
June 5, 1927

Dear Justice Holmes,

Perhaps this will reach you before you leave Washington. It means to tell you what a notable Term October 1926 has been to a student of the opinions of Holmes J. I venture to say that no annual output has been more vigorous, nor sprightlier, and no batch will live longer than what you gave us this Term. And all the gay things you got—the "conjurer's circle" for the bootlegger's claim of immunity from taxation, and the "refined female customers" of Beechnut who were employed to deprive the coarse taste of coarser men for Lorillard brands![1]

If you go into history this summer, Beards' *American Civilization* may interest you.[2] And a fascinating exploration of the imagination as exercised by Coleridge is revealed by Lowes' *The Road to Xanadu*.[3] It's a thrilling book. Perhaps I can see you soon at Beverly Farms.

Always,
F.F.

1. *United States v. Sullivan*, 274 U.S. 259, 263–64 (1927). The defendant, who was engaged in illicit traffic in liquor, had not filed a tax return. Holmes wrote for a unanimous Court: "We see no reason to doubt the interpretation of the [Revenue Act of 1921], or any reason why the fact that a business is unlawful should exempt it from paying the taxes that if lawful it would have to pay. . . . It would be an extreme if not an extravagant application of the 5th Amendment to say that it authorized a man to refuse to state the amount of his income because it had been made in crime. . . . He could not draw a conjurer's circle around the whole matter by his own declaration that to write any word upon the government blank would bring him into danger of the law." In *Beech-nut Packing Company v. P. Lorillard*, 273 U.S. 629, 632 (1927), Holmes's unanimous opinion found that the defendant's use of the trademark was legitimate despite the claim that it had been abandoned. A trademark, Holmes said, "is a distinguishable token devised or picked out with the intent to appropriate it to a particular class of goods and with the hope that it will come to symbolize good will. . . . The fact that the good will once associated with it has vanished does not end at once the preferential right of the proprietor to try it again upon goods of the same class with improvements that renew the proprietor's hopes."

2. Charles A. and Mary R. Beard, *The Rise of American Civilization*, 2 vols. (New York: Macmillan, 1927).

3. John Livingston Lowes, *The Road to Xanadu* (Boston, Houghton, Mifflin, 1927), analyzes Coleridge's poem "Kubla Khan."

Washington, D.C.
June 7, 1927

My dear Frankfurter,

Many thanks for the never failing encouragement. I have felt myself as if things were going well with me this year. I hope and infer that the same is true for you. I also hope that you will be able to drop in on us after we get to Beverly Farms. The two books that you mention are added to a short list of potentialities for a summer which, in view of expecting a lot of *certioraris*, I don't intend to worry over making improving to the mind. The ends are all tucked in so far as I can remember. My trunk sent on by express, and all opinions done are ready to be bound. I hope that the "fury with the abhorred shears" will defer her snip for a time.[1]

Yours as ever,
O.W.H.

1. But the fair guerdon when we hope to find,
And think to burst out into sudden blaze,
Comes the blind Fury with th' abhorred shears,
And slits the thin-spin life.
John Milton, "Lycidas" (64)

Beverly Farms, Massachusetts
June 21, 1927

Dear Frankfurter,

It is a joy to think that we can and shall see you. If you and Luina could make it between 3 and 6 p.m. on Friday or if that doesn't suit, the same hours Saturday it would fit nicely. Those are the only times that we can conveniently this week, which is a little crowded. I won't stop to explain but I get tired more easily than I used to and I have to economize time. If you prefer Saturday telegram Beverly Farms 14. Otherwise I shall expect you Friday.

Affectionately yours,
O. W. Holmes

Beverly Farms, Massachusetts
July 25, 1927

Dear Frankfurter,

Young men will do't
When they come to't

as the bard observes but nevertheless I am a good deal annoyed at the situation.[1] I don't suppose that you could get me another young man as good as you and Corcoran have depicted Sutherland. I think therefore that I shall take him, *non obstant* but before a final decision I should like to know whether you have in mind anyone who will stay single and whom you think fairly equal to the work, if not to Sutherland.[2]

I am taking life pretty leisurely although there are always letters to be answered and although I have gone over 30 odd *certioraris* for next term and have granted one and denied another application for a stay when men are to be executed forthwith. I have read a few books and am rereading Spinoza's *Ethics*, but have no big *piece de resistance* on hand. It seems to agree with me. I hope you also are reasonably well. My compliments to the missus.

Yours ever,
O.W.H.

1. "Young men will do't, if they come to't." *Hamlet*, Act IV: scene 5 (60).

2. Arthur E. Sutherland, Jr. (1902–73), married Margaret Adams on September 10, 1927. Sutherland was Professor of Law at Harvard from 1950 to 1970 and author of several books on constitutional law as well as *The Law at Harvard, 1817–1867* (Cambridge: Harvard University Press, 1967).

Beverly Farms, Massachusetts
July 29, 1927

Dear Frankfurter,

Sutherland it is. I come down. He is so strongly recommended by you, that I waive my objections which after all are more in the interest of society than myself although I shall fear preoccupation and a wish to get back to the beloved one in place of the general availability of a bachelor.

I interrupted Spinoza for the excellent *Life of John Sargent* but have gone back to him again—the *Ethics* in Everyman's Library.[1] His theological machinery and arguments of course leave me unmoved and even bored, but behind that is a conception of the Universe that I share except that I dare not assume that our logic is binding on the Cosmos even if it wears a beard, and that Chauncey Wright taught me half a century or more ago that I could not predicate necessity of it. Spinoza is keen in his analyses of the mind and feelings and comes the nearest of anything I know to my explanation of sympathy, which I never got anyone to attend to. How hard it is for one whose business it is to put results into words, to accept inarticulate impressions as enriching and happy hours as self-justifying—but I try to enlarge my view to that degree and not to worry too much over the absence of big dull books. I read Chesterfield's *Letters* the other day with amusement and approval and the feeling that he put Dr. Johnson in the wrong.[2]

I may have mentioned that I have returned the first batch of *certioraris*—30 or more—examined. To that extent I am willing to bet on my surviving till next term. I hope you are having as good a time as I am—you don't say. Of course Karl Marx is a bore and, as I think, full of fallacies skipping from the interest of England to that of the world as it suits his convenience and treating ownership or control as equivalent to consumption. The Hegelian machinery adds to the tedium.

Yours ever,
O.W.H.

1. Evan Edward Charteris, *John Sargent* (New York: C. Scribner's Sons, 1927); Benedictus de Spinoza, *Ethics* (New York: Dutton, 1925). Introduction by George Santayana; first published in 1910.

2. Charles Strachey, ed., *The Letters of the Earl of Chesterfield to His Son* (New York: G. P. Putnam's Sons, 1925). See pp. lix–lxvi for Strachey's discussion of the conflict between Lord Chesterfield (1694–1773) and Dr. Samuel Johnson (1709–84).

Beverly Farms, Massachusetts
September 9, 1927

Dear Frankfurter,

It must be either a very hurried line or none tonight and I can't wait a minute to tell you how relieved and touched I am by your letter.[1] *The New Republic* I think has been rather hysterical whereas the criticism in your book moved me much, and was only qualified by my necessary suspension of judgment until I should read the proceedings and evidence which I never have done. The talk of the N.R. is on the matter of reasonable doubt.[2] I take it that the jury must have understood that in case of reasonable doubt they were to acquit. If so, the proper tribunal has passed on the matter and this is an attempt to retry the case by the more articulate part of public opinion. In general one doesn't believe in such attempts and it seems quite clear that this one is not due to abstract love of justice but to the undue prominence given to red opinions which interest more than black skins. I repeat that, subject to correction from fuller knowledge, your criticism impressed and moved me much but I cannot but remember that I have seen a murder case tried in half a day in England when the judge I thought very plainly indicated his prejudice which in that case was corrected, I thought rightly, by the jury. I don't understand that anyone who knows about the case denies that there was some evidence against the men and I don't quite see the need of making heroes of them.

I have done 90 odd *certioraris* for next term—read a little, enjoyed much with scruples at want of accomplishment and in the main kept well. I wish I could talk more but once more my thanks.

Affectionately yours,
O.W.H.

1. The letter referred to is missing.
2. "Ominous Execution," *New Republic* 52 (1927): 30. Holmes is commenting here on reaction to the execution of Sacco and Vanzetti. See above, March 18, 1927, and Parrish, *Frankfurter and His Times*, 176–96.

Washington, D.C.
October 8, 1927

Dear Frankfurter,

A thousand thanks for your letter. Probably soon the old pleasure will be on but so far the heat and the oppression of too many things to think about have made it rather wearing. I think everybody is tired this p.m. (I have recently returned from conference.) By the blessing of the Lord we had to adjourn before considering the argued cases so tomorrow I shan't have an opinion to write. But I have not yet got my breath. I hope all is well with you.

Affectionately yours,
O.W.H.

A nice notice of Brandeis in the *Nation* of the 5th.[1] It gave me a thrill of pleasure.

1. Norman Hapgood, "Americans We Like: Justice Brandeis," *Nation* 125 (1927): 330.

Washington, D.C.
November 4, 1927

Dear Frankfurter,

The delay in answering your account of the Cohen celebration meant only that I was hard driven with work.[1] I am deeply pleased that Cohen should have received due honor and am moved by your tale of the event.[2] Also I am glad that things begin well in your academic year. I always ask the young fellows if they have not been stimulated by their contact with you and all that I know always say yes, indeed.

My opinions are written and, except the last two, delivered bar one that elicited a really fine outburst from Butler contra, and led to ordering up the record to be followed perhaps by further argument. I have done all the *certioraris* that had come in last Monday and I have no duty more pressing than to meditate whether to write a dissent on the difference between a tax and a penalty, which opens a hobby.[3] I shall consult with Brandeis before doing much. We agree in result but I don't know whether my mode of approach would have his concurrence.

I should see the dawn of leisure without duty but for a misgiving that I ought to go to the dentist to be looked over which I don't want to do. I have had no time to read but I am half way through a book on the *Rationale of Proximate Cause* by Leon Green, associate professor of law, Yale—a cocky gent, who tells all the courts that they don't know what they are talking about.[4] I am reminded of Sidney Bartlett's comment on an argument of Evarts's—"And through it all there ran a vein of thought, attenuated at times, to be sure, but never wholly lost."[5] The author I think greatly overvalues the significance of his contribution, so far as I have got, but does contribute something for some people toward clearness of thought. I intend to finish the little book and then perhaps struggle with an essay or two sent to me last summer by a German who believes that he is making an important contribution on the theory of possession, stimulated he says by my book. One way or another there will be more to do than there is time for. My blessing on your courses.

Affectionately yours,
O.W.H.

1. The letter referred to is missing.

2. Morris Cohen's students honored him with a dinner on the occasion of his twenty-fifth anniversary at City College New York. See Morris Cohen, *A Dreamer's Journey* (Boston: Beacon Press, 1949), 148–49.

3. *Compania General de Tabacos de Filipinas v. Collector*, 275 U.S. 87, 100 (1927). A Spanish corporation licensed to do business in the Philippines was subject to the tax on insurance for

shipments of goods sold abroad. Taft's majority opinion upheld the plaintiff's suit, which claimed that the tax was a penalty depriving the company of its property without due process and departing from the rules of uniform taxation. Holmes, with Brandeis concurring, based his dissent on this distinction, referring specifically to the precedent, *Allgeyer v. Louisiana*, 165 U.S. 578 (1896), cited by the plaintiff: "It is true that every exaction of money for an act is a discouragement to the extent of the payment required, but that which in its immediacy is a discouragement may be part of an encouragement when seen in its organic connection with the whole. Taxes are what we pay for civilized society, including the chance to insure. A penalty on the other hand is intended altogether to prevent the thing punished."

4. Leon Green, *Rationale of Proximate Cause* (Kansas City, Mo.: Vernon, 1927).

5. Sidney Bartlett (1799–1889) was a leader of the Boston bar. William Maxwell Evarts (1818–1901) served as counsel for President Andrew Johnson during his impeachment trial. He also represented Henry Ward Beecher at the minister's adultery trial. He was Johnson's Attorney General, Secretary of State in the Rutherford B. Hayes administration, and Republican Senator from New York, 1885–91.

Washington, D.C.
November 11, 1927

My dear Frankfurter,

How many times you have touched my heart and not infrequently given me courage when I drooped. You do it again today by your letter and book; except that I droop less as old age brings equanimity.[1] I hope it does, at least for sometimes I am not sure, and life still is exciting. At all events I thank you for one of the things of which I am fondest and happiest in my life. Let me add that from reading most of the parts as they came out I believe you have done a fine and I hope useful piece of work.

Affectionately yours,
O. W. Holmes

1. The letter referred to is missing. The book was Felix Frankfurter and James M. Landis, *The Business of the Supreme Court* (New York: Macmillan, 1927), which the authors dedicated to Holmes.

Washington, D.C.
November 26, 1927

My dear Frankfurter,

If old age has not made me forget what I do not think I could forget, not until a couple of days ago did I know of the Dedication of *The Business of the Supreme Court* when on rereading a letter from Hill I deciphered a word that I didn't understand. Turning to the book I found the connection between the title page and the next not quite cut. I cut it and read for the first time what gave me great pride and pleasure. You certainly get under my hide. I have just finished reading the work of a man who per contra has always had a whack at me when he has mentioned me—and as I have flattered myself always with failure to understand. I mean Zane's *Story of the Law*—there is his usual incredibly egotistic dogmatism but I think he has made a good book in a way that probably we should not envy and yet that is good.[1] I mean you are interested by the story and see the thing as a whole and that means that the book is a work of art, whatever its shortcomings in the way of abstract thinking, accuracy or perhaps proportion. I marvel that one who stops to notice the courtesies of Cornwallis and Washington and the advantages of being born a gentleman should be so unrestrained not to say boorish in his dealings with that large part of the world that does not command his sympathies.[2] Once more I am your debtor.

Affectionately yours,
O. W. Holmes

1. John M. Zane, *The Story of the Law* (Garden City, N.Y.: Doubleday, Doran, 1927).

2. Referring to a dinner party that Washington gave Cornwallis following the British surrender at Yorktown, Zane wrote: "Lord Cornwallis in his gallant way proposed the health of Washington and said many true things of that steadfast soul. Not least striking in his toast was his recognition of Washington's fine generalship and fortitude during the dark days of Valley Forge. It is after all much that one should be born a gentleman. Not only are we indebted to England for our laws, but it would be well if we could remember that originally we were indebted to England for those manners, of which both Washington and Cornwallis were such splendid examples." *The Story of the Law*, 253.

Cambridge, Massachusetts
December 6, 1927

My Justice:

On Thursday the Court and you are celebrating your silver wedding anniversary—the date of taking your seat being the effective date. And what a quarter of a century it has been. Its achievement will remain golden as long as the history of your court and of our country will endure.

And now for the beginning of the second quarter century.

Always devotedly,
F.F.

Washington, D.C.
December 14, 1927

Dear Frankfurter,

Admirably done. Again you make me proud.[1] You spoke the other day of Mrs. Gertrude Bell's letters. I have not seen the book but I have a few admirable ones that she wrote to me in earlier days.[2] I hope you will have a good Christmas and every pleasant thing you wish. The other day I received an opinion by Wu which leads me to infer that he still is alive but I have had no letter from him for I know not how long.

Yours ever,
O. W. Holmes

1. The reference is not clear.
2. Gertrude Lowthian Bell, *The Letters of Gertrude Bell* (New York: Boni and Liveright, 1927). Bell (1868–1926) was a renowned Middle East scholar and traveler.

Washington, D.C.
December 30, 1927

My dear Frankfurter,

You lead me to repeat what perhaps I have repeated before—from what I said to the President when he gave me the Roosevelt medal.[1] "For five minutes you make me believe that the dream of a lifetime has come true." But so long as one writes decisions he is concerned with the future and never can be sure that he won't find out that he really is a damn fool after all. Meantime I appreciate and love your generous attitude and know that it does you honor while reserving judgment as to No. 1. I can't be sure that I didn't write the above quoted sentence to you the other day. I know I thought of it. I am proud to have a word from the wonderful T.C. [Thomas Corcoran]. I thank you again.

Affectionately yours,
O. W. Holmes

1. See above, June 7, 1924.

Washington, D.C.
February 5, 1928

My dear Frankfurter,

Felicitations on the charming, judicious and just notice of your book in *The New Republic.*[1] It gave me joy.

I have a prospect of some leisure this week, but there always is something to do and I always am worried till it is done. However I expect to read some more of the *Greville Diary* and have listened with pleasure to most of Miss Gertrude Bell's correspondence.[2] Do you know Professor Woodruff's *Introduction to the Study of Law* mentioned in the *Cornell Law Quarterly* cracking up Woodruff?[3] I never heard of him before the number was sent to me by Morris Cohen with a good article of his—good but hardly novel to me.[4] He made me want to see Demogue, *Notions fondamentales de droit prive*—I don't remember ever having seen it and I need some smack of thought.[5]

Yours as ever,
O.W.H.

Cohen acutely points out a weakness in the regime of private ownership, the demand for immediate profits. Government can afford to consider the long run.

1. The review, *New Republic* 53 (1928): 329, was written by Cardozo, who noted that the Court was concerned "less and less with tort and contract, more and more with the overshadowing issues of liberty and government."

2. Philip Whitwell Wilson, ed., *The Greville Diary* (New York: Doubleday, Page, 1927). After serving in Parliament, Wilson (1875–1956) joined the editorial staff of the *London Daily News*, and later was a special correspondent for the *New York Times*.

3. Edwin H. Woodruff, *Introduction to the Study of Law* (New York: Baker, Voorhis, 1898). Woodruff (1862–1941) was Professor of Law at Cornell from 1896 to 1927 and Dean of the Law School from 1916 to 1921.

4. Morris Cohen, "Property and Sovereignty," *Cornell Law Quarterly* 13 (1927): 8, 28, 30. Cohen argued for the integration of public law (sovereignty) and private law (property) in the modern state: "Experience has shown all civilized peoples the indispensable need for communal control to prevent the abuse of private enterprise. . . . The wise expenditure of money is a more complicated problem than the mere saving it, and a no less indispensable task to those who face the question of how to promote a better communal life. To do this effectively we need a certain liberal insight into the more intangible desire of the human heart. Preoccupation with the management of property has not in fact advanced this kind of insight."

5. Rene Demogue, *Les Notions fondamentales du droit prive* (Paris: A. Rousseau, 1911).

Washington, D.C.
February 15, 1928

My dear Frankfurter,

Your nomination sounds promising and I have no doubt will continue your successes in that line provided that I live to profit by it.[1] You must tell the lad that I am a very old cove and that my reservation of the right to die or resign grows more ominous every year. But I intend to do my damndest to elude fate for another year. These young chaps nowadays pay me little attentions in the way of helping me on with my coat and rubbers that go to my heart. They also have made out my income tax return since one was required, but I believe that my return is a simple matter beyond perhaps doing two or three sums. Tell him too that last year I called on Corcoran and this year expect to call on Sutherland for some help in vacation probably about September 1. As they draw pay up to October 1 I don't think it unreasonable.

I am much obliged also for Strachey's paper which I have assumed you don't want returned.[2] It transfixed my gizzard. I am expecting Brandeis in a few minutes to confer on one dissent of his and two per me incited by him—a spicy moment.[3]

I haven't read anything of Proust lately. If I get a chance I shall follow your suggestion but I have been pretty busy and haven't quite finished Greville's *Diary* and I am reading a book that M. Cohen's remarks led me to take from the library, Demogue's *Les Notions fondamentales du droit prive*—excellent as far as I have read but not seeming to tell me what I did not know. I am rather bored at not quite feeling free to drop it and yet not getting much new feed from it.

I did not hear of your loss until a few days ago—you have been much in my mind since then.[4]

Affectionately yours,
O. W. Holmes

1. The letter referred to is missing. John E. Lockwood (1904–93) served as Holmes's secretary for the October 1928 Term. Lockwood was an attorney for the U.S. State Department (1941–45). He was a member of the Council on Foreign Relations and for many years was legal adviser to the Rockefeller family.

2. Probably (Evelyn) John (St. Loe) Strachey (1901–63), who was a member of the Labour Party in the 1920s and an active pamphleteer. Strachey's *Revolution and Reason* (London: Parsons, 1925) advocated socialist solutions to Britain's economic problems. He supported the communists in the 1930s but broke with them in 1939 after the Non-Aggression Pact between Hitler and Stalin. He served in the RAF during World War II and in Clement Atlee's Labor government from 1946 to 1951.

3. Brandeis's dissent was *Wuchter v. Pizzuti*, 276 U.S. 13 (1928). Taft's majority opinion in-

quired into a suit between two parties residing in separate states to conclude that the relevant New Jersey statute did not make adequate provision for notification of the nonresident plaintiff who was therefore deprived of his property without due process. Brandeis, with Holmes concurring, held that it was improper for the Court to consider this objection, which was not made or considered by the lower courts or even included in the assignments of error filed with the Supreme Court. Stone dissented separately. Holmes's dissents were *Brimstone Railroad and Canal Co. v. United States*, 276 U.S. 104 (1928), and, probably, *Black and White Taxi Co. v. Brown and Yellow Taxi Co., Id.* at 518. In *Brimstone Railroad*, McReynolds's opinion overturned an Interstate Commerce Commission decision reducing the division of joint rates. Holmes and Brandeis dissented without opinion. On *Black and White Taxi*, see below, April 14, 1928.

4. Frankfurter's mother, Emma Frankfurter, died January 10.

Washington, D.C.
March 15, 1928

Dear F.F.,

Wu asked me to show you the enclosed clipping.[1] I wonder if he takes the "soldiers" too seriously.[2] He says he's worried by too great popularity. Also he desperately wants to come here. I wrote sometime ago that I thought he had better keep his nose to the grindstone and I do think so emphatically. I said I was too old to attempt to initiate a call for him here but that I would contribute to any reasonable scheme. But I can't help fearing that he is too intent on being a great man and wants to eat oats and no hay. I may be wrong and would gladly give him any boost that were good for him but that is where it stands now.

Once more my thanks for all your kindness.

Affectionately yours,
O.W.H.

1. The item referred to is missing.

2. Writing to Laski on May 12, Holmes expressed his concern about Wu: "My last letter from Wu spoke as if his life was in danger—I can't tell how seriously to take it but it makes me uneasy." Howe, ed., *Holmes-Laski Letters*, 1055–56. Whatever the danger may have been, Wu decided to defer the Harvard scholarship offered by Pound and to accept a new assignment to begin codifying the civil law of China. He announced his plans in a letter to Holmes dated May 19: "Lo! the most beautiful of my dreams was fulfilled! I shall devote a whole year to this great task." University of Michigan Law School, *Law Quadrangle Notes* 31 (1987): 17.

Washington, D.C.
March 21, 1928

My dear Frankfurter,

Your news as to Wu is gratifying though privately I doubt if he is not seeking the easier road.[1] Whatever my doubts I am very glad that he should have that chance. If he accepts let me know and if I am alive and no great change has happened I might add say $500 but that is *strictly between ourselves* and not to be hinted to him or anyone else. His address as probably you know is 11 Quinsan Road, Shanghai. I should much prefer that you or Pound should write to him so that he may have the offer in authentic form. Please let me know when it is done. Of course I agree with you about Maitland—everybody does.[2] My work is nearly done, only 4 or 5 *certioraris* to be considered but I am not yet quite freed from the press of work.

Affectionately yours,
O.W.H.

1. The letter referred to is missing.
2. Frederick William Maitland (1850–1906) was Professor of Law at Cambridge and the leading historian of English law in the nineteenth century. A founder of the Selden Society (1887) which supported publication of legal history, he is best known for *Constitutional History of England* (Cambridge: University Press, 1909).

Cambridge, Massachusetts
April 14, 1928

Dear Justice Holmes,

I have just read your dissent in the *Black & White Taxicab* case and I'm all stirred with delight.[1] You have written, if I may say so, a landmark opinion. To think that it has taken a century to expose the fallacy of one of the most obstinate doctrines of your Court! And you have done it with such ineluctable lucidity that only the pertinacity of error can explain persistence in it. At last you have given the means for eventual correction in reason. I'm particularly aroused, because I've been delving a bit into *Swift v. Tyson* and its sequelae, and the more I study the applications of that doctrine the less respect I have for it.[2] My betters tell me to revere Story but I cannot escape a strong scepticism about his intellectual greatness, much as I admire his energy, and his powers of formulation, which gave substance to scattered materials.

Washington must now be at its loveliest.

Always yours,
F.F.

1. *Black & White Taxi Co. v. Brown and Yellow Taxi Co.*, 276 U.S. 518, 533–34 (1928). The Brown and Yellow Company, which enjoyed a monopoly with the Louisville, Kentucky, railroad station, was challenged by the Black and White Company in the expectation that Kentucky law would declare the arrangement illegal. Brown and Yellow rechartered itself in Tennessee and brought suit in federal court in order to avoid the anticipated ruling. Butler's majority opinion sustained the Brown and Yellow strategy by holding that federal courts, in deciding common law questions arising within a particular state, could decide the law without regard to state decisions. Holmes, with Brandeis and Stone concurring, dissented: "The common law so far as it is enforced in a State, whether called common law or not, is not the common law generally but the law of that State existing by the authority of that State without regard to what it may have been in England or anywhere else. It may be adopted by statute in place of another system previously in force. . . . But a general adoption of it does not prevent State Courts from refusing to follow the English decisions upon a matter where the local conditions are different. . . . Whether and how far and in what sense a rule shall be adopted . . . is for the State alone to decide."

2. *Swift v. Tyson*, 16 Peters 1, 18–19 (1842). Justice Joseph Story (1779–1845), writing for a unanimous Court, held that federal courts were bound only by local law, "that is to say . . . by positive statutes of the state, and the construction thereof adopted by the local tribunals." Otherwise, decisions should be guided by "the general principles and doctrines of commercial jurisprudence." Referring to *Swift* in *Black & White Taxicab*, 276 U.S. at 535, Holmes commented that Story was "probably wrong if anyone is interested to inquire what the framers of the instrument meant." Both decisions were overruled by *Erie Railroad Co. v. Tompkins*, 340 U.S. 64 (1938), written by Brandeis.

Washington, D.C.
April 21, 1928

My dear Frankfurter,

Again my thanks. I hoped that you would share my views in the *Taxicab* case. It is the only one that has stirred me much lately. In conference today I have a decision on a point not open to doubt, which a few remarks extended to a page and a half.[1] My brethren express doubt on what I thought obvious and will cut it down to a page to which I have no objection. It is like Franklin's "John Thompson Hatter makes and sells hats" with a picture which his friends by successive eliminations cut down to his name and the picture. I may not have the tale exactly right but very likely you can correct it.[2] It gets on one's nerves after a while always to have something waiting to be done and I shan't be sorry when the arguments end.

I have discovered a third book (after Pepys & Walpole's *Letters*) when you don't want ideas and don't want to waste your time—Disraeli *Curiosities of Literature*.[3] It has been on my shelves uncut since I was a boy. I now put my nose again to the grindstone.

Yours as ever,
O.W.H.

1. Probably *Coffin Brothers v. Bennett*, 277 U.S. 29 (1928), a unanimous opinion denying an appeal from a state decision that held that stockholders in an insolvent bank were not denied due process when the Superintendent of Banks assessed them to pay depositors.

2. Benjamin Franklin told the story of John Thompson to console Thomas Jefferson as the Second Continental Congress proceeded to edit the Declaration of Independence. Franklin advised, "I have made it a rule whenever in my power, to avoid becoming a draughtsman of papers to be reviewed by a public body." The story appeared originally in Jefferson's *Biographical Sketches of Famous Men*, "Anecdotes of Benjamin Franklin" [1818], published in Henry A. Washington, ed., *The Writings of Thomas Jefferson* (Washington: Taylor & Maury, 1853–54).

3. Isaac Disraeli, *Curiosities of Literature*, 3 vols. (1791). Disraeli (1766–1848) was the father of British Prime Minister Benjamin Disraeli; *The Diary of Samuel Pepys, from 1659 to 1869*, 9 vols. (New York: Groscup & Sterling, 1892–1900). Horace Walpole, Sr., *Letters*, 6 vols. (London: R. Bentley, 1840).

Cambridge, Massachusetts
May 22, 1928

Dear Justice Holmes,

I am all exhilarated by your triple-header—your three dissents in the batch of opinions which has just come.[1] One *Black & White Taxi* opinion is glory enough for one Term. But how you have added thereunto the separation-of-powers discussion and those two amazing Tax immunities for patent royalties and on gasoline sold to the Coast Guard! These three dissents have a real wallop! I chortled over the mingling of powers in the I.C.C. "only softened by a quasi." And, the power to tax is not the power to destroy "while this Courts sits," ought forever to reserve for the museum of judicial *dicta* Marshall's utterance. What hold words have on men—I sometimes suspect, particularly on our profession. These are really exciting opinions of yours—like sparkling wine in a dry age.

Your labors will soon be over and the rocks of Beverly Farms and the dunes of Ipswich will again exert their charm.

Always,
F.F.

1. The dissenting opinions were: (1) *Long v. Rockwood*, 277 U.S. 142, 149–50 (1928). McReynolds's majority opinion held the Massachusetts income tax to be constitutionally inapplicable to royalties received by a Massachusetts resident from a patent issued to him by the United States. Holmes, with Brandeis, Sutherland, and Stone concurring, retorted: "Obviously it is not true that patents are instrumentalities of the government. They are used by the patentees for their private advantage alone. . . . Patents would be valueless to their owner without the organized societies constituted by the States, and the question is why patents should not contribute as other property does to maintaining that without which they would be of little use." (2) *Springer v. Philippine Islands, Id.* at 189. Sutherland, writing for the Court, held that

provisions concerning the separation of powers in the Organic Act of the Philippines were violated by statutes transferring from the Governor-General to legislative officers the power to vote shares of stock of government-owned proprietary corporations. Holmes, with Brandeis concurring, urged latitude in determining the dividing line between executive and legislative branches. (3) *Panhandle Oil Co. v. Knox*, *Id.* at 218, 223 (1927). Butler's majority opinion, citing John Marshall's dictum that "the power to tax involves the power to destroy," in *McCulloch v. Maryland*, 4 Wheaton 316 (1819), held that a state could not constitutionally impose a sales tax on gasoline sold by a dealer to the United States for use by Coast Guard vessels and by a Veterans' Hospital. Holmes questioned the relevance of the precedent: "In those days it was not recognized as it is today that most of the distinctions of the law are distinctions of degree. If the States had any power it was assumed that they had all power, and that the necessary alternative was to deny it altogether. . . . But this court which so often has defeated the attempt to tax in certain ways can defeat an attempt to discriminate or otherwise go too far without abolishing the power to tax. The power to tax is not the power to destroy while this Court sits." Brandeis and Stone concurred. McReynolds dissented separately with Stone concurring.

Washington, D.C.
May 26, 1928

My dear Frankfurter,

Again my thanks to you. You touch what has occurred to me: that one might add to this chapter on the part played by fiction an appendix at least on *phrases*—they put water under the boat and float it over dangerous obstacles. I have had my whack at police power dedicated to a public use quasi etc.—one might make a little chapter. I am just back from conference and find 27 or 28 *certioraris* so I must go to work.

Ever affectionately yours,
O.W.H.

Cambridge, Massachusetts
June 13, 1928

Dear Justice Holmes,

I sent Judge Cardozo the rather interesting picture of you, with Brandeis, printed in the [Boston] *Transcript* recently. In reply, he sent me the enclosed letter.[1]

You certainly wound up the Term with a bang. You said what needed to be said about prosecutorial indecencies.[2] It is a serious cause for reflection that with all our improved uses of force and chicane in dealing with crime, our law enforcement is so bad, while in England, where "third-degree"ing and "wire-tapping" are not tolerated, law enforcement is so effective. As Cardozo says, you never wrote better than during the last Term.

I trust *certioraris* won't break in on your leisure and North Shore pleasures for many a day.

Always yours,
F.F.

1. Cardozo's letter to Frankfurter, dated June 3, 1928, reads: "The picture is delightful. The master has a roguish twinkle in his eye. I don't know but that the rogue in him is one of the secrets of his great charm. If it hadn't been for that strain in his make-up, he never could have written some of the great dissents of the last few months—as fine as anything ever written by him or by any one else." Box 33, folder 27, Holmes Papers.

2. *Olmstead v. United States*, 277 U.S. 438, 469–70 (1928). Olmstead had been convicted of conspiracy to violate the Prohibition Act. At the trial, evidence of private telephone conversations between the defendants had been admitted even though it was obtained by means of governmental wire-tapping. The defendants contended that admission of this evidence violated the Fourth and Fifth Amendments. Taft's majority opinion held that the evidence was admissible. Holmes, Brandeis, Butler, and Stone all wrote dissenting opinions. Holmes endorsed Brandeis's lengthy and famous dissent and then added: "The Government ought not to use evidence obtained and only obtainable by a criminal act. . . . It is desirable that criminals should be detected, and to that end all available evidence should be used. It also is desirable that the Government should not itself foster and pay for other crimes, when they are the means by which the evidence is to be obtained. . . . We have to choose, and for my part I think it a less evil that some criminals should escape than that the Government should play an ignoble part."

Beverly Farms, Massachusetts
June 14, 1928

Dear Frankfurter,

You renew my ever recurring gratitude to you for keeping up my courage. For age, like Day and McKenna in former days with my opinions, pulls out here a plum and there a raisin, until one is haunted by a fear that he lags superfluous; not to mix the metaphor, I should have said: has become a mass of sodden dough. I am thankful for Cardozo's letter. Dear Man—I do wish that I had seen or could see more of him. He charmed and impressed me on the one inadequate occasion of our meeting. The *Transcript* portrait I have not seen. I am approaching the feeling of leisure hardly having attained it yet and I have some books: Bertrand Russell's *Philosophy*, Parrington's *Main Currents in American Thought*, Anita Loos' *But Gentlemen Marry Brunettes*.[1] Also my last term cases to be indexed not to speak of daily bills to pay. Which reminds me that I haven't heard from or of Wu whether his apprehensions were well founded and whether he will accept the scholarship. If he accepts let me know.

While at the Touraine I ran through *Genghis Khan* by Lamb.[2] Interesting—it made you say like the Yankee looking at Niagara Falls: What's to hinder?—with his desert horsemen, with their horses and able to take great marches on almost nothing, he always could get there first and so licked everybody. The Rebel General Forrest said he would rather have 15 minutes bulge than a West Point Education or words to that effect.[3]

Sleep gets a chance here and in a minute I shall get into a comfortable position, take a book and see what happens.

Affectionately yours,
O. W. Holmes

1. Bertrand Russell, *An Outline of Philosophy* (London: Allen & Unwin, 1927); Vernon Lewis Parrington, *Main Currents in American Thought*, 3 vols. (New York: Harcourt, Brace, 1927); Anita Loos, *But Gentlemen Marry Brunettes* (New York: Boni and Liveright, 1928).

2. Harold Lamb, *Genghis Khan* (New York: Doubleday, 1927).

3. Nathan Bedford Forrest (1821–77), Confederate General and cavalry raider, was one of the founders of the original Ku Klux Klan in 1866.

Beverly Farms, Massachusetts
June 26, 1928

Dear Frankfurter,

Thanks for the clipping—the portrait—which I had not seen. I should not have known Brandeis.

I suppose I had better wait until Pound's recommendation has been acted on before sending my check. The time is more remote than I realized that it would be. Of course it is doubtful whether I shall be here to welcome Wu in 29–30—to whom should I make the check payable? Of course this will be strictly personal to be applied to Wu not *cy pres*[1] (as I don't suppose there is any great need of it otherwise). I shall be glad to see Cardozo's piece when it comes.[2] I have got to the last 40 pages of Parrington. I have found the book most instructive and interesting in spite of a latent hostility on my part to the implied dogmatism of his continually recurring "exploitation"—a form of thought for which I have devilish little but scorn. Most of the judgments seem to me very sound. But I don't agree at all with his sympathy for the theologically-minded transcendentalists who set such a value on every human soul or with his calling Thoreau a thinker (judging from *Walden* in a memory that is some years old). I suppose on the main point I should find myself in pretty stubborn disagreement with Laski also. I just haven't got to what he says about my father, but from a preliminary glance I should think that he missed, and I shouldn't blame him for it, what I think the fact, that although my governor was largely distracted into easy talk and occasional verse, he had the gift of an insight that was capable of being profound.[3] I think that probably I should hate Parrington's ultimate point of view as one that seems to me sentimental and unreal and at this time noxious but it is long since I have felt so indebted to a writer for a solid and laborious task so faithfully and intelligently performed.

Yours as ever,
O.W.H.

1. As near as possible.

2. Benjamin Cardozo, *The Paradoxes of Legal Science* (New York: Columbia, 1928).

3. Of Thoreau, Parrington (1871–1929) wrote: "Honest, fearless, curiously inquisitive—a masterless man who would give no hostages to fortune—he proved his right to be called a philosopher by seeking wisdom as a daily counselor and friend, and following such paths only as wisdom suggested." And, of Holmes's father, he said: "In the shadow of Emerson and Thoreau, the wit of Back Bay is in danger of being obscured. Unsupported by his physical presence, his writings seem far less vital than they did when the echoes of his clever talk were still sounding through them." Parrington, *Main Currents in American Thought*, 2:400, 451.

Duxbury, Massachusetts
July 11, 1928

Dear Justice Holmes,

The enclosed is from today's *New York Tribune*.[1] This is the silly season, and there is not news, so they have to invent some!

For some writing, I've been rereading the opinions of the last two Terms. I know not how much self-satisfaction your New England conscience permits you to enjoy. But, certainly, no informed mind can read those opinions, as I've been doing, in sequence and not be struck with the fact that yours stand out like the most luminous stars in the sky. And not merely "great causes"—even little bankruptcy cases. I hope the heat has not been your way too much.

Ever yours,
F.F.

1. *New York Herald Tribune*, July 11, 1928: "We hope very much that the report from Washington that Oliver Wendell Holmes will resign from the Supreme Court next October is untrue, for our Nation can ill spare him. . . . His opinions have such freshness, his mind is so pen-

etrating and in tune with the age, and his general view of life has such tang and piquancy that we hope he will stay right where he is as long as his powers permit."

Beverly Farms, Massachusetts
July 13, 1928

Dear Frankfurter,

You continue your kindness and again I thank you. Your article on "Distribution of Judicial Power" came a few days ago but I haven't yet read it as precedence is due to a borrowed book.[1] (I hate to borrow books and always am miserable till I have returned them.) This one—Morison's *Oxford History of the United States* has been begun but rather creeps because of interruptions.[2] It seems to me admirably good though once in a while he ends a sentence with some rather pert snapper. It is interesting to note the new elements considered in the later books such as Parrington's and Morison's—especially the economic one brought forward by Beard with rather mean innuendoes. I am anxious to get at you, and I know I shall have pleasure, but I must do this job. Also *certioraris* have begun to appear—I give them a fraction of time only. I have done 20 odd.

Owen Wister has sent me *The Sun Also Rises* by Hemingway—I infer from what he said stirring garbage—but he thought showing promise.[3]

I wonder if you hear anything from Brandeis. He never writes to me. I hope all goes well with him but can't remember certainly where he is.

I read a trade union report on Russia (after a visit) which was optimistic but leads me to the reflection that if a man does not contribute thought or beauty I do not rejoice at his multiplication which of course will happen none the less.[4]

Yours as ever,
O.W.H.

1. Felix Frankfurter, "Distribution of Judicial Power between United States and State Courts," *Cornell Law Quarterly* 13 (1923): 499. Frankfurter's discussion of diversity jurisdiction focused upon *Swift v. Tyson*, 16 Peters 1 (1842). See above, April 14, 1928.

2. Samuel Eliot Morison, *The Oxford History of the United States*, 2 vols. (London: H. Milford, 1927).

3. Owen Wister (1860–1933), lawyer and novelist, was best known for *The Virginian* (New York: Macmillan, 1902). His friendship with Holmes began when Holmes was on the Massachusetts bench and Wister was a law student at Harvard.

4. American Trade Union Delegation to the Soviet Union, *Russia after Ten Years* (New York: International, 1927).

Duxbury, Massachusetts
September 9, 1928

My dear Justice Holmes,

Have you by any chance read Benet's *John Brown's Body*?[1] It's endlessly long, but I find it vivifying and strikingly pictorial. He manages to give form and immediacy to the panorama of the Civil War and make alive generals and politicians who, heretofore, were merely names to me. Whether these are caricatures rather than portraits I know not. I came to the Benet after Sam Morison's admirable account of the Civil War in his Oxford History which is, indeed, *me judice*, a fine achievement in its entirety.

I hope that your summer has not been too disturbed by *certioraris*. In course of duty, I've been through the opinions of the last term all over again. Your *Black and White Taxi* case opinion (*Swift v. Tyson*) stands out as the term's masterpiece with the Philippine separation of powers, and the two tax dissents (patent royalties and gas for Veteran's Hospital) as close competitors. They are, if I may say so, as pungent and definitive opinions as any you have ever given us.

The present campaign is most exciting even though one of my elder colleagues says it's a race between a live and a dead man. Al Smith in the White House would greatly add to the liveliness of life. And, snobs to the contrary, we'd even survive Mrs. Smith!

Always devotedly yours,
F.F.

1. Stephen Vincent Benet, *John Brown's Body* (New York: Doubleday, Doran, 1928).

Beverly Farms, Massachusetts
September 10, 1928

My dear Frankfurter,

Many thanks for the enclosure and more for your letter. Oddly enough I had yesterday been notified of Benet, *John Brown's Body* and had affirmed that I would not read it without strong compulsion, though the praises were as yours. I may come to it yet. But I am still echoing with the rereading of *Moby Dick* and if any book more realizes the terrors of the world or the abysses of the human spirit, name it. I haven't done as much in the way of improvement as I ought to have done, but have lived, or rather, now that my secretary is here, am living rather an animal life. Getting up late—usually walking and then a long snooze, with solitaire after 9 p.m. doesn't leave much time. I have on hand Volume 2 of a *History of English Literature*—this volume by Cazamian translated by McInnes and the author which was recommended by Laski and which impress me as more subtile and profound than anything of the sort I have seen before.[1] I probably shan't have time to read even this volume through, but I think I shall send for it after I get to Washington. It is worth having.

Well only two weeks more here and then work and the barber. Not being allowed to go to town unattended I haven't had my hair cut since I reached Beverly Farms and I must he desampsonized, even though my wife likes the mop. I hope that all goes well with you. It looks now as if I might outlive Taney which would be accomplished on or about October 21.[2]

Yours always,
O. W. Holmes

1. Emile Legouis and Louis Cazamian, *A History of English Literature*, 2 vols. (New York: Macmillan, 1926–27).

2. Roger Taney (1777–1864), Chief Justice of the Supreme Court from 1835 to 1864.

Washington, D.C.
January 21, 1929

Dear Frankfurter,

The account you give of Mr. Hiss sounds most prepossessing and if he is willing to take the chances I shall hope to have him.[1] He ought to be warned however of the obvious fact that the chances grow more precarious every year. I soon shall be 89, and I may die or feel that I ought to resign. At present however my health seems to be excellent and I have no wish to resign until circumstances change. Probably he has taken the chances into account. I am glad to believe that your importance and value are more recognized with every year and that you are kindling a fire in many a young man.

I have had nothing very thrilling this term although in an opinion that I wrote yesterday I got a chance to make a few observations nearly commonplace that slightly pleased me, if they are not struck out.[2] Some little time ago in consequence of your giving my message to Cardozo, he wrote me a letter that I really regard as one of the superlative successes of my life—so much so that I don't like to talk about it.[3] He like you is generous to me. This to your private ear. I am at leisure today—my work all but two *certioraris* is done and I hope for a chance to read. I took a volume of Heine's poems from the library.[4] I can get the feel of them as I run my eye over them but I need a dictionary a good deal before I have them wholly. My secretary gave me on Xmas *The South Wind* by Norman Douglas which one wonders at the author for writing and oneself for reading—but if one is content with pleasure will give it as it gave the author a chance for sceptical talk about most current creeds in religion or morals.[5] But I shall be looking for a book.

Affectionately yours,
O. W. Holmes

1. Alger Hiss (b.1904), Holmes's secretary, 1929–30, later worked in the state department and was President of the Carnegie Endowment for Peace. In 1947 journalist Whittaker Chambers (1901–61) accused him of being a communist spy. Though the charge was never proven, Hiss was convicted of perjury following sensational congressional hearings that launched the career of Richard M. Nixon (1913–94).

2. Probably *Douglas v. New York, New Haven and Hartford Railroad Company*, 279 U.S. 377 (1929), which was argued on January 16 but not decided until May 13. Holmes's majority opinion upheld a district court decision invalidating a suit brought under the Federal Employers' Liability Act challenging a New York law as discriminating between citizens of New York and citizens of other states. The New York law authorized the court to dismiss an action by a citizen of another state but not an action brought by a citizen of New York. Holmes noted that the federal law was not intended to require state courts to entertain action under it as against an otherwise valid excuse under state law. Taft, Butler, and Van Devanter dissented without opinion.

3. "I was made proud and happy by your message conveyed to me by Felix Frankfurter. I think you must know from him and others that I revere and admire you to the point of adoration. I believe in all sincerity that you are the greatest judge that ever lived though of course it may be that in the stone age or beyond there was juridical genius or achievement beyond our ken today." Cardozo to Holmes, December 14, 1928, Box 38, folder 27, Holmes Papers.

4. German poet Heinrich Heine (1797–1856).

5. Norman Douglas, *South Wind* (New York: Dodd, Mead, 1928).

Washington, D.C.
February 15, 1929

Dear Frankfurter,

A thousand thanks for the book that just has come in—as soon as may be I shall read it.[1] But: 1) Conference tomorrow and I fear I see after it an opinion or dissent to be written. 2) I have not quite finished a little book of Spinoza's—and I have on hand from the library *L'Ombre de la Croix* which I was induced by the wonderful Redlich to take out—also a novel previously lent me by Gerrit Miller, *Dieu protege le Tsar*.[2] 3) I must write at once to Laski who I grieve to learn has had pneumonia and so is not coming here. 4) I must clear my table for action. 5) We begin to sit on Monday therefore I cannot tackle at once what from the look of it I would rather read than any of the forerunners. I thank you very much for the same.

Redlich was here the other night and as delightful and amazing as ever. His notion for a book about the United States in these later years struck me as most amusing and suggestive.

Spinoza is the boy. He is rather tiresome—I don't believe his premises and think his reasoning falls with or without them. But he sees the world as I see it and he alone of all the old ones that I know.

Brandeis has delighted me by an occasional call during the adjournment. I am richer after a talk with him. So no more from your somewhat harassed but affectionate friend.

O.W.H.

1. The book was J. W. N. Sullivan, *The Bases of Modern Science* (New York: Doubleday, Doran, 1929).

2. Joseph Ratner, ed., *The Philosophy of Spinoza* (New York: Modern Library, 1927); Jerome and Jean Tharaud, *A l'Ombre de la Croix* (Paris: Emile Paul, 1917); Louis Dumur, *Dieu protege le Tsar* (Paris: A. Michel, 1928).

Washington, D.C.
February 21, 1929

Dear Frankfurter,

Interest has triumphed over priorities and I have read the book on science that you so generously sent to me. I was absorbed and delighted. It seems to me to do the trick very well and really gives one an idea of the movement and the steps in it. I don't think it necessary to fix the details in my mind if I could have done it. For my purposes the results were enough. They seem to me to confirm the notice that the ultimate remains a mystery and that you may call it matter or force or the thought of God or what you will without getting any [forrader]. Assuming as I do that we are in the universe, that *we* are, in some sense, and not merely *I am* dreaming the whole, I see no reason for expecting to touch bottom. I accept my limitations and bow my head. The scientific men not being metaphysicians are apt to think that *their* ultimate is *the* ultimate for which I see no grounds.

Affectionately yours,
O.W.H.

Washington, D.C.
March 19, 1929

Dear Frankfurter,

As usual I begin with thanks.[1] I was glad to see the civil words of Peirce for I suspected that he regarded outsiders like St. John Green and me with contempt or at least indifference (and I still do).[2] As to young uns—hum/hum. *Hound and Horn* is an imitation of England—the illustrated decor of something—the poetry I thought bad and the criticism I imagined to be an echo in tone.[3] A man doesn't begin to stink until he is well past 21 and until then he is only protoplasm. Not that I didn't learn from what I read and even get suggestions. The remark is *a priori* rather than scientific. I am having a moment nearer to peace of mind than I often do. Several little vexations have disappeared and leisure seems to be ahead. My work is done. Tell Redlich that I began *L'Ombre de la Croix* with suspicion and ended by being deeply impressed. I have sent for the book to own it. I may reread Dewey's *Experience and Nature*, 2nd edition.[4] The strain of the birthday has passed and if I live to my 90th year I shall be proud.

Affectionately yours,
O.W.H.

1. The letter referred to is missing.

2. Probably, Peirce's essay, "Pragmatism" (c. 1906), which referred to the Metaphysical Club, "a knot of us young men in Old Cambridge." See Charles Hartshorne and Paul Weiss, eds., *Collected Papers of Charles Sanders Peirce*, vol. 5 (Cambridge: Harvard University Press, 1934), 7: "It may be that some of our old-time confederates would today not care to have such wild-oats-sowings made public, though there was nothing but boiled oats, milk and sugar in the mess. Mr. Justice Holmes, however, will not, I believe, take it ill that we are proud to remember his membership. . . . Nicholas St. John Green was one of the most interested fellows, a skillful lawyer and a learned one, a disciple of Jeremy Bentham."

3. *The Hound and Horn* was published from 1927 to 1934 by Harvard undergraduates, the best known of whom was Lincoln Kirstein (1907–1996), for many years director of the New York City ballet.

4. John Dewey, *Experience and Nature* (New York: Norton, 1929).

Washington, D.C.
April 9, 1929

Dear Frankfurter,

Of course I thank you for the extract from the *Times* but I don't write, being at leisure and therefore having no time.[1] Now I bother you if ever you should have time to expound Lewis Mumford to me. I am reading with much interest his life of Melville but get a queer impression of the biographer.[2] He talks of actualities in a way that makes me suspect he has not had much contact with them and seems to be conventional with a new set of conventions that despise the old. I know he has written for *The New Republic* but I don't remember to have read what he may have done. Is he a hell of a feller or a gentle priest of an art that he does not practice? Or how otherwise?

Yours ever,
O.W.H.

1. The letter referred to is missing.
2. Lewis Mumford, *Herman Melville* (New York: Harcourt, Brace, 1929).

Washington, D.C.
April 23, 1929

Dear Frankfurter,

Circumstances prevent my writing at length but I thank you for the trouble you have taken.[1] What you say about Mumford shows that I had guessed right in some particulars. With all discounts the book is a fine one and I read it with a feeling that I had gained something. I am delighted at what you tell me of Hackett and not surprised. I have the book and read a few pages before going to bed and should think it a great achievement from what I have read.[2] Everything good that happens to Cohen is a joy to me.[3]

Affectionately yours,
O. W. Holmes

1. The letter referred to is missing.
2. Francis Hackett, *Henry the Eighth* (New York: Liveright, 1929).
3. Morris Cohen became president of the American Philosophical Association in 1929.

Washington, D.C.
May 13, 1929

My Dear Felix,

As you know I build upon your friendship and I thank you for the last expression of it. I think that my wife could not have known freedom from pain again and so am reconciled to her death.[1] I shall work a little longer. The fact but it can't be long.

Affectionately yours,
O.W.H.

1. Mrs. Holmes had died on April 30.

Cambridge, Massachusetts
May 22, 1929

My dear Justice Holmes,

Not for many a long day has an opinion so delighted me as yours in the Becher patent case.[1] It was so neat and piercing an analysis instead of the all too frequent heaviness, particularly in procedural and jurisdictional matters. You deeply satisfied my esthetic appetite.

I have been reading two books of friends with the inevitable conflict between judgment and affection, when reading the books of friends. One is Lippmann's *Preface to Morals*.[2] It has his usual clarity though at times he appears to me clearer than truth and he says some fine things. But somehow—though I would not tell *him* so—he seems to find more dragons to fight than I see, seems to take some forces more horrendous than they appear to me and announces ways to inner peace that, one would suppose, hardly needed argument. But then I probably underestimate the importance of reiteration, of "hearing," as it were, testimony—for on these ultimate issues I prefer silence unless one can add new insight or impressive re-statement of old.

Hackett's *Henry VIII* I've read with gusto. He vitalizes these historic personages—they assume contemporaneous vitality. Hackett's performance is a feat of character no less than a highly imaginative achievement. For he worked like a mole in the British Museum for years and I'm very happy that he can now pay off all his debts and enjoy a care-free period for the play of his spirit without the hard necessity of earning his daily bread by miscellaneous writing. He is a truly gifted person.

The School year is almost at an end—all except the chore part of it, the examinations and it always leaves me wistful to have to part with so many lads with whom I've formed a warm tie. Every year there are these lads that work their way into my heart and head.

And your Term is on its last lap. May we have more and more of your Terms!

Always devotedly,
F.F.

1. In *Becher v. Contoure Laboratories*, 279 U.S. 388, 391 (1929), a machinist, who had been hired to invent a machine, promised to keep secret his invention but then filed for a patent. The question before the Court was jurisdictional: Should the case be handled by state or federal courts? Holmes's unanimous opinion concluded: "It is plain that the suit had for its cause of action the breach of a contract and wrongful disregard of confidential relations, both matters independent of patent law." The case thus fell to the state courts to decide.

2. Walter Lippmann, *A Preface to Morals* (New York: Macmillan, 1929).

Cambridge, Massachusetts
May 29, 1929

My dear Justice Holmes,

I had assumed that you exhausted my capacity for being thrilled by magistral utterance on behalf of sanity in your *Abrams* opinion. But you have done it again and anew. It was like real, prewar champagne to read your *Schwimmer* opinion and not because Mrs. Schwimmer matters at all to me.[1] But the invigoration you give to spacious feeling and the confidence you intensify that man's optimism isn't a menace and may be a fillip to life mean, oh! ever so much to us.

It is a glorious piece of writing. We so need the antiseptic play of your humor and wisdom.

Always yours,
F.F.

P.S. The enclosed is from *The New York Times*.[2]

1. *United States v. Schwimmer*, 279 U.S. 644, 654–55 (1929). The Court majority, in a 6–3 opinion written by Justice Butler, held that Rosika Schwimmer's pacifism made her ineligible for citizenship. Holmes, with Brandeis concurring, dissented: "If there is any principle of the Constitution that more imperatively calls for attachment than any other it is the principle of free thought—not free thought for those who agree with us but freedom for the thought we hate." Sanford dissented separately.

2. Probably an editorial in the *New York Times*, May 29, 1929, which concluded: "Judge Holmes and Judge Brandeis may be said to be the defenders of minorities, of not only theoretic but applied freedom."

Washington, D.C.
May 31, 1929

My dear Frankfurter,

You are generous as you always are and the article gives me more pleasure than articles often do. The things that you have praised show that I haven't lost my interest in the work. It seems to be done at a separate chamber of one's being unaffected by any troubles. Perhaps it will keep on for a year or two but I feel as if my first bell had rung. It really doesn't matter whether the thing keeps on a little longer or not. I am content. I hear rumors of you and Chicago which I hope are not true.[1] I should think it the beginning of the end of the school that we are fond of.

Affectionately yours,
O.W.H.

1. In 1929 Frankfurter considered an offer from the University of Chicago Law School. For several years he had been in conflict with Roscoe Pound, Dean of Harvard Law School, and President A. Lawrence Lowell (1856–1943). In 1927 Lowell served on the panel reviewing the Sacco-Vanzetti case, which concluded that the trial had been conducted properly. The following year Lowell defeated Frankfurter's attempt to gain a Law School appointment for criminal law expert Nathan Margold (1899–1947), an action Frankfurter attributed to Lowell's anti-Semitism. Also, Lowell and Pound tried unsuccessfully to block the appointment of James Landis (1899–1964) to a Law School professorship in 1928. See Baker, *Brandeis and Frankfurter*, 232–33, and Lash, ed., *From the Diaries of Frankfurter*, 124–31.

Beverly Farms, Massachusetts
June 25, 1929

Dear F.F.,

Chapter I–VI of Smut's *Holism and Evolution* I have read and the summaries at the beginning of the other chapters.[1] I feel like the man to the waiter with the bill of fare—I say Mister can't I skip from there to there. I have eaten from there to there. I don't see anything in Smuts except giving a new name to the well known. He seems to think he is telling you something when he bids you not regard matters as a self contained football to be kicked by a force. I thought all educated people understood that whether you called it the action or force, or the I know not what, you were dealing with what you could not limit except by the results. He seems to think he has got to the ultimate realities. I don't see how finite human beings can have any opinion whether they have struck bottom or are on some transitory platform. He calls results that you couldn't have predicted, creative e.g., when 2 colorless liquids turn red when fixed or when matter becomes organic. I thought the root of the whole business was that you couldn't predict anything until it had occurred. Whether such results are expressions of the preexisting character of the I know not what or are new creations seems to me idle speculation, etc., etc., etc. I don't see a damned thing in the job. Of course all formed men incline to reject new theories because they require the trouble of a reformation and old men of course are the worst in that way. Perhaps Smuts is the Messiah from the Cape. But I have the feeling that he is laboriously and verbosely repeating the well known. I think that I shall suspend the reading though I hate to begin a book and not finish it.

Yours ever,
O.W.H.

1. See above, November 26, 1926.

Beverly Farms, Massachusetts
July 9, 1929

Dear Frankfurter,

You hit me where I live—Ruskin thins out, Carlyle is not what he used to be but the *Rejected Addresses* still have the dew of morning on them.[1] Probably I have called your attention to their anticipation of Bergson in two lines (or one I might say):

> *Thinking is but an idle waste of thought:*
> And thought is everything and everything is nought.

I am delighted to have a copy here, as I already have one in Washington.

Thanks to my perennial benefactor and homage to his dame.

Affectionately yours,
O. W. Holmes

1. Horace and James Smith, *Rejected Addresses* (London: Constable, 1929). Originally published in 1812.

Beverly Farms, Massachusetts
August 29, 1929

Dear Frankfurter,

By this mail is returned to you Allen's *Political Thought in the Sixteenth Century* which I have finished reading this day.[1] I am more than ever convinced of its value while I find something which I don't quite like yet find it hard to state in the author. I am very much obliged to you for sending it to me although in general I don't like to borrow books as I am worried until I know they are returned. Allen exemplifies throughout Sumner's thesis that the abstract theories of the philosophers simply reflect the mores of the communities in which they have grown up.[2] I do not yet see the *Laws and Liberties of Massachusetts* but leave that for my secretary when he returns.[3] It connects itself a little with the other book. But just now I don't want any more damned improvement. I hope I shall see you again.

Yours ever,
O. W. Holmes

1. John W. Allen, *A History of Political Thought in the Sixteenth Century* (New York: Barnes & Noble, 1928).
2. William Graham Sumner, *Folkways* (Boston: Ginn, 1907).
3. Max Farrand, ed., *The Laws and Liberties of Massachusetts* (Cambridge: Harvard University Press, 1929). Originally published in 1648.

Washington, D.C.
November 5, 1929

My dear Frankfurter,

Whitehead's noble work already had been sent to me "with the compliments of the author" which made me hope that it really was by his order.[1] I should not tell you this, had I not the purely selfish motive of hoping that you would tell him that I have not written to him because I have not had the chance to read it yet. I expect to very soon, as you may imagine I am keen to do. I am greatly obliged to you. In the circumstances I will if you like send you the Whitehead copy which is not written in. Yours has an inscription. I really am fierce to get at it and, as I expect to circulate my only opinion and to finish my *certs* tomorrow, it seems impending. My case is an attempt to distinguish between the north and northeast side of a hair, to the surprise of Brandeis and myself the majority being on our side, for letting the state tax (a dealing?) bearing regrettable analogies with regrettable decisions that pretty similar matters were interstate commerce.[2] By regrettable I mean disagreed to by B. or me or both. Whether the boys will swallow the little sugar coated pellet of which I just read the proof remains to be seen. I fired my first gun yesterday but it was not a gigantic effort (a mixture of metaphors shows that you have escaped from the material husks and are in the realm of pure intellect).[3]

As usual the new secretary [Alger Hiss] is much to my mind—a very pleasant companion, doing his work well and having just enough of modernist aesthetics to add interest to his talk. I think he likes it though it is hard to be sure.

All goes well enough with me. I hope that it does with you in your new palace. I wonder if any Law School in the world has such an impressive abode.[4]

Affectionately yours,
O.W.H.

1. Alfred North Whitehead, *Process and Reality* (New York: Macmillan, 1929).

2. The tax case was probably *Farmers' Loan and Trust v. Minnesota*, 280 U.S. 204, 216, 218 (1930). McReynolds's majority opinion cited the due process clause to overturn the state's tax of bonds and certificates of indebtedness that had been removed to another state. Holmes, with Brandeis concurring, dissented: "It is not disputed that the transfer was taxable in New York, but there is no constitutional objection to the same transaction being taxed by two states. . . . A good deal has to be read into the Fourteenth Amendment to give it any bearing on this case. The Amendment does not condemn everything that we may think undesirable on economic or sociological grounds."

3. *Wheeler v. Greene*, 280 U.S. 49, 52 (1929). Writing for a unanimous Court, Holmes held that the Federal Farm Loan Board had no power to levy an assessment or to appoint a receiver in order to maintain a suit for the enforcement of the stockholders' liability created by the Federal Farm Loan Act: "The receiver had power to collect the assets of the bank, but the liability of the stockholders is no part of those assets. It is a liability to creditors which creditors may be left to enforce."

4. Langdell Hall at Harvard Law School opened in 1929.

Washington, D.C.
November 22, 1929

Dear Frankfurter,

No—Scott was unknown to me and I gather from a glance or two that I shall be deeply interested.[1] I must finish Huneker's *Promenades of an Impressionist* before I begin it.[2] Whitehead I have postponed. I don't dare to write to him but I may say to you that I believe him to be a great and good man who can speak and write clear and forcible English but whether from his having the mathematician's habit or from my unfamiliarity, his terminology puzzles me and I don't understand one sentence in five. I suspect that if I did fully grasp his theory I should find it belonging to a class that I don't believe or believe in but this is merely a surmise. (Somebody in a horse car to Ned Sohier—"Ned, I smell whores, let's get out!")[3] I am truly delighted to have the Scott book and set up as usual by your kind words. By the by, when you get Hopkinson's picture there may perhaps be photographs of it and I want to get some *and pay for them*.[4] I hope that I may be given the chance.

I rather shudder at being held up as the dissenting judge and more or less contrasted with the Court but I am curious to know whether the publication pays for itself.[5] I should not think there'd be 25 purchasers. I have been as near idling for a week as I ever get. A two hour drive daily until today when I stayed in for fear of a cold and to write letters etc. All sorts of bores bother without right. Today I returned a typewritten tale which I was requested to read and criticize, being assured by the writer that I should find it a relief and that it opened a great boon to mankind. On Monday we come in—I have one brief dissent in which I am alone and yet believe I am right.[6] I have one opinion which dissents may hold up. I dunno till tomorrow. About I.C., Van Devanter, Chief Justice and Butler contra—Van Devanter said he would not delay the case but I rather expect tomorrow he will ask me to wait.[7]

You don't tell me as much about yourself as I could wish. I get the impression that you have quietly grown to be a big figure.

Affectionately yours,
O. W. Holmes

1. Geoffrey Scott, *The Architecture of Humanism* (Boston: Houghton, Mifflin, 1914).
2. James Gibbons Huneker, *Promenades of an Impressionist* (New York: Scribner, 1910).
3. Boston attorney, Edward Dexter Sohier (1810–88).
4. Holmes's portrait was painted by the well-known artist Charles Sydney Hopkinson (1869–1962). It hangs in the reading room of Langdell Hall, Harvard Law School.
5. Alfred Lief, ed., *The Dissenting Opinions of Mr. Justice Holmes* (New York: Vanguard, 1929).
6. In *Safe Deposit and Trust Co. v. Virginia*, 280 U.S. 83, 97, 98 (1929), McReynolds's majority opinion found a state law taxing securities held by a trustee domiciled in another state to be in conflict with the Fourteenth Amendment. Holmes dissented: "Taxes generally are imposed upon persons, for the general advantages of living within the jurisdiction, not upon property, although generally measured more or less by reference to the riches of the person taxed, on grounds not of fiction but of fact. . . . The notion that the property must be within the jurisdiction puts the emphasis on the wrong thing. . . . The place of the property is not material except where inability to protect carries with it inability to tax. But that is an exceptional consequence. One State may tax the owner of bonds of another State."
7. *Superior Oil Company v. Mississippi*, 280 U.S. 390 (1930), was argued October 31, 1929, but not decided until February 24, 1930. See below, March 3, 1930.

Cambridge, Massachusetts
December 2, 1929

My dear Justice,

If I may, I should like to join you in your dissent in the Virginia trust taxing case.[1] The majority have now carried the already unhistorical *Union Re-*

frigerator case to lengths that are wholly out of line with history and the rationale of the taxing power.[2] And Stone's concurrence goes off on too tenuous a technical point. So I'm all for your dissent, and rejoice that you wrote it.

Let's form an offensive and defensive alliance of silence about Whitehead's latest volume. For I do feel confident that he is "a great and good man" and I know that his talk is wise and stimulating. But his book is for me more than obscure and, so far as I can gather his drift, I believe he too is driven by the necessity of filling in the gaps of the "unknowable" or at least certainly the as yet unknown. But as a man he is thoroughly civilized and wholly lacking in the coercions and humorlessness of dogmatism.

I've just had a letter from Wu to say that he will be in Cambridge, "on or before February first." He is evidently in fine form and harnessed to actualities in his judicial work.

As soon as Hopkinson will have finished the final touches on your portrait there will be photographs of it, and you shall have all you may care for. These photographs are taken as matter of course and there will be no charge. We expect the portrait about New Year's.

I'm having a grand time thanks to these very able and responsive lads. Marion joins me in affectionate greetings.

F.F

1. See above, November 22, 1929.

2. In *Union Refrigerator Transit Co. v. Kentucky*, 199 U.S. 194, 211 (1905), the majority opinion, written by Justice Henry Billings Brown (1836–1913), held that the due process clause prohibited *ad valorem* domicile taxations of tangible personal property that was located permanently in another state. Holmes, with Chief Justice White concurring, dissented: "The result reached by the Court probably is a desirable one, but I hardly understand how it can be deduced from the Fourteenth Amendment."

Washington, D.C.
December 7, 1929

Dear F.F.,

You give comfort to one who was howling in solitude (as to my dissent in the Virginia tax). I don't know whether you had the opinion when you wrote. I thought the reasoning sound, and unanswered by anything said.

I forget if I have told you what pleasure I got from Scott's book on architecture, which I shall keep unless demanded within a reasonable time. I shall admit the justice of the demand, if made. Also I am returning or purposing to return the Whitehead. I have read about 100 pages and begin to think that by p. 150 I may have established human relations with the author. His whole attitude however seems to attribute more important cosmic significance to human ultimates than I can and therefore I expect to remain an outsider. Of course a man may say I assume *my* last to be *the* last. I see no reason for or possibility of getting beyond the end. But it seems to me that there is good reason for believing that there is more in the universe than we know or understand and probably more than we can understand. So I bow my head and shut up. I had more to say on other themes but I forget what.

My love to you both.

Affectionately yours,
O.W.H.

Cambridge, Massachusetts
January 14, 1930

My dear Justice,

I have now read the full text of your opinion in *Farmers' Loan and Trust v. Minnesota* and I am, as the modern young things say, "tickled pink."[1] I see no escape from your analysis that existence of a debt depends on the law of the state that created it, and hence, *that* state "can demand a *quid pro quo*" i.e. can tax. The majority reaches its result not by reason but by fiat. And from the point of view of the Court's place in the American scheme of things, in the long run, "they know not what they do."

Not since he has been on the Court, has Brandeis spoken so admirably about the guidance of the presiding judge.[2]

Always devotedly yours,
F.F.

1. See above, November 5, 1929.

2. Chief Justice Taft was ill and no longer able to sit on the Court. He resigned on February 3 and died on March 8. As the senior Associate Justice, Holmes presided until Charles Evans Hughes was confirmed as Chief Justice on February 24. Brandeis had written to Frankfurter on January 9: "O.W.H. is indeed 'to the manner born'—he is presiding with great fondness, alertness and joy. A marked rejuvenescence has been effected; and he is definitely without worry in these unaccustomed duties into his new office. It is several years since we have had so good a C.J." See Urofsky and Levy, eds., *Half Brother, Half Son*, 405.

Washington, D.C.
January 17, 1930

Dear Frankfurter,

This is to thank you for your book on *The Labor Injunction*.[1] I have just had time to read the conclusions rather hastily. They seem to me very wisely and ably stated. I felicitate you on what I doubt not is a noble piece of work and I mean to prove it to myself about the part not yet read as soon as I possibly can but I am somewhat pressed while I have to preside. I was much pleased to have you approve what I said about the Minnesota attempt to tax.

Affectionately yours,
O.W.H.

1. Felix Frankfurter and Nathan Greene, *The Labor Injunction* (New York: Macmillan, 1930).

Washington, D.C.
January 28, 1930

My dear Frankfurter,

You always do happy things. The book came just as I was shut up with a cold and is just the thing for solitary evenings (the reading part of them) and other odd moments.[1] Both the cases I had to write (one only 3 inches long) have been sent out today, and bar some *certs* and my income tax return I shall be pretty free when the doctor lets me go out—if decent weather I hope tomorrow or next day.[2]

Hiss wrote to you accepting the nomination of ______ for next year's secretary if I am alive. Of course he must understand that I reserve liberty to die or resign but I hope not to do either until my 90th birthday.[3] Not meaning hereby that then I will step out one way or tother but that is too far to look ahead. At present I don't go beyond the 89th in my anticipations. I am as interested as ever in the work and want to do it as long as I can. And although I hope that I should receive notice to quit with composure, I still like living. I am wonderfully looked after and Hiss is a marvel of attention. But that has amazed and touched me with all the young fellows of recent years. My homage to Luina. You have all my best wishes.

Affectionately yours,
O. W. Holmes

1. See above, January 17, 1930.

2. The cases were probably *United States v. Wurzbach*, 280 U.S. 396, 398–99 (1930), and *Chesapeake and Ohio Railway v. Bryant, Id.* at 404, 405. In *Wurzbach*, Holmes's unanimous opinion upheld the Federal Corrupt Practices Act: "It hardly needs argument to show that Congress may provide that its officers and employees neither shall exercise nor be subjected to pressure for money for political purposes . . . while they retain their office or employment." The "3 inch" opinion in *Chesapeake*, also for a unanimous Court, held that an action for wrongful death did not fall under the Federal Employers' Liability Act because "the deceased was killed on Monday and there was some evidence that he had been discharged on the Saturday before."

3. Robert Willett Wales (1907–83) was Holmes's secretary for the October 1930 Term. Wales served as counsel for the Treasury Department (1946–52) and later became a partner in the New York firm Cleary, Gottlieb, Steen and Hamilton.

Cambridge, Massachusetts
March 3, 1930

My dear Justice,

Long ago I should have given up wondering how you do it, yet again and again you stir new surprise. Here you've had the responsibility of leading your Court for weeks in open sittings and at conferences and yet you can also find time, or rather make it, to assign to yourself three cases and one such a stinger of a case—the *Minerals Separation*.[1] These patent problems terrify me yet you were able to make clear even to my ignorance what that latest row was all about. Wasn't it god-awful stuff to plow through? Your distillation—to change the figure—is clear and limpid. And in *Superior Oil Company v. Mississippi*, the past compelled you to do some fancy skating but most gracefully did you negotiate the thin ice.[2] This is a truly important opinion and will serve, I believe, as a powerful influence in what I hope will be a check on recent tendencies of the Court on matters affecting state taxation.

Few public men have evoked such spontaneous and warm affection from the public as has Taft. . . . He is a dear man—a true human. I assume that the new C.J. [Charles Evans Hughes] pleases you, because you've always liked him despite a certain rigidity that, I suspect, comes from his rigid Christianity, at least in part so. But he knows the business of the Court, was, when he was on it, aware of the true issues that underlie most of your controversies and has a sense of the Court's place in the stream of history.

Wu is here and full of ferment. His mind is teeming with ideas and books to be written and his tongue gives forth wise and quaintly whimsical talk. And he is a very affectionate person.

I'm reading Plato's *Laws* and much of it seems to me—may I say it—

strange and primitive drool. And in the midst of drool there'll be found a succulent bit of insight. Aristotle's *Politics* I find more gripping.

Always devotedly,
F.F.

1. *Minerals Separation North American Corporation v. Magma Copper Company*, 280 U.S. 400 (1930). In a unanimous opinion Holmes analyzed the processes patented by the two companies to conclude that the differences were so minor as to void the later patent.

2. *Superior Oil Company v. Mississippi*, 280 U.S. 390, 395 (1930). The oil company had tried to avoid paying state tax on gasoline by diverting the shipment to Louisiana before delivering to a Mississippi customer. The company claimed that it was involved in interstate commerce. Holmes's majority opinion found the tax valid: "The importance of the commerce clause to the Union of course is very great. But it also is important to prevent that clause being used to deprive the States of their lifeblood by a strained interpretation of facts." Van Devanter and Butler dissented without opinion.

Washington, D.C.
March 5, 1930

My dear Frankfurter,

As usual you get there first. I was waiting to write to you until I had got a little further into your *The Labor Injunction* which while we sit I rarely have time to look into. I have but begun it but it is my first serious book to be read, and from the beginning I believe it to be first class—really A 1. I didn't assign to myself the three cases—the one on Interstate Commerce, where as you say I was on very thin ice, had been held up a good while for a dissent which ultimately was only noted.[1] But with the patent case, which I took because I thought nobody wanted it and thought I might like to write it, came a letter to be written to the Chief Justice on his retirement and I was as nervous and scared as possible—it rather upset me I think for a day—but as usual the lion's skin came off and I found our old friend the donkey under it. You are right in supposing that I gladly welcome my old neighbor on the Bench, Hughes. I think he will make a mighty good Chief.

I get a line from Wu from time to time, the last yesterday in answer to a caution I ventured on to him and which he received admirably and in a way that relieved and pleased me much.[2] I cannot help fearing that he is in too much of a hurry to get at the generalities and to dodge dreary details but it is hard to be sure about one of a different race and of such different experience. He certainly has remarkable gifts and I hope he won't fritter them. This between ourselves—I have written as much as I cared to say. I suppose I shan't see him until I come to Boston if I live to do it.

I haven't heard from my next year's secretary but I infer that he is arranged with. I wish I could know that my portrait had been received and hung. I am awfully pleased with that whole business except that I don't like to think that Hopkinson still is fussing with it.

I have to write hurriedly—in this week's cases which I hope to deliver next Monday your sharp eyes may detect that I have left the crucial point a little vague as to its precise incidence.[3] I have clear opinions but I said all that I thought safe, to avoid controversy. If I had more time I should write more.

Affectionately yours,
O.W.H.

My homage to the lady Luina.

1. See above, March 3, 1930.

2. Holmes had written to Wu on March 3: "I understand well the effort to help one's inner want of self-confidence by some outward show and I sympathize keenly with the trials that you go through. I had many black years, and find myself often thinking that I was saved by successive moments of great good luck. We see how force of will has carried gifts to achievement. I hope and expect that result for you, but it is not to be easily reached. It takes time, the capacity to want something fiercely and want it all the time, and sticking to the rugged course." Shriver, ed., *Uncollected Papers*, 293–99.

3. *Early v. Federal Reserve Bank of Richmond*, 281 U.S. 84, 88 (1930). Writing for a unanimous Court, Holmes upheld the claim of the Richmond branch to retain the balance of funds against the claim of the Receiver of a bankrupt South Carolina bank. He based his decision on a Federal Reserve circular, "authorized by law and agreed to by the other," stipulating the policies to govern transactions between the two banks.

Cambridge, Massachusetts
March 17, 1930

My dear Justice,

At last Hopkinson is to deliver your portrait! These artist fellers are sovereigns of their moods and their actions are the servitors of their moods. All this time he has been trying to hit the right "background." He has not been fussing with the portrait itself. It is due to arrive at the School this week—a noble frame has already been delivered.

For you to call my work "really A 1" is to be knighted by the King! I'd rather have your "well done" than any one else's in this wide world. You give me reward and spur. Making all allowances for your generosity, enough is left for me to attribute it to quality and not merely your kindness. My deep gratitude.

Soon you will have a new Solicitor General and I miss my guess if he does not add to your joy.[1] He is not a Bowers, nor a Lehmann.[2] But he is a clear and forthright advocate and a beautifully transparent character. Thacher and I are old friends—we were young assistant district attorneys under Stimson in New York two decades ago. Time has seasoned and strengthened Thacher but left him the innocence and purity of boyhood.

Am I right in holding Moody in high esteem?[3] Brief as was his tenure, he left notable opinions behind and showed real power. I happen to be going over the work of the Court from 1906 to 1916 and so have encountered Moody.

Always faithfully,
F.F.

1. Thomas Day Thacher (1881–1950), Solicitor General of the United States from 1930 to 1933 and judge of the New York State Court of Appeals, 1943 to 1948.

2. Lloyd Wheaton Bowers (1859–1910) was Solicitor General, 1909–10; Frederick W. Lehmann (1853–1931) held the position, 1910–12.

3. William Henry Moody (1853–1917), Attorney General of the United States, 1904–1906, and Associate Justice of the Supreme Court, 1906–10.

Cambridge, Massachusetts
March 18, 1930

My dear Justice,

The portrait has come and I'm in the grip of its thrilling qualities. It really is superb and I feared that brush and pigment would be inadequate to convey the glow and esprit and promethean vitality that the subject conveys to us who know him. But I verily believe that Hopkinson has caught the divine spark—you infected him! It's a truly superb and glorious symbol.

Always yours,
F.F.

Cambridge, Massachusetts
March 22, 1930

My dear Justice,

The presentation affair went off admirably—you would have found it right in so far as your own composure would have permitted. It was a feast for the heart to see the place jammed with youth.[1] The Ned Holmes will have brought you details. And I assume that you have seen Learned Hand's piece.[2] But you may not have had Bishop Lawrence's impromptu remarks.[3] It was a good day!

Always,
F.F.

1. The Hopkinson portrait was a gift of the Harvard Law School Class of 1930.

2. Learned Hand, "Mr. Justice Holmes," *Harvard Law Review* 43 (1930): 857: "Carlyle says somewhere that he would give more for a single picture of a man whatever it was, than for all the books that might be written of him. We are fortunate in having a painting which justifies that opinion; it will in part at least preserve the fleeting essence for others who have not had direct acquaintance with the racy speech, the light and shade, the simplicity, the reserve, the dignity, that must some day perish and leave so much the losers such of us as remain."

3. William Lawrence (1850–1941), Episcopal bishop of Massachusetts from 1893 to 1926.

Washington, D.C.
March 25, 1930

Dear F.F.,

A thousand thanks for your enclosure as to the portrait which pleases me down to the ground. I this moment finished *The Labor Injunction* and more than ever think it a first class piece of work. I think that perhaps you have a bias on the labor side and may not show quite so clearly the terrors of a mob let loose as the wrongs to the union. But you have brought out what needed to be brought out and I think that the book ought to have great influence.

I am in the middle of a great case (I hate great cases) and 48 *certioraris* have just come in and, with my secretary's great help, I have sent over 200 birthday letters—no small job.[1] Hence this attenuated line.

Affectionately yours,
O.W.H.

1. In *Wisconsin v. Illinois*, 281 U.S. 179, 197 (1930), Holmes unanimously reaffirmed Taft's earlier unanimous opinion, 270 U.S. 634 (1926), upholding the claims of Wisconsin and five other states against Illinois's diversion of Lake Michigan and Great Lakes water to aid Chicago. Both decisions had been based on the report of a Master; the Master in the original case was Charles Evans Hughes. Holmes wrote: "It has already been decided that the defendants are doing a wrong to the complainants and that they must stop it. They must find out a way at their peril. We have only to consider what is possible if the State of Illinois devotes all its powers to dealing with an exigency to the magnitude of which it seems not yet fully awaked. It can base no defences upon difficulties that it has itself created. If its constitution stands in the way of prompt action it must amend it or yield to an authority that is paramount to the State."

Cambridge, Massachusetts
April 28, 1930

My dear Justice,

And now I have read your opinion in the "great case" and I should be false to my judgment if I did not say it is a great opinion. I verily believe that Aristotle would have liked it—his desire for balance is so finely satisfied. Who was it that said that Homer differs from other writers in that he knew what to leave out. I could not help, as I read your opinion, to reflect on what others might have written.

I have been having a good time lecturing to the heathens at Yale.[1] That's merely formal ungraciousness for they have been the opposite of heathens to me—most kind and friendly. *You* are always so eager about my welfare and so encouraging that I'm tempted to enclose a circular about those lectures. Its fun but I have for once been under the real pressure of work. Next week I shall be a free man—only my regular work will remain and that too will soon be over.

I wish the President would give you Learned Hand or Cardozo as a colleague and call it a day![2] And the 1929 term will also enable us to see you here.

Devotedly yours,
F.F.

1. Felix Frankfurter, *The Public and Its Government* (New Haven: Yale University Press, 1930).

2. Justice Sanford had died on March 8, the same day as Taft. Hoover nominated John J. Parker (1885–1958), a North Carolina circuit court judge, to replace Sanford but the Senate refused to confirm, citing Parker's bias in cases involving labor unions and blacks. Owen J. Roberts (1875–1955), a University of Pennsylvania law professor and one of the prosecutors in the Teapot Dome scandal of 1924, was confirmed on May 20.

Washington, D.C.
May 2, 1930

Dear F.F.,

A thousand thanks for your letter which as usual gives encouragement that I wanted. If I have cheered you, you have cheered me a thousand fold. I have time for but a word. A line from Wu says that he is not well. I am anxious and hope that it is nothing serious. I wish that I could have heard your lectures though I used to say I wouldn't go to hear the Apostle Paul or anybody but myself which last I couldn't avow.

Affectionately yours,
O.W.H.

Cambridge, Massachusetts
May 28, 1930

My dear Justice,

You have the property of the great masters in Art and of the greatest artist Nature. The familiar hits one with fresh power and gives new, exhilarating relish. One re-reads a great poem, sees an old favorite Rembrandt, hears a well-known Bach and it's new and wonderful all over again. So, with your dissent in the Baldwin case.[1] I thought I knew your views and even your words. Yet, it comes as a fresh and original experience. Your speech has the accent of brave truth and luminous insight into the society of a Union of States. And it means everything to us younger and less discerning ones that you give us the guidance of your vision and the courage, for days of doubt, of speaking the truth as we see it.

Devotedly yours,
F.F.

1. *Baldwin v. Missouri*, 281 U.S. 586, 595–96 (1930). The majority opinion, written by McReynolds, held that the due process clause invalidated the attempt of Missouri to tax assets being transferred by will, the testatrix and the legatee being domiciled in Illinois. Citing *Farmers' Loan and Trust v. Minnesota*, 280 U.S. 204 (1930), McReynolds observed in conference: "The result here ought to be clear to an unclouded mind." Holmes, with Brandeis and Stone concurring, responded with a vigorous dissent: "I have not adequately expressed the more than anxiety that I feel at the ever increasing scope given to the Fourteenth Amendment in cutting down what I believe to be the constitutional rights of the States. As the decisions now stand, I see hardly any limit but the sky to the invalidating of those rights if they happen to strike a majority of this Court as for any reason undesirable. I cannot believe that the Amendment was intended to give us *carte blanche* to embody our economic or moral beliefs in its prohibitions. . . . Very probably it might be good policy to restrict taxation to a single place, and perhaps the technical conception of domicil may be the best determinant. But it seems to me that if the result is to be reached it should be reached through understanding among the States, by uniform legislation or otherwise, not by evoking a constitutional prohibition from the void of 'due process of law,' when logic, tradition and authority have united to declare the right of the State to lay the now prohibited tax." See above, November 5, 1929, and Urofsky and Levy, eds., *Half Brother, Half Son*, 429–30.

Washington, D.C.
May 29, 1930

My dear Frankfurter,

As usual when I was feeling sad and finished, there came a letter from you putting new heart into me. I shall be up to see you in Boston or at Cambridge after my arrival due Thursday June 5. I must have one more glimpse of the new Law School but I want to do it without notice. Just sneaking in and out again—perhaps seeing you and a casual law student. Don't mention it.

Affectionately yours,
O.W.H.

Beverly Farms, Massachusetts
July 12, 1930

My dear Frankfurter,

When your letter arrived an hour ago I had been thinking of you and hoping for another glimpse of you and Luina. Far be it from me to bore you but if you are still in the neighborhood, which I can't tell from the postmark, and you feel like it, you will be most welcome at luncheon. I am sure to be at home and need notice only to insure the victuals.

Thanks for the case. I think Cardozo has it all his own way.[1] The use made of the provision by the mortgagee is wholly outside of the manifest purpose of such a stipulation. If you ever write to Cardozo, I wish you could tell him that I entreat him if he ever happens to be in this neighborhood, as I think I heard some hint that he might be, to let me see his noble face. Luncheon at 1:00 or I could put him up at a pinch. I don't want to die without seeing him again.

By the blessing of the Lord, we have finished Trotzky and the *certs* were returned a week or more ago.[2] Now I am returning to *Process and Reality* which I have begun over again and now think I understand so far.[3] I feel healthy after reading in it which I didn't when listening to the autobiography of Trotzky. I meant to write more but my secretary is taking me to walk.

Always yours,
O.W.H.

1. Cardozo's minority opinion in *Graf v. Hope Building Corporation*, 171 N.E. 884, 896 (1930), objected to allowing a foreclosure in equity of a loan, over 90 percent paid off, which had a lapsed payment due to clerical oversight: "There is no undeviating principle that equity shall enforce the covenants of a mortgage, unmoved by an appeal *ad misericordiam*, however urgent or affecting. The development of the jurisdiction of the chancery is lined with historic monuments that point another course."

2. Leon Trotsky, *My Life: An Attempt at an Autobiography* (New York: Scribner, 1930).

3. Alfred North Whitehead, *Process and Reality* (New York: Macmillan, 1929).

Cambridge, Massachusetts
July 30, 1930

My dear Justice,

"F.P." probably has written you of a recent House of Lords decision following your line on landowners' liability for injury to infant trespassers, leading to F.P.'s footnote reference, in the official reports ([1929] A.C. 358, 380), to your opinion in the *Britt* case, 258 U.S. 268.[1] But I wonder if someone has also told you that the highest Court of South Africa, having before it a provision in the South Africa Act similar to the limitation in our Constitution against diminution of judicial salaries, refused to follow the decision in *Evans v. Gore* and instead based its ruling on your dissent.[2] You will recognize almost your words: "The prohibition is directed against the diminution of the salaries of judges as such, and cannot be construed to protect from the incidence of a tax of general applicability." *Evans v. Gore* always did seem to me—in the forum of reason—close to the end of the limit.

I assume that you are deep in *certioraris*—I hope not too deep. Someday next week, I should like to intrude upon them if I may. This time I'll come alone—any day, either noon or evening that you can conveniently have me. But *please* consult wholly your convenience.

Always devotedly,
F.F.

1. *Robert Addie v. Dumbreck* [1929] A.C. 358 at 380. Frederick Pollock and Holmes had recently discussed Holmes's opinion in *United Zinc and Chemical Company v. Britt*, 258 U.S. 268 (1921). See Howe, ed., *Holmes-Pollock Letters*, 2:239–42. Also, see above, March 28, 1922.

2. *Evans v. Gore*, 253 U.S. 245 (1920). See above, February 5, 1921.

Beverly Farms, Massachusetts
September 19, 1930

My dear F.F.,

Thank you for the notice which I was glad to see. It comes *apropos* since I hope to have Hale here at luncheon on the Sabbath.

Something that Dr. Cohn said to Hill led me to see my doctor about my back—*per quod* x-ray yesterday and today the conclusion that there is nothing to be done but grin and bear it.[1] It is as little a burden as one could expect and I am glad to compromise on it.

I am on my last batch of *certs* and have done in all close to 200 and am within a day's work of the end here. My love to you both.

Affectionately,
O.W.H.

I am greatly obligated to you for your kindness to Mary.[2]

1. Alfred Einstein Cohn (1879–1957), physician and medical researcher, was Frankfurter's close friend and author of *Medicine, Science and Art* (Chicago: University of Chicago Press, 1931) and *No Retreat from Reason* (New York: Harcourt, Brace, 1948).

2. Annie Mary Donellen Coakley (1899–1985) managed Holmes's household from the mid-1920s until his death in 1935. *Washington Post*, June 3 and 19, 1985.

Washington, D.C.
October 7, 1930

My dear F.F.,

Your letter as always makes life worth living—a matter on which I am capable of doubt for myself.[1] I thank you for it and for the flowers that cheered my room at the Touraine (For the last, perhaps Luina?). There is still a lot of stuff to be handled but I have only a few *certs* and I have hanker for many books most of which must wait for better days.

What do you know about Llewellyn, Professor at Columbia?[2] I haven't read his pamphlets but he seems pretty categorical and seems to think Pound the end of the limit. Has he things to say? I am glad to believe that your fame now grows constantly.

Affectionately yours,
O.W.H.

1. The letter referred to is missing.

2. Karl N. Llewellyn (1893–1962), Professor of Law at Yale, Columbia, and Chicago and advocate of judicial realism, which held that decisions were shaped by the personal biases of the judge, rather than socioeconomic influences as Roscoe Pound would have it. Llewellyn had just published his best-known book, *The Bramble Bush* (New York: n.p., 1930), a collection of his lectures to first-year students at Columbia.

Washington, D.C.
October 17, 1930

Dear Frankfurter,

Thank you so much for just what I wanted about Llewellyn.[1] Frank's book my secretary has been reading to me for some days.[2] It has ideas but too many words, I think, and seems to show some confusion about the emotional reaction of judges as if it were all to be set against the rules. Whereas the greater part of such reactions are in aid of them. I should make a number of criticisms of detail especially the above, but the lad is thinking hard and has done solid work. We have nearly reached the chapter on codification. Frank's prejudice against the rules seems to forget how great a body of conduct is determined by them and how many cases they keep out of Court. This is but a hurried note but I may add, with regard to the use of words, when we speak of *law* we think of something aimed at future conduct and therefore mean the rules not the act, the judgment that verifies them.

Yours,
O.W.H.

If you know Frank don't show him this criticism, which is not a judgment, and does not do justice to the work that he has done.

1. The letter referred to is missing.

2. Jerome N. Frank, *Law and the Modern Mind* (New York: Brentano's, 1930), a significant statement of the philosophy of judicial realism. As a judge on the United States Circuit Court of Appeals for the Second Circuit from 1941 to 1957, Frank (1899–1957) often cited his own work.

Washington, D.C.
November 8, 1930

My dear Frankfurter,

My secretary has just finished reading aloud to me your Yale lectures—*The Public and Its Government*. I think them admirable and wish that every young man in the country might read them. Again and again they sting me with pleasure, not to speak of the almost awe I feel for your familiarity with so much as to which I feel myself ignorant. By some mistake I missed the inscription until today though of course I assumed the book came from you. Thank you again and felicitations incidentally on the good taste of the printing. To Luina also on being the dedicatee of such a book.

Affectionately yours,
O. W. Holmes

Washington, D.C.
December 23, 1930

My dear Frankfurter and Luina,

Thank you for the ∞ time. You have sent me just what I want for my secretary to read to me.[1] Especially handy at this moment when (*entre nous*—I don't want it to get into the papers) I am housed with lumbago—getting better but keeping me in for a day or two. It could be quite delightful if some of the judges didn't write opinions and send them around. But these have been alleviated by a book or two and another promised that feed my baser nature. You know the poem:

There was a young lady of Joppa
Who came in society cropper
She went to Ostend with a military friend
The rest of the story is not proper

Let us draw a veil. A Merry Christmas and happy New Year to you both.

Affectionately yours,
O. W. Holmes

1. The letter referred to is missing.

Washington, D.C.
January 27, 1931

My dear Frankfurter,

Your letters bring my misgivings to a point on which please regard what I say as strictly between ourselves or ourselves and Rose if that is necessary.[1] Of course I accept your nomination without question, but each year adds a little to the burden on the Camel's back. And even assuming, as I hardly can, that I shall be in as good condition next year as this, I grow more uncertain whether I ought to hold on. The brethren are all kind and give no hint that they would like to drop me and some I am pretty sure would like me to stay but my uneasiness increases and the fear that I am not pulling my weight. Can I leave the matter open until a little later? It would be more natural for Rose to want a definite answer now. In that case I could only say that if I keep on I should be glad to have him, but could not promise, even subject to the uncertainties of life, and he must use his own judgment. In any event I must reserve my liberty to die or resign.

Of your generous sending I am reading in *The Stuffed Owl* with great delight.[2] The Burroughs and Santayana are waiting.[3] I have had a cold that has kept me in for a day or two because I must take every precaution to live six weeks. Also there has been a lot of work to do. So I am a little below par but cheerful. My love to you both.

Affectionately yours,
O.W.H.

1. The letters referred to are missing. Horace Chapman Rose (1907–90), Holmes's secretary, 1931–32, was for many years associated with the firm Jones, Day, Reavis & Pogue of Washington, D.C. During the Eisenhower Administration, he served as Undersecretary of the Treasury.

2. D. B. Wyndham Lewis, *The Stuffed Owl: An Anthology of Bad Verse* (London: J. M. Dent, 1930).

3. Probably Edgar Rice Burroughs, *Tarzan the Invincible* (New York: Grossett, 1931), and George Santayana, *The Realm of Matter* (New York: Scribner, 1930).

Cambridge, Massachusetts
February 6, 1931

My dear Justice,

Rose—next year's lad—fully understands, and he is unabated in his eagerness to come next Fall. Why should he not be? I wish I could nominate myself for Wales's succession. Of course, the ninety-first year will be the ninety-first year! But I, who watch your opinions, with affection to be sure, but also, I'm confident, with scientific scrutiny, find the power and fire of old wholly unimpaired. And only the other night I happened to see John W. Davis, and he volunteered his clear judgment to the same effect.[1] "There has never been anything like it," was his parting word.

I'm so glad that you find amusement in *The Stuffed Owl*. I had hoped that it would be new to you and attain a place on your shelves.

My friend Dr. Cohn phoned me from New York of his exhilarating visit—he had to tell me about it, it could not be left to mere paper. I envy him, I told him, his joy and hope myself to drink from the fresh springs which fed him, before very long.

I speak as a zealous student of your Court's work when I say that I could not, at pistol's point, find warrant in the remotest degree, for any concern of yours as to your share of the Court's work. The quality and quantity of the output disprove such concern *in toto*. So—write on! Luina sends her love.

Always,
F.F.

1. John W. Davis (1873–1955) was Solicitor General from 1913 to 1918, United States Ambassador to England from 1918 to 1921, and Democratic nominee for President in 1924. He also represented the Topeka Board of Education in *Brown v. Board of Education*, 347 U.S. 483 (1954), the landmark school desegregation case.

Washington, D.C.
February 7, 1931

Dear Frankfurter,

Santayana is returned herewith on the notion that you may want it though I kept the anthology of bad verse because *I* wanted it. If you desire, I will replace it.

Santayana comes nearer to hitting me than most philosophers but I dislike him. He patronizes, as being rich with the past experience of a Catholic although no longer believing in the Church. He has the openness to all thought that is anti-dogmatic and yet he sneers like a dogmatist. I take back or qualify the "dislike" above. He is a good sauce to have on hand, but not a food. He writes like a gentleman but I doubt if he quite is one. Good reading anyhow.

I infer that you got my answer about the secretary, Rose. I would like a jaw with you this hour. The Sabbath seems sadly imminent. But I will cheer up.

Affectionately,
O.W.H.

Washington, D.C.
March 1, 1931

Dear Frankfurter,

Before your letter came I had heard that my nephew was coming on and invited him and his wife and my cousin Mary Clark and her husband to luncheon at 1:30. Also my secretary [Robert W. Wales]. Laski as you probably know will be with me Saturday and Sunday night. I inevitably shall be very tired in the evening and therefore suggest that you join the luncheon party, 1:30 Sunday March 8, which will be my dinner. I intend to follow this with a letter to Palfrey asking him to the same luncheon which will close the table unless some very exceptional man turns up to make 10.

Yours,
O.W.H.

Cambridge, Massachusetts
May 16, 1931

My dear Justice,

And now I have read the full text of your opinion in the New York–New Jersey Delaware River controversy.[1] It's as fine an opinion as you have written in interstate litigation and yours are indubitably the best writings also in that field. What I truly marvel at is the speed and compactness with which you assimilated the vast body of details that the Delaware River case involved. It really is, if I may say so, an A 1 opinion.

And your Term is on the home stretch. Soon you'll be in these parts, and I hope that Luina and I may come to see you at your convenience. We want to do so, with eagerness. Have you been reading anything of excitement? And what is your verdict on Cohen's *Nature and Reason*?[2]

Laski has been here to our delight.

Always devotedly,
F.F.

1. *New Jersey v. New York*, 283 U.S. 336, 342 (1931). Holmes's unanimous decision upheld New Jersey's suit enjoining New York from diverting water from the Delaware River to increase the supply to New York City. Drawing from the master's report, Holmes urged compromise between the parties: "A river is more than an amenity, it is a treasure. It offers a necessity of life that must be rationed among those who have power over it. . . . Both states have real and substantial interests in the river that must be reconciled."

2. Morris Cohen, *Reason and Nature* (New York: Harcourt, Brace, 1931). Holmes expressed his opinion in a letter to Laski: "I heartily agree with his repudiation of the irrationalists etc., but. . . . I have no faith that reason is the last word of the universe." See Howe, ed., *Holmes-Laski Letters*, 1314–15.

Laguna Beach, California
August 4, 1931

My dear Justice,

The two enclosures may not be without interest—a recent note from Leslie Scott and a report of scientific vindication of one of your father's insights.[1]

It has been pleasant along these Pacific shores—the elements have been benign and we have been feeling unduly favored of the Gods as we read of Eastern heat. But the year round, I should find this pleasantly sunny climate unendurable—it is meant, I believe, for people who are temperamentally "external" not "internal." I should miss the dolorous fall, the stingingly tonic winter and the thrill of the burst of spring. But it serves my present purposes well—in my cool, quiet study I work away on the mass of materials the Harvard group has been turning up in our crime survey. It's my job to piece the whole together into a synthetic report.[2]

I have heard from Laski regarding your Life.[3] That you should put such confidence in me arouses feelings not for words and yet I do not wish to remain wholly silent. I have of course many lacks for the task but none that devotion, complete sympathy, absorbed preoccupation with the main interests and labors of your life, and whole-souled dedication to the enterprise can give. And I do believe that I shall bring considerable understanding to your significance not only for Law, but for the civilization of which law is only one, very important expression. I shall say no more except that I'm bowed with zest and humility.

I hope the heat has been merciful to you and that the damned *certs* have not been an avalanche. Luina joins me in affectionate greeting.

Always devotedly,
F.F.

1. The enclosures are missing. Sir Leslie Frederic Scott (1859–1950) was a Conservative M.P. from 1910 to 1929. In 1922 he also served as Solicitor General.

2. See above, December 8, 1926.

3. See Howe, ed., *Holmes-Laski Letters*, 1320–21.

Cambridge, Massachusetts
September 13, 1931

My dear Justice,

Always your responses exquisitely fit the occasion. "He has done it again," I said to my wife, as I finished the reading of your American Bar Association letter.[1] Indeed, you seem to me to have expressed some of your old *apercus* with fresh pithiness.

I hope that you really are indulging yourself and, *pro tem*, have banished Duty.

Always devotedly,
F.F.

P.S. Please do not bother to acknowledge this. I write because I have an urgent feeling to do so.

1. Holmes was awarded the American Bar Association Medal which he acknowledged in a letter published in the *American Bar Association Journal* 17 (1931): 715–17: "The law tries to embody things that men most believe and want. But beliefs and wants begin as vague yearnings and only gradually work themselves into words. Those words at first cannot fully express what they aim at. Some of us have tried to make clearer what the aims are or should be, using

history, economics and philosophy as our aids. If we have helped to throw light upon the general scope of the subject, or of some part of it, we have so far helped our fellows along a predestined road and have been of use."

Cambridge, Massachusetts
October 22, 1931

My dear Justice,

Sometime ago I sent my friend Nevinson a copy of the *Mr. Justice Holmes* volume.[1] Today I have a letter from him in which he says: "How very good of you to send me the book on the really Grand Old Man! I do wish I could come over to see him again! The water is wide, I cannot get o'er, and neither have I wings to fly! That is the beginning of one of our ancient English songs and I often sing it with regret. I have never met anyone who so delighted me and filled me with such reverent admiration as your great judge. If you are writing to him, please tell him so and ask him to remember me. How kindly and courteous he always was in receiving me, an unknown stranger and one entirely ignorant of everything in his own line of knowledge." I have always accounted Nevinson a dear fellow and his autobiography, particularly the second volume thereof, *More Changes and More Chances*, one of the gayest, most spirited of books.[2]

I see that your Court has had several of those beastly I.C.C. cases.[3] They are like the mumps—something to get through with. The Term, I hope, is happily underway. And I trust you have settled the great issue: ready-made vs. tailor-made pants![4] Luina joins me in affectionate greetings.

Always,
F.F.

1. Felix Frankfurter, ed., *Mr. Justice Holmes* (New York: Macmillan, 1931).

2. H. W. Nevinson, *More Changes, More Chances* (New York: Harcourt, Brace, 1925). Nevinson (1856–1941) was a renowned war correspondent and military historian.

3. *Western Pacific California Railroad Co. v. Southern Pacific Co.*, 284 U.S. 47 (1931); *Chicago, Rock Island & Pacific Railroad Co. v. United States, Id.* at 80; *Louisiana Public Service Commission v. Texas & New Orleans Railroad Co., Id.* at 125; *United States v. Baltimore & Ohio Railroad Co., Id.* at 195. Holmes wrote none of these opinions; he joined Stone's dissent in the *Rock Island* and *Baltimore & Ohio* cases.

4. Holmes was growing increasingly infirm and had to be fitted for new clothes in October.

Washington, D.C.
October 23, 1931

Dear F.F.,

Your letter brings the usual joy. I am surprised and delighted by what you quote from Nevinson. He is one chap who goes straight to one's heart. Two days ago was Ball's Bluff day when I was knocked out 70 years ago—humanly speaking, a long time. The trousers issue—tailor or ready-made—is postponed to the adjournment. I can get on till them without being embare-assed. (Do you get me?)

I have felt stupid and muddle-headed at the oral arguments. They always bother me, but the dear Brandeis helps me to understand what the question is when I know that I am capable of an opinion. I think too I am gradually recovering from the exhausted feeling with which I arrived here. So things seem cheerful. Rose rivals his predecessors in attentions that I have no right to demand. We have read a good deal. Craven's *Men of Art* gave me much pleasure even if a trifle conscious.[1] We stopped Lawrence, *Lady Chatterley's Lover*, in transition, a thing I have rarely done—this time, I think, at Rose's suggestion.[2] Not enough lubricity to relieve it from being dull. I am surprised that reviewers found him worth talking about.

One word more and then a rest. I hope that when I next sit I shall feel all right. Such pretty days that I fain would skip to the Soldiers Home or Virginia. I wish we could dine together. My love to Luina.

Affectionately yours,
O.W.H.

1. Thomas Craven, *Men of Art* (New York: Simon & Schuster, 1931).
2. D. H. Lawrence, *Lady Chatterley's Lover* (New York: W. Faro, 1930).

Cambridge, Massachusetts
December 3, 1931

My dear Justice,

I have now read in cold blood the two opinions in the Wisconsin tax case and more than ever I appreciate your occasional phrase in past cases: "But for the views of my Brethren I should have supposed the matter was clear."[1] I am bound to say that Roberts's opinion does not become more convincing on a re-reading, while your dissent is one of the closest-knitted bits you've done. And I glory over the beauty of "They form a system with echoes of different moments" etc. I ask myself, and cannot answer, why should Hughes go off in this case as he did?

Stimson writes me what a delightful visit he had with you, in viewing historic scenes.

Have you seen a little book on *Mrs. Bell* by Mrs. Drown?[2] And did your conscience really take you to the end of that dullard Goodhart?[3] Goethe had his like in mind when he wrote, "*Grau ist alle Theorie*," except that Goodhart wasn't *Theorie*, but jejune pedantry. Luina bids me send her affectionate greetings.

Always devotedly,
F.F.

1. *Hoeper v. Tax Commission of Wisconsin*, 284 U.S. 206, 219 (1931). Justice Roberts's majority opinion, with which Chief Justice Hughes concurred without opinion, overturned a provision of the state's income tax that authorized assessment against a husband of a tax computed on the combined total of his and his wife's incomes and augmented by surtaxes resulting from the combination. Noting that the law allowed married persons to file separate returns and to divide the tax proportionately, Holmes, with Brandeis and Stone concurring, dissented: "This case cannot be disposed of as an attempt to take one person's property to pay another person's debts. The statutes are the outcome of a thousand years of history. They must be viewed against the background of the earlier rules that the husband and wife are one and that one the husband; and that as the husband took the wife's chattels he was liable for her debts."

2. P. C. S. Drown, *Mrs. Bell* (Boston: Houghton Mifflin, 1931).

3. Arthur Lehman Goodhart, *Essays in Jurisprudence and the Common Law* (Cambridge: University Press, 1931). Goodhart (1891–1978), an American-born scholar spent his professional life at Cambridge and Oxford. A good friend of Pollock, he edited the *Law Quarterly Review* from 1926 to 1975.

Washington D.C.
December 7, 1931

My dear Felix,

The usual message of good cheer comes from you—I won't say to save me from despair but at least as I was thinking more than ever that I am finished. Why not? As Emerson said at a good deal earlier age, "It is time to be old." And then this day also comes a line from Brandeis. He never fails to offer a strong hand. I am fortunate in my friend. My love to Luina.

Affectionately yours,
O. W. Holmes

Washington, D.C.
December 26, 1931

My dear Frankfurter,

You rightly surmised that I should be much moved and impressed by Mr. Thompson's address.[1] It reaffirms all that I felt when he came to see me in the Sacco & Vanzetti affair. His must be a beautiful and powerful nature. I wish I knew him better. It is strange how words embodying postulates that one does not accept can lift up the heart as one feels the end draw near. The numerous thanks I owe you, including thanks for yesterday, I don't intend to express now. But I want to tell you at once that what you sent comes as a *sursum corda*.[2]

Affectionately yours,
O. W. Holmes

1. William G. Thompson (1864–1938), Boston lawyer and defense counsel for Sacco and Vanzetti in the later stages of the case. Holmes met Thompson in 1927. The address was likely *Commonwealth of Massachusetts v. Nicola Sacco and Bartolomeo Vanzetti: Defendant's Brief* (Boston: Ellis, 1927).

2. Lift to the heart.

Cambridge, Massachusetts
January 12, 1932

My dear Justice,

It would be less than the truth for me to deny that your retirement from the active work of the Court removes one of the linchpins of my world.[1] But I would be even less deserving of your friendship than I am if I failed to bow to the inevitable with grace and gratitude. I shall say no more for surely heart speaks to heart—except to add that your leave-taking, like all else I've ever known of you, was in the grand manner.

Luina joins me in devoted love.

F.F.

1. Holmes resigned from the Supreme Court of the United States on January 12. On February 15 President Hoover nominated Benjamin Cardozo as Holmes's successor; the Senate confirmed the nomination on February 24.

Washington, D.C.
February 24, 1932

My dear Frankfurter,

Your letter as usual brought joy. Also it sent me to the Library to inquire for Schneider.[1] I have brought home 2 volumes not promising to read them but intending to try them. I have various others on hand. The Sherlock Holmes not quite though nearly finished.[2] *Mainsprings of Men* by Whiting Williams, recommended in *World Chaos* (lent me by Gerrit Miller, suggestive rather than the last word).[3] Walter Lippmann's new book etc.[4] Idleness as usual is pretty busy. I think I am feeling rather stronger than when I came down here. It doesn't matter except as affecting one's spirits. Like you I rejoice in Cardozo. I think they all will love him. I don't know why I find writing comes hard but with this apology I shut up. My love to Luina.

Affectionately yours,
O.W.H.

1. Hermann Schneider, *History of World Civilization* (New York: Harcourt, Brace, 1931).
2. Arthur Conan Doyle, *The Complete Sherlock Holmes*, 2 vols. (New York: Doubleday, 1930).
3. Whiting Williams, *Mainsprings of Men* (New York: C. Scribner's Sons); William McDougall, *World Chaos* (New York: Covici, Friede, 1931).
4. Walter Lippmann, *Interpretations, 1931–32* (New York: Macmillan, 1932).

Cambridge, Massachusetts
March 21, 1932

My dear Justice:

Sometime ago, the Yale University Press, as will appear from the enclosure, asked me to bring together in a volume, some of the papers which were published on the occasion of Brandeis's seventy-fifth. Now that the volume is going through the press, it occurs to me that the carnal in Brandeis would care for nothing so much as a few words from you. That, would, I know, be the ultimate word on his work. And so I venture to put it to you, emphasizing however as strongly as I can, that you must not regard this as a chore to be done, a new duty to be assumed, but only something to be written if and as the spirit moves you during the next week or so.[1] A page or less will do. But—and this is the most important part of my remarks—please do not regard this as something that ought to be done, but only as an expression of your views of Brandeis and his labors that you might find some pleasure in making. Of course, Brandeis knows nothing of this—he does not even know of the projected volume. If you happen to be at all interested in the nature of the papers to be included, your lad, Rose, will know them.

Winter has been with us an unconscionable length of time but at last the sparkling Spring is in the air. This season of the year, one attends many so-called banquets—the annual dinners of the law clubs. These experiences give me an ever new joy of life with these youngsters. They seem to me to be so much more mature and freer in spirit than my crowd was, when we left the School. Each year Luina and I think there never again will be such fine lads but nature is versatile and generous. Luina and I send our affection.

F.F.

1. Holmes wrote the introduction to Felix Frankfurter, ed., *Mr. Justice Brandeis* (New Haven: Yale University Press, 1932), ix: "In the moments of discouragement that we all pass through, he always had the happy word that lifts up one's heart. It comes from knowledge, experience, courage, and the high way in which he has always taken life."

Washington, D.C.
March 25, 1932

My dear Frankfurter,

You do not expect from me a critical analysis of Brandeis and I assume that a few words of general appreciation are enough. These I enclose—they are meager but I trust superlatives. If not satisfactory send them back and I will try again but I hardly can write at length.

I am beginning to wonder what I shall do when my secretary's year is up if I am still alive and kicking. It is not a place for a young lawyer who wants to rise. Mrs. Codman once said that she might be able to get one, but I mention it to you before doing anything—but I doubt if you can help.[1]

Affectionately yours,
O.W.H.

1. Anna Kneeland Crafts Codman (1869–1962) was a summer neighbor and close friend of Holmes. She served as President of the Alliance Francaise and received France's Legion of Honor after World War I. Frankfurter arranged for a succession of clerks to continue assisting Holmes: Donald Hiss (1907–89), brother of Alger Hiss, who later became well known for his expertise in tariff and international trade laws, served in 1932–33. He was followed by Mark DeWolfe Howe (1906–67) and Holmes's last secretary, James Henry Rowe, Jr. (1909–85).

Washington, D.C.
March 30, 1932

My dear Frankfurter,

Your letter leads me into temptation. I feel as if I ought not to let a young lawyer waste his time in being my intelligent valet. For a good deal of the work comes to that plus letters, accounts, etc., a good deal of reading aloud and taking a drive with me. But I won't discuss that, and I very much wish to have a young man if I live and remain in fair condition. What would be the salary? I suppose my investments have shrunk a good deal but unless I am mistaken I shall be able to afford the pay and I should not want to hold him down or [ ] expectations. I should like to keep this open until later because I necessarily am a little uncertain how it will be with me six months and more ahead.

Affectionately yours,
O. W. Holmes

Cambridge, Massachusetts
May 23, 1932

My Justice,

There never was doubt about the deep pleasure that appreciation from you would bring to Brandeis, and in his own shy way he has revealed it. But Mrs. Brandeis comes right out with it. I quote from a note I have from her about the book: "Justice Holmes' little word—so beautiful and moving—is the crowning point of it all." I am so glad that you wrote it.

Spring has burst upon us with resplendent glory—she will be all ready for you. The snap in the air will be gone—wholly gone—and I hope that Washington's heat will restrain itself until after your departure.

Another School year is at an end—they seem to be flying faster. A certain seriousness is in the air these days, but I am confident that the effect of these trying times upon our youth is tonical, all to the good. In the boom and flush days there was something hollow and tawdry about it all, a feeling of manna perpetually falling into mouths of the darlings of the Gods. Life seems tougher and less meretricious—something fit for hardy natures is now confronting this generation. And their talk and their aspirations, both, seem more masculine, there seems more fire in their belly. This is not a projection of my own pious wishes. I've seen these boys very intimately and I have that new sense about them very clearly. Luina and I send you affectionate greetings.

Always devotedly,
F.F.

Washington, D.C.
May 25,1932

Dear F.F.,

Your letter delights me by saying that Brandeis and Mrs. B. were pleased by my few inadequate words and also by what you say about the young men and how they take the hard times.

I expect to reach Beverly Farms June 9 and hope that after allowing a day or two to get into shape you and Luina will come over to luncheon.

Affectionately yours,
O.W.H.

Beverly Farms, Massachusetts
July 12, 1932

My dear Felix,

Some misgiving I had lest your silence had made it impossible for you to decline but I understand that that is the Governor's affair and that you had spoken fully and freely to him.[1] I hope it won't be a [ ] and will come out to your satisfaction. When the [tangle?] is over you and Luina will come to luncheon I hope. My love to you both.

Affectionately yours,
O. W. Holmes

1. Frankfurter had declined Governor Joseph Ely's (1881–1956) nomination to the Massachusetts Supreme Judicial Court. See Parrish, *Frankfurter and His Times*, 210.

Cambridge, Massachusetts
July 13, 1932

My dear Justice,

You have been so kind and generous through this judge business that I do not trust myself to give even intimations of the depth of my gratitude. Long before this episode you had put winds in my sail strong and well-directed enough for a lifetime. But now I know more profoundly than ever how exquisite is your tenderness and how powerful the inspiration for me to draw upon.

Devotedly and gratefully,
Felix Frankfurter

Washington, D.C.
November 12, 1932

My dear Felix,

This is really a blank paper on which you can write what you like. I am empty except for murder cases. The serious in literature is apt to bore me. On returning Dreiser's *American Tragedy* to G. Miller, unread, I wrote Truth be damned—give me Oppenheim.[1] Hiss has just finished reading to me *The Fountain* (by Morgan), an able writer but the metaphysics of screwing your neighbor's wife don't interest me.[2] I repeat, I am an empty bottle and suppose I need washing out. I hope I may see you before long. Homage to Luina.

Affectionately yours,
O.W.H.

I am glad to believe from Brandeis that you are not likely to accept the Massachusetts judgeship.

O.W.H.

1. Theodore Dreiser, *American Tragedy* (New York: Boni and Liveright, 1925). Edward P. Oppenheim (1866–1946) was a mystery writer. See *Shudders and Thrills, the Second Oppenheim Omnibus* (Boston: Little, Brown, 1932).

2. Charles Morgan, *The Fountain* (New York: Knopf, 1932).

Washington, D.C.
November 26, 1932

My dear Frankfurter,

You are now a highlight and I have dropped into the final obscurity. I haven't written because I find it so hard to write—physically at least. I hope I shall see you before you go to Oxford.[1] When? I am inclined to agree with Brandeis against Attorney General/Solicitor Generalship and I surmise that is settled.[2] For me I see no achievement ahead but leisure and some amusements though I begin to see Oppenheim as finite and the end of joy in Murders—not quite yet however. When there is a chance of seeing you let me know. My love to Luina.

Affectionately yours,
O. W. Holmes[3]

1. Frankfurter was George Eastman Visiting Professor at Oxford for the 1933–34 academic year.

2. Frankfurter declined the position of Solicitor General offered by Franklin Roosevelt.

3. This was the last letter from Holmes to Frankfurter.

Oxford, England
October 30, 1933

My dear Justice,

We have dug in, as it were—the transplantation seems to be effective but it all feels very unreal when we begin to be self-conscious about it. We're having a truly good time, people are kindness itself without fuss and feathers and apparently with much casualness. The English are very imaginative in their hospitality and we find it all, thus far, exciting. And so we sniff at the new sounds and sights and smells for there is the smell of centuries about the place. Time here tells—the soothing beauty of the quads, the sturdy, enduring Norman well, the very Hall that Wolsey built, to get down to more modern days, how the feeling and authority of age, the conquests of time, imperceptibly get into one's blood, and under one's skin.[1] But all this is very old stuff to you—you who know Oxford well and saw these sights and sniffed this very air before I was born. But each new visitor to America is, for himself, a Columbus and so it is for us at Oxford. Not that we have not seen it before. But this time we are a part of it—we are outside-insiders.

And I trounce along in my cap and gown to lectures as tho' I had always done, and eat my dinners "in Hall" and drink my series of tonics and spirits as tho' I had not lived for a decade under a Prohibition regime. Essentially this is a man's world but Luina is having an exhilarating time, all on her own. O yes, I do some work, lecture and have a seminar; but essentially my function seems to be to live. From this happy midst we send you our love.

Felix

1. Thomas Wolsey (c. 1473–1530), English cardinal and statesman, served as senior bursar of Magdalen College until 1500 when, according to legend, he had to resign his post for spending college revenues without proper authority for the completion of the great tower.

Oxford, England
November 23, 1933

Our dearest Justice,

This is Thanksgiving Day and my voltage of patriotism is therefore higher, and my thoughts of America more lively. And so they inevitably turn towards you as the most distinguished possession of my country, the finest symbol I can claim as friend.

We're having a grand time for we've been resolved to be what we are and not imitative Englishmen. And they seem to like it. There is no doubt that Luina is what they call "a great success." My lectures seem to go well and I show talent for the common room rituals when the Madeiras and the port is passed! Which reminds me that your friend Leslie Scott has been most kind to me. He had me for one of the grand nights of the Inner Temple where all the bigwigs of Bench and Bar—and also the Archbishop of Canterbury—did justice to nine courses of delicious wines![1]

The other day I heard that you were the Senior Bencher of Lincoln's Inn. What a glory and for an American at that.

I trust you have been reading much "improving" and unimproving literature.

Our affection to you,
Felix F.

1. The Archbishop of Canterbury was Cosmo Gordon Lang (1864–1945).

Cambridge, England
February 27, 1934

My dear Justice,

Here I am, in the old study of Maitland and the most natural impulse is to write to you. It would be so even if I had not just finished two short series of lectures in Cambridge on our Supreme Court. And for me the core of the Supreme Court's wisdom and philosophy—its effective share in our political scheme of things—is really the distillation of your opinions, indeed of your juristic outlook for more than sixty years.

And so I send you this affectionate word of greeting, from Cambridge, England where you are as much cherished as you are in Cambridge, Massachusetts.

Always with affectionate devotion,
Felix F.

Oxford, England
May 7, 1934

My dear Justice,

For a brief space I should like to be the boss of the universe. I would transplant you for a short stay to Palestine.[1] Luina and I were, enchanted. Nobody had told us, or at least made us feel that the land has compelling beauty—beauty of contour and color, marvelous atmospheric lucidity, endless varieties of majestic and lovely views. I'm a pedestrian, unimaginative lawyer, and nothing of the mystic is in me. But there is something poignant and magical about Palestine, in its very air, that makes one feel that the utterances of the prophets, the songs of the ancient poets were indigenous, they could not have come from any other soil, they are *there* now. And the achievements of the scientific modern man—the reclamation of what was desolate and infertile and squalid—make a combination of the glories of the past and the triumphs and hopes of the present quite unique, I believe, certainly in our time. And how you would revel in those endless fields of red, luscious anemones. A don here tells me that the fields of Marathon also bloom with these anemones—like glorious, passionate poppies—but Palestine has them in greater and richer abundance. Well, it was a great experience and Aaron Aaronsohn recurred to memory all the time for the place is full of great lads like him. It's hard to talk about what we saw and felt for it really sounds so incredible. But it was a most inspiring and glorious adventure for us.

Now we're back here for the home-stretch as it were. And I'm at my duties again—mostly dining out in the various Colleges and "jawing"—the Englishman's informal method of education. One's patriotism becomes more alert here and I think I have not been lacking in that talent for port which makes Englishmen respect in an American! Seriously, though, our days are very full and very happy for the people here and in London and in Cambridge have been most kind and friendly to us.

I've been seeing Lewis Einstein recently and of course we have talked much and lovingly of you.[2] And whenever I see Maurice Amos he holds forth on you with eloquence.[3]

Which reminds me that I should have written you long ago that I have two or three lads from among whom to select the fortunate one who is to come to you next year. I haven't yet made up my mind who is the best of three good ones. My wife asks me to give you her love.

Always devotedly,
F.F.

1. Frankfurter's visit to Palestine deepened his pride in being Jewish, and increased his determination to work for a modification of British policy. See Parrish, *Frankfurter and His Times*, 242.

2. Lewis Einstein (1877–1949), diplomat and scholar, corresponded frequently with Holmes. See Peabody, ed., *Holmes-Einstein Letters*.

3. Sir Maurice Sheldon Amos (1872–1940) served in the judiciary in Egypt and later as Professor of Comparative Law, University College, London. His principal work was *The English Constitution* (London: Longmans, Green, 1930).

Cambridge, Massachusetts
October 8, 1934

Our dearest Justice,

Greetings to you from Luina and me. We assume that you are having some lovely autumn days in Washington. Even Cambridge has tang in the air, that exhilarating feel and ebullience that we missed in the sticky Oxford climate.

I was of course delighted to have you speak so warmly of your last year's lad, young Howe. He is, I know, all you think of him. But God or nature is kind and keeps on producing a great variety of admirable lads. And so, I'm sure, you will find your new one. He will I'm sure! [ ] Something very good can come out of Montana—culture even, for young Rowe has read not a little and reflected. And he is looking forward to your year with you ever so much.

We saw dainty Sarah Palfrey married.[1] She was an exquisite looking bride and had that look of charming unspoiled girlishness that is so charming in Sarah, with all her world-wide fame. Incidentally, my wife greatly admired your wedding present to Sarah—an unusually well-shapen pitcher.

The Law School is well under way and your interest and encouragement all these years leads me to tell you that my courses are better attended than ever. Our fondest love to you.

Always,
F.F.

1. Sarah Hammond Palfrey was the daughter of John Gorham Palfrey.

Cambridge, Massachusetts
December 12, 1934

Our dear Justice,

Under separate cover, care of Dempsey alias Rowe, I'm sending you the latest book by Francis Hackett, *Francis I*. I know you don't care for biography, but Hackett's *Francis* is different.[1] Anyhow, you are under no obligation to him or to me to read it, if after savoring it you find it not to your taste.

I have been most derelict in not telling you how deeply touched I was by your new recondite interests and learning. Since when have you taken to reading Kansas papers and how did you discover the capricious fact of my birthday? Be that as it may, your telegram delighted both of us. Is there better news ever than "to talk about nothing in particular." No wonder that lover thanked God for it.

I've been deep in the dreary details of *certiorari*—that game of legal checkers which you so fortunately and cosmically have put behind you. But I keep on, watching the performances of "the lads," and reporting thereon for those who will not read. And, really, "the lads" are doing well if I may say so, humbly speaking as a student of the natural history of the Supreme Court. But what a tantalizing person you are. How feeble and futile you make us all feel, every time one touches a subject on which you wrote, whether up here or later in Washington. I've had such new experience recently—worrying about some problems only to find that you had said all there was to be said forty years ago. Verily, we have been living on and off you jurisprudentially for half a century.

It's stinking cold up here and Luina envies you the milder climate. She and I join in affectionate devotion to you.

F.F.

1. Francis Hackett, *Francis I* (London: Heineman, 1934)

Day Telegram to O. W. Holmes, Jr., from St. Timons Island, Christmas 1934

Our dear Justice:

Three people who adore you would like to say that they revere you if you weren't so snooty about such things. We're here in the sunshine off the coast of Georgia and have definitely determined to kidnap you and take you to California with us. Confidentially, there ain't no Santa Claus but life is good.

Elizabeth Ellis, Luina and Felix

Reply from Washington, D.C., December 25th, to Felix, Luina Frankfurter and Elizabeth Ellis.

Why should I spend money sending wires to Boston. Of course there is a Santa Claus. Don't be sentimental. Merry Xmas.

O. W. Holmes

FREQUENTLY CITED WORKS

Baker, Leonard. *Brandeis and Frankfurter: A Dual Biography.* New York: Harper & Row, 1984.

Baker, Liva. *Felix Frankfurter: A Biography.* New York: Coward-McCann, 1969.

———. *The Justice from Beacon Hill: The Life and Times of Oliver Wendell Holmes.* New York: Harper, 1991.

Bickel, Alexander, M., and Benno C. Schmidt, Jr. *History of the Supreme Court of the United States: The Judiciary and Responsible Government, 1910–1921* (New York: Macmillan, 1984).

Gordon, Robert W., ed. *The Legacy of Oliver Wendell Holmes, Jr.* Stanford: Stanford University Press, 1992.

Hirsch, H. N. *The Enigma of Felix Frankfurter.* New York: Basic Books, 1981.

Holmes, Oliver Wendell. *Collected Legal Papers.* New York: Harcourt, Brace and Howe, 1920.

———. *The Common Law.* Boston: Little, Brown, 1881.

———. *The Occasional Speeches of Justice Oliver Wendell Holmes; Compiled by Mark DeWolfe Howe.* Cambridge: Harvard University Press, 1962.

Horwitz, Morton J. *The Transformation of American Law, 1870–1960: The Crisis of Legal Orthodoxy.* New York: Oxford, 1992.

Howe, Mark DeWolfe, ed. *Holmes-Laski Letters: The Correspondence of Mr. Justice Holmes and Harold J. Laski, 1916–1935*, 2 vols. Cambridge: Harvard University Press, 1953.

———. *Holmes-Pollock Letters: The Correspondence of Mr. Justice Holmes and Sir Frederick Pollock, 1874–1932*, 2 vols. Cambridge: Harvard University Press, 1941.

———. *Justice Oliver Wendell Holmes: The Proving Years, 1870–1882.* Cambridge: Harvard University Press, 1963.

Kramnick, Isaac, and Barry Sheerman. *Harold Laski: A Life on the Left.* New York: Penguin, 1993.

Lash, Joseph P. *From the Diaries of Felix Frankfurter.* New York: Norton, 1975.

Lerner, Max, ed. *The Mind and Faith of Justice Holmes: His Speeches, Essays, Letters and Judicial Opinions.* Boston: Little Brown, 1943.

Novick, Sheldon M. *Honorable Justice: The Life of Oliver Wendell Holmes.* Boston: Little Brown, 1989.

Parrish, Michael E. *Felix Frankfurter and His Times: The Reform Years.* New York: Free Press, 1982.

Peabody, James Bishop, ed. *The Holmes-Einstein Letters: Correspondence of Mr. Justice Holmes and Lewis Einstein, 1903–1935*. New York: St. Martin's Press, 1964.
Phillips, Harlan B. *Felix Frankfurter Reminisces.* New York: Reynal, 1960.
Polenberg, Richard. *Fighting Faiths: The Abrams Case, The Supreme Court and Free Speech.* New York: Viking, 1987.
Shriver, Harry C., ed. *Justice Oliver Wendell Holmes: His Book Notices and Uncollected Letters and Papers.* New York: Central Book, 1936.
Urofsky, Melvin I. *Felix Frankfurter: Judicial Restraint and Individual Liberties.* Boston: Twayne, 1991.
Urofsky, Melvin I., and David W. Levy, eds. *"Half Brother, Half Son": The Letters of Louis D. Brandeis to Felix Frankfurter.* Norman: University of Oklahoma Press, 1991.
White, G. Edward. *Justice Oliver Wendell Holmes: Law and the Inner Self.* New York: Oxford, 1992.
———. *Intervention and Detachment: Essays in Legal History and Jurisprudence*. New York: Oxford, 1994.

SUBJECT INDEX

Aaronsohn, Alexander, 34, 35 n.6, 48, 50, 276; *With the Turks in Palestine* (1916), 35 n.6
Acheson, Dean, xxiv & n.39
Adams, Henry, *Democracy: An American Novel* (1925), 187, 188 n.1
Adams, John, 120
Adamson Act, 56 n.3, 69, 71 nn.3 & 5, 91 n.2
Adler, Edward A., 44, 45 n.2
Aeschylus, *Prometheus Bound*, 119, 173
Alice in Wonderland, 127
Allen, John W., *A History of Political Thought in the Sixteenth Century* (1928), 242
American Bar Association, 15, 16 n.2, 44 n.1, 50 n.2, 127; medal given to Holmes, 264 & n.1
American Civil Liberties Union, xviii
American Political Science Review, 68
Ames, James Barr, 29 & n.2, 141, 142 n.4, 186
Amos, Sir Maurice, 276, 277 n.3
Antin, Mary: *From Plotzk to Boston* (1899), 12 n.4; *Promised Land* (1912), 9 & n.1, 10, 11 n.1, 12nn. 3 & 4
anti-semitism, xii, xiii, xix. *See also* Harvard University
Aristotle, 254; *Metaphysics*, 120; *Politics*, 250
Astor, Lady, 107, 108 n.5
Aubrey, John, *Brief Lives, Chiefly of Contemporaries, 1669–1696* (1898), 165, 167
Austen, Jane, *Pride and Prejudice* (1813), 157

Baker, Leonard, *Brandeis and Frankfurter: A Dual Biography* (1984), xl
Baker, Liva, xi, xiii, xxxix, xli
Balzac, Honoré de, 206
Barbour, Tom, 56, & n.1, 114
Barbour, Willard T., *The History of Contract in Early English Equity* (1914), 29 & n.2, 38
Barbusse, Henri, *Le Feu* (1917), 104, 105 n.2
Bartlett, Sidney, 218, 219 n.5
Beale, Joseph Henry, 115, 116 n.3
Beard, Charles, 80 n.2; *An Economic Interpretation of the Constitution* (1913), 53, 232
Beard, Charles and Mary, *The Rise of American Civilization* (1927), 213
Beck, James Montgomery, 131 & n.4, 164, 165 n.3
Becker, Carl L., 191; *The Declaration of Independence* (1922), 192
Bell, Gertrude Lowthian, *The Letters of Gertrude Bell* (1927), 221 & n.2, 222
Benét, Stephen Vincent, *John Brown's Body* (1928), 233
Benjamin, Robert M., xxiv, 132 & n.1, 146, 147, 154
Bentham, Jeremy, 135
Bernstein, Irving, "The Conservative Mr. Justice Holmes" (1950), xxxv & n.88
Beveridge, Albert J., 121, 122, 147 n.2; work on *Abraham Lincoln*, 187, 188 n.2, 189, 191, 204; *Life of John Marshall* (1916–19), 34 & n.2, 121, 187
Beverly Farms, xx
Bickel, Alexander M., xxx, xxxvi, xxxvii & n.95; *The Unpublished Opinions of Mr. Justice Brandeis* (1957), xl

Biddle, Francis B., 3, 4 n.4; *Mr. Justice Holmes* (1942), xxxiii
Bigelow, Henry J., 115, 116 n.1
Black, Hugo, xxvi
Blum, John M., xl
Boston Evening Transcript, 82 & n.3, 108, 179 & n.1, 228, 229
Bowen, Catherine Drinker, *Yankee from Olympus* (1944), xxxii & n.78, xxxiv n.85, xli, 177 n.1
Bowers, Lloyd Wheaton, 252 & n.2
Brand, Charles H., 127 n.1
Brandeis, Elizabeth, 151 n.4
Brandeis, Louis, 13, 16 n.7, 115, 183; biography, xv, xxxvi, xxxvii, xl; due process, comments on, xxv, 108, 110; nomination to Supreme Court, 40 n.3, 50; relationship with Felix Frankfurter, xiv, xxiv n.41, 153; treatment in press, 217, 228, 230, 240 n.2
RELATIONSHIP WITH HOLMES: assistance to Holmes, 266, 267; friendship with Holmes, 95, 116, 140, 168, 193, 234, 236, 266, 267; Holmes's opinion of, 194, 269, 270 n.2, 272; Holmes's opinion of Brandeis's decisions, 64, 101, 103, 148, 149, 150, 153, 164, 169, 171, 177, 243; influence on Holmes's work, 68, 99, 133, 137, 162, 184, 198, 218, 223; opinion of Holmes, 247 & n.2, 271
SUPREME COURT DECISIONS: *Abrams v. United States*, xviii, 75, 77; *Buck v. Bell*, xx; *Pennsylvania Coal Co. v. Mahon*, xxiii, xxiv; votes, 59 n.3, 70 n.1, 72 n.1, 84 n.1, 87 n.1, 91 n.3, 95, 100 nn.2 & 3, 101 n.2, 105 n.3, 106 n.2, 133 n.1, 134 n.1, 138, 148 nn.1 & 2, 151 n.4, 162 n.2, 165 n.7, 168 n.2, 197 nn.2 & 3, 209 n.3, 212 n.1, 219 n.3, 223 n.3, 226 n.1, 227 n.1, 228 n.1, 229 n.2, 244 n.2, 255 n.1, 267 n.1
Bridgewater Treatises on the Power, Wisdom and Goodness of God as Manifested in the Creation (1833–36), 29, 30 n.4
Brown, Dorothy Kirchwey, 34, 35 n.5
Brown, Henry Billings, 246 n.2
Brown, LaRue, 34, 35 n.5
Brown, P. C. S., *Mrs. Bell* (1931), 267
Browning, Elizabeth Barrett, *Aurora Leigh* (1857), 67, 68
Bryce, James, *Modern Democracies* (1921), xx & n.27, 113
Buckland, William Warwick, *A Textbook of Roman Law from Augustus to Justinian* (1921), 162, 163 n.5
Bundy, Harvey H., 55 & n.3
Bunn, Charles, 62 & n.2, 63, 64
Burdon, Richard. *See* Haldane, Lord
Burroughs, Edgar Rice, *Tarzan the Invincible* (1931), 261
Butler, Pierce, 163 n.3, 206 n.4, 207, 209 n.3, 212 n.1, 218, 228 n.1, 229 n.2, 235 n.2, 240 n.1, 245, 250 n.2

Campbell, Ivar, 48 & n.2
Cardozo, Benjamin, xix n.25, 76 n.2, 111–13, 182; appointment to Supreme Court, 268, 269; Frankfurter's opinion of, xix, 108, 254; Holmes's opinion of, 109, 110, 256 & n.1; "Law and Literature" (1925), 185, 186 & n.1, 187; observations on Supreme Court, 222 & n.1; opinion of Holmes, 51 & n.1, 155, 180, 181 n.1, 185, 186 n.1, 228, 229 & n.1, 234, 235 n.3; *The Paradoxes of Legal Science* (1928), 230
Carlyle, Thomas, 35, 242; *The French Revolution* (1848), 158, 161
Cazamian, Louis. *See under* Emile Legouis
Century, 189
Cervantes, *Don Quixote*, 189, 190
Chadbourn, Erika S., xxxviii n.102, xxxix n.107
Chafee, Zechariah, 77 n.3; "A Contemporary State Trial—The United States versus Jacob Abrams" (1920), 86, 88 n.6
Chandler, Peleg Whitman, 68, 69 n.9
Charteris, Evan Edward, *John Sargent* (1927), 215
Chayes, Abram L., xxx
Child Labor Acts, 72 & n.1, 142 n.2
Choate, Rufus, 68, 69 n.9

Christie, Loring, 7 & n.2, 9, 15, 29, 42, 129
Cicero, 125
citizens, rights of, 99, 100 n.3, 128 n.2
Clark, Austin H., 192 & n.1
Clark, Mary, 262
Clarke, John H., 75 n.1, 86; Supreme Court decisions, 59 n.3, 70 nn.1 & 2, 72 n.1, 75 n.1, 84 n.1, 87 n.1, 91 n.1, 95 n.4, 96, 97 n.2, 99 n.2, 101 n.2, 106 n.2, 110 n.1, 132 n.2, 133 nn.1 & 2, 134, 135 & nn.3 & 4, 137, 138 n.2, 141 n.5, 142 n.2, 143 n.2
Clarke, Stanley, 7 & n.2
Clayton Antitrust Act, xxii, xxiii, 100, 101 n.2, 103, 132 n.2
Coakley, Annie Mary Donellen, 258 & n.2
Coar, John Firman, *The Old and New Germany* (1924), 167
Codman, Anna Kneeland Crafts, 270 & n.1
Cohen, Benjamin V., xxx
Cohen, Morris Raphael, 8 n.1, 238 & n.3; friendship with Frankfurter, 76, 102, 199; "History and Value" (1914), 24, 25 n.3, 27, 28; Holmes's opinion of, 24, 26, 27, 28, 30, 238; honored by students, 218 & n.2; *Law and the Social Order* (1933), 30 n.2; opinion of Holmes, 103, 104 n.2; "Property and Sovereignty" (1927), 222 & n.4; readings recommended by Cohen to Holmes, 30, 96, 222, 223; *Reason and Nature* (1931), 263 & n.2; visit with Holmes, 178
Cohn, Alfred Einstein, 257, 258 n.1, 261
Coke, Sir Edward, 18 & n.2
Cole, G. D. H., *Social Theory* (1920), 94 & n.3
Coleman, William L., xxx
Columbia Law Review, 108
common law, 70 n.1, 103, 171 n.2, 226 n.1
Conrad, Joseph, *The Rescue*, 121
contract law, 33 & n.2, 38, 143 n.3, 151 n.4
Coolidge, Calvin, 174
Corcoran, Thomas Gardner, xvii, xxx, 198, 205, 207, 208, 211, 215, 221, 223
Cornell Law Quarterly, 222
Cosmopolitan, 74
Cosmos Club, 164
Coulanges, Numa Denis Fustel de, *Les Origenes du systeme feodal* (1890), 27, 28 n.2
Cowan, Arthur W. A., xxxvi
Craven, Thomas, *Men of Art* (1931), 266
Criminal Appeals Act, 178 n.2
criminal law, 61 n.1, 116 nn. 2 & 3, 162 n.1, 185 n.1, 228, 229 n.2
Croce, Benedetto, *Aesthetic as Science of Expression and General Linguistics* (1909) 51, 52 n.3, 120
Croly, Herbert, 120, 123, 130; "The Paradox of Lincoln" (1919), 83, 84 n.3; *Progressive Democracy* (1914), 23, 25
Currie, David P., xxx
Curtis, Charles Pelham, 68 & n.5, 177, 178 n.4
Curtis, Ellen Amory, 43 & n.5
Curtis, Laurence, 105 & n.1, 110, 111, 154; "Judicial Review of Commission" (1921), 122
Cythereia: or, New Poems upon Love and Intrigue, 139

Dante, 158, 173
Darwin, Charles, 117, 118
Davies, W. H., *Collected Poems* (1916), 64 & n.1
Davis, James J., *The Iron Puddler* (1922), 165
Davis, John W., xxiv n.38, 261, 262 n.1
Day, William R., 25 n.2, 26 n.3, 33 n.2, 59 n.3, 69, 71 n.4, 80 n.3, 84 n.1, 91 n.2, 99 n.2, 111, 133 n.2, 134, 138 & n.3, 143 n.2; response to Holmes's opinions, 229
Declareuil, Joseph, *Histoire Generale du droit francais* (1925), 204
"deliberate speed," 32, 33 n.1
Del Vecchio, Giorgio, *The Formal Bases of Law* (1919), 28 & n.3
Demogue, Réné, *Les Notions fondamentales du droit prive* (1911), 222, 223
Denby, Charles, Jr., 178, 179 n.4, 195

Denison, Winfred, 9, 10 n.2, 11, 12, 16
Desborough, Lady, 35, 36 n.2
Devens, Charles, 90, 91 n.2, 177
Dewey, John, *Experience and Nature* (1929), 237
Dicey, Albert Venn, 156 & n.3; *Law and Public Opinion* (1905), 186
Disraeli, Isaac, *Curiosities of Literature* (1791), 226
Doughty, Charles Montagu, *Travels in Arabia Desert* (1925), 187, 190
Douglas, Norman, *The South Wind* (1928), 235
Douglas, William O., xxvi
Doyle, Arthur Conan, *The Complete Sherlock Holmes* (1930), 269
Dreiser, Theodore, *An American Tragedy* (1925), 273
due process, xxi, xxiii; Brandeis's view of, xxv, 108, 110; Cardozo's view of, 108; Hand's view of, 108, 122; Holmes's view of, 108; McKenna's view of, 111; relating to property, 219 n.3, 224 n.3, 227 n.1, 246 n.2; relating to state powers, 59 n.2, 133, 183 n.2, 199 n.2, 212 & n.1, 244 n.2, 255 n.1. *See also* Fourteenth Amendment
Duguit, Leon: *Law in the Modern State* (1919), 83; *Les Transformations du Droit Public* (1913), 13, 13 n.3
Dumur, Louis, *Dieu protege le Tsar* (1928), 235
Dworkin, Ronald, xxxix

Earle, George H., *Does Price Fixing Destroy Liberty?* (1920), 95 & n.2
Eastman, Max, 130, 131 n.1
Edelman, Peter, xxx
Edgerton, Henry W., "Relation of Mental States to Negligence" (1926), 201, 202 n.1
Ehrlich, Eugen, 107, 108 & n.2, 110; *Die juristische Logik* (1918), 77 & n.2, 79; *Grundlegung der Soziologie des Rechts* (1913), 31 & n.2, 32, 33
Eighteenth Amendment, 81, 94 & n.4, 97 n.1, 143 n.2, 193 n.2
Einstein, Albert, 114, 115 n.5, 117, 118 & n.2
Einstein, Lewis David, xxxvii n.94, 122, 276, 277 n.2; *Tudor Ideals*, 121, 123 n.4
Eliot, Charles W., 36, 75 n.4
Ellis, Elizabeth, 15, 16 n.5, 278, 279
Ely, Joseph, 272 n.1
Emerson, Ralph Waldo, 267
Espionage Act, 106 n.2
Evarts, William Maxwell, 218, 219 n.5

Fall, Albert B., 143 n.3
Faquet, Emile, 190
Farrand, Max, *The Laws and Liberties of Massachusetts* (1929), 243
Federal Corrupt Practices Act, 249 n.2
Federal Employers' Liability Act, 61 n.2, 64 n.2, 162 n.1, 235 n.2, 249 n.2
Federal Farm Loan Act, 244 n.3
federal government, powers of, 23 n.3, 162 n.1, 179 n.3
federalism, 23, 66 n.3, 72 n.1, 90 n.3, 91 n.3, 95 n.4, 142 n.2, 226 n.1
Ferrero, Guglielmo, *The Greatness and Decline of Rome* (1907–1909), 164
Fifth Amendment, xxiii, 213 n.1
Figgis, John Neville, 82; *Churches in the Modern State* (1913), 54 & n.3
Fish, Frederick P., 130, 131 n.1
Fliegende Blatter, 79, 80 n.5
Ford, Franklin, 13 & n.2, 21
Forrest, Nathan Bedford, 230
Fourteenth Amendment, xvii, xxiii, 77 n.1; compensation, 128 n.2, 209; free speech, 99, 100 n.3, 153 n.1; incorporation of Bill of Rights, 185 n.1; property, 100 n.4, 146 n.2, 245 n.6; state powers, 100 n.4, 146 nn.2 & 3, 147, 198, 245 n.6
Fourth Amendment, 80 n.4, 171 n.4, 229 n.2. *See also* due process
Frank, Jerome, xxvii, 258, 259 & n.2
Frankfurter, Emma, 223, 224 n.4
Frankfurter, Felix:
  ACADEMIC CAREER: Cambridge University, 275; Cornell Law School, 186, 191; Harvard Law School, xii, xiv–xvi, xviii, xxviii, 10, 11, 12 n.5, 14, 17, 20, 34, 42, 65, 77, 78 & n.1, 85, 89, 90 n.4, 163 & n.2, 167,

277; Oxford University, xxviii, 273, 274; University of Chicago Law School, 241 & n.1; views of academics and legal education, 14, 15, 44 n.1; Yale University, 254, 259

ARTICLES: "The Business of the Supreme Court of the United States: A Study in the Federal Judicial System" (with James M. Landis, 1925), 188, 189 n.1; "The Business of the Supreme Court of the United States: A Study in the Federal Judicial System; Pt. IV Federal Courts of Specialized Jurisdiction" (1926), 200 & n.2; "The Compact Clause of the Constitution—A Study of Interstate Adjustments" (with James M. Landis, 1925), 183 & n.1; "The Constitutional Opinions of Justice Holmes" (1916), xvii, 51 & n.1; "Distribution of Judicial Power between United States and State Courts" (1923), 232 & n.1; "Economic Elements" (with Harold Laski), 75 n.4; "The 'Law' and Labor" (1921), 102 & n.2; "The Law and the Law Schools" (1915), 43, 44 n.1; "Mr. Justice Brandeis and the Constitution" (1932), xxxvii n.93; "Mr. Justice Holmes" (1926), 200; "Municipal Liability for Tort" (1917), 65, 66; "Petty Federal Offenses and the Constitutional Guaranty of Trial by Jury" (with Thomas G. Corcoran, 1926), 201, 202 n.2; "Power of Congress over Procedure in Criminal Contempts in 'Inferior' Federal Courts—A Study in Separation of Powers" (with James M. Landis, 1924), 175; "Twenty Years of Mr. Justice Holmes' Constitutional Opinions" (1923), xxiv n.41, 123, 154 & n.1; "Wilson and Roosevelt" (1916), 59 & n.1; "The Zeitgeist and the Judiciary" (1912–13), 19, 20 & n.1

BIOGRAPHY, BACKGROUND, AND PERSONAL QUALITIES: education, xii; Jewish religion, xi; personality, xi, xiv, xxxi; political nature, xxv, & n.46; travel in Europe, 94 n.2; travel in Palestine, xxviii, 276, 277 n.1; World War I, 68, 73 & n.1

BOOKS: *The Business of the Supreme Court* (with James M. Landis, 1928), 159, 160 n.2, 219 & n.1, 222 & n.1; *The Case of Sacco and Vanzetti: A Critical Analysis for Lawyers and Laymen* (1927), 211 & n.1, 216; *Criminal Justice in Cleveland* (with Roscoe Pound, 1922), 140, 141, 146; *The Labor Injunction* (with Nathan Green, 1930), 248, 250, 253; *Mr. Justice Brandeis* (1932), 269, 270; *Mr. Justice Holmes* (1931), 265; *Mr. Justice Holmes and the Supreme Court* (1938), xxx, xxxi, 142 n.1; *The Public and Its Government* (1930), 254, 259; *A Selection of Cases under the Interstate Commerce Act* (1915), 26, 36, 37 n.1

CAREER IN PUBLIC LAW: advisor to Franklin Roosevelt, xxviii; career goals, 11, 14, 15, 21; Hornblower, Byrne, Miller, and Potter, xii; litigation, 151 n.4; Massachusetts Supreme Judicial Court, xxviii, 272 & n.1, 273; U.S. Solicitor General, xxviii, 273, 274 n.2; U.S. Supreme Court, xxxi; War Department, xii, xv, 11, 17 & n.1; Wilson Administration, 71 n.1, 74 n.2, 130

FRIENDSHIPS: with Brandeis, 130, 144, 197; explanations for friendship with Holmes, xiii, xiv n.8; with Holmes, xi, 21, 71, 130, 141, 200, 218, 220, 234, 273; opinion of Holmes, xxvi; reassuring Holmes, 179, 193, 199, 213, 214, 229, 231, 249, 251, 252, 254, 257, 261, 265, 266; tendency to impose views on Holmes, xvii

FUNDAMENTAL BELIEFS: personal philosophy, 124, 130; political philosophy, 47, 48, 129

JUDICIAL PHILOSOPHY: judicial restraint, xviii, 20 n.1, 20, 21, 63, 86,

Frankfurter, Felix: (*continued*)
209; tendency to read own views into decisions, 103
LEGAL IDEAS AND WORK: administrative law, 42, 106, 141, 142 n.1, 197; civil liberties, xviii, xxvi n.48; labor, xv, xxiii, 25, 71, 86, 151 n.4, 253; social reform, 14, 21; tort, 66, 67 n.2
UNPUBLISHED WORK: Harvard Survey on Crime and Law in Boston, 210 & n.5, 264. *See also* Holmes, Oliver Wendell, Jr., official biographers
Frankfurter, Leopold, 46, 47 n.1
Frankfurter, Marion Denman, xvi, xxix, xxxvii, xlii, 76 nn.1 & 2, 123, 130, 160, 274, 275, 277
Frankfurter, Solomon, 108, 109 n.2
Franklin, Benjamin, 226, 227 n.2
Frazer, James G., *Pausanias and Other Greek Sketches* (1900), 135, 136 n.7
freedom of speech, 99, 100 n.3, 136 n.4. See also [Index to Court Cases], *Abrams v. United States*
Freeman, 123
Freund, Paul, xiv, xv, xxiii n.38, xxiv nn. 39 & 40, xxxiii, xxxvi, xxxviii, xl n.109
Friendly, Henry J., xxiv n.39
Froude, James Anthony, 158, 159 n.6
Fuller, Lon, xxxv & n.87
Fuller, Margaret, 35
Fuller, Melville Weston, 72 n.2, 180

Garrison, Lindley M., 11, 12 n.6
Gates, Sylvester, 197 & n.3, 199
General Strike (U.K.), 201, 202 n.3, 203
Gennap, Arnold Van, *La Formation des legendes* (1910), 121 & n.4
Gibbon, Edward, 27
Gilmore, Grant, xxxviii, xxxix
Gilmore, Helen, xl
Girard, Paul Frederic, *Manuel Elementaire du Droit Romain* (1896), 162
Gloucester Harbor, 192
Goethe, Johann Wolfgang von, 64, 267; *Faust*, 96, 168
Goodhart, Arthur Lehman, *Essays in Jurisprudence and the Common Law* (1931), 267 & n.3
Goodwin, Richard N., xxx

Graham, Philip L., xxx
Gray, John Chipman, xii, xiii, 63
Gray, Nina, xxxii
Green, Leon, *Rationale of Proximate Cause* (1927), 218
Green, Nicholas St. John, 237 & n.2
Grenfell, Ethel. *See* Desborough, Lady
Griswold, Erwin, xxxvii & n.95
Gross, Milton, *Nize Baby* (1926), 204

Hackett, Francis, 51 & n.5, 79, 80 n.2, 140, 158, 159 n.3; *Francis I* (1934), 278; *Henry the Eighth* (1929), 238, 239; *Story of the Irish Nation* (1922), 140
Haldane, Lord, 15, 16 n.2, 117, 118 & n.2, 121
Hale, Richard Walden, 176
Hale, Sheldon, 40, 45, 69, 70
Hale, William Bayard, *The Story of a Style* (1921), 120, 121 n.3
Hall, G. Stanley, 82, 84 n.1
Hamilton, William Hale, 170 & n.3
Hand, Learned, 61 & n.1, 76 n.1, 88, 108, 127, 164, 182, 200, 254; "Mr. Justice Holmes" (1930), 253; promotion to Court of Appeals, 180 & n.3
Harcourt, Brace and Howe, 107
Harcourt, Sir William, 158, 159 n.5
Hard, William, "The Eyes of the Law on Labor" (1920), 89, 90 n.2, 91
Harding, Warren G., 94 n.4
Harlan, John Marshall, 26 n.2
Harrington, James, *The Commonwealth of Oceana* (1656), 58, 59 n.1, 91 & n.4
George L. Harrison, 41 & n.2
Hart, Henry M., xxiv n.39, xxxix
Harvard Lampoon, 82 & nn 2 & 3
Harvard Law Review, xvii, 39, 44, 51 & n.1, 52, 65, 86, 107, 154, 200, 201
Harvard Law School, Langdell Hall, 244 & n.4, 256; Holmes papers, xxxiii, xxxiv, xxxvi, xxxvii; students, 186, 270. *See also* Eliot, Charles; Frankfurter, Felix; Hill, Arthur; Holmes, Oliver Wendell, Jr.; Howe, Mark; Laski, Harold; Perkins, Thomas Nelson; Pound, Roscoe; Wu, John C. H.
Harvard University, 85; anti-semitism, xix, 241

Harvey, George B., "The Passing of State Rights" (1920), 94
Hegel, George Wilhelm Friedrich, 17, 94, 113, 118, 120, 216
Heine, Heinrich, 234
Hemingway, Ernest, *The Sun Also Rises* (1926), 232
Henderson, Gerald, *The Position of Foreign Corporations in American Constitutional Law* (1918), 72, 73 n.1
Henderson, Lawrence J., *The Fitness of the Environment* (1913), 29, 30 n.3
Henry, John, Cardinal Newman, *An Essay in Aid of a Grammar of Assent* (1870), 3, 4 n.3
Higgins, Henry Bournes, "A New Province for Law and Order: Industrial Peace through Minimum Wage and Arbitration" (1915), 39 & n.2
Hill, Arthur D., 42, 43 n.1, 46, 50, 62, 63, 81, 159, 160, 219, 255
Hillman, Sidney, 86, 87 n.2
Hirsch, H. N., *The Enigma of Felix Frankfurter* (1981), xvi n.14, xxv n.47, xl
Hiss, Alger, xvii, 234, 235 n.1, 243, 248
Hiss, Donald, 270 n.1
Hobbes, Thomas, 113, 135, 165; *Leviathan* (1651), 58, 59 n.1
Hoffding, Harold, *A History of Modern Philosophy* (1924), 204, 205 n.1
Hohfeld, Wesley N., 136, 137 n.1
Holdsworth, W. S., *A History of English Law* (1909), 8 & n.2
Hollinger, David, xiii, xlii
Holmes, Abiel, xxii
Holmes, Edward Jackson, 67, 68 n.1, 252, 262
Holmes, Fanny, xiii, xiv, xvi, xxvii, 52, 54, 58, 84, 85, 86, 89, 98, 106, 139, 176, 238, 239 & n.1
Holmes, Oliver Wendell, Sr., xiii n.8, 202, 231 & n.3, 263
Holmes, Oliver Wendell, Jr.
ARTICLES AND ESSAYS: "Learning and Science" (1895), 24, 25 n.4; Memorial Day Address, 60, 61 n.1; "Path of the Law" (1897), 116, 117 n.2; "Privilege, Malice and Intent" (1894), xxiii, 86, 87 n.4, 102; "The Soldier's Faith" (1895), 60, 61 n.1
BIOGRAPHY: *American Law Review*, 19, 20 n.2; Civil War, xi, xxix, 22, 58, 68, 156 n.1, 164, 266; death, xxviii; Harvard Law School, 13 n.1, 30 n.2; New England heritage, xi, xxix, 110, 156, 158, 231; observations on old age, xiii & n.7, 74, 84, 154, 164, 175, 203, 204, 205, 214, 219, 223, 224, 229, 234, 241, 248, 260, 266, 267; Supreme Judicial Court of Massachusetts, xxxvi, xxxviii, xxxix, 101 n.2, 121 & n.6, 129 & n.1, 177; U.S. Supreme Court, Chief Justice, xxvii, 247 & n.2; U.S. Supreme Court, retirement from, xxvii, 268 & n.1; U.S. Supreme Court, speculations on resignation, 179, 180 & n.1, 183, 231 & n.1
BOOKS: *Collected Legal Papers* (1920), xii, 27 & n.1, 90, 91 n.1, 97, 103, 104 n.2, 107, 122, 123, 124 n.1, 127 & n.1; *The Common Law* (1881), xii, xxi, 4, 30 n.2, 117 n.2, 170, 201; *James Kent's Commentaries on American Law* (1873), xii; *Public Writings* (ed. Sheldon Novick, 1994), xli; *Speeches* (1900), 4 n.4
FRIENDSHIPS: appreciation for younger generation of scholars, xvi, 6, 23, 25; Brandeis (*see also* Brandeis, Louis); Frankfurter, advice regarding career, 12, 13. *See also* Frankfurter, Felix
FUNDAMENTAL BELIEFS AND OPINIONS: academic freedom, respect for, 78; academic life, opinion of, 12, 13; civil rights and liberties, commitment to, xviii, xxvi, xxxviii n.100, 240 n.1; history, appreciation for, 44, 117, 118 n.4, 144, 159, 164, 172, 173; labor, attitude toward, 26 nn. 1–3, 53, 56, 70, 87 n.4, 104; polity, view of, xxii, 92, 108, 188; politics, disinterest in, xxv; property rights, commitment to, xxiii & n.38; religion, atti-

Holmes, Oliver Wendell, Jr. (*continued*) tude toward, 83; social welfare, opinion of, 8; sovereign power, view of, 54 n.3
INFLUENCE: legal writings, 4, 86, 102, 116, 170, 201; opinions, 257, 278
JUDICIAL PHILOSOPHY: xi, xxi, xxii, xxiv, xxv & n.47, xxvi, 26 n.1, 40, 44, 64, 87 n.4, 110, 160, 186, 194, 221, 259; judicial restraint, xii, xviii, xx n.28, xxi, xxii, 19, 87 n.4, 133, 209, 212 n.1; opinion of German legal writings, 204
OFFICIAL BIOGRAPHERS: xxix, xxx, xxxi, xxxvii, xl, xli; Felix Frankfurter xxix, xxxii–xxxvii, 264; Grant Gilmore, xxxviii, xxxix; Mark Howe, xxxii–xxxvi
PERSONAL PHILOSOPHY: 3, 5, 24, 27, 29, 35, 36, 53, 57, 60, 70, 78, 88, 124, 133, 168, 187, 203, 215, 232, 236; Malthus, xii, 89, 202, 210, 211 n.2; science, 236
RECOGNITION: American Bar Association Medal, 264 & n.1; concern with reputation, xii, xiii, xv, 244; Harvard Law School, Phi Beta Kappa Lecture, 74 n.1; Harvard Law School, portrait, 244, 246, 251, 252; Lincoln's Inn, senior bencher, 275; Roosevelt Memorial Association Medal, 174 n.1, 221; U.S. Supreme Court, 25th Anniversary, 220
SECRETARIES, CRITERIA: xvi, 40, 42, 62, 178, 195, 215
Holmes-Frankfurter correspondence, xiv–xvii, xix, xx, xxviii–xxx, xxxii, xxxiii, xxxvi, xxxvii n.97, xxxviii, xli, xlii, 129, 131; missing letters, xiv, xix
Homer, xxi, 119, 120, 122, 173, 254; *Odyssey* 192
Hopkinson, Charles Sydney, 244, 245 n.4, 246, 251, 252
Hornblower, Byrne, Miller and Potter, xii
Horwitz, Morton, xxii
Hough, Charles Merrill, 107, 108 n.3, 108, 109, 110; "Admiralty Jurisdiction—of Late Years" (1924), 170, 171 & nn.1 & 3
Hound and Horn, 237 & n.3
Hours of Service Act, 62 n.2
House, Edward M., 74 n.2
House of Truth, xiii, 3, 10 n.3, 18 & n.3, 22 n.1, 61 n.1, 162
Howe, Mark DeWolfe: *The Common Law* (edited, 1963), xxxviii n.100; Harvard Law School, xxxiii; *Holmes-Laski Letters* (1953), xxxiv, xxxv n.89, xxxvi, xli, xlii, xxxiv; *Holmes-Pollock Letters* (1941), xxxi, xxxii, xxxv; Holmes's biographer, xv, xxxii–xxxv, xxxvi n.90; Holmes's secretary, xvii, 270 n.1, 277; *Justice Oliver Wendell Holmes: The Proving Years, 1870–1882* (1963), xxxv n.90; *Justice Oliver Wendell Holmes: The Shaping Years, 1841–1870* (1957), xxxvi n.90; *Occasional Speeches* (1962), xxxiv, & n.86; "The Positivism of Mr. Justice Holmes" (1951), xxxv; publications regarding Holmes, xxxi–xxxiv, xxxv n.87, xxxvi–xxxix, xli; *Touched with Fire: Civil War Letters and Diary of Oliver Wendell Holmes, Jr.* (1946), xxxiii
Howe, Mark Antony DeWolfe, xxxii
Howe, Mary Manning (Mrs. Fanuiel Adams), xxxi, xxxiv, xxxviii, & n.102, xl
Hudson, Manley, 111, 112 & n.2, 113
Hughes, Charles Evans, 28 & n.4; as advocate, 95, 96 n.2, 115 n.3; as Chief Justice, 247 n.2, 249; Holmes's opinion of, 250; Holmes's retirement, xxvii; as Master, 253 n.1; presidential race, 59 n.1; Supreme Court decisions, 26 nn.2 & 3, 31 n.3, 49, 267 & n.1
Huneker, James G.: *Painted Veils* (1920), 96 & n.3; *Promenades of an Impressionist* (1910), 244
Hunt, William Morris, xxi, 92, 196 & n.5
Hurst, Willard H., xxiv n.39
Huxley, Leonard, *Life and Letters of T. H. Huxley* (1900), 47, 48 n.1

Illinois Law Review, 28, 86, 122
Inner Temple, 275

interstate commerce, 100 n.5, 141 n.6, 143 n.3, 153 n.2, 169 n.5, 171 & n.4, 243, 250 n.2, 263 & n.1. *See also* Interstate Commerce Act and Interstate Commerce Commission
Interstate Commerce Act, 36, 62 n.5, 64 n.3, 135 n.3, 167 n.1
Interstate Commerce Commission, 59 n.3, 61 n.2, 70 n.2, 115, 165 n.7, 169 n.4, 194 n.3, 197 n.1, 224 n.3, 227, 265
Iowa Law Bulletin and Weekly Review, 122, 123
Ireland, 121 & n.7, 124, 126

Jaffe, Louis L., xxiv, n.39
James, Henry, 93 & n.2; *The Golden Bowl*, 87; *The Letters of Henry James* (1920), 86, 88 n.8
James, Henry (1879–1947), *The Letters of William James* (1920), 98, 99 n.4
James, William, xxi, 3, 24, 36, 98, 118 n.3, 155; *Pragmatism* (1907), 98
Jenks, Edward, "English Civil Law" (1916), 61, 62 n.3
Jews, religion and culture, 10, 12 n.2, 56
Johnson, Alvin, 80 n.2; "Is Revolution Possible?" (1919), 76 & n.2, 77
Josephson, Matthew, xiv
Journal of the American Bar Association, 123

Kaneko, Count Kentaro, 162, 163 n.3
Kant, Immanuel, 203
Kelly, Edmond, *Twentieth Century Socialism* (1910), 51, 52 n.6
Kennedy, Margaret, *The Constant Nymph* (1925), 191
Keynes, John Maynard, 136; "When the Big Four Met" (1919), 81 n.2
Keyserling, Hermann, *Travel Diary of the Philosopher* (1925), 186, 189, 190, 191
Kimball, Day, 81, 82 & n.1, 83, 98, 111
King, Gertrude, 3 & n.1, 5 & n.1, 30
Kingsley, Charles, 47, 48 n.1
Klarman, Michael J., xxvi n.49
Kocourek, Albert, "The Hohfeld System" (1920), 136, 137 n.2. *See also* Wigmore, John Henry and Albert Kocourek
Kurland, Philip B., xxx

labor and labor unions, 25, 26 nn.1–3, 76 n.2, 85, 86, 87 nn.1 & 3, 101 n.1, 104, 130, 139, 165 n.3
labor legislation, xx, 56, 61 n.2, 69, 71 nn.3 & 5, 71, 72, 91 n.3, 102 n.2, 103 n.3, 128 n.2, 151 n.4
Labori, Fernand, 15, 16 n.3
Lamar, Joseph, 25 n.2, 40 & n.3, 114, 115 n.4
Lamb, Harold, *Genghis Khan* (1927), 230
Landau, Lloyd H., 92 & n.2
Landis, James, xxiv n.39, 241 n.1
Lane, Franklin K., 114 & n.2, 115
Lao Tzu, 171
Lash, Joseph, xxv
Laski, Harold, xx, 54 n.3, 83, 135, 264; friendship with Frankfurter, 76; Harvard College, xix, 45 n.1, 65, 77 n.3, 82, 87 137, 201; London School of Economics, 88 & n.9; Parliament, 152
FRIENDSHIP WITH HOLMES: xv, xxxix, 81, 123; correspondence between, xv, xxiv, xxxi, xxxiv, xxxv n.89, 45 n.1, 62, 66, 85, 90, 107, 153, 189, 193, 235; Holmes's disagreement with, 54, 113, 120, 231, 188; Holmes's opinion of, 44, 53; Holmes, readings recommended by Laski to, 56, 89, 93, 96, 127, 157, 165, 184, 187, 196, 204, 234; Holmes, visits with, 57, 262; opinion of Holmes's work, 50 & n.1. *See also* Howe, Mark
PUBLICATIONS: "The Apotheosis of the State" (1916), 54 n.3; *A Defense of Liberty against Tyrants* (1924), 171, 172 n.6; *The Foundations of Sovereignty* (1921), 121, 122, 123, 141, 142 n.4; *A Grammar of Politics* (1925), 177, 188; "Responsibility of the State of England" (1919), 135, 136 n.5
Law Quarterly Review, 97, 141, 199, 267 n.3

Lawrence, Alfred Tristam, 109 & n.5
Lawrence, D. H., *Lady Chatterley's Lover* (1930), 266
Lawrence, Bishop William, 253 & n.3
Leach, W. Barton, 164 & n.1, 178, 179 n.5
legal education, 11, 12 n.5, 14, 44 n.1, 137 nn.1 & 2
legislative law, 14
Legouis, Emile, and Louis Cazamian, *A History of English Literature* (1926–27), 234
Lehmann, Frederick W., 252 & n.2
Leif, Alfred, *The Dissenting Opinions of Mr. Justice Holmes* (1929), 244, 245
Lemaitre, Jules, *Jean Racine* (1905), 189, 190
Lepaulle, Pierre G., 134, 135 n.1, 194, 196
Lerner, Max, xxxv n.89
Lever Act, 95, 96 n.2, 143 n.3
Levy, David W., xiv, xl
Lewis, D. B. Wyndham, *The Stuffed Owl: An Anthology of Bad Verse* (1930), 260, 261, 262
Lewis, Sinclair, *Arrowsmith* (1925), 195
libel, 65, 66 n.5, 162 n.2
Liberator, 130
Library of Congress, xxxi, xxxvii, 140
Lippmann, Walter, xiii, 49, 164, 197, *Drift and Mastery* (1914), 23, 25; *Interpretations, 1931–32* (1932), 269; *A Preface to Morals* (1929), 238
Littell, Philip, 158, 159 n.2, 165, 203, 204
Llewellyn, Karl N., 258 & n.2
Lockwood, John E., 223 & n.1
Lodge, Sir Oliver, 82, 84 n.1
London Nation, 111
Loos, Anita, *But Gentlemen Marry Brunettes* (1927), 229
Lotze, Hermann, *Microcosmus: An Essay Concerning Man and His Relation to the World* (1885), 158
Lowe, Robert, Viscount Sherbrooke, 158, 159 n.6
Lowell, A. Lawrence, xviii, 241 n.1
Lowell, Amy, 49 & n.1
Lowell, John, 23 & n.1
Lowes, John L., *The Road to Xanadu* (1927), 213, 214 n.3
Lurton, Horace H., 31 n.3

Macauley, Thomas Babbington, *History*, 125
McDougall, William, *World Chaos* (1931), 269
Mack, Julian, 16 & n.7
McKenna, Joseph, 94, 178 & n.2; Frankfurter's opinion of, 63, 102, 108, 111; Holmes's opinion of, xvii, xxv, 110, 112, 229; Supreme Court decisions, 19 n.1, 26 n.2, 33 n.2, 40, 41 nn.4 & 5, 48 & n.5, 49, 62 n.5, 64 n.3, 70 n.2, 72 n.1, 84 n.1, 95 n.4, 97 n.2, 99, 100 n.2, 102 n.3, 108 n.1, 110 n.1, 133 & n.2, 134 & n.1, 135 n.3, 143 n.2, 170 & n.2
MacLaurin, Charles, *Post Mortem* (1922), 187
McReynolds, James C., 31 & n.1; Holmes's opinion of, 110; Supreme Court decisions, 71 n.4, 84 nn.1 & 2, 91 n.2, 94 n.4, 98 n.2, 102 n.3, 114 n.3, 133 n.2, 134 n.1, 138, 141 n.6, 162 n.2, 168 n.2, 169 nn.4 & 5, 172 n.5, 197 n.1, 199 n.3, 206 n.4, 207, 224 n.3, 227 n.1, 244 n.2, 245 n.6, 255 n.1
Maitland, Frederick William, 225 & n.2, 275
Malone, Dumas, xxxii
Mallock, William H., 124 & n.3
Manchester Guardian, 135
Mansfield, John H., xxx
Marshall, John, 227, 228 n.1
Marston, George, 32 & n.2
Martha's Vineyard, 190
Marx, Karl, 216
Masefield, John, *William Shakespeare* (1911), 148
Mason, Alpheus T., xxxvii, xl n.109
Mason, Jeremiah, 68, 69 n.9
Massachusetts Constitutional Convention, 68 & n.5
Matthews, Nathan, "The Valuation of Property in the Roman Law" (1920–21), 104

Maurois, Andre, *Ariel, ou La Vie de Shelley* (1923), 164
Meiklejohn, Alexander, 170 & n.3
Mellins, Judith, xxxix n.107
Melville, Herman, xxi; *Moby Dick*, 107, 109, 113, 117, 118, 232
Meredith, George, 87, 88 n.8; *Diana at the Crossways* (1909), 109 & n.4
Metaphysical Club, 161 n.1, 237 n.2
Meyer, Agnes Elizabeth Ernst, *Chinese Painting as Reflected in the Thought and Act of Li Lung-mien* (1923), 165
Miller, Alice Duer, 60, 61 n.2
Miller, Gerrit, 235, 269, 273
Miller, Perry, xxxv
Milton, John: *Aeropagitica*, 76; "Lycidas," 214
Milwaukee Leader, 106 & n.2
Mitchell-Innes, Alfred, 18 & n.3
Monroe, William Adam, 160 & n.5
Moody, William Henry, 252 & n.3
Mooney, Thomas J., 71 n.1, 130, 131 n.2
Monday P.M. Club, 34, 35 n.1, 36
Morgan, Charles, *The Fountain* (1932), 273
Morgan, John Hartmann, *John Viscount Morley* (1924), 196
Morison, Samuel Eliot, xxxv, *The Oxford History of the United States* (1927), 232, 233; *Prologue to American History* (1922), 145
Morton, James M., 149 & n.2
Muirhead, James, *Historical Introduction to the Private Law of Rome* (1886), 172
Mumford, Lewis, *Herman Melville* (1929), 238
Murray, Gilbert, *Euripides and His Age* (1913), 173

Nagel, Charles, 156, 157 n.1
Narcotic Drug Act, 138 n.3
Nation, 217
National Prohibition Act, 210 n.4, 229
negligence, 19 n.1, 138 n.2
Nevinson, Henry W., 265 & n.2, 266; *Essays in Freedom and Rebellion* (1921), 135, 136 n.7; *More Changes, More Chances* (1925), 265
New England Calvinism, xxii
New England Quarterly, xxxv n.88
New Republic, 44, 51, 56, 57, 67, 76, 79, 80, 81, 89, 106, 140, 165, 238; Frankfurter's articles, xvii, xxiii n.37, 102, 200; Frankfurter's book, review of, 222; Holmes, articles about, xvii, 103, 149, 200; Holmes's opinions, comments on, xxiv, 150; writers, Holmes's opinion of, 30; Sacco-Vanzetti, 216
New York Evening Post, 122
New York Herald Tribune, 231 & n.1
New York Times, 237, 240
New York Workmen's Compensation Act, 69, 70 n.1
New York World, 86
Nicely, James, 146, 147 n.1, 155
Novick, Sheldon, xli
Noyes, Frances (Mrs. Edward L. Hart): *Mark* (1913), 51

O'Connell, Cardinal William Henry, 111
Oedipus Tyrannus, 55
Olds, Irving S., 9, 10 n.3
Oppenheim, Edward P., 273, 274

Palfrey, John Graham, xxix, xxxi, xxxii, xxxiii, 174 & n.2, 262, 277 n.1
Palmer, A. Mitchell, 86
Parker, John J., 254 n.2
Parrington, V. L., *Main Currents in American Thought* (1927), 229, 230, 231, 232
Parrish, Michael, *Frankfurter and His Times: The Reform Years* (1982), xl
Pascal, Blaise, 187, 189; *Provinciales*, 190, 191
patent law, 168 n.1, 201 n.1, 227 & n.1, 240 n.1, 249, 250 n.1
Patten, Simon, *The Development of English Thought* (1899), 53
Patterson, Edwin W., 122, 123, 124 n.1
Peabody, James B., xxxvii n.94, xxxviii n.99
Peckham, Rufus, 138 & n.4
Pegler, Westbrook, xxxv n.87
Peirce, Charles Sanders: *Chance, Love and Logic* (1923), 161 & n.1; "Pragmatism" (1906), 237
Pepys, Samuel, *Diary* (1892–1900), 226
Percy, Lord Eustace, 21, 22 & n.1

Perkins, Thomas Nelson, 77 & n.3, 78 & n.1, 89, 90 & n.4
Philbrook, Francis S.: "A Genial Skeptic" (1921), 123, 124 n.2, 125, 126, 127 & n.3
Pierce, Frederick, *Understanding Our Children* (1926), 202
Pilgrim's Progress, 191
Pitney, Mahlon, 94, 147 & n.3; Frankfurter's opinion of, xxiii, 86, 102, 111; Holmes's opinion of, 147, 177; Supreme Court decisions, xxii, 26 n.1, 31 n.3, 48 n.4, 59 n.3, 70 n.1, 71 n.4, 79, 80 n.4, 84 n.1, 87 n.1, 91 nn.2 & 3, 94, 98 n.2, 101 n.2, 102, n.3, 133 n.1
Plato, 113; *Laws*, 249; *Republic*, 33; *Timaeus*, 120, 122
Plautus, 172
Pluncknett, Theodore F. T., *Statutes and Their Interpretation in the Fourteenth Century* (1923), 151
Plunkett, Edward, *Book of Wonder* (1913), 17 n.2
Plutarch, 172
Poe, Charles K., 54, 55 & n.1
Polakoff, Sol, 65 & n.2
police powers, xxiii, 74, 75 n.3, 101 n.1, 146, 147, 148, 212, 228
Political Science Quarterly, 127
Pollock, Sir Frederick, xxxi, 68, 97 & n.2, 141, 142 n.4, 148, 199 n.5, 257, 267 n.3
Pound, Cuthbert, 191 & n.6
Pound, Roscoe, 40, 97, 135, 141, 142 n.4; comments on Holmes's decisions, 38, 76, 116; "Courts and Legislation" (1917), 68 & n.4; *Criminal Justice in Cleveland* (1922), 140, 141, 146; criticized by John Zane, 206; criticized by Karl Llewellyn, 258 & n.2; "Equitable Relief against Defamation and Injuries to Personality" (1916), 52 & n.7; Frankfurter's position at Harvard Law School, role regarding, 10, 11, 17, 89, 90 & n.4, 241 n.1; Harvard Law School, 50; "Interests of Personality" (1915), 37 n.4; *Interpretations of Legal History* (1923), 150; *An Introduction to the Philosophy of Law* (1922), 131; "Law in Books and Law in Action" (1910), 36, 37 & n.3, 39; "The Maxims of Equity" (1921), 122; observations on legal education, 14; *Outline of Lectures on Jurisprudence* (1914), 34, 35 n.7; *Readings in Roman Law* (1906), 162; sociological jurisprudence, 8 & n.4, 10, 11, 32, 36; *The Spirit of the Common Law* (1921), 131, 137; "The Theory of Judicial Decision" (1923), 155; John Wu, regarding, 157, 207, 225, 230
Powell, Thomas Reed, xxiv n.40
procedure, 31 n.3
property, rights of, 18 & n.2, 25 n.2, 36, 37, 87 n.4, 91 n.4, 146 n.1, 148 nn.1 & 2
Proust, Marcel: 223; *Du cote de Chez Swann*, xxi, 156; *Swann's Way*, 203, 204
Public Utilities Act, 128 n.2

Quesney, Francois, 120

Radcliffe, William, *Fishing from the Earliest Times* (1921), 139
Rait, Robert S., *Memorials of Albert Venn Dicey* (1925), 186
Rauh, Joseph L., Jr., xxx
Redlich, Josef, 106, 107 & n.1, 144, 207, 208 n.1, 235, 236, 237
Reinach, Solomon, *Orpheus: A General History of Religions* (1909), 83, 84 n.4
Renan, Ernest, *The History of the Origins of Christianity* (1890), 83, 84 n.4
Repplier, Agnes, *Counter-currents* (1916), 57 & n.2, 58
Requin, Edouard J., "Our Faith in Foch" (1918), 72, 73 n.2
Revenue Act, 194 n.3, 213 n.1
Rhodes, James F., *History of the United States, 1877–1896* (1919), 79, 80 n.2
Richardson, Eliot L., xxx
Riesman, David, xxiv n.39
Roberts, Owen J., 254 n.2, 266, 267 n.1
Robertson, John Mackinnon, *Elizabethan Literature* (1914), 34, 35 n.3
Robinson, Edward, *Public Authorities and Legal Liability* (1925), 196

Rockefeller, John D., 77
Rogat, Yosal, xxii n.34, xxxviii n.100
Rolland, Romain, *Jean Christophe* (1904–12), 16, 17 & n.1
Roosevelt, Franklin D., xxviii, xxxi, 274 n.2
Roosevelt, Theodore, 7, 50, 59 n.1, 130
Rose, Horace Chapman, 260, 261 & n.1, 262, 266, 270
Rousseau, Jean-Jacques, *Confessions* (1782), 168, 169
Rowe, James Henry, Jr., xvii, xxviii, 270 n.1, 277, 278
Rugg, Arthur Prentice, 180 & n.2
Ruskin, John, 119 & n.3, 242; *Seven Lamps of Architecture*, 165
Russell, Bertrand: *An Outline of History* (1927), 229; *What I Believe* (1925), 183

Sacco-Vanzetti case, xix, xx n.28, 211, 216, 217 & n.2, 241 n.1, 268 & n.1
Sacks, Albert M., xxx
Sainte-Beuve, Charles Augustin: *Causeries du lundi*, 153, 154, 156, 157, 158, 161, 175; *Port Royal* (1840–59), 184, 187, 188, 189
Sallust, 125
Sanford, Edward T., 147 n.3, 151 n.4, 163 n.3, 168 n.2, 169 n.4, 185 n.1, 206 n.4, 207, 212 n.1, 240 n.1, 254 n.2
Santayana, George, xxvii; *Character and Opinion in the United States* (1920), 98, 99 n.3; *The Realm of Matter* (1930), 261, 262; *The Unknowable* (1923), 168
Sargant, Sir Charles Henry, 181 & n.1
Saunders, Sir Edmund, 74, 75 n.2
Schindler, Rudolf, 135 & n.2
Schneider, Hermann, *History of World Civilization* (1931), 269
Schwimmer, Rosika, *Great Musicians as Children* (1929), xxix
Scott, Geoffrey, *The Architecture of Humanism* (1914), 244, 246
Scott, Sir Leslie Frederic, 263, 264 n.1, 275
Scott, Sir Leslie F., and Alfred Hildesley, *The Case of Requisition: In re a Petition of Right of De Keyser's Royal Hotel* (1920), 104, 105 n.4
Sedgwick, Arthur G., 20 n.2, 83
Sedgwick, Ellery, 10, 12 n.3
Sedgwick, Henry Dwight, *Marcus Aurelius* (1921), 171, 172
Sedition Act, 75 n.1
Seneca, 172
separation of powers, 227 & n.1
Sergeant, Elizabeth Shepley: *Fire under the Andes* (1927), 196 n.3; "Justice Touched with Fire" (1925), 196 & n.3, 209, 210
Shakespeare, 39, 145 & n.2, 158; *Hamlet*, 47, 203, 215; *Macbeth*, 164; *Midsummer Nights Dream*, 145; *Romeo and Juliet*, 145; *Taming of the Shrew*, 187
Shattuck, George Otis, 190, 191 n.2
Shaw, George Bernard, 67 & n.4; *Back to Methuselah* (1921), 118
Shaw, Lemuel, 93 & n.1
Sheehan, Canon Patrick Augustus, 11, 12 n.7
Sherman Anti-Trust Act, xvi, 8, 37 n.5, 84 n.2, 95 n.5, 143 n.3, 163, 164 n.2
Shirley, John M., *The Dartmouth College Causes and the Supreme Court of the United States* (1877), 158
Sichel, Edith Helen, *The Renaissance* (1914), 34
Sidgwick, Ethel, *Herself* (1912), 43
Smellie, Kingsley B. S., 199 & n.4
Smith, Adam, 119, 199 n.3
Smith, Al, 233
Smith, Horace and James, *Reflected Addresses* (1929), 242
Smuts, General Jan, *Holism and Evolution* (1926), 208 & n.4, 241, 242
sociological jurisprudence, 77 & n.2, 201
Sorel, George, *Reflections on Violence* (1912), 53, 54 n.2
Soviet Union, 232
Spengler, Oswald, *Der Untergang des Abendlandes* (1918), 175, 176
Spillenger, Clyde, xxx, xl
Spinoza, Benedictine de, 235, 236; *Ethics* (1925), 150, 215, 216
spiritualism, 83
Springfield Republican, 77
Stammler, Rudolf, 157, 158 n.2; *Theory of Justice*, 203

state governments, powers of, 99, 183 n.2. *See also* due process; Fourteenth Amendment
Stephens, William D., 131 n.2
Stimson, Henry L., xii, xiii, 267
Stone, Harlan Fiske: appointment to Supreme Court, 178 n.2; Supreme Court decisions; 199 nn.2 & 3, 209 n.3, 212 n.1, 223 n.3, 226 n.1, 227 n.1, 229 n.2, 246, 255 n.1, 265 n.3, 267 n.1
Storey, Moorfield, 50 & n.2
Story, Joseph, 130, 158, 225
Strachey, Charles, *The Letters of the Earl of Chesterfield to his Son* (1925), 216
Strachey, John, *Revolution and Reason* (1925), 223 & n.2
Strachey, Lytton, *Queen Victoria* (1921), 106, 107 n.2, 109
Sullivan, J. W. N., *The Bases of Modern Science* (1929), 235, 236
Sunday, Billy, 62 & n.4, 63
Supreme Court, 95, 126, 127 n.1
Sutherland, Arthur E., 215 & n.2, 223
Sutherland, George, 193; Supreme Court decisions, 148 n.1, 153 n.1, 163 nn.2 & 3, 168 n.2, 169 n.4, 206 & n.4, 207, 212 n.1, 227 n.1

Tacitus, *Histoire*, 172
Taft, William Howard, xiii, xxvii, 114 n.1, 193, 247; "Adequate Machinery for Judicial Business" (1921), 127 n.2; Frankfurter's opinion of, 117; Holmes's opinion of, 119, 127, 132, 140, 249, 250; Supreme Court decisions, 132 n.2, 133 n.1, 135 n.3, 138, 139 n.1, 141 nn.5 & 6, 142 n.2, 146, 151 n.4, 152, 172, 178, 218 n.3, 223 n.3, 235 n.2, 245, 253 n.1
Tarde, Gabriel, *Les Transformations du droit* (1893), 33
Tawney, R. H.: *The Acquisitive Society* (1920), 92 & n.1; *The Establishment of Minimum Rates in the Chain-Making Industry under the Trade Boards Act of 1909* (1914), 54
taxes: federal government's power, 152 n.1, 184 n.2, 213 n.1; Frankfurter's discussion of, 245–47; Holmes's discussion of, 19, 20, 218 & n.3, 227 n.1, 244 & n.2, 245 n.6, 247, 255 n.1, 267 n.1; Supreme Court decisions, 33 n.1, 42, 43 n.2, 104 n.1, 110 n.1, 113 n.2, 118 n.4, 137 n.4, 146 n.2, 169 n.5, 183 n.2, 184 n.2, 199 n.3, 201 n.1, 218 n.3, 227 & n.1, 244 n.2, 245 n.6, 249, 250 n.2, 255 n.1, 267 n.1; taxation of judges, 105 n.3
Taylor, Henry Osborn, *The Medieval Mind* (1911), 119
Tennyson, Alfred Lord: "Crossing the Bar," 79, 80 n.1; *Idylls of the King* (1859), 3, 4 n.2
Thacher, Thomas Day, 252 & n.1
Tharaud, Jerome and Jean, *A l'Ombre de la Croix* (1917), 235, 237
Thayer, Ezra Ripley, 15, 16 n.6, 31 & nn.4 & 5, 45, 46 n.1; "John Chipman Gray (1839–1915)," 31 n.4
Thayer, James B., xii
Thayer, William Roscoe, *Theodore Roosevelt: An Intimate Biography* (1919), 130, 131 n.3
These Eventful Years, 177
Thompson, William G., *Commonwealth of Massachusetts v. Nicola Sacco and Bartolomeo Vanzetti* (1927), 268
Thucydides, *History of the Peloponnesian War*, 175, 176
Tittle, W., "Glimpses of Interesting Americans" (1925), 189
Tocqueville, Alexis de, *Ancien Regime* (1856), 165, 168
Tolstoy, Leo, *La Guerre et la paix*, 175
tort, 77 n.1, 116 & n.2, 138, 171 n.2, 181
Tourtoulon, Pierre de, *Les Principes philosophiques de l'histoire du droit* (1908), 96, 97 n.3
trademark, 48 & n.4, 49, 50, 172 n.5, 213 n.1
Transportation Act, 197 n.1
Trotsky, Leon, 129 & n.2, 131; *My Life: An Attempt at an Autobiography* (1930), 256
Tufts, James H., "The Legal and Social

Philosophy of Mr. Justice Holmes" (1921), 117, 118 & n.3, 122, 123
Turner, Joseph Mallard William, 145, 176

Ulysses, 71
Untermeyer, Louis, *Including Horace* (1919), 79, 80 n.2
Urofsky, Melvin I., xxvi n.49, xl
Urofsky, Melvin, and David Levy, xiv; "*Half Brother, Half Son*" (1991), xl; *The Letters of Louis D. Brandeis* (1971–78), xl
U. S. Coal Commission, 157 & n.3

Valentine, Robert G., xiii, 60, 61 n.1, 64, 65, 66
Valentine, Sophia French, 60, 61 n.1
Van Devanter, Willis, 31 n.3, 66 n.3, 70 n.2, 71 n.4, 80 n.3, 89, 91 n.2, 94 & n.4, 98 n.2, 102 n.3, 105 n.3, 110, 140 n.3, 141 n.5, 235 n.2, 245, 250 n.2
Veblen, Thorstein: *Theory of Business Enterprise* (1904), 52 n.5; *Theory of the Leisure Class* (1899), 51
Verlaine, Paul, 55 & n.4
Versailles Peace Conference, 74 n.2
Vinogradoff, Paul, *Custom and Right* (1925), 205, 206 & n.2
Virgil, xxvii
Virginia Sterilizing Act, xx, 212, 213 n.2
Volstead Act, 95 n.4, 97 n.2
Vorenberg, James, xxx

Wales, Robert Willett, 249 & n.3, 251, 262
Wallas, Graham: *The Art of Thought* (1926), 206; *The Great Society* (1914), 30 n.1, 56; *Human Nature in Politics* (1908), 30; *Our Social Heritage* (1921), 113
Walpole, Horace, *Letters* (1840), 226
Warren, Charles, *The Supreme Court in United States History* (1922), 148
Warren, Earl, 33 n.1
Webb-Kenyon Act, 65 & n.3, 66
Webster, Daniel, 158
West, Rebecca, xxxv n.89
White, Edward D., 15, 58, 90, 94, 115 n.4, 126, 160 n.4; death, 65, 160; Frankfurter's opinion of, 114 & n.1, 115; Supreme Court decisions, 19 n.1, 33 n.2, 61 n.1, 65 n.3, 69, 71 n.3, 80 n.4, 91 & n.3, 94 n.4, 96 n.2, 98 n.2, 100 nn.2 & 3, 102 n.3, 110, 114 n.3, 246 n.2
White, G. Edward, xiii, xvi, xvii, xxvii, xxxix n.105, xlii
Whitehead, Alfred North, 199; *Process and Reality* (1929), 243, 244, 246, 256; *Science and the Modern World* (1925), 197
Whittier, Charles A., 155, 156 n.1
Wickersham, George, 107, 108 n.4
Wigglesworth, Richard, 42 & n.2
Wigmore, John Henry, 28 & n.2, 29, 86, 89 n.1, 133, 155; "Abrams v. United States: Freedom of Speech and Freedom of Thuggery in War-Time and Peace-Time" (1920), 85 & n.2, 88
Wigmore, John Henry, and Albert Kocourek: *Primitive and Ancient Legal Institutions* (1915), 33; *The Rational Basis of Legal Institutions* (1923), 150, 151 n.5, 155
Williams, Whiting, *Mainsprings of Men* (1925), 269
Williston, Samuel, 63 & n.2
Wilson, Edmund, xxii, 188 n.1
Wilson, Philip Whitwell, *The Greville Diary* (1927), 222, 223
Wilson, Woodrow, xv, xvii, 67, 160; criticism of, 94 n.4, 100, 121, 121 n.3; Frankfurter's opinion of, 59 n.1, 78 n.1; Frankfurter's work for, 71 n.1, 74 n.2, 130; labor legislation, 56 n.3, 61 n.2, 71 & n.1, 100; treatment of radicals, 80 n.6
Winfield, Percy Henry, 152, 152 n.2; *The History of Conspiracy and Abuse of Legal Procedure* (1921), 151 & n.2
Wister, Owen, 232 & n.3
Wolsey, Thomas, 274 & n.1
women's rights, 41 nn.4 & 5
Woodruff, Edwin H., *Introduction to the Study of Law* (1898), 222 & n.3

World War I, xiv, xv, xvii, xxxix, 48, 68, 73 & n.1, 75 n.1, 104, 105 nn.1 & 2, 117, 131, 141 n.5, 144, 177, 194 n.4
World War II, xxxiii
Wu, John C. H., 157 & n.1, 189, 246, 254; Frankfurter's opinion of, 249; Holmes's friendship with, 164, 166, 171, 174, 180, 203; Holmes's opinion of, 166, 168, 173, 225, 250, 251 n.2; legal career, 174 n.1, 184 & n.1; proposal to teach at Harvard Law School, 207 & n.2, 208, 210, 221, 224 & n.2, 225, 229, 230
Yale Legal Realists, xxvii
Yale Review, 185

Zane, John M.: "A Legal Heresy" (1919), 88, 89 n.2, 135, 136 n.6; review of *Custom and Right*, 206 & n.2; *The Story of the Law* (1927), 220 & n.2
Zangwill, Israel, 10, 12 n.4; *War of the Worlds* (1916), 56
Zimmern, Sir Alfred, 194 & n.5
zionism, 74 n.2, 208 n.4

INDEX TO COURT CASES

Abrams v. United States, xviii & n.19, 75 & nn.1 & 2, 85, 86, 97, 185 n.1, 199 n.5, 240
Adair v. United States, xi, 26 & n.2
Adkins v. Children's Hospital, xx, 26 n.2, 150, 151 n.4
Admiralty Commissioners v. S.S. Amerika, 68 & n.3
Alaska Fish Co. v. Fish, 103, 104 n.1
Alexander Milburn Co. v. Davis-Bournonville Co., 200, 201 n.1
Allgeyer v. Louisiana, 218, 219 n. 3
American Banana Co. v. United Fruit Co., 37 & n.5, 38
American Bank and Trust Co. v. Federal Reserve Bank, 115, 116 & n.2
American Railway Express v. Levee, 163 & n.1
American Steel Foundries v. Tri-City Trades Council, 132 & n.2
Arizona Employers' Liability Cases, 102 & n.3
Atlantic Coast Line v. Daughton, 153 & n.2

Bailey v. Drexel Furniture Co., 141, 142 n.2
Baldwin v. Missouri, 255 & n.1
Baltimore and Ohio Railway Co. v. Wilson, 61 & n.2
Bartels v. Iowa, xxvi & n.48, 153 n.1
Becher v. Contoure Laboratories, 239, 240 n.1
Beech-nut Packing Company v. P. Lorillard, 213 & n.1
Bi-metallic Investment Co. v. Colorado, 42, 43 n.2
Birge-Forbes Co. v. Heye, 79, 80 n.3
Black and White Taxi Co. v. Brown and Yellow Taxi Co., 223, 224 n.3, 225, 226 & nn.1 & 2, 227, 233
Block v. Hirsh, 107, 108 & n.1, 111, 112
Bohring v. Ohio, 151 n.1
Brimstone Railroad and Canal Co. v. U.S., 223, 224 n.3
Brown v. Board of Education, 33 n.1, 262
Brown v. Gerald, 44, 45 n.4
Brown v. United States, 115, 116 & n.2, 117 n.2
Buck v. Bell, xx & n.28, 211 n.2, 212 & n.2
Burrill v. Locomobile Co., 137 & n.4

Cami v. Central Victoria, 184 & n.2
Chesapeake and Ohio Railway v. Bryant, 248, 249 n.2
Chicago, Burlington and Quincy Rail Road v. McGuire, 26 n.2
Chicago, Rock Island and Pacific Railroad Co. v. Cole, 77 & n.1
Chicago, Rock Island and Pacific Railroad Co. v. United States, 265 & n.3
Chicago Junction Case, 167, 168 n.2, 169 & n.4
Child Labor Tax Case, 141, 142 n.2
China, The, 170, 171 n.2
Clark Distilling Co. v. Western Maryland Railroad Co., 65 & n.3, 67 n.3
Coffin Brothers v. Bennett, 226, 227 n.1
Colorado v. Toll, 182, 183 n.2
Compania General de Tabacos de Filipinas v. Collector, 218 & n.3
Coppage v. Kansas, 25, 26 nn.1 & 3
Craig v. Hecht, 162 & n.2

De La Rama v. De La Rama, 51, 52 n.2
Denver v. Home Savings Bank, 24, 25 n.2

Deutsche Bank Filiale Nurnberg v. Humphrey, 206 & n.4, 208, 209
Diaz v. Gonzales, 150, 151 n.6
Direction der Disconto-Gesellschaft v. United States Steel Corporation, 180, 181 n.4
Douglas v. New York, New Haven and Hartford Railroad Company, 234, 235 n.2
Druggan v. Anderson, 193 & n.2
Duffy v. Charak, 24, 25 n.2
Duplex Co. v. Deering, xxii, xxiii, 100, 101 & n.2, 102 & n.2, 103

Early v. Federal Reserve Bank of Richmond, 251 & n.3
Edwards v. Chile Copper Co., 200, 201 n.1
Edwards v. Douglas, 194 & n.3
Electric Boat Company v. United States, 167, 168 n.1
Erie Railroad Co. v. Public Utility Commission, 98 & n.2, 100, 101 n.1
Erie Railroad Co. v. Tompkins, 226 n.2
Evans v. Gore, 104, 105 n.3, 257 & n.2
Ex parte United States, 61 & n.1
Ex parte Uppercu, 42, 43 n.2

Farmers' Loan and Trust v. Minnesota, 243, 244 n.2, 247, 248, 255
Federal Baseball Club v. National League, 142, 143 n.3
Federal Trade Commission v. American Tobacco Company, 171 & n.4, 172
Federal Trade Commission v. Beech-Nut Co., 133, 134 n.1
Five Per Cent Discount Cases, 68, 69 n.6
Forbes Boat Line v. Board of Commissioners, 139 & n.3
Fort Smith and Western R.R. Co. v. Mills, 88, 89 n.3, 91 n.2
Frese v. Chicago, Burlington & Quincy Railroad Company, 161 & n.1
Frick v. Pennsylvania, 183 n.2

Gast Realty Co. v. Schneider Granite Co., 44, 45 n.5
Gilbert v. Minnesota, xix, 99, 100 nn.2 & 4
Gitlow v. New York, xviii n.21, 184, 185 n.1, 199 n.5
Goldsmith Grant v. United States, 102 & n.3
Gooch v. Oregon Short Line R.R. Co., 135 & n.3
Graf v. Hope Building Corporation, 256 & n.1
Grogan v. Walker and Sons, 142, 143 n.11
Gsell v. Insular Collector of Customs, 34, 35 n.2

Hammer v. Dagenhart, 72 & n.1, 141, 142 n.2
Hanover Star Milling Co. v. Metcalf, 48 & n.4, 49, 50 & n.1
Heim v. McCall, 128 & n.2
Hicks v. Guinness, 194 & n.4
Hitchman Coal and Coke Co. v. Mitchell, 86, 87 n.1
Hoeper v. Tax Commission of Wisconsin, 266, 267 n.1
Hoke v. United States, 40, 41 n.5
Howat v. Kansas, 139 & n.1
Hughes v. Samuel Brothers, 65, 66 n.4

Illinois Central Railway Company v. Peery, 61 & n.2

Jackman v. Rosenbaum Co., 146 & n.2, 147
Johnson v. Root Manufacturing Co., 51, 52 n.2

Kansas City Western Railway Co. v. McAdow, 44, 45 n.5
Kawananakoa v. Polybank, 135, 136 n.6
Kinnane v. Detroit Creamery Co., 96 n.2
Knickerbocker Ice Co. v. Stewart, 91 & n.3
Knights v. Jackson, 146 & n.1

Lamar v. United States, 44, 45 n.5
Leach v. Carlile, 135 & n.4
LeHigh Valley R.R. Co. v. United States, 69, 70 n.2
LeRoy Fibre Co. v. Chicago, Minneapolis and St. Paul Railway Co., 18, 19 n.1
Lewellyn v. Frick, 182, 183 n.2
Liverpool Navigation Co. v. Brooklyn Terminal, 77 & n.1
Local Government Board v. Arlidge, 43 & n.3
Lochner v. New York, xi, 199 n.2
Long v. Rockwood, 227 & n.1, 233

Los Angeles v. Los Angeles Gas Corp., 128 & n.2
Louisiana Public Service Commission v. Texas & New Orleans Railroad Co., 265 & n.3
Louisville and Nashville Railroad Co. v. Ohio Valley Tie Co., 61 & n.2
Louisville and Nashville Railroad Co. v. Sloss-Sheffield Steel & Iron Co., 194 & n.3
Louisville and Nashville Railroad Co. v. United States, 58, 59 n.3
Lumber Underwriters v. Rife, 33 n.2

McCardle v. Indianapolis Water Company, 209 & n.3
McCray v. United States, 72 & n.2, 141, 142 n.3
McCulloch v. Maryland, 228 n.1
McDonald v. Mabee, 68, 69 n.6
Mackenzie v. Hare, 40, 41 n.4
Mail Divisor Cases, 79, 80 n.3
Maine Railroad and Coal Co. v. United States, 127, 128 n.2
Massachusetts State Grange v. Benton, 208 & n.3, 209
Meyer v. Nebraska, 153 & n.1
Michaels v. Hillman, 86, 87 n.3
Milwaukee Publishing Co. v. Burleson, 106 & n.2
Minerals Separation North American Corporation v. Magma Copper Company, 249, 250 & n.1
Minneapolis and St. Louis R.R. Co. v. Winters, 64 & n.2
Missouri v. Holland, 89, 90 & n.3
Morrisdate Coal Co. v. United States, 142, 143 n.3
Motion Picture Patents Co. v. Universal Film Co., 69, 70 n.2
Mount Hope Cemetery v. Boston, 129 & n.1, 131
Mt. Vernon-Woodberry Cotton Duck Co. v. Alabama Interstate Power Co., 44
Murphy v. United States, 210 & n.4
Mutual Life Insurance Co. v. Liebing, 142, 143 n.3

National Association of Window Glass Manufacturers v. United States, 164 & n.2
National Prohibition Cases, 94 & nn.1, 2, & 4
Newberry v. United States, 114 & n.3
New Jersey v. New York, 263 & n.1
New York Trust v. Eisner, 118 & n.4
New York v. Jersawit, 164, 165 n.4
New York v. Sage, 42, 43 n.2
Nickel v. Cole, xxiii n.37, 110 & n.1, 112
Noble State Bank v. Haskell, xi, 74, 75 n.3
Northern Securities Co. v. United States, xi n.2, 94, 95 n.5, 125

O'Neil v. Northern Colorado Irrigation Co., 58, 59 n.2
Oklahoma v. Texas, 93 & n.3, 94, 140 & n.3
Olmstead v. United States, 228, 229 n.2
Otis v. Parker, 99, 100 n.4, 147

Panhandle Oil Co. v. Knox, 227, 228 n.1, 233
Peck v. Tribune Co., 65, 66 n.5
Pennsylvania Coal Co. v. Mahon, xix, xxiii, xxiii n.38, xxiv nn.40 & 41, 148 & n.2, 149, 150
Pennsylvania Fire Insurance Co. Gold Issue Mining Co., 68, 69 n.6
Peoria and Pekin Union Railway Company v. United States Interstate Commerce Commission, & Minneapolis & St. Louis Railroad Company, 164, 165 n.7
Pine Hill Coal Co. v. United States, 142, 143 n.3
Pipe Line Cases, 64 & n.3
Pitney v. State of Washington, 49 n.5
Plant v. Woods, 100, 101 n.2
Portsmouth Harbor Land and Hotel Co. v. United States, 148 & n.1
Prestonettes, Inc. v. Coty, 171, 172 & n.5

Queen Insurance Company of America v. Globe & Rutgers Fire Insurance Company, 164, 165 n.4, 171 & n.3

Railroad Co. v. Strout, 138 n.2
Rast v. Van Deman and Lewis, 48 & n.5
Rex v. United States, 79, 80 n.4
Reynolds v. Shipping Federation, 181 & n.1
Robert Addie v. Dumbreck, 257 & n.1

Safe Deposit and Trust Co. v. Virginia, 245 & n.6, 246
Sage v. Hampe, 23 & n.3
Sanitary District of Chicago v. United States, 178, 179 n.3
Santa Fe Pacific v. Fall, 142, 143 n.3
Schenck v. United States, 199 n.5
Schlesinger v. Wisconsin, 198, 199 n.3
Silverthorne Lumber Co. v. United States, 79, 80 n.4
Sloan Shipyards v. U.S. Fleet Corp., 140, 141 n.5
Slocum v. New York Insurance, 31 & n.3
South Pacific v. Jensen, 169 n.5
Southern Pacific Co. v. Berkshire, 98 & n.2
Southern Pacific Co. v. Jensen, 68, 69 n.8, 70 n.1, 91 n.3
Spaulding and Bros. v. Edwards, 152 & n.1
Springer v. Philippine Islands, 227 & n.1, 233
Springfield Gas and Electric Co. v. Springfield, 127, 128 & n.2
St. Louis-San Francisco R.R. Co. v. Middlekamp, 113 & n.2
Stafford v. Wallace, 140, 141 n.6
Stark Bros. Co. v. Stark, 103, 104 n.1
Straus v. Victor Talking Machine Co., 70 n.2
Superior Oil Company v. Mississippi, 245 & n.7, 249, 250 & n.2
Swift v. Tyson, 225, 226 n.2, 232, 233

Tanner v. Little, 48 n.5
Tedrow v. Lewis and Son Co., 96 n.2
Texas & Pacific Railway v. Gulf, Colorado & Santa Fe Railroad, 197 & n.1
Texas Transportation Co. v. New Orleans, 169 & n.5
Trimble v. City of Seattle, 18 & n.2
Truax v. Corrigan, 132, 133 n.1
Tyson and Brothers v. Banton, 212 & n.1
Tyson v. Banton, 75 n.3

Union Pacific Railway Co. v. McDonald, 138 n.2
Union Refrigerator Transit Co. v. Kentucky, 245, 246 n.2
United States v. Baltimore & Ohio Railroad Co., 265 & n.3
United States v. Behrman, 138 & n.3
United States v. Cohen Grocery Co., 95, 96 n.2
United States v. Colgate and Co., 84 & n.2
United States v. Darby, 72 n.1
United States v. Holte, 24, 25 n.2
United States v. Illinois Central Railroad, 164, 165 n.7
United States v. Pennsylvania R.R. Co., 62 & n.5, 63
United States v. Robbins, 196 & n.2
United States v. Schwimmer, xxix n.62, 240 & n.1
United States v. Storrs, 210 & n.4
United States v. Sullivan, 213 & n.1
United States v. United States Steel Corp., 84 & n.1
United States v. Walter, 161, 162 n.2
United States v. Weissman, 177, 178 n.2
United States v. Wurzbach, 248, 249 n.2
United States, Interstate Commerce Commission, National Council of Traveling Salesmen's Associations v. New York Central Railroad, 166, 167 n.1
United Zinc and Chemical Co. v. Britt, 137, 138 n.2, 139, 257 & n.1

Vegelahn v. Guntner, 100, 101 n.2, 125
Virginia v. West Virginia, 33 n.1

Washington v. Dawson and Co., 169 & n.5
Weaver v. Palmer Brothers, 198, 199 n.2
Wedding v. Meyler, 96, 97 n.2
West Coast Hotel v. Parrish, 151 n.4
Western Maid, 133 & n.2, 134, 135, 171 n.1
Western Pacific California Railroad Co. v. Southern Pacific Co., 265 & n.3
Western Union Telegraph Co. v. Czizek, 170 & n.2
Western Union Telegraph Co. v. Speight, 95, 96 n.1
Wheeler v. Greene, 243, 244 n.3
White Oak Co. v. Boston Canal Co., 139 & n.3
Willoughby v. Chicago, 23 & n.3
Wilson v. New, 68, 69 n.7, 71, 91 n.2
Wisconsin v. Illinois, 253 & n.1, 254
Wuchter v. Pizzuti, 223 & n.3

UNIVERSITY PRESS OF NEW ENGLAND publishes books under its own imprint and is the publisher for Brandeis University Press, Dartmouth College, Middlebury College Press, University of New Hampshire, Tufts University, Wesleyan University Press, and Salzburg Seminar.

Library of Congress Cataloging-in-Publication Data

Holmes, Oliver Wendell, 1841–1935.
Holmes and Frankfurter : their correspondence, 1912–1934 / edited by Robert M. Mennel and Christine L. Compston.
p. cm.
Includes index.
ISBN 0–87451–758–3
1. Holmes, Oliver Wendell, 1841–1935—Correspondence. 2. Frankfurter, Felix, 1882–1965—Correspondence. 3. Judges—United States—Correspondence. 4. United States. Supreme Court—Biography. I. Frankfurter, Felix, 1882–1965. II. Mennel, Robert M. III. Compston, Christine L. IV. Title.
KF8745.H6A433 1996
347.73′1′0922—dc20
[347.30710922] 96-597

♾